At Stalingrad the German Sixth Army was annihilated in five months of the most savage fighting in World War II. Of the 330,000 men Hitler threw into that battle, fewer than 7,000 returned.

How the battle for Stalingrad looked from the inside is now told for the first time by Marshal Vasili Chuikov, who commanded the 62nd (Siberian) Army and was the chief Russian officer responsible for the city's defense.

As war history, Chuikov's book could not be more authoritative. Chuikov was in the city with his men, and his account of the yard-by-yard fighting in the factories and in the streets is written with a vividness and immediacy few generals could manage. At the same time, his frankness in analyzing Soviet strengths and weaknesses, and his devastating criticism of Stalin and some of the Soviet generals is extraordinary among books from the Russian side.

Illustrated with authentic battle maps and rare photos from Russian sources, and with an introduction by Hanson W. Baldwin, military editor of **The New York Times**, **The Battle for Stalingrad** is the most important and revealing book to appear about Russia at war.

"The most complete account yet published of the epic battle of Stalingrad ... a stirring narration of military achievement against staggering opposition."

—*Baltimore Sun*

Related Reading in
Ballantine War Books

With more than 60 titles in print, Ballantine Books publishes the largest list of nonfiction military histories available in paperback. Below are some titles of special interest to the readers of this book:

STALINGRAD, Heinz Schröter $.75
The German side. Too frightening for the German people, this harrowing account of the defeat of the Wehrmacht could not be published until after the war! (*4th printing*)

STUKA PILOT, Hans Ulrich Rudel $.75
Air war on the Russian front by Germany's most decorated pilot, veteran of 2500 sorties at Leningrad, Moscow and Stalingrad (*9th printing*)

DEFEAT IN THE EAST, Juergen Thorwald $.75
1945: the collapse of Hitler's Germany and the Russian drive on Berlin. (Original title: Flight in Winter)

PANZER LEADER, Heinz Guderian $.75
The classic account of German tanks in World War II—by the commander of Hitler's Panzer Corps in Russia. Over 400 pages, abridged. (*6th printing*)

For a complete list of Ballantine Books, or to order by mail, write to: Dept. CS, Ballantine Books, 101 Fifth Avenue, New York, N.Y. 10003

THE
BATTLE
FOR
STALINGRAD

VASILI I. CHUIKOV

Marshal of the Soviet Union

Introduction by
HANSON W. BALDWIN

Translated from the Russian by
HAROLD SILVER

BALLANTINE BOOKS • NEW YORK

CONTENTS

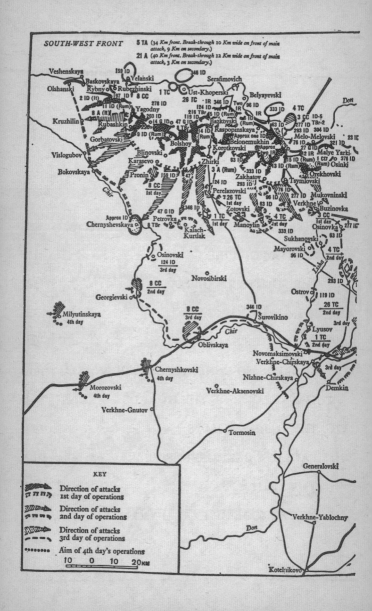

SOUTH-WEST FRONT

5 TA (34 Km front. Break-through 10 Km wide on front of main attack, 9 Km on secondary.)

21 A (40 Km front. Break-through 12 Km wide on front of main attack, 3 Km on secondary.)

Veshenskaya
Baskovskaya
Olshanski   Rybny   Rubezhinski
2 ID (It)   97 ID   8 CC
11 ID (Rum)
8 A (It)   278 ID
Kruzhilin   Yagodny
293 ID
Kubashkin   14 G ID
226 ID   8 TbR
9 ID (Rum)
Gorbatovski
Blinovski   Bolshoy
Karasevo
Vislogubov   Pronin
Bokovskaya   8 CC
1st day
Chir
Approx 1D   47 G ID
Chernyshevskaya   2 TbR   Petrovka
Kalach-
Kurtlak
Osinovski
124 ID
3rd day
Novosibirski
Georgievski   8 CC
2nd day
Milyutinskaya   8 CC
4th day   3rd day
Oblivskaya
Chernyshkovski
4th day
Morozovski
4th day
Verkhne-Gnutov

159 ID   Yelanski   346 ID
Serafimovich
1 TC   Ust-Khoperski
26 TC   1R 346 ID   Belyayevski
1R   96 ID
1R Twr
216 TbR 45 ID (Rum)   4 TC
119 ID   1R   333 ID   3 CC DD-5
Bazkovski   63 ID   277 ID   TBr-2
4 G ID (Rum)   Raspopinskaya   293 ID   304 ID   23 TC
Approx one ID   76 ID   Melo-Melovski   321 ID
Belonemukhin   8 G ID   Malye Yarki
Korotkovski   12 IR   1 CD   378 ID
Approx   15 ID (Rum)   Osinki
Zhirki   3 ID (Rum)   Orekhovski
3 A (Rum)   333 ID   Tsymlovski
Zakhatov   293 ID   76 ID
124 ID   277 ID   Mukovninski
Perelazovski   96 ID   Verkhne-
7 26 TC   63 ID   Buzinovka
Zotovski   4 TC
346 ID   1st day   Osinovka   277 IC
1 TC   Manoylin   333 ID   1st day
1st day   1st day   Sukhanovski   63 ID
Mayorovski   4 TC
96 ID   2nd day
Liska
293 ID
346 ID   Ostrov   119 ID
Surovikino   26 TC
2nd day
3rd day
Lyusov
Chir   1 TC
2nd day
Novomaksimovski
Verkhne-Chirskaya   3rd day
Nizhne-Chirskaya   Demkin
Verkhne-Aksenovski
Tormosin

Don

Generalovski

Verkhne-Yablochny

Kotelnikovo

KEY

Direction of attacks
1st day of operations

Direction of attacks
2nd day of operations

Direction of attacks
3rd day of operations

Aim of 4th day's operations

10   0   10   20 Km

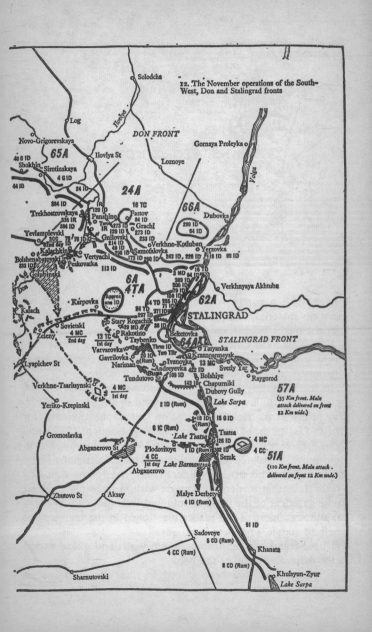

12. The November operations of the South-West, Don and Stalingrad fronts

TRANSLATOR'S NOTE

I have made a number of very minor cuts in the translation, omitting material (*e.g.*, occasional lists of names) which I thought might be distracting for the non-Russian reader.

I have in most cases avoided the questionable practice of "translating" names of factories, etc., preferring *Barrikady* and *Krasny Oktyabr* to *Barricades* and *Red October.*

In transliterating Russian place and proper names I have, by and large, followed the practice used in the *Russian Glossary* of the Permanent Committee on Geographical Names for British Use (Royal Geographical Society, London, 1942) and the *Dictionary of Russian Geographical Names* by M. B. Bolostnova, translated and transliterated by T. Deruguine (New York, 1958). This practice differs from that followed in *The Times Atlas,* but readers who might wish to trace place names in the gazetteer of the latter should find little difficulty in doing so, although most of the places mentioned in the text are too small, of course, to appear in atlases.

I have transposed all distances into yards and miles, except in the maps at the end of the book.

All footnotes have been added by the translator, unless otherwise indicated.

INTRODUCTION

by Hanson W. Baldwin

At STALINGRAD, as Winston Churchill wrote, "the hinge of fate" turned.

Stalingrad and the campaign of which it was a part was a decisive battle of World War II. It was the high-water mark of German conquest; after January 31, 1943, when Field-Marshal Friedrich von Paulus surrendered what was left of the German 6th Army, the paths of glory for Hitler and his legions led only to the grave.

In late June, 1942, Stalingrad, strung along the west bank of the Volga for some thirty miles where the great river makes its sweeping loop to the west, was the third industrial city of the Soviet Union. The front then was far away. The Nazis had been halted at the gates of Moscow in November and December, 1941, and the war of Blitzkrieg had been turned into the war of attrition. Pearl Harbor had brought the United States, with all its immense potential, into the war, and in North Africa, despite Rommel's victories, British armies still held the gateway to Egypt and the Suez Canal. Hitler faced the specter that even he dreaded—war on many fronts.

Yet the USSR was sorely hurt and German armies still held a 2,300-mile front deep within the Russian "motherland." The Reich that was to last a thousand years mobilized new units and called on sixty-nine satellite divisions—Rumanian, Italian, Hungarian, Finnish, Spanish, Slovak—to bolster German strength for a gargantuan effort.

For the 1942 campaigns Hitler substituted economic for military goals. His eyes shifted from Moscow to the oil fields of the Caucasus. The *Drang nach Osten* (push to the East), which had lured the Kaiser, influenced his plans for the German armies.

The basic German objective in the great seven-months campaign, of which the battle for Stalingrad was a key part, was the oil of the Caucasus and penetration of that great mountain barrier. Russian armies in the Don bend—where the river looped far to the east within a few miles of the westward-looping Volga—were to be destroyed. Stalingrad was originally envisaged as a means to a more grandiose end; the Russians were to be deprived of its "production and transportation facilities" and traffic on the Volga was to be interrupted either by actual seizure of the city or by artillery fire. The city was not a key objective.

At the start of "Operation Blau" in late June, 1942, about 100 Axis divisions had been concentrated in Southern Russia opposite about 120 to 140 Soviet divisions. Army Group A was to drive deep into the Caucasus; Army Group B, of which the 6th Army was a part, was to clear the banks of the Don of all Soviet forces and hold the long northern flank of the great Caucasian salient, from Voronezh, the pivot point of the operation, through Stalingrad southward toward Rostov.

The huge German offensive had sweeping initial success; Russian forces were shattered, Voronezh fell, and the 6th Army drove eastward into the loop of the Don. Through the gateway of Rostov and across the Kerch strait, Army Group A drove deep into the Caucasus.

But late in July, 1942, Hitler, who fancied himself a master strategist and who handled every detail of military operations on the Russian front, shifted the *schwerpunkt,* or main weight of attack, northward from the Caucasus toward Stalingrad. Stalingrad gradually became an end in itself; Hitler came to realize that the city on the Volga dominated a key part of the exposed northern flank of the southern offensive. In General Franz Halder's words he understood, too late, that "the fate of the Caucasus will be decided at Stalingrad."

August, 1942, was a black month for Soviet Russia and for the Allies. In the West the Dieppe raid was repulsed bloodily. In the Caucasus German tanks captured the Maikop oil fields and the Nazi swastika flew on the Caucasus' highest peak—18,481 foot Mount Elborus. On August 23rd, after a 275-mile advance in some two months, Panzer Grenadiers of the German 6th Army reached the Volga on the northern outskirts of Stalingrad and the long trial by fire started.

The five-month battle in and around Stalingrad—the subject of this book—was only a part of a far vaster drama played across an immense stage of steppes and forests and mountains. As the southern campaign progressed, the vast spaces of the Russian land—which had defeated Napoleon—muffled the German blows. Army Groups A and B were engaged in divergent attacks, each with weak and insecure flanks, separated by some fifteen hundred miles of hostile "heartland." Logistics, the problem of supply which can make or break the best-laid plans of any general, became more and more important the deeper the Germans drove into Russia. And as stiffening Soviet resistance, plus their own difficulties, slowed the German advance Hitler milked more and more troops away from the vital northern flank of the deep salient —the hinge of the whole operation from Voronezh to Kletskaya—to re-enforce Paulus's 6th Army at Stalingrad. This flank, which held the key to the safety of the German forces at Stalingrad and in the Caucasus, was held by the Hungarian, Italian, and Rumanian armies with only slight German support, the weakest of the Axis forces in the most important area. And south of Stalingrad, almost to the communications bottleneck at Rostov, there was an open flank of hundreds of miles, patrolled for many weeks by only a single German motorized division. The front was, in truth, "fluid."

Except at Stalingrad. In July and early August Stalingrad might have been easily captured, but the German *schwerpunkt* then was toward the Caucasus or was just shifting toward Stalingrad. From September on, as Paulus, ever obedient to Hitler's orders, drove the steel fist of the 6th Army squarely against the city on the Volga, resistance stiffened. The German advantage of mobility was lost in the street fighting, and the battle of Stalingrad became a vicious, no-quarter struggle for every building, each street.

When the main German attack to seize the city started in mid-September, Paulus and his 6th Army, with the 4th Panzer Army on the southern flank, held with five corps (about twenty divisions in all) the forty-mile isthmus between the Don and the Volga. From eight to fourteen of the German divisions fought in the city and its suburbs. Paulus was opposed in Stalingrad by the 62nd (Siberian) Army, commanded by Lieutenant-General Vasili Chuikov (the author of this book), who originally commanded some five to eight divisions (subsequently re-enforced). Moscow created a special Stalingrad Front (equivalent to an Army Group) commanded by Andrey Yeremenko and elements of the 64th Soviet Army, astride the Volga, and the 57th Army faced the 6th Army outside Stalingrad and the German 4th Panzer Army south of the city.

These were the forces that asked no quarter and gave none in one of the bloodiest battles of modern times. Stalingrad, between September, 1942, and February, 1943, became a Verdun, a symbol to both sides; for Hitler it was an obsession. In its battered factories, from its cellars and sewers, from rooftops and smashed windows and piles of rubble, Paulus and Chuikov fought a battle to the death.

At first the Germans were on the offensive, inching forward yard by yard here, reaching the Volga there. Front lines were inextricably confused; there were few flanks, no rear; fighting was everywhere.

But by mid-November, with the Battle of El Alamein lost in Egypt, Paulus was almost through. On November 19th, when the iron blast of winter had hardened the steppes, some half-a-million Soviet troops and fifteen hundred tanks, concentrated on the flanks of the Don and Volga bends, struck. The first blows broke through the vulnerable northern flank held by Germany's hapless allies, and by November 22nd, the Don Front (Rokossovski) and Yeremenko's Stalingrad Front, with some seven Russian armies, had closed their pincers at Kalach on the Don bend, encircling in the isthmus between the Don and Volga and in Stalingrad more than two hundred thousand soldiers of the German 6th Army, a few units of the 4th Panzer Army, elements of two Rumanian divisions, Luftwaffe units, a Croat regiment and some seventy thousand noncombatants, including Russian "Hiwis" (voluntary laborers who aided the Germans) and Russian prisoners. When the encirclement was complete the Germans in the Caucasus had pushed to within seventy-five miles of the Caspian Sea.

The *Kessel,* or encirclement, originally covered an area about the size of the state of Connecticut, not only the city of Stalingrad itself but large areas of frozen, wind-swept open steppe westward to the Don. Hitler called it "Fortress

Stalingrad" and forbade any attempt at breakout; where the German soldier had set foot he must remain.

The rest is history—sanguinary, brutal history—the slow, and then the rapid, death of an army and of a city. An airlift was organized to supply Paulus on November 25th, and in the bitter winter weather of December, Manstein, possibly the ablest German commander of World War II, attempted to break through the Russian encirclement to relieve Stalingrad. He almost succeeded; his Panzers driving along the Kotelnikovski-Stalingrad railway reached to within thirty miles of the 6th Army's outposts by December 21st, but Paulus, obedient to Hitler's stand-fast orders, made no effort to break out. By Christmas Day all hope had gone; Manstein was in full retreat and the last days of agony of the 6th Army had started.

On January 31, 1943, a dazed and broken Paulus surrendered in the basement of the Univermag department store in what was left of Stalingrad. But Hitler was right in the long run, the 6th Army did not die in vain. Until the end of December Hitler had forbidden the withdrawal of Army Group A deep in the Caucasus, though the northern flank of the great salient on which its safety depended was in shreds. But in January, while the 6th Army died, Manstein—repulsed in his attempt to relieve Stalingrad—fought desperately and successfully to hold open the gateway to safety at Rostov, as Germany's conquering legions in the Caucasus withdrew in a brilliant but precipitate retreat across the mouth of the Volga and the Kerch strait from the conquests they had so briefly held.

The 6th Army, ordered to fight to the death, undoubtedly diverted Russian divisions from concentrating against the Rostov gateway and prevented, by their sacrifice, an even greater Soviet triumph. Army Group A in the Caucasus escaped to fight again, and the war's ultimate end was still two long years away.

The Battle of Stalingrad was ever more important politically and psychologically than it was militarily. An entire German army was destroyed for the first time in World War II; of some 334,000 men, only about 93,000 survived to surrender (plus some Rumanians and 30,000 to 40,000 German noncombatants and Russian "auxiliaries" and civilians).

The shock upon the German mind was terrific; the myth of invincibility had been forever broken. After the Battle of Moscow and the entry of the United States into the war the Germans had no hope of unconditional victory. After Stalingrad they had little hope of conditional victory, of a negotiated peace with Stalin.

Hitler at Stalingrad attempted to achieve unlimited aims with limited means; he became obsessed with his own infallibility. His lust for global power recoiled in blood and death from the ruins of Stalingrad; from then on, the German tide was on the ebb.

Soviet military history—like all Soviet history—hews to the party line: it does not hesitate to make black white; it sets out to prove a point, not to accumulate and relate the facts. Truth, in terms of dialectical materialism, is relative; it is what the party says it is.

These faults, which were even carried to such an extreme as to obliterate totally from the record the names of Russians who cast their lot with the West (such as Vlasov), were particularly pronounced under Stalin. But, since his death, the gradual "thaw" which has influenced Soviet life and mores has affected even the writing of military history.

The official Russian history of World War II, now being published—though still reticent in many areas—is refreshingly frank as compared to the polemical sketches of a decade ago. However, there have been relatively few book-length memoirs or authoritative personal accounts by Soviet wartime leaders; it was safer to be inconspicuous than to bring down the possible wrath of official displeasure by putting anything on the record.

In fact, the historian of the Russian front has found, until recently, very little grist for his mill; the German records are excellent but one-sided. Of the available Russian material, accounts published in military magazines were perhaps the best, though most of them were brief and devoid of details. A few official Soviet accounts, which had been written for official use only but which had fallen into U.S. hands, presented a somewhat less biased picture. A notable example of this kind of document, which deals with the battle for Stalingrad, is a study of the battle under the title *Combat*

Experiences, published with the sponsorship of the Red Army's general staff in the spring of 1943 for a restricted military audience. A translated copy of this document—which, unlike most publicly available Soviet history, admits mistakes and is relatively frank—is in the files of the Office of the Chief of Military History of the United States Army in Washington, D.C.

To these sparse sources this book by Marshal Chuikov is a very welcome and an important addition. During the battle Chuikov commanded the 62nd (Siberian) Army, which was directly responsible for Stalingrad's defense; he might be called, in Western parlance, "the Rock of Stalingrad." Chuikov is now, at writing, commander in chief of Soviet land forces, and his book makes it obvious that he pays obeisance to Premier Khrushchev.

As judged by Western military memoirs *The Battle for Stalingrad* appears episodic, fragmented, and far from complete. But by past Soviet standards it ranks high. It provides very considerable new insight into the battle in the city itself, and there are many surprising flashes of frankness. The memoir adds materially to our knowledge of a struggle which was the beginning of the road to ultimate Allied victory.

Occasional frank tributes to German combat effectiveness, open criticism of some Soviet commanders, admissions of tactical mistakes and of very heavy casualties, accounts of confusion and supply and medical deficiencies would all seem to attest to the essential validity of this account.

More than a thousand soldiers of the 13th Guards Infantry Division reached Stalingrad with no rifles. The Soviet system of political endorsement of military orders is described.

The narrative makes clear that Stalingrad was in truth a *Rattenkrieg,* or "war of the rats"; its horrible hardships and bitter fighting are implicit in Chuikov's account, although the pitiless nature of the struggle and the atrocities on both sides that accompanied and followed the battle are glossed over.

Mother Volga was always at the back of the Russian defenders in the Stalingrad battle; it was at once comfort and agony. For all supplies had to be ferried somehow across this great river to the rubble heaps and cellars of Stalingrad, and the wounded had to be removed across the same water route. Chuikov's description of some of the expedients resorted to during the period of major supply difficulties from November 12th to December 17th, before the river was frozen solid but while it was full of huge cakes of floating ice, provides a kind of thumbnail tribute to the strengths of the Russian soldier—the strength of mass, of unending dogged labor, of sweat and blood, of love for Mother Russia, of courage.

Chuikov contributes, too, specific details of battle orders issued by him and by other unit commanders, and he fills in gaps in the West's knowledge of the Russian units that fought in the Stalingrad campaign. There are interesting and informative sections dealing with the contributions of Russian women, as soldiers and auxiliaries, to the defense of Stalingrad.

On the whole, *The Battle for Stalingrad* adds materially to the data on Stalingrad; indeed, it presents from the Russian point of view more detail of the battle in the city itself than any other volume in English.

The book, of course, does not entirely escape from the inevitable polemical fetters which handicap every Soviet historical work—despite the new liberalism. The author time and again pays sycophantic tribute to political commissar Khrushchev, who was the Communist Party representative at the Stalingrad Front headquarters east of the Volga, but who never once—as far as this book indicates—entered the shattered city of Stalingrad during the fighting. The real architects of the great Russian victory in the Stalingrad-Caucasus campaign—the then Generals Georgi Zhukov, Alexander Vasilievski, and Nikolai N. Voronov—receive no credit. Stalin is conspicuous by his absence. German losses and German troop strengths are exaggerated, and, despite frequent mention of heavy Russian casualties, the reader will search in vain for that rarest of all statistics: specific figures of Soviet casualties. And one will find no appreciation of the "big picture" or of the contribution to final victory of the United States or Great Britain.

Despite these weaknesses—inevitable in the Soviet literature of war until communism changes its stripes—this book is an addition to history, a chronology of a famous victory, and a study in command and tactics.

Despite the dialectical cant with which Moscow has tried,

until recently, to cloak Soviet military concepts, all soldiers in all armies draw common lessons from the common heritage of war. Marshal Chuikov shows himself in his memoirs to be a perceptive and vigorous commander. And despite his Communist ideology, he sums up his experiences at Stalingrad—one of the world's great battles—in terms often used at military schools everywhere:

1. Use historical examples, but don't repeat them blindly.
2. Don't stand on your dignity; listen to your subordinates and don't encourage them to be yes-men.
3. Don't cling blindly to regulations.

Stalingrad—its name now changed by one of those ironic twists of which Communist policy is so full to Volgograd—stands today restored, enlarged, a monument to disaster and to triumph, a symbol of man's inhumanity to man, a site of awful carnage, of fierce patriotism and burning loyalties, a city which will forever live, like Troy, in the tears and legends of two peoples.

New York

CHAPTER I

BAPTISM OF FIRE

THE OUTBREAK of war between Germany and the Soviet Union found me in China, where I was military attaché and chief military adviser to Chiang Kai-shek.

At the beginning of the war, when the armies of Nazi Germany managed to advance deep into the heart of the Soviet Union, the pro-Fascist elements in China openly rejoiced at our defeats and harped on them and on the 'imminent collapse' of the Soviet state and its armed forces.

British and American representatives in China did not spare my feelings. Only the French military attaché, I thought, was sincere in commenting that a Soviet victory was the sole way of rescuing France from Nazism.

I tried as hard as I could to return home quickly and take part in our fight against the Nazi invaders. I had far less to do now in China, since the Japanese and Chinese, by mutual consent as it were, had broken off active operations as from June 22, and all eyes were on the fighting taking place on the Soviet-German front.

After the Japanese attacks on Hong Kong and Pearl Harbor, Kuomintang headquarters was flooded with British and American military missions. The Americans and British courted Chiang Kai-shek and his followers as if they were rich widows, and tried to get as many Chinese divisions out of them as possible, for use in defence of imperialist interests. Chiang Kai-shek, in return, wanted as many dollars as possible.

The Chiang Kai-shek leaders did everything they could to complicate our relations with Japan. A number of times Chiang Kai-shek proposed to the Soviet government that they should immediately wage a joint campaign against the Japanese. Other provocative moves were also made. For example, the Chiang Kai-shek press claimed that the Soviet Union was giving 'colossal aid' to China in the fight against the Japanese, aid which, of course, we were not giving and could not give. One of the newspapers even published a report to the effect that I had been talking to some Chinese correspondent or other and had made the same claim in the course of conversation. It was necessary, finally, to put a stop to such provocations by Chiang Kai-shek, and the Soviet government decided to recall its military attaché from China.

I arrived in Moscow at the beginning of March 1942. I reported back on my work in China, and immediately requested to be sent to the front. I wanted to get to know the nature of modern warfare as quickly as possible, to understand the reasons for our defeats, and to try to find out where the German army's tactical strength lay and what new military techniques it was using.

In May I was appointed Acting Commander of the reserve army spread out over the Tula region, where, during May, June and early July it underwent intensive military training.

One day I stayed on at H.Q. until midnight and then set

off back to my quarters. I did not notice what state the driver, Grinev, was in. He started up the car with a jerk, and it rapidly began to gather speed.

'Grinev, don't drive so fast,' I warned him, but he appeared not to understand me. The car was gaining in speed all the time, and at a bend in the road it overturned. Trying to crawl out from under the wreckage I lost consciousness. Who picked me up and how I was taken home I don't remember.

'You have injured your spine,' the doctor told me. 'You'll have to stay on your back.'

For a few days I lay on a special bed, strapped down by the shoulders and legs, being given traction treatment. However, healthy and hardy by nature, I was on my feet again in a week, though I walked with a stick.

At the beginning of July an order came through from G.H.Q. renaming the reserve army the 64th Army, and transferring it to the Don. At that time the South-Western front, after an unsuccessful offensive in the region of Izyum and Barvenkovo, was rapidly moving eastward under pressure from the attacking German armies. Fighting was going on in the region of Rossosh and at the approaches to Lugansk, and was coming close to Voronezh. We realized that we would have to engage battle for the first time somewhere on the Don or between the Volga and the Don. The Army quickly entrained and set off for its new assembly positions.

I went to Balashov with the Army H.Q. by train, but then, so as to get to know the situation at the front as soon as possible and talk to the men at the front, Konstantin Kirkovich Abramov, the Member of the Military Council,[1]

---

[1]The term Military Council (or War Council) occurs frequently, and the following explanation may be helpful: 'In units above division level, authority (was) always vested in a Military Council which was normally composed of three men: one, the Commanding General; two, his Chief of Staff; and three, a gentleman always referred to in Russian as "The Member of the Military Council". Before the War, the Member of the Military Council was always a highly trusted member of the Communist Party ... during the War ... the Member of the Military Council more often than not filled the role of Deputy to the Commanding General dealing mainly with political and strategic questions ...' (Seth, R., *Stalingrad—Point of Return*, London, 1959, p. 92).

and I transferred to a light truck and went on ahead of the train to Front[2] H.Q.

We followed the railway line and called in at the big stations, so as to have a clear picture of the movement of our troop trains. The enemy was systematically bombing all these stations in an attempt to stop the movement of our troops.

At Frolovo Station we met 21st Army H.Q. The Chief of Staff received us warmly, but much though he would have liked he could not enlighten us about the situation. Where the front line was, where neighbouring armies were and where the enemy was—he did not know. The only thing I found out from him was that Front H.Q. was on the Volga.

21st Army H.Q. was on wheels: signals and supplies were all mobile, in motor vehicles. I did not like such mobility. In everything here one could sense a lack of firm resistance at the front, a lack of tenacity in battle. It seemed as if someone were running after the Army H.Q., and in order to escape pursuit everyone, from the Army Commander downwards, was always ready to make another move.

We spent the night at Frolovo and the next morning we went on towards the Volga. Passing through villages, stations and groups of houses we noticed how peaceful everything was. The corn was being harvested, cattle were grazing, hairdressers' shops, cinemas and theatres were functioning. Only at night did anti-aircraft guns occasionally open fire at odd enemy planes.

On 16 July 1942, we arrived at Stalingrad Front Headquarters. Here we learned that after the unsuccessful offensive by our troops towards Kharkov from the region of Izyum and Barvenkovo, the enemy had counter-attacked and reached a line running through Chernyshevskaya, Morozovsk and Chernyshkovski, where he had been brought to a halt by forward detachments of the 62nd Army, and had begun to build up men and material for a further offensive.

On the western bank of the Don, along a line through Kletskaya, Kalmykov, Surovikino and Peshcherski, the 62nd Army was preparing for defensive action. Its H.Q. was on the eastern bank of the Don, at Kamyshi Farm, some thirty-five to fifty miles away from the troops.

Men of the 64th Army were now beginning to detrain: the

---

[2]Roughly equivalent in Russian to Army Group.

112th Division at Kotluban, Kachalino and Filonovo Stations; the 214th Division at Donskaya, Muzga and Rychkov, and the 29th Division at Zhutovo. The remainder were on the banks of the Volga.

From the troop trains, the regiments and battalions marched to the Don in echelons.

Units of the 229th Infantry Division and the Army Headquarters staff were particularly delayed *en route*. The last troop trains, in which they were travelling, arrived only on July 23.

On July 17 we received instructions from Stalingrad Front H.Q.: 'The 64th Army, consisting of the 229th, 214th, 29th and 112th Infantry Divisions, the 66th and 154th Motorized Infantry Brigades, and the 40th and 137th Armoured Brigades, will on the night of July 19 proceed to the Surovikino, Nizhne-Solonovski, Peshcherski, Suvorovski, Potemkinskaya, Verkhne-Kurmoyarskaya Front. It will consolidate this front, and by firm defensive action will prevent an enemy break-through to Stalingrad. Forward detachments, consisting of one regiment with artillery from each division, will be moved to the River Tsimla . . .'

Front H.Q. obviously possessed extremely limited information about the enemy, who was mentioned in this order only in general terms.

The instructions given us were clearly impracticable, since the units concerned had only just left the troop trains and set off westward towards the Don, not in military columns, but in whatever order the troop trains had delivered them. The first units of some divisions were already approaching the Don, while rear ones were still in trains on the banks of the Volga. Generally speaking, the rearmost parts of the Army and army stores were still, in fact, in the Tula region, waiting for railway carriages.

Army troops would not only have to be reassembled after leaving the troop trains, they would also have to cross the Don. The Nizhne-Solonovski, Peshcherski, Suvorovski line of defence mentioned in the instructions was a day's journey from the Verkhne-Chirskaya and Nizhne-Chirskaya Don crossings, and the forward positions on the River Tsimla were thirty miles beyond the main ones. After leaving the trains, the troops would have a march of 125 miles or more.

After I had studied the instructions I immediately pointed out to the Chief of Staff at Front H.Q. that to carry them out in the time given was impossible, as parts of the Army which were to carry out these tasks had not yet arrived. The Chief of Staff replied that the instructions had to be carried out, but then he thought it over and proposed that I should call in to see him the following day.

Next morning, however, he did not appear at H.Q., and no one was able to tell me when he would be there. What was I to do? I went to see the officer in command of the operations section at Front H.Q., Colonel Rukhle, and showing him that it was impossible to carry out the instructions according to schedule, asked him to report to the Front Military Council that the 64th Army could occupy its line of defence not earlier than July 23.

Colonel Rukhle immediately, without reporting to anyone, with his own hand altered the date for the occupation of the line of defence from July 19 to July 21. I was astounded. How could the officer in command of operations, without the knowledge of the Commander, change the date of the operation? Who was in command of the Front?

While endeavouring to reassemble the troops who were now crossing the steppe westward to the Don, I called in at 62nd Army H.Q., at Kamyshi Farm.

62nd Army Commander, tall, well-built Major-General V. I. Kolpakchi, and Divisional Commissar K. A. Gurov, the Member of the Military Council, with dark brows and shaved head, acquainted me with the situation.

The 62nd Army was at this time in defensive positions in the big elbow of the Don, along a line through Kletskaya, Yevstratovski, Hill 181.4,[1] Krasny Rodnichok, Starikovski, Surovikino, Hill 117.4, State Farm No. 79 and Verkhne-Solonovski. Its job was to prevent the enemy from breaking through to the Don and farther east.

On the right flank of the 62nd Army, from Kalmykov to Verkhnyaya Gusynka, the 33rd Guards Division had entrenched itself.

Farther south, the line through Slepikhin, Hill 165.4 and

[1]On Soviet military maps hills are numbered according to their height (in metres) above river level.

Krasny Rodnichok was held by regiments of the 181st Infantry Division.

Farther south still, from Verkhnyaya Osinovka to Hill 117.4, the 147th Infantry Division was consolidating its positions.

The very left flank of the Army, from State Farm No. 79 to Nizhne-Solonovski Farm, was being defended by the 196th Infantry Division, which was to be relieved by units of the 64th Army.

Each division in the first line of defence was reinforced by one tank battalion and one anti-tank regiment.

In the second line of defence the 62nd Army had the 192nd and 184th Infantry Divisions, three separate tank battalions, ten artillery regiments of the Reserve High Command, one 'Katyushi'[2] regiment and four regiments of students from military institutes.

In accordance with instructions from Stalingrad Front H.Q., the 62nd Army had posted forward infantry detachments with artillery and tanks to a line bringing in the Rivers Tsutskan and Chir and Tormosin Farm.

Spirits were quite high at 62nd Army H.Q. Major-General Kolpakchi, the Army Commander, assured me that in the next few days he was going to try to probe the enemy forces facing him and occupy the village of Chernyshevskaya.

Contact with our neighbour on the right, therefore, had been established, but about our neighbour on the left I still had no information, apart from the boundary line drawn on the map at Front H.Q. operations section.

While I was travelling about I saw people crossing the scorched and waterless steppe from west to east, eating the last of their rations, suffocating with the heat. When they were asked where they were going and what they were looking for, they invariably gave the nonsensical reply that they had to look for someone across the Volga or in the Saratov region.

In one of the gullies in the steppe, near Sovietski State Farm, I came across two divisional staffs supposedly looking for 9th Army H.Q. They consisted of a number of officers

---

[2]*Katyusha* (or *gvardyeyski minomyot*—guards' mortar): a vehicle-mounted, multiple rocket-launcher. The Germans called them 'Stalin organs'. For further information see Seth, ibid., p. 182.

travelling in some three to five trucks filled to overflowing with cans of fuel. When I asked them where the Germans were, where our units were and where they were going, they could not give me a sensible reply. It was clear that to restore to these men the faith they had lost in their own powers, and to improve the fighting power of the retreating units, would not be easy. The first need was to stop the enemy, then to launch a powerful attack and smash his forward units, and then . . . all else would undeniably follow.

This situation, of course, was having a bad effect on the morale of the 64th Army troops moving west to the Don.

Seeing the situation and weighing up the information I had gleaned among 62nd Army units about the enemy, I decided to occupy a line on the west bank of the Don from Surovikino to the village of Suvorovskaya with two infantry divisions (the 229th and 214th), one marine infantry brigade (the 154th) and one armoured brigade. The left section of the front (Potemkinskaya to Verkhne-Kurmoyarskaya) was to be defended by the 29th Division. In the second line of defence, on the River Chir, where the 62nd and 64th Armies met, the 112th Infantry Division was deployed. The Front Command endorsed this decision.

To the left of the 64th Army, on the Don south of Verkhne-Kurmoyarskaya, the defence was in the hands of the neighbouring front, with which the 64th Army had had no communication.

On the evening of July 19, Lieutenant-General Gordov arrived at 64th Army H.Q., which was at Ilmen-Chirski Farm, with instructions to take over command of the 64th Army. He had hitherto been in command of the 21st Army. I was appointed his deputy.

This was my first encounter with General Gordov. His hair was turning grey, and he had tired grey eyes which seemed to see nothing, and whose cold glance seemed to say: 'Don't tell me about the situation, I know everything, and there's nothing I can do if that's how fate has turned out.'

When he was acquainted with my decisions Gordov did not make a single important alteration, endorsed them and instructed that they should be carried out. The Commander did, however, make substantial changes with regard to the Army's reserves. He ordered the 112th Infantry Division to be moved, not to the junction point of the 62nd and 64th Armies, but to the outer defences of Stalingrad, along the River Myshkova from Logovski to Gromoslavka. The 66th Marine Infantry Brigade, the 137th Armoured Brigade and the four regiments of military students were moved to the River Aksay, on the Army's left flank.

This decision of General Gordov's meant that all the Army's reserves were now on the east bank of the Don, and the 64th Army's defences across the Don were left without a second line and without reserves.

Gordov would not tolerate any objections from his subordinates.

On the morning of July 21, I went out to the defence positions and spent that day and the next with Divisional Commanders reconnoitring the country and selecting positions. Not a regiment or a division had actually arrived yet—they were still on the march from the stations where the troop trains had deposited them, and they arrived to take up their positions late and under-strength.

The 229th Infantry Division, for example, which was to defend the Army's right flank, marched from Stalingrad (about 125 miles), reached the line of defence on July 22, and proceeded to relieve the 62nd Army units only at noon on July 24, and then with only five battalions and two batteries of artillery—the remainder were still east of the Don.

On the previous day, July 23, the 214th Infantry Division took up defensive positions from State Farm No. 79 to Kruchinovski Farm; the same day, to the left, along the River Solok to its confluence with the Don, the 154th Marine Infantry Brigade began to deploy.

The appearance of our units and the build-up of the 64th Army along the line of defence was, beyond doubt, closely followed by the enemy. His Focke-Wulf reconnaissance planes circled overhead for hours, and we could not go into action against them because the Army had no artillery and our fighter planes were occupied in another sector of the front, presumably on the right flank of the 62nd Army, which was already engaged in stubborn, unsuccessful defence action in the Kletskaya-Kalmykov region. In order to strengthen this extremely dangerous flank on the right, the

62nd Army Commander made an urgent decision to move the 196th Infantry Division from his left flank between Surovikino and Nizhne-Solonovski. This left another section of the 64th Army's defensive positions exposed.

The battle in the big elbow of the Don, the battle for the Volga, began. At first sight such a statement may seem strange. How can one talk about the battle for the Volga stronghold when Hitler's forces were still far beyond the Don, and there had not yet been any sign that Hitler's path to Caucasian oil lay through the Volga rather than through Rostov-on-Don? A careful analysis of the plans of the German Supreme Command, or rather of Hitler himself, shows clearly, however, that this was the case.

After the dismissal of von Brauchitsch, Hitler himself, as we know, took over as Commander-in-Chief of Germany's land forces. As the Chief of Staff of the Southern Army Group, Infantry-General Sonderstein, and Major-General Doerr, have indicated in their memoirs, Hitler issued instructions to the Supreme Command of the land forces as early as November 1941, to the effect that: 'Given suitable weather conditions, it would be expedient to use all available forces for an attack southward to Stalingrad, or a rapid break-through along the line of Maykop and Grozny, so as to improve the army's oil supplies, since our oil resources are limited'.

Later, in the spring of 1942, this aim was formulated in Order No. 41, on the subject of the summer offensive by the Southern Army Group. It read as follows:

1. GENERAL AIM OF THE 1942 CAMPAIGN

The original overall plans for the campaign in the east remain in force; the main aim remains to safeguard the position on the central sector, take Leningrad in the north and establish communication by land with the Finns, and in the south accomplish the break-through to the Caucasus.

This task can be carried out only by breaking it down into stages, as the situation after the end of the winter campaign and the availability of forces, resources and transport, must be taken into account.

In the first place, therefore, all available forces must be concentrated on carrying out the main operation in the southern sector, with the aim of destroying the enemy west of the Don, so as then to seize the oil region of the Caucasus and cross the Caucasus Mountains.

II. PLAN OF OPERATIONS

A. The immediate task of the ground and air forces after the end of the season of bad roads is to create the conditions for accomplishing the main operation.

For this purpose it is essential to stabilize and consolidate the entire eastern front and the regions in the rear, and by so doing release as many forces as possible for the main operation, and at the same time be in a position to beat off any attack by the enemy on other fronts.

Wherever, in accordance with my instructions, offensive operations are conducted for this purpose with a limited aim, it is also necessary to ensure the use in all cases of all available means of attack by ground and air forces, so as to obtain quick, decisive successes with superior forces. Only in this way, before the beginning of the big operations in the spring of this year, will our troops' unswerving confidence in victory be strengthened and the enemy troops be convinced that we have decisive superiority.

B. In conducting these operations the next tasks are to clear the Kerch Peninsula and occupy Sevastopol. Air and then naval forces will blockade the Black Sea ports and the Kerch Strait with the aim of creating suitable conditions for these operations.

In the south, the enemy, who has driven a wedge on both sides from Izyum, must be thrown back to the Donets and destroyed.

The operations needed in order to even out the front line in its central and northern sectors, can be planned and carried out only when the military operations now in progress and the period of the bad roads are over. However, as soon as conditions permit, the forces needed to accomplish this should be detached from the front.

C. The main operation on the Eastern Front. Its aim, as has already been indicated, is to smash and destroy the Russian armies in the region of Voronezh and south of it, and also to the west and north of the River Don. In view of the fact that the formations necessary for this will come into existence only gradually, this operation falls into a series of successive, but inter-connected and complementary, attacks. Their distribution in time from north to south must be arranged, therefore, in such a way as to ensure that as many ground, and in particular air, forces as possible are concentrated for each of these attacks in a decisive direction.

The starting point for the whole of this operation should be an out-flanking attack or break-through from the region south of Orel in the direction of Voronezh. Of the two Groups of panzer and motorized armies which are to carry out the outflanking manœuvre, the northern-most must be the stronger. The aim of this break-through is to take the town of Voronezh. Some of the infantry divisions will rapidly have to equip a powerful line of defence from the point where the offensive began (Orel) towards Voronezh, and the panzer and motorized formations will at the same time have to continue to attack with their left flank from Voronezh along the Don to the south, so as to act in coordination with the troops carrying out the break-through, for example, eastward from the region of Kharkov. Here the main task is not to force the Russian armies to retreat, but to destroy them, in conjunction with the attacks made by the motorized formations down the River Don.

The third attack to be made as part of this operation needs to be organized in such a way that the forces making the attack down the Don join up in Stalingrad with forces attacking from the region of Taganrog and Artemovsk, between the lower reaches of the River Don and Voroshilovgrad across the Donets to the east. *These forces should then join up with the Panzer Army advancing on Stalingrad.* [Author's italics.]

If during this operation, in particular as a result of capturing bridges intact, there is a possibility of establishing a bridgehead eastward or southward across the Don, it must be exploited. *At any event, it is essential to try to reach Stalingrad or at least to expose it to our heavy fire, so that it loses its importance as a centre of war industry and of communications.* [Author's italics.]

While these operations are proceeding it is essential not only to take into account the need to protect the north-east flank of the attacking armies, but to begin equipping positions on the River Don. Particular importance must be attached to setting up powerful anti-tank defences. Positions must be provided with all necessary equipment for their possible use in winter-time.

The defence of the positions on this front along the Don, a front which will constantly grow as operations develop, will be allocated primarily to formations of allied troops, so as to use German troops to establish a powerful barrier between Orel and the River Don, and also in the Stalingrad isthmus; individual German divisions which are disengaged should be concentrated as a mobile reserve behind the front line on the River Don.

D. For the aim of the operation to be achieved it is essential to ensure that the advance beyond the Don is carried out rapidly, because there is only a brief period of favourable weather.

In accordance with these instructions the 1942 summer campaign in the south was divided into four stages.

First Stage. Break through to and seize Voronezh with the 2nd Field and 4th Panzer Army.

Second Stage. Smash the Soviet army west of the Don. To carry out this task the 6th Army was brought up, after breaking through to the east from the region east of Kharkov. At the same time the 4th Panzer Army swung southward along the Don from the region of Voronezh, to destroy the Soviet troops west of the Don, in conjunction with the 6th Army.

Third Stage. Launch an offensive south-east along the Don to Stalingrad with the 6th Field Army and the 4th Panzer Army, with a simultaneous attack by the 17th Field Army and 1st Panzer Army from the region east of Taganrog and

Artemovsk across the lower Donets and then north-east up the Don.

The two Army Groups, in accordance with the plan of operations, were to meet in the region of Stalingrad, so as to put the town's war industry and extremely important communications network out of action.

Fourth Stage. Capture the oil of the Caucasus. This was the ultimate aim, but the road to the Caucasus ran, not the shortest way through Rostov, but through Stalingrad.

In the process of carrying out these instructions, various amendments had to be made, because no general can forecast in detail what his adversary is going to do. In any battle fundamental corrections and changes are made by the strength or weakness of the enemy's will-power.

When it came to implementing Order No. 41, therefore, Hitler himself was compelled to make a number of corrections as a result of operations by the Soviet armed forces. The vigorous defence of Voronezh, where the German success was not decisive, the skillfully accomplished manœuvre by our forces and their withdrawal to north and south across the Don, the mistake in appraising Soviet forces north of Rostov, and a series of other events all upset Hitler's plans.

Abandoning consistency in conducting his operations, that is, instead of trying to reach the Volga with his main forces in the third stage of his operations, and then turning these forces to the job of capturing the oil of the Caucasus, Hitler soon decided to carry out the two operations at the same time.

In Order No. 45, on 23 July 1942, therefore, he set out the following tasks:

Army Group A to advance southward across the Don, with the aim of taking possession of the Caucasus with its oil resources;

Army Group B[1] to attack Stalingrad, smash the enemy concentration there, take the town and cut off the isthmus between the Don and the Volga.

---

[1]Now consisting of the 6th Field Army and the 4th Panzer Army, plus the 6th Rumanian Army Corps and reinforcements. (*Author's note.*)

Tanks and motorized troops were then immediately to strike along the Volga to Astrakhan and bring traffic on the main channel of the Volga to a halt.

For the seizure of Stalingrad three Army Groups were formed.

The Northern Group consisted of four infantry, two armoured and two motorized divisions, which were to launch their attack on July 23 from the region of Golovski and Perelazovski towards Verkhne-Buzinovka, and take Kalach.

The Central Group consisted of two infantry divisions and one armoured division, which were to attack on July 25 from the region of Oblivskaya and Verkhne-Aksenovski, through Staromaksimovski and break through to Kalach.

Both of these Groups, together with the 6th Army, were to encircle and destroy the main Soviet forces in the big elbow of the Don, force a crossing over the Don and advance to the Volga.

The Southern Group consisted of two infantry divisions, one armoured division, one motorized division of the 4th Panzer Army and two Rumanian infantry divisions. The Army Group was to cross the Don on July 21 at the village of Tsimlyanski, establish a substantial bridgehead on the south bank of the river, and prepare to attack Stalingrad from the south.

An analysis of the details of this situation shows that the German operations, particularly those of the Central Group, were aimed at a line which our armies were not yet ready to defend. Carrying out non-stop air reconnaissance, the enemy could clearly observe the columns moving up and the deployment and defence preparations of our units—in other words, the enemy was in the picture about the sectors of the front occupied by the 62nd and 64th Armies.

Waiting for my first military encounter with the German forces, I felt that, inexperienced as I was in battle against such a strong and experienced enemy, I would have to go through a great deal before things got better, if I survived.

I tried to find out as much as I could about the enemy's tactical methods, and chatted to many officers who had already had experience of battle. Unfortunately they had not all correctly weighed up the enemy, some of them simply did not understand his tactics and on occasion reckoned their obvious failures as great successes.

I knew that I could not study the enemy by sitting at Army H.Q., without seeing the field of battle. I tried to use every available opportunity, therefore, of being out in the field, so as to learn from experienced commanders.

Returning at 5 a.m. on July 22, I learned that Gordov had been summoned to Moscow the previous evening; he returned twenty-four hours later as Commander of the Stalingrad Front, and once again I was without an Army Commander.

64th Army H.Q. had already received orders from Front H.Q. for the 66th Infantry and 137th Armoured Brigades to move up to the village of Tsimlyanski on the west bank of the Don. Their task was to strike at and destroy the flank and rear of the enemy Army Group which had crossed the Don at this point. On Gordov's instructions this detachment assembled on the night of July 23 in the village of Suvorovski (the 137th Armoured Brigade was without heavy and medium tanks, as the bridge across the Don would not take their weight; it therefore joined this detachment with one motorized infantry battalion with fifteen T-60 tanks). My fears that Front H.Q. was under-estimating the strength of the enemy's Army Group at Tsimlyanski were confirmed.

In fact, as later became known, the German 48th Panzer Corps had crossed the Don in the Tsimlyanski area on July 21.

I was new at the front, but I could see that to send such a detachment, in effect one reinforced infantry brigade, to march some sixty miles out of contact with any Army, and moreover, ahead of positions which had been prepared to meet an enemy offensive, was a senseless, risky and useless venture.

On the morning of July 23 I telephoned Front H.Q., and failing to have this order revoked, I flew straight to Suvorovski in a PO-2 and handed over the order to the two brigades. I put the 66th Brigade Commander in charge of the detachment.

At 10 a.m. on July 23 the detachment set off to carry out its mission.

On my return journey, I decided to fly along the Army's Front, so as to examine our troops' positions from the air.

South-east of Surovikino we met a German aeroplane, a Ju 88, which turned and came in to attack us.

Our PO-2 was completely unarmed; the Ju 88 had a cannon and machine-guns. A cat-and-mouse game began.

The Ju 88 attacked us ten times or so. It looked as though the enemy's cannon and machine-gun fire would cut our plane to pieces in the air. To land in the bare steppe was out of the question, as we would become sitting targets and would soon have been shot to bits.

My pilot, taking his bearings from the sun, headed eastward, trying to find some small village behind which we could hide for a while from the bird of prey pursuing us ... But the steppe was bare. After the ninth or tenth successive attack, I don't remember exactly, our plane struck the ground and split in two.

As we were flying at ground level, the pilot and I were relatively unhurt by the crash. We were merely thrown out of the cockpits; I had a bump on the forehead and the pilot was bruised on the knees.

Our pursuer, seeing our plane burst into flames, presumably decided that we had been killed. Circling round, he headed west and was lost over the horizon.

We were soon picked up in the steppe and taken by car out of the danger area by Captain A. I. Semikov, an officer from the operations section at 62nd Army H.Q., afterwards made a Hero of the Soviet Union.

On July 24, forward detachments of the 229th and 214th Divisions and the 154th Marine Infantry Brigade of the 64th Army reached the River Tsimla. On the same day they were outflanked by the enemy on both sides, found themselves in a very difficult position and began to fight their way out into the bare steppe under pressure from the enemy's 51st Army Corps and under incessant bombardment from the air.

The previous day, the enemy had launched a general offensive against the 62nd Army's sector of the Front. Starting from the region of Bokovskaya, with four infantry, two armoured and two motorized divisions, the enemy quickly smashed the forward detachments of the 62nd Army and threw them back to the main line of defence, broke through

33

the front in the Kletskaya and Yevstratovski area, and began to advance towards the village of Tsymlovski.

On July 24 the enemy broke through the Front in the region of Kalmykov and began to advance on Manoylin.

After two days of fighting the enemy detected a weak spot in the 62nd Army's defences, encircled two infantry divisions and one armoured brigade in the region of Yevstratovski, Mayorovski and Kalmykov, and broke through to the region of Verkhne-Buzinovka, Osinovka and Sukhanovski.

In the centre, the three divisions of the 62nd Army continued to hold the line from Kalmykov to Surovikino, in the face of one very extended infantry division, the 44th.

These three 62nd Army divisions were doing nothing, while other parts of the front were in need of men to repulse the enemy's attacks.

The 64th Army, although occupying its line of defence as instructed by Front H.Q., was under-strength. Only the 214th Infantry Division, under the command of General Biryukov, and a marine infantry brigade, under the command of Colonel Smirnov, seemed to be in a somewhat better state than the others: they were at full strength and had had almost three days in which to organize their defence.

The 66th Infantry and 137th Armoured Brigades, moved by order of Front H.Q. from Suvorovski to Tsimlyanski, came under an enemy flank attack and might have perished to no purpose.

When I learned that the enemy had gone over to the offensive I repeatedly urged Front H.Q. to return these brigades to their previous positions. Gordov hated listening to proposals from subordinates, but after a battle of words with him on the telephone I finally got my way, and at 5 p.m. on July 24 the brigades were brought back to Nizhne-Chirskaya.

I also moved the 112th Infantry Division to the right bank of the Don, into defensive positions on the lower reaches of the River Chir. This time Gordov was in agreement.

On 25 July 1942, commanding operations by units of the 64th Army, I had my first baptism of fire on the front.

We were defending, the Germans were attacking. The initiative lay in the hands of the enemy, who, it must be said, had prepared for this offensive thoroughly. The 64th Army had only just consolidated this line of defence, was without well-equipped positions, and without well-organized transport of military stores and rations. The Army's rear stretched as far back as Tula.

The enemy's main attack, with two infantry divisions and one panzer division, fell on our right flank, where the 229th Infantry Division was defending about nine miles of front, with only five battalions in all—its remaining four battalions were on the way. This Division's front-line and rear units included the 137th Armoured Brigade, which had five heavy tanks, ten T-34's and twenty T-60's.

The battle began in the early morning.

The enemy started by throwing one infantry division with tanks against the centre of the 229th Infantry Division, against positions held by the 783rd Regiment.

In spite of the enemy's numerical superiority our battalions firmly repulsed his infantry and tanks. Ten tanks were put out of action and in the sector defended by the 783rd Regiment some 600 enemy soldiers were killed.

In the afternoon the enemy managed to drive a wedge into our defences as far as point 155.0 and seized State Farm No. 79. The Division's command post, which was at that time at point 155.0, was attacked by enemy tommy gunners. The Divisional Commander had to abandon his position rapidly, and as a result lost communication with the 783rd Infantry Regiment and the 2nd Battalion of the 804th Infantry Regiment. An officer from Divisional H.Q. sent to the area with a tank did not return, and was presumably killed.

So ended 25 July 1942, my first day of battle.

On July 26, at 5 a.m., after preparing the way with artillery and air attacks, the enemy again threw infantry and tanks into the battle. From my observation post (six miles north-west of Nizhne-Chirskaya) I counted more than eighty enemy tanks going into the attack under cover from artillery and mortar fire. The main attack was delivered through point 118.3, against a dairy farm held by units of the 783rd Infantry Regiment.

I could see the enemy's tanks, covered from the air, cutting into our military formations. One group of German tanks fell upon our KV's. Battle was joined. Our heavy tanks withstood the attack, but our light T-60's crawled along the gullies, not engaging battle.

Early in the battle the Commander of the 783rd Infantry Regiment was killed and the Commissar wounded; the Regiment began to retreat to the east.

The Divisional Commander immediately threw into the battle two battalions of the 804th Regiment, which had only just arrived. This was an attempt to halt the enemy's advance, but time was already running out. The battalions came under fire from enemy tanks and flung themselves to the ground. At 1 p.m. they were attacked by enemy infantry and tanks. Not having been able to dig themselves in, they could not hold off the attack, abandoned Hills 161 and 156, and moved back to the village of Savinski.

Mortar salvos and the artillery bombardment by the 214th Division in this sector caused the enemy heavy losses, but his units nonetheless continued to advance. At noon he threw in two groups of tanks. One, consisting of some forty tanks, pursued the battalions which had retreated to the banks of the River Myshkova; the other advanced towards Nizhne-Chirskaya.

It became clear during the afternoon that our defences on the right flank of the 229th Infantry Division had been broken. The enemy was advancing rapidly towards the River Chir between the 64th and 62nd Armies. Our Army had no reserves on the west bank of the Don. The 66th Infantry and 137th Armoured Brigades, which I had brought up from the Minayev region, were moving towards Nizhne-Chirskaya. Tired out with useless marches, the marine infantry moved slowly, and the tanks were running out of fuel. In order to drive the enemy back, and in particular to protect the junction point of the 64th and 62nd Armies, I decided to move the 112th Infantry Division, which was resting in the region of Logovski village after a night's march, and ten KV tanks of the 137th Armoured Brigade, quickly across the Don railway bridge. Their job was to occupy a line of defence from Staromaksimovski along the River Chir to its confluence with the Don and consolidate itself in positions of vantage. The junction point between the 62nd and 64th Armies had to be quickly and reliably protected, and an enemy flank and rear attack prevented.

This manœuvre was only partially successful; the enemy forestalled us. The 112th Infantry Division managed to cross the river and reach the railway line from Rychkovski to Lyapichev. We also succeeded in moving up part of the 66th Marine Infantry Brigade with a battery of artillery; the units of the 137th Armoured Brigade, however, ran out of fuel and did not even reach Nizhne-Chirskaya. To defend the junction point of the 214th and 229th Divisions, instead of tanks we had to use battalions of the 66th Marine Infantry Brigade, which were soon attacked from the air, and then by tanks. The marines took cover and began to beat off enemy attacks.

It looked as though we would succeed after all in halting the enemy and closing the gap, but panic appeared among the troops. It broke out not at the front but in the rear. Among the medical ambulance battalions, artillery park and transport units on the right bank of the Don, someone reported that German tanks were a mile or two away. This report was certainly an act of provocation and at this time it was enough to make the rear units rush for the crossing in disorder. Through channels unknown to me the panic was also communicated to the troops at the front.

I sent staff officers who were with me and my Artillery Commander, Major-General Braut, to the crossing, to try to stop the mass of people and vehicles rushing towards the Don. But all was to no avail: the enemy's aircraft had already spotted the multitude of men and machines at the crossing and begun to bomb them.

General Braut, Lieutenant-Colonel Sidorin, in command of operations, Colonel Burilov, in command of army engineering, and other army staff officers were killed in the bombing.

Towards evening the bridge across the Don at Nizhne-Chirskaya was destroyed by enemy air attack and sank. The 214th Infantry Division and two marine brigades of the 64th Army were left on the west bank of the Don without a crossing. Colonel Novikov, Army Chief of Staff, and Divisional Commander Abramov, the Member of the Military Council, learning of the position at the Front, towards evening on July 26 took a hasty and unnecessary step. Without my knowledge (I was still at Nizhne-Chirskaya) they issued an order by radio: 'The 214th Infantry Division, the two infantry brigades and the 137th Armoured Brigade are to retreat across the Don'. I learned of this order only when I returned to Army H.Q. at night on July 26, when units were already on the move. I was horror-stricken at the thought of what would happen when they reached the river during the night, without a single crossing to use.

What was needed was not to withdraw across the Don, but to organize defences on the west bank, anchoring both flanks at the river. We mobilized every possible means of communication to inform the troops of this decision. I do not remember what means of communication were available to us, but the troops received this order, and the retreat to the Don took on a more or less organized character.

The 112th Division, which had crossed the railway bridge with ten KV tanks to the west bank of the Don, was also instructed to strike south-west from the Rychkovski region, to throw the enemy back across the River Chir, and by so doing to close the gap and provide a reliable defence for the junction point with the 62nd Army. On the right of the 112th Division were regiments of the 229th Division, which had retreated under enemy attack.

On the afternoon of July 27, the regiments of these two divisions engaged in long and bitter fighting with the enemy, aiming towards the railway bridge and further north along the banks of the Don.

As a result of these measures towards evening on July 27, the breach made by the enemy was closed along the whole 64th Army front.

Many years have passed since all this happened, but I am still not ashamed to remember my baptism of fire on the Don. The enemy broke through the 64th Army's first line of defence, but was unable to carry his attack through any farther. He was halted.

Three days of fighting are a short period of time, but for me, who had not been long at the front, that short period of time had proved to be very important in every respect.

The 64th Army had had to retreat with losses. The first defeats, however, had not discouraged me. I believed that the time would come when Hitler's arrogant generals would also have to drain to the dregs the bitter cup of defeat by the Red Army.

The enemy's success could be explained largely by the fact that he launched the offensive when our troops were not yet assembled in regiments and divisions. But what would have happened if we had had two or three days in which to organize our defences, to assemble our regiments, battalions and divisions, to dig in, to organize proper cover and communications, and bring up military supplies and provisions?

There is only one answer—the enemy would not have succeeded in breaching the 64th Army's defences so quickly.

Observing how the Germans carried out their artillery preparation against the 229th Infantry Division's sector, I saw the weak points in their tactics. In strength and organization this artillery preparation was weak. Artillery and mortar attacks were not coordinated or in depth, but only against the main line of defence. I saw no broad manœuvre with artillery cover in the dynamic of battle.

When I was a student at the Frunze Academy I studied many battles and German operations on the western front in the first world war. I knew the views of the German generals about the role of artillery in future war (for example, the views of von Bernhardi). In the first days of the battle on the Don, therefore, I was expecting close combined operations between the enemy's artillery and ground forces, a precise organization of the artillery barrage, a lightning-fast manœuvre of shell and wheel. But this was not the case. I encountered the far from new method of slow wearing-down, trench by trench.

If at this time we had had a deeper defence structure (not five, but all ten battalions) and bigger anti-tank reserves, we could have not only beaten off the attack, but soundly thrashed the enemy.

The German tanks did not go into action without infantry and air support. On the battlefield there was no evidence of the 'prowess' of German tank crews, their courage and speed in action, about which foreign newspapers had written. The reverse was true, in fact—they operated sluggishly, extremely cautiously and indecisively.

The German infantry was strong in automatic fire, but I saw no rapid movement or resolute attack on the battlefield. When advancing, the German infantry did not spare their bullets, but frequently fired into thin air.

On July 27, when one regiment of the 112th Division counterattacked at Novomaksimovski Farm, the enemy's infantry did not engage battle at all and retreated. Only on the next day, when tank units had come up, did it fight for the positions it had abandoned without battle the previous day.

The German forward positions, particularly at night, were beautifully visible, being marked by machine-gun fire, tracer bullets, often fired into empty space, and different-coloured rockets. It seemed as if the Germans were either afraid of the dark or were bored without the crackle of machine-guns and the light of tracer bullets.

Any enemy troop manœuvre could be clearly followed by the columns of motor vehicles moving across the steppe with their headlights on.

The enemy's air force worked most accurately in battle. Combined operations and communication between the enemy's air and ground forces were very good. One could feel that the German pilots were familiar with the tactics of their own ground forces and ours.

One would very often see something like this: when German infantry had to take cover from our artillery or rifle and machine-gun fire, in a few minutes German aircraft would fly up, usually assault planes. Flying in a closed circle they would attack our military formations and artillery positions.

In modern warfare victory is impossible without combined action by all types of forces and without good administration. The Germans had this kind of polished, co-ordinated action. In battle the different arms of their forces never hurried, did not push ahead alone, but fought with the whole mass of men and technical backing. A few minutes before a general attack, their aircraft would fly in, bomb and strafe the object under attack, pinning the defending troops to the ground, and then infantry and tanks with supporting artillery and mortar fire would cut into our military formations almost with impunity.

These were the first deductions I came to about the enemy's tactics. I came to them not as a casual observer, and not so that I could talk about them afterwards. No, far from it. I had to know how the Nazi generals organized for battle, see the enemy's strong points, detect the weak ones and find his Achilles heel.

Now, therefore, many years afterwards, remembering my constant attempts to observe the enemy and discern his battle tactics I can see that I did not do this for nothing. To observe the enemy, to study his strong and weak points, to know his habits and customs, means to fight with one's eyes open, to take advantage of his mistakes and not expose one's own weak spots to dangerous attack.

From July 26 to the end of the month the main military operations of our units were on the Army's right flank, in the region of Bolshaya Osinovka, Yeritski and Verkhne-Chirskaya. In this sector the enemy tried to break through the military formations of the 229th and 112th Divisions to the north-east, emerge at the rear of the 62nd Army, and reach the Don crossings in the region of Logovski and Kalach.

I spent the whole of this time at an observation post on Hill III.I, north of Rychkovski Station and was in constant communication with the Commanders of the 229th and 112th Divisions and with the remaining troops through Army H.Q.

The battle was going with varying degrees of success. For several days the enemy threw into the attack units of the 51st Army Corps, reinforced with tanks. On some days as many as a hundred of his tanks went into action at the same time, while on this sector we had only ten. Our units, however, particularly the 112th Division, beat back the attacks and themselves counter-attacked.

This continued for four days. Early on the morning of July 31, regiments of the 229th and 112th Divisions, supported by the ten tanks and by aircraft, launched an attack and threw the enemy back across the River Chir. On the evening of the same day a radio telegram assessing our operations was intercepted: 'Units of the 51st Army which had crossed the River Chir at Surovikino have been smashed'. This was a report from some Nazi officer of Group B to his H.Q. He was probably a Gestapo agent, as it was signed with an X.

During this fighting I used every opportunity to question as many prisoners as possible, and through them to try to find out the mood of the enemy troops. I can only tell the truth and say that the prisoners firmly held their tongues, and sticking to their oath, maintained a stubborn silence. But not all ...

Somehow or other a Nazi fighter pilot was brought to me. He had been put out of action and made a forced landing north of Novomaksimovski. The prisoner said that German airmen were not afraid of Soviet fighters, as the technical superiority of the Messerschmitt was obvious: it was nearly fifty miles an hour faster and one and a half times better armed. He praised our airmen highly, however, for their courage, fortitude and fearlessness.

'The Luftwaffe is the big fist in battle,' the pilot said. 'Both the airmen themselves and the ground forces have faith in it. If we hadn't had the Luftwaffe we would not have had such successes in the West or the East.'

This was how a German airman spoke, after just being shot down.

When I asked him what he thought about the end of the war, he shrugged his shoulders and said:

'The Führer made a mistake about Russia. He and many other Germans did not expect the Russians to have such staying power, so it's hard to say about the end of the war.'

In the thick of the fighting on the Don, General Kolpakchi, Commander of the 62nd Army, telephoned me at my observation post. But the telephone call was from 64th Army H.Q. I was surprised, as heavy fighting was in progress on the 62nd Army sector. The enemy had advanced with powerful forces, taken Verkhne-Buzinovka, broken through on the right flank and encircled two divisions.

Kolpakchi told me over the telephone that he had been relieved of his post as Army Commander. Lieutenant-General A. I. Lopatin had been appointed to the command in his place.

General Lopatin was an ex-cavalryman and had recently been in command of an army which, in the retreat to the Don, had got so dispersed in the steppe that it had been very difficult to reassemble it.

The following day Major-General M. S. Shumilov arrived at 64th Army H.Q. He told me he had been sent to take over command of the Army, and that I was to report to Gordov.

At this time an order was received from Front H.Q., signed by the Chief of Staff, Major-General Nikishev, instructing the 62nd and 64th Armies to launch a simultaneous attack and destroy the enemy Group in the region of Verkhne-Buzinovka and on the River Chir. The 64th Army was to be reinforced by the 204th Infantry Division and the 23rd Armoured Corps.

The order was received at 2 p.m. on July 28, and the attack was scheduled to begin at 2 a.m. on July 29—twelve hours later.

Much of this short order was incomprehensible. We inquired by telephone where to find the 204th Division and the 23rd Armoured Corps, and were given the vague reply:

'Look for them between the River Don and the River Liska.'

We felt that Nikishev himself had no idea where they were.

We talked things over and decided to look for them in all directions.

Together with Z. T. Serdyuk, the Member of the Military Council, I took the road through Rychkovski, Novomaksimovski, Tuzov, Lysov and Zhirkov. Other comrades went off in other directions.

We drove across the steppe the whole night looking for the units that had been attached to the 64th Army. We searched the whole morning and not until nearly noon on July 29 did we find one armoured brigade of the 23rd Corps. The Commander of the brigade had had no instructions and had made no preparations for an attack.

Looking for the 23rd Corps H.Q., which was alleged to be at 'Pobyeda Oktabrya' State Farm, we called in *en route* at Volodinski Farm, where the 62nd Army's command post was situated.

Stout, fair-haired and outwardly very calm, General Lopatin entertained us to a good dinner, and told us that the 62nd Army could not and would not carry out the order from the Chief of Staff at Front H.Q., as the units were not ready, military supplies had not been brought up, and the Front Military Council had not confirmed the order.

Lopatin, as I had suspected, was in a far from confident frame of mind. He had no hope of being able to destroy the enemy's forces at Buzinovka. He doubted whether his half-encircled units on the right flank would hold out.

During our comings and goings between the Don and the 62nd Army's defences, the enemy's fighters and assault planes were constantly overhead. They shuttled backwards and forwards, flying east and back as calmly as if they were at home. We did not see any of our own planes the whole day.

The Nazi marauders, therefore, singly or in pairs, frequently dived and machine-gunned cars and other vehicles. These planes were obviously returning from military missions, and having unloaded their bombs on some target to the east, on the return journey they emptied their machine-gun belts at targets moving along the roads.

We spent the whole day meandering about the steppe, being shot at and bombed, and returned to 64th Army Headquarters empty-handed.

On the evening of July 30, I handed over command of the Army to General Shumilov and left for Front Headquarters at Stalingrad, where I spent two days waiting to see Gordov. I found loitering about the town and waiting for I knew not what, at a time when important events were taking place at the front, extremely disagreeable. On the evening of August 1, I finally went in to see Gordov. He was listening to a report from Air Commandant General T. T. Khryukin.

Gordov was in a gay, even jesting, mood.

'The enemy has been pinned down in our defence positions,' he said, 'and he can now be wiped out with a single blow.'

Contrasting Gordov's mood with that of Lopatin, and remembering the vain search in the steppe for the divisions that were not there, I came to the conclusion that the Front Commander did not know the situation at the front. He took wishful thinking for reality, and did not realize that a new threat, a large-scale attack, was imminent from the region of Tsimlyanski through Kotelnikovo.

General Gordov would not listen to my report.

'I know the situation at the front as well as you,' he affirmed, and, after a pause, asked me to explain why the right flank of the Army had withdrawn across the River Chir during the fighting on July 24-26.

'That withdrawal,' I answered, 'was forced upon us by pressure from superior enemy forces. The division was defending at only half-strength; the remainder was on the way, and it had no reinforcements . . .'

'Submit a written report,' he interrupted. 'A written one.'

'I have no military map or documents here,' I replied. 'I should like permission to return to the Army. I will write the report there and send it by special messenger.'

Gordov agreed to this proposal and I immediately returned to the Army.

After my meeting with Gordov I did not have to go back to see him again. Even then in the days of the fighting in the big elbow of the Don, it was as clear as daylight that the Commander of the Front and his H.Q. were too much in a hurry to imagine that the enemy was pinned down. Subsequent events completely refuted such an analysis, and I ought to say a little more about this here.

In the first place, it must be said that from the very start of the fighting in the elbow of the Don the enemy held the initiative firmly in his hands, and he was not pinned down, as Gordov and Nikishev tried to persuade themselves and their subordinates.

In certain sectors the enemy really did suffer big losses and was held back. In this connection one cannot but mention the 33rd Guards Division, which was defending to the south-west of Manoylin.

On July 21, for example, when the enemy had broken the resistance put up by forward detachments of the 62nd Army on the banks of the Rivers Tsutskan and Chir and hurried to make himself room for manœuvre, regiments of the 33rd Guards Division stuck to their positions and compelled the enemy to withdraw.

Next day the enemy again attacked the Guards' positions, this time with two divisions, one armoured and one infantry. The Guards did not waver. With anti-tank guns and rifle fire, grenades and bottles of incendiary mixture, they first destroyed the enemy's tanks and then turned their rifle fire on the infantry.

Those who took part in this battle tell of one tank attack after another. Individual tanks managed to break through our defences, but were then destroyed by our second line of defence. In one day's fighting the Guards of the 33rd Division put out of action and burned out fifty tanks and killed several hundred of the enemy.

In the centre of the defences held by this Division, in the sector where the main German blow fell, a position was held by the 76th Artillery Battery, under the command of Lieutenant Sery, a very young officer, and the officer in charge of an administrative platoon, Lieutenant Nedelin.

'Each platoon had 200 high explosive shells,' Nedelin told me. 'Our job was to stop the enemy from crossing our line of defence. Every gunner knew this clearly. Early in the morning of July 22, a big column of tanks appeared, and not far behind was a column of trucks with supplies and fuel.

'Our battery first opened fire on the trucks. Some of them burst into flames, the others turned back and drove away into the steppe. Meanwhile some twenty enemy tanks deployed and came into the attack. Ahead of us were two infantry platoons, but they did not succeed in halting these tanks, and the battle approached our battery's firing positions. At the first salvo from our guns the German tanks stopped, though not one of them had caught fire. The high explosive shells were very good against trucks, but they were not very effective against tanks.

'Nonetheless, the battery commander repeated the order— "Fire!" and we started to fire at point-blank range. A duel began between our four guns and those of the enemy's twenty tanks. We could not understand why the enemy did not immediately overrun our battery. Seeing that we were firing non-stop, the enemy must have thought our forces were strong in this sector ...

'Twin-engined aeroplanes soon appeared over the battlefield and began to bomb and machine-gun our battery. Heavy artillery shells, fired from behind the enemy's lines, were falling all round the battery. We were given no order to withdraw, and in any case we couldn't—there was nowhere to withdraw to, and we couldn't move across open steppe under constant air and artillery bombardment.

'We thought it over and decided to stay where we were and fight to the last shell.

'Everything was blowing up with a thunderous noise all about us. The thick steppe grass was on fire. The flames took away our last defence—the camouflage over our guns. The

Germans were clearly not short of supplies, but, knowing how small ours were, we economized every shell.

'About 4 p.m. the gun commander began to report that shells were running out. The battery had six shells left ... three ... and finally the last one. Then on our side everything fell silent. But even after we had stopped firing the enemy again plastered us with a great tornado of firing, and only then came in to attack us.

'A few dozen rifle bullets against an avalanche of tanks were quite pointless. We stayed in our emplacements, covered in earth, and waited for the end to come.

'The enemy's tanks came right up to the dug-outs, still firing. Our battery commander, Sery, was killed. Only a few men were still alive. I don't remember anything else: I was wounded by fragments from a shell which burst not more than a couple of yards away ...'

This is only one of the many episodes which testify to the fact that the Guards of the 33rd Division fought to the last shell, to the last bullet.

The anti-tank riflemen of this Division also fought valiantly. The exploit of the four anti-tank riflemen led by Pyotr Boloto, whom I later had occasion to meet, is well known. They had only two anti-tank rifles between them, and thirty tanks were heading for the hillock they were defending. This unequal battle went on the whole day. Their accurate firing sent fifteen enemy tanks up in flames. The remainder turned back.

Such determination on the part of the soldiers of the 33rd Guards Division really made it possible to imagine that the enemy had been pinned down. In fact, three German divisions were literally stuck and were involved in a (for them) very unprofitable battle which went on for several days on a very narrow sector of the Front. Advantage should have been taken of this situation by immediately counter-attacking against the flanks of the attacking German Group, throwing in nearby divisions and utterly smashing the enemy. But this did not happen. Neighboring divisions continued to remain on the defensive, waiting for something or other to happen. Meanwhile the enemy called off his attacks, threw his forces against the right flank of the 62nd Army, and on the morning of July 23 launched a new offensive. After several hours he managed to break through the defences of the 192nd Infantry Division in the sector from Kletskaya to Yevstratovski.

In this way, after battles lasting two days, the Germans captured Verkhne-Buzinovka, Osinovka and Sukhanovski, and encircled the 192nd and 184th Infantry Divisions and the 40th Armoured Brigade. Pressing home his attack, the enemy's forward units reached the Don between Golubinski and Mostovski Farms towards evening on July 26.

In spite of the courage of individual units of the 62nd Army and their stubborn resistance, the initiative remained firmly in the hands of the Germans.

Weighing up the position facing the 62nd and 64th Armies, the Commander of the Front took the decision on July 26 to launch concentrated attacks from north to south and from south to northwest, using the 1st and 4th Armoured Armies and part of the 21st and 64th Armies, so as to cut off and destroy the enemy forces which had broken through, and restore the situation.

The direction in which these attacks were to be made was chosen correctly, and had they been carried through the enemy Group which had broken through in the region of Verkhne-Buzinovka, Osinovka and Sukhanovski would undoubtedly have been encircled and smashed. But for success in battle beautifully drawn maps count for very little. A good strategic or operational plan needs to be implemented in good time, needs good tactics and the flexible handling of armies. But when a decision is taken late, it will inevitably be carried out in haste. In such cases there will as a rule be a lack of organization and co-ordination.

Six 62nd Army divisions were at full strength, and had even been reinforced, but to all intents and purposes it was only the 196th Infantry Division which went into battle against the enemy Group. The 192nd and 184th Infantry Divisions and the 40th Armoured Brigade stayed, as it were, bound hand and foot, north of Manoylin, waiting to be rescued from north or south at some time or other.

The 33rd, 181st and 147th Infantry Divisions and their reinforcements remained on their line of defence from Kalmykov to Surovikino, staring across, as we have seen, at one extremely drawn-out German division, the 44th.

What is more, all the armies were not instructed to counter-attack at the same time: the 196th Infantry Division launched its attack at 6 a.m. on July 26, the 1st Armoured Army went into action on the morning of July 27, and the 4th Armoured Army was able to go on to the offensive only on July 29.

Haste brings in its wake other mistakes in the organization of battle. The concentration on the west bank of the Don took place primarily during the day, without observing the elementary rules of camouflage. The region to the west of Kalach is open ground and the enemy was able not only to see what forces were moving up from the east, but also to count the number of tanks reaching the west bank of the Don. Finally the regions where the counter-attack was to begin were not given air and artillery cover.

As the counter-attack was so badly organized, the armies involved were unable to destroy the enemy forces which had broken through and, after suffering heavy losses, had to withdraw to the east bank of the Don.

In a special battle-order (No. 20) from 62nd Army H.Q., on July 28, General Lopatin wrote:

> From July 23-25, after unsuccessfully attacking on the right flank and in the centre of the 62nd Army, the enemy went over to the defensive, trying to keep the right flank of the Army half encircled, and at the same time attacked from the River Chir line with the 51st Army Corps, supported by 70-100 tanks, trying to break through to the region of Kalach.
>
> The 62nd Army is firmly holding its defensive positions, and together with the 1st Armoured Army and the 21st Army is completing the encirclement of the enemy Group at Verkhne-Buzinovka.

That is how the Commander of the 62nd Army estimated the position at the front and rear of his Army on July 28. This reminds me of the anecdote about the man who caught a bear. 'Bring it over here,' someone said. 'I can't,' he replied, 'it won't let me.'

Two days later the Commander of the Stalingrad Front, Lieutenant-General Gordov, in his Order No. 00160, instructed the 196th Infantry Division (that is, the whole section of the 62nd Army involved in the counter-attack) to take up a line of defence from Yevseyev to Manoylin, and prevent any enemy advance southwards. He had abandoned active operations by the 62nd Army and simply put it in defensive positions.

This was the end of the battle on the west bank of the Don.

In the fighting from July 23 to August 14, the 62nd Army suffered extremely heavy losses and soon withdrew to the east bank of the Don, to all intents and purposes without the division which it had comprised. They had been encircled by the enemy and fought their way out in small groups. The 62nd Army contained divisions which had previously been in the 1st Armoured Army, which handed over its troops to the 62nd Army and ceased to exist. It also contained one division (the 112th) which had previously been part of the 64th Army.

On the night of August 16, the 4th Armoured Army, which had occupied a bridgehead on the Malo-Kletski, Malo-Golubinski front, also withdrew across the Don under pressure from superior enemy forces.

The Germans were in full possession of the big elbow of the Don.

CHAPTER II

THE SOUTHERN GROUP

I ARRIVED back at the Army on August 1, and started collecting documents and writing a report on the fighting which had taken place on July 24-26. On the morning of August 2, however, I was sent for by General Shumilov.

At the house where Shumilov was living and working I found the whole Army Military Council, discussing a report by the Chief of Staff on the position on the left flank.

The information was disturbing. The 4th Panzer Army had crossed the Don at Tsimlyanski, had concentrated several divisions (including two panzer divisions) on the left bank, and had been attacking eastward, cutting the Stalingrad-Salsk railway. It was obvious that from the region of Tsimlyanski the enemy would direct his main attack towards the Volga, outflanking the 64th Army and the whole Stalingrad front from the left.

General Shumilov proposed that I should go to the southern sector, clarify the situation, and take such measures on the spot as the situation might demand. I asked:

'Is the Front Military Council in agreement with this?'

I was given an affirmative reply and I unhesitatingly agreed, and was even pleased to be released from writing the useless report for Gordov.

I was accompanied by an aide-de-camp, G. I. Klimov, orderly Revold Sidorin, drivers Kayum Kalimulin and Vadim Sidorkov, and some signallers. We set off south in three trucks, one of which contained radio transmitting equipment.

I called in *en route* at 214th Division H.Q. (in the village of Verkhne-Ruberzhny), where I was met by Divisional Commander General N. I. Biryukov. I had not seen him since July 24. Biryukov gave me a report on the situation, which was suspiciously quiet. Over the whole of the Division's sector from Nizhne-Chirskaya to the village of Gorodskoy the enemy was not even making attempts to force a crossing of the Don, and was not carrying out active reconnaissance.

Sitting with Biryukov near a haystack and drinking Don water with ice obtained from I have no idea where, we suddenly found ourselves under fire from the enemy's heavy guns. Thirty or so shells exploded not far from us. When things had quietened down I said good-bye to Biryukov and went off southward to the village of Generalovski, to the headquarters of the 29th Infantry Division of the 64th Army.

The 29th Division occupied positions to the south along the River Aksay, from the village of Gorodskoy to Novoaksayski. To the north of it, along the Don, the defence was in the hands of the 214th Division. To the south, from Potemkinskaya to Verkhne-Kurmoyarskaya, a cavalry regiment attached to the Army was defending. The left flank of the 29th Division was exposed.

I also knew that defences were being prepared along the River Myshkova, but that was in the rear, to the north of the River Aksay.

I stayed overnight at 29th Divisional H.Q. and on the morning of August 3 I went on to reconnoitre in the vicinity of Verkhne-Yablochny and Kotelnikovo. I had with me two squads of infantry, borrowed from 29th Divisional H.Q. They travelled in two lorries. Visibility in the steppe was perfect—about five miles.

Approaching the village of Verkhne-Yablochny from the north we saw two columns of infantry with artillery approaching from the south. They proved to be the 13th Infantry Division, under the command of Colonel Lyudnikov, and the 157th, commanded by Colonel Kuropatenko, retreating to the north.

Both divisions were under-strength and were going to join the army of General Trufanov. Attacked by the enemy in the region of Tsimlyanski and Remontnoye, they had suffered heavy losses, and having no communications with the Army, decided to retreat northward to Stalingrad. Retreating with them were two 'katyushi' regiments led by Deputy Army Artillery Commander, Major-General Dmitriev.

Lyudnikov and Kuropatenko could say little about the situation farther south. The enemy's attacks had shaken them severely. I realized this immediately, and taking both divisions under my command, decided to put them in a sector where they could pull themselves together. The divisions were ordered to withdraw behind the River Aksay and occupy and prepare defence positions there. Smirnov's 154th Marine Infantry Brigade took up positions behind these divisions as a second line of defence, from Verkhne-Kumskaya to a crossroads nearly eight miles to the north. I set up my improvised Southern Group Headquarters at the village of Verkhne-Kumskaya. One of the officers of Trufanov's Army H.Q. was appointed Chief of Staff.

I then got in touch with Stalingrad Front H.Q. and through the duty officer reported in detail on the situation in the southern sector. I could not establish communication with 64th Army H.Q.

Front H.Q. informed me that the 208th Siberian Infantry Division, freshly arrived at the front, was detraining at Chilekov and Kotelnikovo Stations, and proposed that I should also take this division under my command. I asked where its H.Q. was, but could get no definite answer.

On the morning of August 4, after confirming my order to Divisional Commanders Lyudnikov, Kuropatenko and Smirnov to prepare defences along the River Aksay in the sectors they had occupied, I went out as on the previous day to reconnoitre via Generalovski and Verkhne-Yablochny to the south-west.

On the roads in the steppe we kept coming across men and vehicles belonging to Lyudnikov's and Kuropatenko's divisions. To some extent I found this reassuring—it meant that the enemy was not in the vicinity. But at Verkhne-Yablochny the local inhabitants told me that there were Rumanians in the region of Verkhne-Kurmoyarskaya, crossing to the left bank of the Don.

Near Gremayachi Station we again met men and transport retreating southward along the railway. With difficulty I found an officer in the crowd and from him heard the serious news that the previous day a number of troop trains depositing units of the 208th Division at Kotelnikovo Station had suddenly been attacked by enemy planes and tanks. Groups of survivors were retreating back along the railway line. I could not find out what had happened to the Divisional Commander, Regimental Commanders and Chief of Staff.

Near Nebykovski Station a battalion which had deployed in a line facing south, was digging trenches. The officer in charge reported that, on hearing from the men retreating from the south that enemy tanks had appeared in Kotelnikovo, he had decided on his own initiative to establish a defence position. Where the Regimental or Divisional Commanders were he did not know. I approved his action, instructed him to hold retreating stragglers, and promised to put him in touch with the nearest H.Q., which I hoped to find at Chilekov Station.

As we approached the station we saw a number of troop trains. Units of the 208th Division were detraining. The news of the destruction of four troop trains at Kotelnikovo had not yet reached them. Alongside the railway line and around the troop trains were crowds of men, kitchens smoking and carts scattered about.

I found the officer in charge of one of the troop trains, in rank a Major but acting as Battalion Commander, and briefly explained to him the situation in the south; I instructed him to post strong covering detachments on high ground at Nebykovo village, to move the remaining troops away from the station and await instructions from Divisional H.Q. I then went off with my group to Dairy Farm No. 1, just over a mile west of Chilekov Station.

There we set up our radio equipment so as to get into contact with Front H.Q. The call sign, I remember, was 'Acoustic'. It was noon and there was not a cloud in the sky. Units of the 208th Division were in the farm buildings round about us. After about a quarter of an hour aide-de-camp Klimov reported that 'Acoustic' was answering. On my way to the building where we had set up the radio equipment I spotted three aircraft formations, nine in each. They were heading north, straight towards us. I thought they were ours . . .

Suddenly there was the roar of explosions. The planes were bombing Chilekov Station and the troop trains being unloaded there. I could see the carriages and the station buildings on fire, with raging flames rapidly leaping from one building to another.

I ran to the radio transmitter and ordered the operator to transmit a message that our troops were being bombed at Chilekov Station. Watching the 'Acoustic' warning signal being transmitted I did not notice one of the formations coming in from the north to bomb our farm; having dropped their bombs the planes then circled round and dived down on us with their guns blazing. It was painful to watch men who had just arrived and had not yet seen the enemy, being knocked out of action. All this happened because the area where the troop trains were to be unloaded was not given air cover. Front H.Q. had not seen to it.

Our radio was damaged, and there I was without communications.

Only in the evening, near Biryukovski Station, did we finally find the Divisional Commander, Colonel Voskoboynikov. I remember his pale face and quivering voice. He was suffering from shock. The death of his men had had a terrible effect on him.

'Comrade General,' he said, 'I am a Soviet Commander and I cannot go on after the loss of my units; it's difficult to reassemble them and their morale is shattered. I can therefore no longer consider myself in command of the division.'

I could not leave him without attention in this frame of mind. I stayed for a few hours, and when Voskoboynikov had come to his senses I saw him together with the Chief of Staff and the head of the Division's political section. I made all three undertake to get in touch with the units which had dispersed from stations between Zhutovo and Abganerovo, withdraw them by night across the River Aksay, organize defences from the village of Antonov to Zhutov No. I Farm and organize urgent reconnaissance in front of the Division's positions and on the left flank.

From the information I possessed it could be assumed that the Germans, not wishing to engage battle with our units deployed along the railway as far as Kotelnikovo, had decided to make a wide detour towards the Volga through Plodovitoye and Tinguta. We later discovered that columns of tanks of the enemy's 48th Panzer Corps were, in fact, heading in that direction from the vicinity of Kotelnikovo. This was why I had asked the 208th Divisional Command to carry out urgent reconnaissance, so as to find out where and how the enemy was moving his main forces in this area.

Night had already fallen when we turned back to our improvised Southern Group H.Q.

Fortunately the moon was shining and we travelled without headlights across the moonlit steppe. Near a crossroads about six miles south of Generalovski we spotted a cavalry patrol. Our squad of infantry went ahead in one of the vehicles to meet the patrol.

'Halt! Who goes there?'

They answered, and everything went off smoothly.

It was a patrol from a cavalry regiment which had retreated from Verkhne-Kurmoyarskaya Station. The officer in charge of the patrol told us that strong enemy forces had been crossing the Don at that point since early morning.

'Tell the Regimental Commander,' I instructed him, 'to carry out reconnaissance along the front from Potemkinskaya to Verkhne-Yablochny, to observe the enemy's operations and any possible approach by enemy units from the area of Kotelnikovo. Tell him to keep in touch with me through 29th Division's H.Q. in the village of Generalovski.'

Returning to Generalovski, I learned that the 29th Division, on instructions from Front H.Q., was rapidly withdrawing from its defensive positions and moving eastward to the region of Abgenerovo Station.

For two days the men who had accompanied me had been so exhausted that they were literally asleep on their feet. We therefore stayed in the village till morning.

The next morning, August 5, we were awakened by the crash of explosions from the steppe: enemy planes were bombing and machine-gunning columns of the 29th Infantry Division moving eastward along the northern bank of the River Aksay. The withdrawal had not been given air or artillery cover, and the division lost more men on the march than it had done in battle.

On the same morning the Commander of the cavalry regiment was instructed to occupy the line of defence abandoned by the 29th Division, taking in Chausovski and Generalovski. One cavalry regiment was, of course, very little with which to defend such a sector, but we had no other resources at our command. It was obvious, however, that the enemy was not preparing to attack us on this sector; his forces were moving off to the north-east.

Reconnaisance also made it clear that the enemy units which had crossed the Don at Verkhne-Kurmoyarskaya were also heading to the north-east, sending out small covering detachments to the River Aksay. These detachments were obviously designed to protect the left flank of the main force advancing from Kotelnikovo to Stalingrad by an encircling movement from the south-east.

It was somewhat disturbing that enemy forces, though quite small Rumanian units for the most part, were attacking our cavalry's positions. There was also another disturbing factor—the advance of the enemy's main forces to the northeast. It was obvious that, preparing an attack from the south, he was wheeling round the flank and rear of the whole Stalingrad front and cutting communications with our base.

Reconnaissance also showed us that the main German forces, after the capture of Kotelnikovo, were not taking the short cut along the railway but were heading via Pimen-Cherni, Darganov and Imantsevo, emerging in the vicinity of Tinguta, Plodovitoye and Abganerovo.

I contacted Front H.Q., reported on the situation that had

arisen in the south, and received a categorical order to hold the positions on the River Aksay with all the forces I could muster.

I received no other instructions or guidance, though I learned from men who travelled to the Army's rear, from telephonists and other 'grapevine' sources, that an extensive regrouping of our armies was taking place in our rear, and that 66th Army H.Q. was moving to the vicinity of Abganerovo.

The Southern Group which I was commanding was acting as a detachment on the River Aksay. I was waiting for an attack by the German and Rumanian forces, which must be aware of the regrouping of our armies. A German attack northward from the region of Kruglyakova and Zhutovo Station could smash the 64th Army's manœuvre.

I warned the troops under my command to prepare for a stubborn defence of the River Aksay line, and went round checking on the state of readiness of artillery and mortars for action, and so as not to be caught unawares by a surprise attack I sent out reconnaissance units in all directions.

The 154th Marine Infantry Brigade and two 'katyushi' regiments were held in reserve in the gullies, carefully camouflaged.

The attack by the German and Rumanian troops came on the evening of August 5, at the junction point of the divisions commanded by Lyudnikov and Kuropatenko. The main attack was delivered along a five-mile front. The enemy's infantry managed to cross the Aksay and drive a small wedge into our formations. Enemy tanks, for the moment, remained on the south bank, obviously until ferries had been prepared.

It was clear that the German and Rumanian troops, now that they had established a bridgehead on the north bank of the Aksay, would try to bring up tank ferries during the night, and would launch an attack on the morning of August 6, with their main body of troops. I say it was clear that this was how the enemy would behave, and this is where I see the first small, but nevertheless concrete result of my personal experience in the fighting from July 25-30 on the right bank of the Don.

Believing their tactics and methods to be infallible, the Germans followed exactly the same pattern here as when they had crossed the Don: air attack, then artillery, then infantry, then tanks. They did not know any other order in which to attack. When, on the evening of August 5, our reconnaissance and observers detected a concentration of infantry, artillery and transport ahead of our defence positions, there was no need for us to stop and wonder very long—we knew that the enemy was going to act as we expected.

I decided to frustrate this attack.

My plan was a simple one—to make an early dawn artillery attack on the positions from which the enemy was going to attack, and to counter-attack quickly so as to throw the enemy back across the Aksay.

We undertook no complicated manœuvres, except for moving up the two 'katyushi' regiments into suitable firing positions. Our artillery and mortars would open fire on previously reconnoitred targets, for which the range had been carefully found. After the artillery, the infantry would go into the attack. We had no tanks and I had no air cover on which to count, as I had been unable to establish contact with the air force.

To be quite frank, I was afraid of conducting even a simple operation with the troops I had collected during the retreat—I had no idea what they were capable of. However, I thought that if for some reason or other our attack did not succeed, or did not take place at all, our line of defence would still remain unaffected.

The enemy's tanks, the main danger facing us, were still on the other side of the Aksay. But if they were ferried across during the night our counter-attack would obviously be doomed to failure, because we not only had no anti-tank artillery—we did not even have any anti-tank grenades. It was a risky situation, but doing nothing might make it even worse.

When darkness fell the enemy behaved quite unconcernedly: his vehicles moved about with headlights on, not the slightest worried about our aeroplanes. The tanks did not move, waiting for ferries to be brought up. 'That means,' I thought, 'that the enemy is reckoning on throwing in his armour when the Luftwaffe is over our heads, when his artillery has put our firing positions out of action, and when the infantry has started to move forward. The Germans intend using the usual order and flattening our trenches with their caterpillars. But that's not how it's going to be!'

During the night I visited Divisional Commanders Lyudnikov and Kuropatenko and gave them my plan of action for the morning of August 6. They understood at once and started to prepare for the attack.

In banking on surprise we were fully justified. As soon as day broke, our artillery opened fire on the concentrations of enemy troops, and from our observation post we could see enemy infantry, followed by transport and artillery, scattering out of the gullies and other shelter. The masses of men and artillery rushing south, back across the Aksay, stopped the tanks from being ferried across.

Almost without loss, therefore, we broke the enemy attack planned for August 6. It was considerably more difficult, however, to attack and throw back the enemy infantry which had since the previous evening been deploying in the steppe, and which had already to some extent dug itself in; it took us almost until evening to do it.

In the fighting on August 6, the enemy suffered heavy losses in men killed, wounded and taken prisioner. We captured eight guns, many rifles and much ammunition.

I had satisfied myself that the retreating troops I had collected had not lost their fighting spirit and fought well: they moved into the attack rapidly and met the enemy without panic and staunchly. That was the most important thing of all.

So, for the first time, we not only stood up against the enemy, but soundly beat him.

Towards the end of the day, when I reported to Front H.Q. about the progress of the day's fighting, I learned that fierce fighting had been going on at the same time in the region of Abganerovo and Tinguta, where the 64th Army had been moved. The enemy had been unsuccessful there also, and had been firmly repulsed.

Finally, I learned that our Front was under the command of Colonel-General Andrey Ivanovich Yeremenko, whom I had known personally since 1938, when we were serving in the Belorussian military district. There we had often carried out military exercises together. The same night I sent him a note with some proposals—not to confine ourselves to passive defence, but on every suitable opportunity to counter-attack. I proposed that the troops under my command should counter-attack through Chilekov towards Darganov or Pimen-Cherni.

I received no reply to this note, and am not even sure whether Yeremenko received it.

I soon discovered that a military stores depot on the bank of the Volga had been blown up. There was a threat of 'bullet starvation', and the threat grew. Previously we had received as many supplies as we were able to transport, but now some of the trucks we sent for ammunition returned empty.

On August 7 the enemy attacked again in the same direction. Towards noon he managed to drive a three-four mile wedge into our defences.

In order to close the gap we decided to counter-attack again, smash the enemy and throw him back across the Aksay. We decided to do this, not in the daytime when enemy planes were particularly active, and not in the morning, as we had done on August 6, but two hours before sunset, when the enemy's planes had hardly any light left, and when his tanks, separated from the infantry, were still on the other side of the river.

This time it was not a frontal but a flank attack, with Lyudnikov attacking from north-west to south-east, and Kuropatenko from north-east to south-west, the two attacks converging on a single point.

This plan, orally worked out and agreed with Lyudnikov and Kuropatenko, was completely successful. The enemy was again soundly beaten and thrown back.

We took several dozen prisoners.

In our positions on the Aksay we fought for about a week. The German and Rumanian troops attacked nearly every day. They would drive a wedge into our lines, but we would immediately counter-attack and throw them back.

In these battles we worked out our own special methods and our own tactics.

The enemy usually attacked between 10-12 noon. He would have to spend two to three hours crossing the Aksay and approaching our forward defences, which were in fact reinforced outposts. The infantry attack would be supported by artillery and two or three formation of aeroplanes, nine in each.

Our outposts, opening fire with support from our artillery, would slowly retreat towards the main defence positions. In such a situation the enemy could not select the moment to attack, and had to spend a further two or three hours in reaching our main positions. To break through our main positions he had to stop, bring up men and guns, and organize communications and administration. By nightfall, therefore, the attackers had not succeeded in breaking through our defences, and they did not like, and possibly were unable, to fight by night. We would then counter-attack either in the evening or at dawn, when the enemy's planes were on the ground. Our artillery and mortars would go into action and our units would counter-attack swiftly and strongly at the enemy's weakest point and throw him back to where he started from.

This pattern was repeated several times.

On August 12, Front H.Q. instructed the Southern Group to take over the 66th Marine Infantry Brigade, which somewhat strengthened the rather thin ranks of the Southern Group, particularly on the right flank. Using natural obstacles—river, ravine and gully—we established firm defensive positions.

At the same time, units of the 64th Army, reinforced by Tanastishin's Mechanized Corps, were engaged in bitter defensive fighting against the Germans' 4th Panzer Army, which had advanced from the south to the neighbourhood of Plodovitoye and Abganerovo.

It was clear that the German generals, using their beloved pincer movement, would try to seize Stalingrad from west and south and simultaneously encircle our forces west and south-west of the city. These were obviously contributory factors to the slight withdrawal of the Southern Group to the River Myshkova.

We received the order to withdraw on August 17 from Front H.Q. Group H.Q. immediately drew up a plan for the withdrawal to the new positions.

I was confident that the Southern Group's forces could be disengaged and withdrawn without loss. I therefore gave final

61

instructions and went to bed, so that in the early hours of the morning I could be with the troops withdrawing to their new positions. At midnight the Deputy Commander of the Front, Lieutenant-General Philip Ivanovich Golikov, arrived. He got me out of bed when our troops had already started to move.

He was told the plan and organization for the withdrawal, showed me the line of defence more precisely on the map, and seeing that we had taken the measures necessary for any attempt by the enemy to pursue the retreating troops, he also went to sleep.

The troops moved quickly, successfully completed their withdrawal during the night, and occupied their new defensive positions without the loss of a man.

It took the enemy a long time to detect our withdrawal to new positions. It was not until evening on August 18 that reconnaissance aircraft appeared over the River Myshkova. The enemy did not, however, try to attack our units in their new positions, presumably not considering it expedient to do so. At this time events of fundamental importance were taking place elsewhere—through the area of Vertyachi towards Stalingrad on the right flank of the 64th Army, and through Plodovitoye and Tundotovo towards Stalingrad on its left flank. In the battles in these areas considerably more troops and technical backing were involved than on the River Aksay. I believe, however, that in that sector also our Command could have been more active and could have tried, if not to wrest the initiative completely out of the enemy's hands, at least to upset his plans. For example, at the moment when the main forces of the 4th Panzer Army began their advance from Kotelnikovo to Abganerovo along the railway, we could have probed the weak points in his flanks, where units of Hitler's satellites were acting as covering detachments, and could have delivered a powerful attack on them. Similarly, an attack could have been made purely by the Southern Group and the 214th Division, which was doing nothing on the Don, from the vicinity of Verkhne-Kumski and Antonov towards the Aksay, coming out at the rear of the enemy's main forces, and again upsetting and possibly shattering his plans.

In other words, what was needed was not just defensive action to beat off German attacks, but offensive action by some of the forces at the disposal of Front H.Q. In fact, facing us were the exposed flank and rear of the 4th Panzer Army. We should not have waited for events to catch up with us in those places where the enemy had superior numbers, but should have struck at the enemy's most vulnerable points. This would have been possible when the 64th Army, under General M. S. Shumilov, was putting up a stiff resistance in the region of Plodovitoye and Abganerovo, was dealing the enemy a series of powerful blows, and even forced him temporarily to suspend his offensive.

On August 19, after the Southern Group had withdrawn to its new defence positions, I went to 64th Army H.Q. to explain the general position. When I arrived to see General Shumilov at Verkhne-Tsaritsynski I also found there Lieutenant-General Golikov, Deputy Commander of the Front.

We had a meal together and I learned that the Front Military Council had already decided to incorporate the troops of the Southern Group into the 64th Army. General Golikov proposed that I should remain with the Army as Deputy Commander. I agreed. The Group H.Q. would be incorporated into Army H.Q.

The troops of the former Southern Group were ordered by the Front Commander to move from the right flank and strengthen our units in the main line of attack of the 4th Panzer Army.

On August 24, at Shumilov's request, I went out to the vicinity of the village of Vasilievka, where bitter fighting had been reported against the attacking enemy. Approaching from the village of Ivanovka, the driver, Kayum Kalimulin, drove at such a furious speed that we suddenly found ourselves between our positions and the Germans'—under fire from both sides. I was wearing a foreign raincoat. Scampering back in our vehicle from the German positions we were met by our own soldiers with such suspicion that, had I not spoken to them in colloquial Russian, we would probably have been met with hand grenades, and my raincoat would have been riddled with machine-gun bullets.

To the north of Vasilievka I found the observation post of the Artillery Commander of the regiment which had been attached to Kuropatenko's division. Enemy tanks and infantry were approaching, but for some reason or other the regiment was not doing anything about it.

'Why aren't you firing at the enemy?' I asked the Commander.

He was somewhat embarrassed.

'We're running out of ammunition.'

This was the answer usually given by commanders about to retreat.

'I order you to load the guns immediately and open fire!'

'On which group?'

'On the enemy's reserves.'

From the observation post we could clearly see large groups of enemy infantry coming up from the neighbourhood of the village.

The first salvo burst, then the next, and the approaching enemy reserves began to scatter along the gullies, while men, horses and carts and vehicles were rushing out of them. The Germans clearly did not like our accurate fire.

The Divisional Commander suddenly appeared at the observation post. There and then we organized additional fire by the division's artillery, and the infantry regiments launched a counter-attack. Fighting then went on for two hours, and we retook the villages of Vasilievka and Kaplinka. The enemy withdrew southward in disorder. In the fighting here also we saw no particular pertinacity by the enemy in battle. One had only to fire at them accurately and they were not slow in showing their heels.

The next day I went to Lyudnikov's so-called divisional command post. It was a slit trench about a yard and a half wide and six yards long. It was so cramped that I was not anxious to crawl into it when Lyudnikov invited me.

Heavy artillery shells were bursting all about us, but I stayed out of the trench and could not take my eyes off the counter-attack being launched by our troops.

The main forces involved in the counter-attack—a battalion of tanks with some of Lyudnikov's infantry—had only just gone into battle. I could see the German tanks and infantry falling back under pressure from our troops. But after twenty to thirty minutes German aeroplanes flew in and started diving. Our tanks and infantry stopped and fired from where they were. A gun battle began between the German tanks and ours. Neither side came any closer. This went on for several hours.

Seeing that the situation was firmly in hand on this sector, I informed Shumilov of the position, and went on to the 29th Division's sector, to Yurkin State Farm, about six miles north of Abganerovo.

Before we reached Abganerovo we stopped near a burnt-out T-34 tank to have a snack. We were extremely hungry but we did not have much food. No sooner had we sat down, opened some tinned food and started eating, however, than immediately in front of me, not more than a yard away, I saw a decayed and blackened human hand sticking up out of the grass. The others followed my glance, and suddenly none of us had any appetite. We stood up, and leaving the food spread out on the newspaper, got back into our truck . . .

At 29th Division's command post I again met General Golikov, who obviously did not like just sitting at Front H.Q. From here we watched enemy planes bombing their own infantry. This happened after a short skirmish, when our units rapidly withdrew from the positions being bombed by the enemy, enticing the enemy's infantry into advancing quickly. German planes, flying in groups of twenty to thirty, then bombed their own troops for more than half an hour. The German infantry and tanks scattered from their own bombs, sending up dozens of white rockets to tell the planes they were bombing their own men. But the planes carried on until they had no bombs left.

This was a simple, but intelligent and rapidly executed manœuvre.

On the same day, near Yurkin State Farm, I was able to watch six-barrelled mortars at work. The trajectory of the missiles was clearly visible against the sky, heading towards the sector occupied by Lyudnikov's division. The mortar salvos sounded like the creak of a cart that needed oiling followed by powerful explosions.

In the evening I decided to go back to the Army's command post, in a gully six miles north of Zety.

Heading towards the station, we saw a long line of Red Army men who had crossed the railway line and were retreating northward. There was no firing to be heard; nor could we see from whom the men were retreating. The three of us left our truck, stopped the men, led them behind the railway embankment and set them digging themselves in. We soon found platoon and company commanders of Lyudnikov's division and ordered them to hold the position the men had occupied. We could not reach Lyudnikov's command post because it was already growing dark, and in the darkness we might run into the Germans.

Near a railway crossing we met one of the Army's political staff (I don't remember his name). He told us that Shumilov and the whole Army H.Q. were sitting at telephones trying to find me, as they had no idea where I had gone. I suddenly realized that I had not rung Army H.Q. for about ten hours.

General M. S. Shumilov, and his senior deputies, Z. T. Serdyuk and K. K. Abramov, Members of the Military Council, and Chief of Staff M. S. Laskin, were very attentive towards me. We had somehow quickly found a common language, worked together amicably and harmoniously, and were concerned for one another's welfare. (This friendly relationship existed the whole time I was with the 64th Army.) And now they had lost me!

They had good reason to be concerned, of course. At that time such 'peripatetic' generals sometimes did fail to return—having been killed or taken prisoner.

When I came into the dug-out and Shumilov saw me he shouted:

'He's turned up!'

He immediately telephoned the Chief of Staff at Front H.Q. and told him I had reappeared.

The Member of the Military Council was soon in the dug-out, and they all began to scold me, but I could see an ill-concealed pleasure on their faces. Not having had news from me for a long time, they had apparently given Lyudnikov and other commanders instructions to search for me on the battlefield, even if only to find the wrecked vehicle. But I had come back hale and hearty, under my own steam.

The days of the fighting between the Don and the Volga gave rise to outstanding mass heroism by the Soviet people.

The unsuccessful action waged by our armies on the right bank of the Don did not break the spirit of the Soviet troops.

The 62nd and 64th Armies grew steeled and mature. In these battles officers and men alike learned how to hit the enemy and inflict losses on him, in spite of his great numerical superiority.

It was during these days that the exploit of sixteen guardsmen, led by a young Communist, Lieutenant V. D. Kochetkov, took place. Ordered to occupy positions on one of the heights, the men knew that until reinforcements arrived they would have to wage a stiff battle, and pledged one another their word not to retreat a step.

A small group of enemy infantry began the attack, unsuccessfully attacking the hillock four times; a company of machine-gunners was then thrown in. This attack was also beaten off.

At dawn the following day twelve enemy tanks moved into the attack. The sixteen men had not a single anti-tank rifle among them, and many of them were wounded. The officer in charge was badly wounded. They bound one another's wounds and waited for the enemy to approach . . .

A battle to the death began. One of the men threw himself with a bunch of grenades under the tracks of the first tank. The tank blew up. A second man followed, then a third, and a fourth . . . Four tanks stood blazing on the battlefield. The German tank crews' nerves could not stand it. Some of the tanks turned back, but two of them continued to move forward relentlessly.

Of the sixteen heroes, only four were still alive—Chirkov, Stepanenko, Shukmatov and young Lieutenant Kochetkov. They could have hidden in a dug-out, escaped down a ravine. But this would have meant surrendering their position to the enemy and opening up a path to the Volga for him. The three men laid the dying lieutenant under cover, took handfuls of grenades and threw themselves under the German tanks, destroying them.

When reinforcements arrived, on the slope of the hill they found six burnt-out German tanks. The defenders had fought against superior forces and perished without retreating a step.

Young Lieutenant Kochetkov managed to tell the story of what had happened before he died.

On another sector, near Malye Rossoshki, twenty-five miles

west of Stalingrad, thirty-three soldiers of the 62nd Army, led by the deputy political instructor, a Komsomol member called Leonid Kovalev, found themselves completely encircled, but made no attempt to retreat. Seventy German tanks stormed their position. Their supplies of provisions ran out. They were thirsty, but did not have a drop of water. But they did not waver, and in the battle which ensued they burnt out twenty-seven tanks and killed more than 150 of the enemy.

So, day by day, mass heroism grew, and the Soviet troops stiffened their resistance.

Encountering increasing opposition at the approaches to Stalingrad, the German Command began to build up its forces. The scale and intensity of the battle grew day by day. New enemy troops crossed the Don principally at Nizhni Akatov, Vyertyachi and Nizhne-Chirskaya, where all attempts by the 62nd Army to throw back the enemy units which had crossed the Don had been unsuccessful.

The four corps which made up Paulus's 6th Army were preparing for a new offensive from bridgeheads on the east bank of the Don. The 8th Army Corps was to attack through Kotluban and Kuzmichi to Yerzovka, covering the entire operation from the north; the 14th Panzer Corps was to attack the town directly through Rossoshka and Gumrak, and the 24th Panzer Corps was also to attack the town from the area of Kalach through Karpova. Meanwhile the 4th Panzer Army would continue to attack from the south.

In planning to reach the Volga north of the city, the attackers were also trying to conduct a deep outflanking movement to the right of the 62nd Army. They were obviously trying to carry out a precise plan for the encirclement of the 62nd and 64th Armies, by driving pincers from west and south to the banks of the Volga.

Under orders from Hitler to take Stalingrad by August 25, the German hordes, regardless of losses, tore through towards the Volga. 23 August 1942 proved to be a tragic day for the city, when, with several infantry divisions and one panzer division, and at the cost of enormous losses, the enemy managed to break through the 62nd Army's defences between Vertyachi and Peskovatka. The enemy's forward units, supported by a hundred tanks, reached the Volga north of the village of Rynok. Along a corridor five miles in width the Germans poured several infantry, motorized and panzer divisions.

An extremely dangerous situation had arisen. The slightest confusion, the slightest sign of panic, on our side, would have been fatal. This is what the Germans were banking on. With the deliberate intention of sowing panic, and, as a result of it, breaking through to the city, on August 23 they turned some 2,000 bombers on the town. Never before in the entire war had the enemy attacked in such strength from the air. The huge city, stretching for nearly thirty-five miles along the Volga, was enveloped in flames. Everything was blazing, collapsing. Death and disaster descended on thousands of families.

But the response to the enemy attacks was not panic or alarm. At the call of the Front Military Council and the Party organizations in the city, the soldiers and citizens replied by closing their ranks. The famous Barrikady (Barricades) and Krasny Oktyabr (Red October) tractor factories and the power station, became bastions of defence. The workers forged guns and fought for the factories alongside the soldiers. Grey-haired veterans of the defence of Tsaritsyn, foundrymen and tractor engineers, Volga boatmen and stevedores, railwaymen and shipbuilders, office workers and housewives, fathers and children—all became soldiers, and each and every one turned out to defend their city. Help soon came to them from military units belonging to Colonels Sarayev, Gorokhov and Andryusenko, and Lieutenant-Colonel Bolvinov.

The fighting grew more and more intense. Every step forward the Germans made was at the price of huge losses. The nearer they came to the city, the more intense became the fighting, the more fearlessly did the Soviet troops fight. During these days of fighting our defence was like a spring, which increases its resilience under pressure.

The Germans reached the Volga north of the city on August 23, but they were unable to widen their breakthrough. The villages of Rynok, Spartanovka and Orlovka, where defences were organized in time, became insurmountable obstacles for them. In the battles on the northern outskirts of the city hundreds and thousands of workers took part, shoulder to shoulder with the men of the 62nd Army. Here the Germans were held.

To the south, on the 64th Army's sector, the Germans were unable to break through to the Volga. They were firmly beaten back by our counter-attacks.

The weakest point in the defence at this time was in the area of Kotluban and Konny Stations, on the 62nd Army's right flank. If the enemy had turned even two divisions along the railway line southward from Konny, they could easily have reached Voroponovo Station, at the rear of the 62nd and 64th Armies, and could have cut them off from the city.

But the German generals obviously wanted to kill two birds with one stone, rapidly taking the city and encircling the 62nd and 64th Armies. They were so obsessed with this aim that they did not notice the mounting resistance being put up by the Soviet armies, and the lengthening of the German front and communications; all this again finally upset the plans of the German strategists. They had banked on sowing panic and confusion by their barbarous bombing attack, but in this they had miscalculated. The population of the city had sustained this savage attack.

The 62nd and 64th Armies' defensive positions at the end of August stretched from the village of Latashanka through Rynok, Orlovka, Sovietski, Lyapichev and then south-east along the Yerik and Myshkova Rivers as far as Vasilievka, then through Yurkin State Farm and along the railway line to Tundutovo Station.

The 46th Panzer Corps, attacking on the right flank of the 4th Panzer Army, at the end of August found itself blocked by defences on the Chervlenaya River (now the Volga-Don Canal). It marked time here for about a week. At the end of August this Corps was transferred to the 4th Panzer Army's left flank, in the vicinity of Abganerovo. From there, developing an attack through Zety towards Basargino Station, it was to join up with the 6th Army. A real threat of encirclement developed for the 62nd Army and two divisions of the 64th Army.

The manoeuvre was detected by our reconnaissance in time, however, and the Front Commander instructed the 62nd and 64th Armies to take up new defence positions through Rynok, Orlovka, Novaya Nadezhda State Farm, Bolshaya

Rossoshka and Malaya Rossoshka, the east bank of the River Rossoshka, the east bank of the River Chervlenaya, Novy Rogachik and Ivanovka.

On the night of August 29, with Colonel Borzhilovski of army engineering, I went out to reconnoitre the River Chervlenaya line. We spent the night in the village of Peschanka, with General Aleksandrov, Chief of Staff of the 64th Army's rear units. Early in the morning of the 30th we went out on reconnaissance.

In the Novy Rogachik area, we saw some units of the 62nd Army retreating, while fighting was already taking place in the Karpovka area. The 64th Army's units were some eighteen to thirty miles from this position, and I was very worried whether they would be able to withdraw to their new line of defence in good time, as the Southern Group had done on August 17.

During the day we met General Golikov, who, on instructions from the Front Commander, was also reconnoitring these positions. Golikov was pleased to have found someone to whom to hand over this sector, and I was also pleased that there and then he was able to attach to me a reserve regiment of anti-tank artillery, with which I could cover a crossing of the River Chervlenaya.

Enemy reconnaissance planes appeared overhead on the evening of August 30 and dropped a few bombs on the anti-tank artillery regiment's batteries.

I informed Shumilov about my reconnaissance and the position on the new line of defence, and also about the neighbouring 62nd Army. From then on through the night and until noon the following day we did not close our eyes, waiting for the appearance of the units withdrawing to the new defence positions. On the morning of August 31 it was clear that our units had not been able to disengage themselves unnoticed from the enemy: the rumble of bomb and shell explosions confirmed our fears.

The withdrawal of the 64th Army's units had coincided with the beginning of a new attack by panzer divisions of the 48th Corps. His tanks and planes carried on an unflagging attack against the withdrawing units. Crossing the River Chervlenaya, the regiments of the 64th Army immediately set about occupying positions for battle. The Army command post was in Karavatka gully, and the Army H.Q. was at Gornaya Polyana State Farm. The 62nd and 64th Armies' flanks met at the village of Novy Rogachik. On its left flank the 64th Army joined up with Tolbukhin's 57th Army. The enemy decided against attacking our new positions immediately.

On September 1 the Germans were obviously bringing up their forces and occupying positions from which to launch a further offensive, and on September 2 they subjected our rear, our artillery positions and communications to heavy bombing. Our emergency signals post was put out of action. The Germans clearly knew the disposition of our communications and even of our command posts.

On the morning of September 3, after fierce bombing and Artillery preparation, the Germans launched an attack along the whole of this front. Towards noon they managed to cross the River Chervlenaya on the Army's left flank. The Front Commander ordered us to restore the position immediately. General Shumilov was ordered to go to Hill 128.2 and personally lead the counter-attack. Shumilov left and wasted several hours on this hill, under incessant mortar fire and air attack. Abramov, the Member of the Military Council, and I, with signals and administration, remained at the command post. Around midday General Golikov arrived. When he had familiarized himself with the situation and given a number of oral instructions from the Front Military Council, he went on along the front. Half an hour later a bombing attack began. The enemy's air reconnaissance must have detected our command post and promptly sent in bombers. We had no right to move anywhere else: our communications were from here and our troops were being administered from here. In any case, to move in the open steppe under a bombing attack was out of the question.

We therefore had to carry on working in the dug-outs, with a nine-inch thick roof of poles and earth over our heads.

My tiny desk with telephones stood opposite Abramov's. Our six square yards of space with walls of earth and a low ceiling reminded me of a ready-prepared grave. It was hot, stuffy and dusty. Soil poured through cracks between the poles in the roof.

72

After sitting like this under bombardment for several hours, we began to grow accustomed to it and took no notice of the roar of engines and the explosion of bombs.

Suddenly our dug-out seemed to be thrown into the air. There was a deafening explosion. Abramov and I found ourselves on the floor, together with the overturned desks and stools. Above us was the sky, choked with dust. Lumps of earth and stones were flying about, and around us people were crying out and groaning.

When the dust had settled a little, we saw an enormous crater some six to ten yards from our dug-out. Round it lay a number of mutilated bodies, and scattered about were overturned trucks and our radio transmitter, now out of action. Our telephone communications had also been destroyed.

The Army's emergency signals post was near the village of Yagodny, over a mile south of the main command post. I decided to go and maintain contact with our units from there.

I sent for my truck, and with Klimov, my aide-de-camp, and Kayum Kalimulin, the driver, I set off. But we had scarcely emerged from the gully when the enemy's aeroplanes again started peppering our command post with small bombs. We could see Ju 88's coming in for low-level attacks, dropping some ten or a dozen bombs each on the gully, and then going after individual vehicles. One Junker came after us. We were saved, and I say this without embarrassment, by firmness and calculation.

Not taking my eyes off the Junker, I shouted to the driver: 'Drive straight ahead and don't turn off!'

When I saw the first bomb leave the plane I ordered him to turn sharp right. The vehicle swung round ninety degrees at full speed. By the time the bombs hit the ground we were already over a hundred yards away.

The Junker dropped about a dozen bombs, but not one of us was hurt. Our vehicle's battery, however, had a hole in it and the electrolyte was running out; the engine would not start. All this happened about 350-550 yards from our command post.

While Kayum was tinkering with the engine, I climbed to the top of a hillock, and from the region of Tsybenko village I saw German tanks approaching. There was a group of ten in front, then ten more, and about a hundred in all, coming out of the valley of the Chervlenaya. The column was heading along the road northward towards the village of Basargino.

It was clear that while the Luftwaffe had been attacking our troops and the Army's command post, the tanks had been able to overcome the defences in the region of Varvarovka and Tsybenko. They were now less than a mile and a half from our command post. Our artillery opened fire on them, and I decided not to go on to the emergency signals post. I returned on foot to the shattered command post, and again met General Golikov, who had obviously come back to find out what was left of the command post.

Communication had already been re-established with Army H.Q., and we learned that the Germans had broken through the 64th Army's defences not only in the vicinity of Tsybenko, but also near the village of Nariman.

Things were going no better on the 62nd Army's sector. There, after breaking through the defences on the River Rossoshka, the enemy had reached Basargino.

Until darkness fell I stayed at the command post, and only at nightfall did Shumilov summon us to a new one, in a wood three miles west of Beketovka.

The 62nd and 64th Army units made a bitterly-fought retreat to the last positions, towards Stalingrad.

An endless stream of people was moving along the roads. Workers from collective and state farms were escaping with their families. They were heading for the Volga crossings, driving their cattle with them, carting away their agricultural equipment—anything of value, so that nothing would fall into enemy hands.

I would like here to quote some reminiscences contained in a letter from Dmitri Ivanovich Soloviev, Director of RKKA[1] 13th Anniversary State Farm (stock-breeding). After evacuating their farm near Kharkov, he and the other members camped temporarily near Prudboy Station, on Marinovski Collective Farm, thirty-four miles west of the Volga.

'We kept in touch with military units,' writes Soloviev, 'so

_____
[1] Workers' and Peasants' Red Army (renamed Soviet Army in 1946).

74

as to find out what was going on at the front, and whether there was any danger of our falling into the hands of the Nazis with all our possessions.

'We heard rumors that the Germans had already crossed the Don. Someone started to agitate for us to stay where we were and not try to cross the Volga. The Germans, said some, were just people like us.

'The headquarters of an armoured unit with which we were in touch went off somewhere or other. Nazi planes dropped bombs and leaflets on us, and dived low to machine-gun us.

'I decided that during the night of August 28 we would set off for the Volga. We hadn't enough workers and drivers. Several traitors, led by a mechanic called Missyura, went off allegedly to reconnoitre, and did not return.

'On August 28, after nightfall, our column moved out of Prudboy. There was not a soul on the road, and we had no idea what the position was.

'At Prudboy Station we met an officer called Karpenko in charge of a company of sappers, who mined the roads and bridges after we had gone. He told me that the only path that had not been mined now lay through Rogachinski State Farm. But summer nights are very short, and by dawn the column had gone less than ten miles. During the day we hid in stooks of corn, behind banks and in haystacks. We had no rest from German planes and their machine-guns. The first victim was a driver, Osip Serikov, who fired back with a rifle he had found in a field.

'In the evening I set out in a truck along country paths to reconnoitre a way to Basargino, where, according to some peasants we met, there were no Germans. The village had not, in fact, yet been occupied. When I came back to the column I found that the train of horse-drawn carts with barrels of petrol and paraffin and spare parts was missing. The workers told me that Kopachev, the man I had left in charge, had taken the carts back to Prudboy. The traitors knew that without fuel we would have to abandon all the farm's machinery to the enemy. But they made a mistake. We decided to set off after them, and if, when we found them, the drivers ran away, we would transfer the fuel and spare parts to the truck.

'Everyone knew that the roads and bridges had been mined, so I asked for volunteers. I took with me two of the many volunteers who came forward—driver Malashich (who was later killed at the front and posthumously named Hero of the Soviet Union) and driver Sosyura (now living at a collective farm near Kharkov). We made detours round roads and bridges. The train of carts was already back where we had started from, and the drivers were peacefully asleep. Revolver in hand, I went round ordering them back. I did not find Kopachev, who had run away. Towards dawn we returned to the column with the carts, but we could not go on till the following night. The German planes never let us alone, shooting at us, dropping leaflets and at night flares.

'On the morning of August 31 we arrived at Basargino. During the day we were attacked by German planes and one woman and two children were killed.

'In the evening the column set off in the direction of Voroponovo Station. After nightfall we met some army officers in a truck, who told us that if we hurried we could get into the city.

'At dawn on September 1 the column stopped in a wood on the outskirts of the city. I set off on foot to reconnoitre. The city was in flames. The streets were barricaded with poles, wire and bricks. The park, where a meeting of Communists setting off for the front was being held, addressed by Comrade Khrushchev, was pitted with craters.

'In a dug-out near the mouth of the River Tsaritsa I met someone from Kharkov, called Demchenko, who promised to help us to cross the Volga. We had to clear a way through the city ourselves, so that the trucks, tractors and carts could get through. This took us about twenty-four hours.

'We waited for three days near the main crossing before we had the chance of a ferry across the Volga. We were being bombed the entire time. People stayed in cellars, hardly ever going out . . .'

This letter throws some light on conditions at this time, and on the frame of mind of Soviet citizens who, not hesitating to risk their lives, did everything they could to try to help their country in its fight against the enemy.

In the bitter days of retreat Soviet officers and men did

not lose heart, and continued to fight back. We tried to understand the enemy more fully, his tactics and habits.

On September 5, the enemy captured Voroponovo Station, and bringing up reserves, tried to carry on a non-stop offensive in the direction of Sadovaya Station. The enemy's attack here was doubly dangerous because this was the junction point of the 62nd and 64th Armies. With a group of Army staff officers in three vehicles I went to the village of Peschanka, just over a mile from Voroponovo Station, to try to strengthen our defences in this sector.

From the north-west corner of Peschanka we could clearly see Voroponovo Station and the enemy's anti-aircraft guns, infantry and tanks. Seven of our Ilyushins appeared overhead. We watched them bombing the anti-aircraft batteries and tank concentrations.

With our eyes on this battle, we did not notice the approach of a number of German Ju 88's from the south. They spotted our vehicles and came in to attack us.

Fortunately, we were close to a good dug-out, in which General Aleksandrov, Chief of Staff of our rear, had two or three days before had his headquarters. We did not have to stop and think before diving into the dug-out for cover, and I must admit, only just in time. It is difficult to say how many planes bombed the western side of the village, but it seemed to us then that every bomb exploded near our dug-out. The bombing lasted about ten minutes.

When the dust had settled, we saw that half of our dug-out roof was missing. It was surprising that none of our group was injured by the bombs or fragments of wood from the roof.

When we came out of the dug-out we saw German tanks attacking the Verkhnyaya Yelshanka cattle-yards from the direction of Voroponovo. Some twenty-five tanks, followed by infantry, were engaged in the attack. They were met with fire from our tanks, which had been well hidden and camouflaged in and to the south of the village of Verkhnyaya Yelshanka.

The first salvo sent seven German tanks up in flames, and the rest promptly turned back and raced off at full speed.

'Bravo our tanks—that was a splendid ambush!' I thought,

and decided to go down and see the crews. When I got there I unexpectedly met the commander of the unit, Colonel Lebedev, with whom I had served in Kisselevichi in 1937. I had been commander of a mechanized brigade, and Lebedev of a battalion.

Our meeting was brief, and the last—Lebedev, not leaving his tanks, was killed at the approaches to the city.

Returning to H.Q. via Gornaya Polyana State Farm, we saw a number of Junkers in circular formation diving at a grove, obviously having spotted the concentration of troops and transport there. Some of our large-calibre anti-aircraft machine-guns were firing at the enemy aircraft. In an orchard near the road stood a lorry with a machine-gun. One Junker detached itself from the circle and came in to attack the lorry. The two machine-gunners did not flinch and opened fire. The tracer bullets could be seen riddling the body of the plane; it tried to climb out of its dive, but failed. Not more than a hundred yards from the machine-gunners the plane buried itself in the ground.

Having broken our outer defence ring and compelled our troops to withdraw to the inner ring round the city itself, the enemy threw in fresh troops at the junction point of the 62nd and 64th Armies, along the railway line from Karpovka Station to Sadovaya. He was trying to take the city rapidly at all costs.

The 62nd Army and the right flank of the 64th Army were faced with about eighteen enemy divisions—between ten and twelve infantry, three panzer and three motorized. These units possessed up to about 600 tanks. They were supported from the air by more than 500 planes of the 4th Air Force.

The total number of enemy sorties on this sector was as many as a thousand a day, not counting raids on the city.

The enemy had many times the number of troops in the 62nd Army, whose units were severely depleted. The total number of guns (including front-line artillery) supporting the 62nd Army was 723. The enemy had twice as many. We had no more than eighty tanks, compared with the enemy's six hundred or so.

Resistance by the 62nd and 64th Armies was growing stiffer, and the enemy's rate of advance, in spite of his absolute superiority in numbers, had been slowed down and could now be measured in hundreds of yards a day. But even this slow rate of advance, which was costing the enemy enormous losses, was a serious danger to us.

As a result of bitterly-fought battles, on September 10 the enemy managed to drive our units back to the outskirts of the city. To the south of Stalingrad, at Kuporosnoye, the enemy reached the Volga. The 62nd Army was cut off from its neighbours to right and left. The period of bitter street fighting began.

The month and a half of fighting which had begun at the other side of the Don on July 23 had taught me a great deal. During this time I had studied the enemy well enough to be able to predict his operational plans.

Pincers driven in depth towards a single point—that was the enemy's main tactic. With superiority in air power and tanks, the enemy was able to penetrate our defences relatively easily, drive in his pincers, and make our units retreat when they seemed to be on the point of being surrounded. No sooner would a stubborn defence or counter-attack stop or eliminate one of the pincers, than another one would appear and try to find a foothold elsewhere.

That was how it had been at the other side of the Don. When the wedge driven by the German 51st Army Corps had been stopped at the River Chir, a second one had appeared in the vicinity of Verkhne-Buzinovka. That was how it had been in the south. When the 64th Army and the Southern Group were beating off attacks from the south and south-west at the beginning of August, a second group approaching the Volga to the north of the city did nothing for a week.

The enemy stuck to the same pattern in his tactics. His infantry went into an attack whole-heartedly only when tanks had already reached the target. The tanks, however, normally went into an attack only when the Lufwaffe was already over the heads of our troops. One had only to break this sequence for an enemy attack to stop and his units to turn back.

That was how it had been on the Don, when the 112th Division for several days in succession beat off attacks in the area of Verkhne-Chirskaya and Novomaksimovski. Enemy planes had been afraid to fly too close to our position, as we had a powerful concentration of anti-aircraft artillery here, covering the railway bridge across the Don.

That was how it had been on the River Aksay, when the enemy's tanks were unable to give their infantry any support, so that the infantry was quickly thrown back.

That was how it had been at Plodovitoye and Abganerovo, and in other sectors.

The enemy could sustain our sudden attacks, particularly by artillery and mortar fire. We had only to organize a good artillery bombardment on an enemy concentration and the Germans would scatter in panic.

The Germans could not stand close fighting; they opened up with their automatic weapons from well over half a mile away, when their bullets could not cover half the distance. They fired simply to keep up their morale. They could not bear us to come close to them when we counter-attacked, soon threw themselves to the ground, and often retreated.

Their communications between infantry, tanks and aeroplanes were good, especially through the use of rockets. They met their aeroplanes with dozens, hundreds of rockets, pinpointing their positions. Our troops and commanders worked out this signalling system and began to make use of it, frequently leading the enemy to make mistakes.

Analysing the enemy's tactical and operational methods, I tried to find counter-measures and counter-methods. I thought a great deal, in particular, about how to overcome or reduce the importance of German superiority in the air, and its effect on the morale of our troops. I remembered battles against the White Guards and White Poles in the Civil War, when we had to attack under artillery and machine-gun fire, without any artillery support of our own. We used to run up close to the enemy, and his artillery would be unable to take fresh aim and fire on rapidly approaching targets. A short, sharp attack would decide a battle.

I came to the conclusion that the best method of fighting the Germans would be close battle, applied night and day in different forms. We should get as close to the enemy as possible, so that his air force could not bomb our forward units or trenches. Every German soldier must be made to feel that he was living under the muzzle of a Russian gun, always ready to treat him to a fatal dose of lead.

Those were the ideas which took shape in my hours of reflection about the fate of the city for which such fierce fighting was taking place. It seemed to me that it was precisely here, in the fighting for the city, that it was possible to force the enemy into close fighting and deprive him of his trump card—his air force.

On 11 September 1942, I was summoned to Stalingrad and South-Western Fronts Military Council (the one Military Council was covering both fronts), to see Comrades Khrushchev and Yeremenko. I had known Nikita Sergeyevich Khrushchev as Secretary of the Moscow Committee of the Communist Party, as Secretary of the Central Committee of the Communist Party of the Ukraine and as Member of the Front Military Council; I knew Andrey Ivanovich Yeremenko, as I have said, from the days when we had served together in the Belorussian military district.

I said good-bye to Shumilov, Abramov, Serdyuk, Laskin and other comrades and set off from Beketovka for Front H.Q., at Yamy, on the left bank of the Volga.

At each ferry across the Volga and its channels I have to wait an hour or two. The ferries are working irregularly. At the moorings crowds of people and vehicles are waiting. There are groans from the wounded, who cannot be ferried across during the day because of the bombing and machine-gunning by enemy aircraft, or after nightfall because of the lack of transport, or delays.

Waiting for a ferry I go into some of the dressing-stations. The faces of the wounded are anxious, strained. In their eyes I read the same questions: 'How are things in the city? Are our troops retreating or not? Will transport come soon?'

At these dressing-stations I see many things wrong—the wounded are not being fed, they are lying in the open, they are asking for water. Their blood-soaked and dust-covered bandages look like a gaudy reproduction. I approach the medical staff and keep asking the same question: 'Why?' I know beforehand, however, that I will not hear anything in reply that I do not already know. 'We haven't slept for several days; in the daytime we are bombed, and at night so many wounded arrive that we don't know how to cope!' I ask them to hurry. They say they will and then go on working as slowly as before.

I grow more and more agitated, but I realize that the doctors, nurses and orderlies can do no more than they are doing. They are on their feet the whole time, without sleep, are probably hungry and so exhausted that they are incapable of working any faster. They are worn out.

Near one of the crossings there is a hospital. I go into the operating theatre. They are operating on a soldier who has been wounded in the buttock by splinters from a mine. The faces of the surgeon and the nurses are whiter than their gowns. I can see that everyone is exhausted from work and lack of sleep. The wounded man is groaning. Near the table is a basin with blood-stained gauze. The surgeon glances at me and goes on with his work. I watch the operation through to the end and then ask him:

'Why did you cut away nearly the whole buttock?'

'If I leave any flesh,' he replies, 'the man will die of gas gangrene. He won't come back from the dead . . .'

Another soldier, with a head wound, is laid on the table. He is mumbling something incoherent. They take off, or rather rip off, the bandages. The pain must be frightful, but he does not cry out, just goes on groaning. The same sort of thing is happening on other tables. I feel suffocated and have a nasty taste in my mouth. Leaving the hospital I go and sit in my jeep and drive on.

At night I cross the Volga.

I look round at the west bank and see it in flames. The glow lights up the road. There is no need to switch headlights on. Bends in the road frequently bring me back almost to the Volga. German shells frequently fly over the city, over the river, and explode on the left bank. The Germans are systematically bombarding the roads leading to the city from the east. Anyone without experience of war would think that in the blazing city there is no longer anywhere left to live, that everything has been destroyed and burnt out. But I know that on the other side of the river a battle is being fought, a titanic struggle is taking place.

I had a premonition that it would not be long before I was in that flame-covered city. Without asking, I could see from their eyes that my aide, G. I. Klimov, the driver, Kayum Kalimulin, and the orderly, Revold Sidorin, were thinking the same.

At midnight we reached the village of Yamy, or to be more precise, the place where the village had been until recently. German long-distance artillery had destroyed it, and the remains of it had been used by our troops in the rear to make dug-outs and for fuel. Of course, Front H.Q. was not to be found, and I could not find anyone who knew where it had gone to.

I do not remember exactly how long we spent driving around the village; it must have been about two in the morning when we chanced upon the dug-out of the Chief of Staff of the 64th Army's rear, General Aleksandrov. I got him out of bed and he accompanied me to H.Q.

Front H.Q. was underground, in dug-outs, well-camouflaged from the air with bushes. The duty officer told me that the Members of the Military Council and the Chief of Staff had only just gone to bed. He did not know why I had been summoned to H.Q. and suggested that I should also rest until morning. There was nothing for me to do but agree, and I went to spend the night at General Aleksandrov's.

When I realized that I had done everything I needed to do for the day, that is, I had found H.Q., and that it was not my fault that I had not received my orders there and then, I suddenly felt terribly hungry, and ravenously ate a combined dinner and supper.

That night I slept well and peacefully, though at the other side of the Volga, five to six miles away, a battle was raging. It was a month and a half since I had slept so 'far' from the battlefield.

I arrived at Front H.Q. at exactly 10 a.m. on September 12, and was received immediately by A. I. Yeremenko and N. S. Khrushchev.

The conversation was brief. I had been appointed Commander of the 62nd Army. Nikita Khrushchev added some more brief comments.

The basic theme was that the Germans had decided to take the city at any cost. We should not and could not surrender it to them, we could not retreat any further, there was nowhere to retreat to. The 62nd Army's Commander, General Lopatin, did not believe that his Army could hold the city. Instead of fighting to the death, instead of dying in the attempt to keep the enemy from the Volga, he had been withdrawing units. He had therefore been relieved of his post, and the Army had been temporarily put under the command of the Chief of Staff, General N. I. Krylov. The Front Military Council, with the agreement of G.H.Q., had proposed that I should take over command of the Army.

He underlined, in saying this, that he knew of the successful operations of the Southern Group in soundly beating the enemy on the River Aksay, and so protecting our troop movements in the danger area.

I took this as a compliment, a compliment which also meant obligations for me.

Finally, Nikita Khrushchev asked me:

'Comrade Chuikov, how do you interpret your task?'

I had not expected to have to answer such a question, but I did not have to think for long—everything was clear.

'We cannot surrender the city to the enemy,' I replied, 'because it is extremely valuable to us, to the whole Soviet people. The loss of it would undermine the nation's morale. All possible measures will be taken to prevent the city from falling. I don't ask for anything now, but I would ask the Military Council not to refuse me help when I ask for it, and I swear I shall stand firm. We will defend the city or die in the attempt.'

They looked at me and said I had understood my task correctly.

We had finished our business. They invited me to stay for lunch. I declined. We said good-bye. I wanted to be left alone as quickly as possible, to ponder on whether I had not rated myself and my powers too highly. I had for some time been expecting to be sent to take over the defence of the city, was ready to do so, wanted to do so. But now that it had happened, I felt very acutely the full weight of the responsibility placed upon me. I had been honoured with a gigantic and extremely difficult task, since the enemy was already on the outskirts of the city.

I left the dug-out of the Military Council and called in to

see General T. F. Zakharov, Front Chief of Staff, to find out where the command post of the 62nd Army H.Q. was.

We collected our things, not taking too much, even leaving the beds behind—not wanting to overload the truck. I told Revold to stay on the left bank, find the 62nd Army's rear administration and join it. He looked at me with tears in his eyes.

'What's the matter?' I asked.

He was silent, turned away. I understood. I could not but remember how he had come to be my orderly.

Revold, a lad of sixteen, was the son of a Communist, Lieutenant-Colonel Timofey Sidorin, whom I had known before the war when he was on the operations staff at Belorussian military district H.Q.

After war broke out I met Sidorin on the Stalingrad front. He was in charge of the operations section at 64th Army H.Q. On 26 July 1942 he was killed near one of the Don crossings. I had seen him with his son several times—they were inseparable. On the evening of July 26 the lad came to find me at our command post, and reported:

'Comrade Commander, I have brought the body of Lieutenant-Colonel Sidorin . . .'

Knowing that Revold was Sidorin's son, I was at a loss for a moment what to say. The Member of the Military Council, Divisional Commissar Abramov, who was sitting with me, answered over his shoulder:

'Hand the body over to the Commandant at H.Q. and tell him to get a grave ready, and see to an orchestra and everything else for the funeral.'

Abramov had not met Revold before, and spoke to him so abruptly without any idea of what the lad was going through at that moment.

Waiting till Revold had gone, I said to Abramov:

'Do you realize who that lad is and what you said to him? He's Sidorin's son . . .'

Abramov looked at me wide-eyed.

'Good gracious! . . .' he exclaimed, and ran out after him.

I was not present at the funeral. I was getting ready to go out to my observation post the following morning, and was already sitting in my vehicle, when I saw Revold. He was lying on the ground, his shoulders convulsed with sobs. He had lost his father and he was alone, which made things even worse for him. I thought quickly and shouted to him:

'Sidorin! Fetch a tommy-gun and as much ammunition as you can, then get in here. You're coming with me.'

Revold leaped to his feet, shook himself, straightened his shirt and flew like a shot to carry out my order. He was soon back and calmly sat down in the truck. We chatted as we drove along and I learned that his mother had been evacuated to somewhere in Siberia. I carefully asked him if he did not want to join her. His eyes filled with tears and I realized that I had made a mistake and aggravated his wound. He replied firmly:

'No. If you send me away I still won't leave the front. I'll avenge my father and the others.'

From then on Revold Sidorin had never left me. He was calm, even cheerful, in battle, was not afraid of anything. Sometimes, however, in the evenings, he would start to sob, and secretly wept for his father ...

Looking at him now, I agreed to take him with me into the blazing city.

CHAPTER III

MAMAYEV KURGAN[1]

ON THE evening of September 12 we arrive in our truck at Krasnaya Sloboda and make for the ferry. One T-34 tank has already been loaded on to the ferry and a second is being loaded. They will not allow my truck on. I present my documents as Commander of the 62nd Army and drive on to the boat.

The deputy commander of a tank formation introduces himself. I ask him how things are going.

'Yesterday evening,' he answers, 'we had about forty tanks, with only half of them or so in working order—the remainder are out of action but are being used as stationary

---

[1]Mamayev Mound or Hill.

firing positions. I am now taking up two more tanks, but how many have been put out of action and burnt out today I don't know.'

Our ferry skirts round the sandy spit of land jutting out north of Golodny Island and heads for the central landing-stage. Shells occasionally burst on the water. They are firing aimlessly. It is not dangerous. We come in close to the bank. From a distance we can see that as our ferry approaches, the landing-stage fills with people. They are bringing the wounded out of trenches, craters and dug-outs, and people are crowding round with bundles and cases. Until the ferry approached they have been taking cover in trenches, shell holes and bomb craters.

All these people have stern faces, black with dust and streaked with tears. Children, racked with thirst and hunger, no longer cry, but merely whimper, trailing their little hands in the water ... One's heart contracts and a lump comes into one's throat.

Our vehicle quickly drives off the ferry and we head for the 62nd Army's command post; they have told me at Front H. Q. that is in the valley on the River Tsaritsa, not far from its mouth.

The streets of the city are dead. There is not a single green twig left on the trees: everything has perished in the flames. All that is left of the wooden houses is a pile of ashes and stove chimneys sticking up out of them. The many stone houses are burnt out, their windows and doors missing and roofs caved in. Now and then a building that is still standing collapses. People are rummaging about in the ruins, pulling out bundles, samovars and crockery, and carrying everything to the landing-stage.

We follow the railway line along the bank of the Volga to the mouth of the Tsaritsa, then along the valley as far as Astrakhanski Bridge but cannot find the command post anywhere. It is growing dark. No one I ask has any idea where the Army command post is.

We pass through barricades put up in the streets and are amazed at them. Who could have made such 'fortifications'? Not only will they not hold back enemy tanks—the bumper of a lorry will knock them down.

Near the station we meet an officer. He turns out to be the

Commissar of a sapper unit. We are delighted to find that he knows where the Army command post is. He gets into the truck and guides us to the foot of Mamayev Kurgan.

We leave the truck and go up the hill on foot. In the darkness I clutch at bushes, scratch myself on all kinds of thorns. Finally I hear the long-awaited shout of a sentry:

'Halt! Who goes there?'

I have arrived at the command post. I go along a gully, striding and jumping over trenches and entrances to dug-outs. At the end of it all I find myself in the dug-out of the Army Chief of Staff, General N. I. Krylov, who has been Acting Commander. He is a thick-set, stocky man with a determined face.

Krylov's dug-out, strictly speaking, is not a dug-out at all, but a broad trench with a bench made of packed earth along one side, a bed made of earth on the other, and a table made of earth at the end of the bed. The roof is made of brush-wood, with bits of straw sticking through it, and on top of the straw a layer of soil about twelve to fifteen inches thick. Shells and mortar bombs are exploding nearby. The explosions make the dug-out shake and soil runs down through the ceiling on to the spread-out maps and on to the heads of the people inside.

There are two people in the dug-out—General Krylov, with a telephone in his hand, and the telephonist on duty, Elena Bakarevich, a blue-eyed girl of about eighteen. Krylov is having strong words with someone or other. His voice is hard, loud, angry. The telephonist is sitting near the entrance with headphones on, answering someone:

'He is speaking on the other telephone . . .'

I take out my papers and put them in front of Krylov. Continuing to tell somebody off, he glances at the papers, then finishes the conversation, and we introduce ourselves. In the poor light of a paraffin lamp I see a vigorous, stern and at the same time friendly face.

'You see, Comrade Commander,' he says, 'without my permission the commander of an armoured formation has transferred his command post from Hill 107.5 right to the bank of the Volga. In other words, the formation's command post is now behind us. It's disgraceful . . .'

I agree with him that it is disgraceful and sit down at the

table. The telephone rings continually. Elena Bakarevich hands the telephone to Krylov. He is giving instructions for the following day. I listen, trying to understand the meaning of the conversation: I have decided not to interfere. I listen to Krylov and at the same time study his working map, the marks and arrows on it, trying to feel my way into the events taking place. I realize that he has no time to give me a report on the situation in peace and quiet. I have to trust Krylov; I do not disturb his operations or alter his plans for tomorrow, because in any case, necessary or not, there is nothing I am capable of changing.

The Americans say 'time is money'. During those days we might well have said 'time is blood'. Time wasted had to be paid for with the blood of our men. Krylov obviously understood my wishes; while speaking on the telephone he marked the sector under discussion in great detail with a sharp pencil on the map and explained to the commanders the tasks they were to carry out, thus enabling me to see the military situation. I felt that we had found a common language.

Nikolay Ivanovich Krylov and I were inseparable throughout the period of the battle for the city. We lived in the same dug-out or trench, slept and ate together if circumstances permitted, and washed together by the Volga, taking no notice of enemy fire.

He was the Army Chief of Staff and senior deputy. In that difficult time we got to know each other very well, and we never disagreed in our assessment of events, however complicated the situation might become. He was able to carry out decisions so efficiently that subordinate commanders always felt in discussions with him that no other decision could have been possible.

I found his military experience in the defence of Odessa and Sevastopol, his profound knowledge, organizational talent and ability to work with people, particularly valuable. He had exceptional integrity, sense of sympathy and devotion to duty.

I sent the Front Military Council a telegram announcing my arrival to take over command of the 62nd Army, and got down to work. First of all I decided to clarify why the commander of the armoured formation had moved to the bank of the Volga without permission, when the order had gone out: 'Not a step back!' I asked for him to be called on the telephone.

'The commander of the armoured formation on the telephone,' said Elena Bakarevich, handing me the receiver.

I told him who I was and asked him why he had moved his command post without authorization. The General began to explain that he had been compelled to do so by mortar fire, losses in men, the instability of the units under him at the front, and a variety of other causes. I was interested to know whether communications with the Army command post existed when he had taken his decision. He answered:

'I don't know. Now, may I explain . . .'

It was clear that you could not get at such people over the telephone, and I ordered the General, together with the Commissar of his unit, to come and see me immediately on Mamayev Kurgan.

Divisional Commissar, Kuzma Akimovich Gurov, the Member of the Army Military Council, came into the dug-out, and we greeted each other. We had met before, and he already knew why I was here. I merely added that I had come to stay.

He answered simply: "That's right. Nothing more needed to be said—we understood each other.

The officers in charge of the various headquarters sections and their deputies came to the dug-out and introduced themselves.

Soon I was told that the Commander and Commissar of the armoured formation had arrived. I immediately invited them into the dug-out, and asked everyone present to stay. I asked the Commander:

'What would your attitude be, as a Soviet General, in command of a military sector, if one of your subordinate commanders and headquarters left the front without your permission? How do you regard your own action—the unauthorized transfer of a formation's command post to the rear of the Army's command post?'

I received no reply to my question. Both the commander and the commissar of the formation felt thoroughly ashamed of themselves. This was obvious from their eyes.

I warned them in no uncertain terms that I considered

theirs an act of cowardice, and would regard any similar act in the future as treachery and desertion on the field of battle. I ordered them to have their command post back on Hill 107.5 by 4 a.m.

Gurov endorsed my decision with his brief: 'That's right'. He ordered the Commissar to see him in his dug-out: I do not know what they talked about, but when we met again, Gurov said:

'Let us work like that in future as well . . .'

The Deputy Commander of the Front, Lieutenant-General P. I. Golikov, arrived. I was very pleased to see him on Mamayev Kurgan at the time when I was taking over command of the 62nd Army.

We had seen each other many times on the field of battle. He was constantly on the move, personally knew the position in all the armies on our front, always looked at the situation sensibly and expressed his views frankly about the progress of a battle and the fighting in general. This time also Golikov gave me valuable information and advice.

I introduced the commander of the tank formation to him and explained the reason for his being summoned to the command post. Lieutenant-General Golikov in turn reprimanded him severely, telling him squarely that such action undermined the fighting efficiency of the armies.

Golikov soon left, promising to report to the Front Military Council that the Army needed several fresh divisions.

I spent until about two in the morning watching Krylov at work getting to know my deputies, and learning the basic facts of the situation, though there were still many details I had not yet grasped.

On the night of September 12 the situation was as follows. The 62nd Army was under attack from the 6th Field Army and several divisions of the 4th Panzer Army. Individual enemy units had reached the Volga north of Rynok and south of the city at Kuporosnoye. Our Army was being pressed back to the Volga from the front and the flanks by a powerful arc of German armies.

To the north, the sector from Latishanka to point 135.4 was occupied by the 16th Panzer Division, facing southward.

The enemy's 60th Motorized Infantry Division occupied the sector to the left, from point 135.4 to 147.6. From point

147.6 through 108.8 to Hill 129.1, facing eastward, was the 389th Infantry Division.

From Hill 129.1, taking in Gorodishche, the 100th Infantry Division was deployed.

These four reinforced divisions occupied a front extending about twelve and a half miles, but were not showing signs of any particular activity. They had obviously been fairly depleted in previous battles, were being built up again, and were temporarily on the defensive.

A shock group of three infantry divisions (295th, 76th and 71st) with heavy reinforcements was in action further south, along a front of just over three and a half miles, taking in Gorodishche, Aleksandrovka and the hospital. This attack was being directed towards Mamayev Kurgan, Central Station and the central landing-stage. The sector from point 147.5 to the suburbs of Minina and Kuporosnoye, along a front of three and a half miles, was occupied by the southern shock group, consisting of four divisions—24th Panzer, 94th Infantry, 14th Panzer and 29th Motorized Infantry. This thrust was being made directly eastward, with the aim of reaching the Volga.

The enemy's nearest reserves, according to our reconnaissance information, were in the neighborhood of Gumrak (one division)and Voroponovo, Karpovka and Malaya Rossoshka (two or three divisions).

The whole group, consisting of between eleven and fourteen divisions, with reinforcements, in action against the 62nd Army, was supported by the 4th Air Force, consisting of a thousand operational aircraft of all types. This powerful group of German armies had the straightforward task of taking the city and reaching the Volga, that is, of fighting their way forward some three to six miles and throwing us in the river.

The number of divisions and brigades which made up the 62nd Army does not give an accurate and full picture of its numerical strength. For example, on the morning of September 14, one armoured brigade had only one tank; two other armoured brigades had no tanks at all and were soon moved across to the left bank to be re-formed. The composite regiment of Glazkov's division on the evening of September 14 had about a hundred infantry, that is, less than a normal company; the total number of men in the next division to his was not more than 1,500, and the number of infantry in the division was not more than in a normal battalion. The motorized infantry brigade had 666 men, including no more than 200 infantrymen; the Guards Division of Colonel Dubyanski on the left flank had no more than 250 infantrymen. Only one division, that of Colonel Sarayev, and two infantry brigades, were more or less up to strength.

The 62nd Army had no integrated communications with neighbours to left and right. Both our flanks were anchored at the Volga. While the Germans were able to fly up to three thousand sorties a day, our air force could not retaliate with even a tenth of that number.

The enemy had firm mastery in the air. This dispirited our troops more than anything, and we feverishly thought about how to take this trump card out of the enemy's hand. But how, by what tactical method? The question was not easy if one remembers that the city's anti-aircraft defences had already been substantially weakened. Part of the anti-aircraft artillery had been destroyed by the enemy, and what remained of it had been moved to the left bank of the Volga, from where it could cover the river and a narrow strip along the right bank. From dawn to dusk, therefore, German planes were over the city, over our military units and over the Volga.

Watching the Luftwaffe in action, we noticed that accurate bombing was not a distinguishing feature of the German airmen: they bombed our forward positions only where there was a broad expanse of no-man's-land between our forward positions and those of the enemy. It occurred to us, therefore, that we should reduce the no-man's land as much as possible—to the throw of a grenade.

But above all it was necessary to raise the fighting spirit of the Army. And it was essential to achieve this as rapidly as possible. Losses in battle, retreats, the shortage of ammunition and provisions, difficulties in replenishing men and material—all these lowered the morale of our troops. Many of them had begun to want to get across the Volga as quickly as possible, and get away from this hell.

To anticipate events a moment, when I met the former 62nd Army Commander on September 14, I was staggered by the hopelessness he felt, his sense of the impossibility and pointlessness of fighting for the city. I felt it necessary, politely of course, to propose that he should appear as soon as possible before the Front Military Council and simply leave the army. His feeling of depression had undoubtedly communicated itself to his subordinates, of which fact I was soon convinced when, on the pretext of illness, three of my deputies (for artillery, tanks and army engineering) left for the opposite bank of the Volga.

The Party organizations and the Army's political department were doing their utmost to raise the military spirit of the troops. My military assistants and friends—Generals Krylov and Pozharski, Colonel Vitkov, Brigade Commissar Vasiliev and others—did a great deal to help. We were quickly able to overcome the despondency. The commanders and political workers in the units understood that we had to fight for the city to the last man, to the last round.

On that day we received an order from the Front Military Council which had a tremendous rallying influence on all the troops. The words of the order—'The enemy must be destroyed at Stalingrad!'—became sacred to all soldiers, commanders and political workers of the 62nd Army.

The Party organizations of the Army and of the whole Front, under the leadership of the Member of the War Council, N. S. Khrushchev, worked untiringly among the troops, explaining to every soldier the meaning and purpose of the words of this order. Hundreds of Communists went to the front line, and a relentless battle was waged against the appearance of any sign of panic or cowardice. Communists were in the forefront, in the most crucial sectors of the fighting.

By 2 a.m. we had drawn up a plan of operations for the next two or three days. We could now have some sleep till dawn. I felt hungry: I had not eaten since morning.

'Do you ever eat here, or do you go without?' I asked Krylov.

'Yes, let's have something to eat,' Gurov answered for him.

Our aides somewhere or other got hold of some bread, some tinned food and some cold tea. When we had had a bite we went to bed, all of us alike wondering what tomorrow would bring.

We had decided, above all, to defend the ferries from the enemy's artillery fire, to achieve which we would put up a stiff defence on the right and left flanks, and attack the centre to occupy Razgulyayevka Station and the railway from it to the south-west as far as the sharp bend near Gumrak. This would make it possible to straighten out the front in the centre and, using the railway embankment as an anti-tank obstacle, to go ahead afterwards and occupy Gorodishche and Aleksandrovka. A tank formation, reinforced with infantry, was set aside for this purpose; it would have the support of the major part of the Army's artillery. The regrouping would take place on September 13, and the attack the day after.

We were awakened early in the morning by heavy enemy artillery fire and bombing.

At 6.30 a.m. the Germans attacked with an infantry division and forty to fifty tanks from the vicinity of Razgulyayevka. The attack was aimed through Aviagorodok[1] towards Central Station and Mamayev Kurgan.

On both flanks of our Army the enemy confined himself to holding actions, from the north attacking an infantry brigade were one of his battalions, aiming towards Orlovka, and on the left flank throwing individual battalions against the positions held by our composite regiment.

In the centre and on the left flank the battle went on all day. The enemy brought up fresh reserves and intensified the attack. His artillery and mortars pounded our units. His planes flew non-stop over the battlefield.

From Mamayev Kurgan both the ground and air fighting were clearly visible. We saw about a dozen planes—our own and the enemy's—burst into flames and crash to the ground. In spite of stubborn resistance by Soviet forces on the ground and in the air, the enemy's numerical superiority gave him the upper hand. Our command post, right at the top of Mamayev Kurgan, was showered with artillery shells and mortar bombs. I was working with Krylov in the same dug-out and from time to time we went out together to the

---

[1] The aerodrome 'townlet' or 'settlement'.

stereoscopic telescope to observe the battle. A number of dug-outs were destroyed, and there were losses among the Army H.Q. staff.

Our telephone wires were constantly being broken, and radio communication worked with long and frequent interruptions. We threw all our signallers into the job of repairing communications. Even the telephonists on duty repeatedly had to abandon the telephones and climb out to find and repair damage to the lines. On September 13 I managed to speak to the Front Commander by telephone only once. I briefly reported on the situation to him and asked him to let me have two or three fresh divisions in the coming days—we had nothing to beat off the enemy's attacks with.

Despite all the efforts of our signallers, by 4 p.m. we had almost completely lost contact with the troops.

The situation was now somewhat disturbing. Although the enemy battalion which had attacked from the north towards Orlovka had been wiped out by our infantry brigade, at the centre of the Army's positions our units had suffered losses and had been forced to withdraw eastward, to the western edge of a wood, west of the Barrikady and Krasny Oktyabr workers' settlements.[1] The Germans had taken Hill 126.3, Aviagorodok and the hospital. On the left flank our composite regiment had abandoned the machine and tractor station east of Sadovaya Station. On the remaining sectors individual attacks had been beaten off and sixteen enemy tanks had been burnt out.

What happened afterwards we discovered only by messengers and through Army H.Q. signals officers. All the enemy's attacks in the latter part of the day were beaten off.

Before darkness fell I had to decide whether to carry out the plan of active defence we had drawn up the previous day, or, in view of the new enemy attack, to take more decisive action. There could be no delay, as we could only carry out the regrouping of our forces under cover of darkness—it would have been impossible in daylight because of the enemy's air raids.

---

[1] Separate factory workers' residential districts. Alexander Werth describes them as 'garden cities' (*The Year of Stalingrad*, London, 1946, p. 205).

We decided to counter-attack. In order to forestall the enemy, the counter-attack was scheduled to start early on the morning of September 14. We knew that the Army's potential was very restricted, and that we could not allocate large forces to the counter-attack, but we were sure that the enemy knew this and that the last thing he was expecting was active operations on our part. We remembered Suvorov's dictum—'to surprise is to conquer'. We were not counting on any rapid victory, but on surprising the enemy and upsetting his plans. It was important for our attack to be sudden, however partial and temporary a measure it might be, so as to take the initiative out of his hands.

The order to counter-attack was communicated to the troops at 10.30 p.m. It laid down precise objectives for every unit.

The 38th Motorized Brigade, reinforced by a motorized infantry company, and with an artillery battery attached to it, was to direct its attack to the south-east of Razgulyayevka. Sarayev's division, one regiment strong, was to counter-attack towards Hill 126.3 and then Hill 144.3.

The composite regiment, with one armoured brigade attached, would attack in the direction of Aviagorodok and Hill 153.7. The detached 92nd Infantry Brigade was ready to counter-attack towards the hospital and Hill 153.7.

All units taking part in the counter-attack were directed to cooperate closely and keep in close touch with one another.

The remaining units were firmly to hold the line they were occupying.

The counter-attack was to be supported by three anti-tank artillery regiments, three artillery regiments from G.H.Q. Reserve and three 'katyushi' regiments.

The day spent on Mamayev Kurgan had shown that to direct the troops from this command post was impossible. The incessant breaks in communication resulting from enemy fire led to a loss of efficiency in directing the troops. We decided to transfer the command post to the valley of the River Tsaritsa. We left an Army observation post on Mamayev Kurgan. Front H.Q. had given permission to move the command post two days before.

All of us at the command post, from private to commander, had nothing to eat on September 13. Breakfast was prepared for us in a cottage on Mamayev Kurgan itself, but an enemy bomb sent the cottage and the breakfast up in flames. An attempt was made to cook dinner in a field kitchen, but it was destroyed by a direct hit from a mortar bomb. After that our cook decided not to bring out any more food to no purpose and simply left us to go hungry. To stop any more economies of this kind at the expense of our stomachs, we sent Glinka, the cook, and Tasya, the waitress, in the first contingent to the new command post, for which they were very grateful.

CHAPTER IV

NOT A STEP BACK

TOWARDS DAWN on September 14 the Army command post moved to what was known as the Tsaritsyn bunker. This was a large tunnel-cum-dug-out, divided into ten sections, the ceilings and walls of which were faced with planks. Earlier, in August, this had been Stalingrad Front H.Q. The roof of earth was over ten yards thick; only a bomb weighing a ton or more could have penetrated it, and then not everywhere. The bunker had two exits, the lower one leading to the bed of the River Tsaritsa, and the upper one into Pushkin Street.

Krylov and I left Mamayev Kurgan before dawn on September 14. Gurov had left earlier. Accompanying us as guide through the city was the Deputy Commander of the Army's armoured and motorized troops, Lieutenant-Colonel M. G. Weinrub. German night-flying aircraft were circling overhead, picking out and bombing targets by the light of the fires.

We made our way through the ruins of destroyed streets, and nearly half a mile from the new command post my vehicle and the one containing Krylov and Weinrub got tangled up in telephone wires and came to a halt. We were held up three or four minutes and in that time a dozen or so small bombs exploded not far away from us. Fortunately no one was hurt, and we reached our destination safe and sound.

There was no time to rest. Once we had arrived I had to check on communications, and on the troops' state of preparedness to counter-attack. Everything was going according to plan. The enemy's troops, apart from the night-flying aircraft, were either asleep or preparing for action the following day.

At 3a.m. our artillery preparation began, then at 3.30 our counter-attack. I telephoned the Front Commander and reported to him that our counter-attack had started and asked him to cover our operations from the air at sunrise. He promised to do this and gave me the glad news that the 13th Guards Infantry Division was being attached to us from G.H.Q. Reserve; the division would start to assemble at the Volga crossings towards evening that day, in the vicinity of Krasnaya Sloboda.

I immediately sent Colonel Tupichev, who was in command of army engineering, with a group of Army H.Q. staff officers to Krasnaya Sloboda to meet the Guards Division, and Krylov and I again began to get into touch with our units and to find out what the position was.

We found that at the centre of the Army's sector our counter-attack had at the beginning met with some success, but as soon as day broke the enemy brought the Luftwaffe into action; groups of fifty to sixty aircraft flew in bombing and machine-gunning our counter-attacking units, pinning them to the ground. The counter-attack petered out. At noon the enemy threw large infantry and tank formations into the battle and began to press our units back. Their attack was directed towards Central Station.

This was an exceptionally strong attack. In spite of enormous losses, the enemy broke through. Lorry-loads of infantry and tanks tore through into the city. The Germans obviously thought that the fate of the city had been settled, and they all rushed to reach the Volga and the centre of the city as rapidly as possible, and to grab some souvenirs for themselves. Our soldiers, snipers, anti-tank and artillery men, hiding in and behind houses, in cellars and block-houses, saw drunken Germans jumping down from their lorries, playing mouth-organs, shouting like mad and dancing on the pavements.

Enemy troops perished in their hundreds, but fresh waves of reserves flooded into the streets. Enemy tommy-gunners infiltrated into the city east of the railway towards the station, and occupied the 'specialists' houses'.[1] Fighting was going on half a mile from our command post. There was a danger that the enemy would occupy the station, cut through the Army and reach the central landing-stage before the 13th Guards Infantry Division arrived.

Fierce fighting was also taking place on the left flank, around Minina suburb. Our right flank was also giving the enemy no rest. The situation was growing more difficult with every hour.

I had a small reserve still intact—a single heavy armoured brigade consisting of nineteen tanks. It was on the Army's left flank, on the southern outskirts of the city. I ordered one battalion of this brigade's tanks to be sent immediately to the command post. It arrived two hours later, with nine tanks. General Krylov had already formed two groups consisting of staff officers and a guard company. The first of these groups, reinforced with six tanks, was put under the command of Communist I. Zalyuzik, who was in charge of the Army's operations section. It was given the task of blocking the streets leading from the railway station to the landing-stage. The second group, with three tanks, under Lieutenant-Colonel Weinrub, was sent to the specialists' houses, from which the Volga and the landing-stage were under fire from the enemy's heavy machine-guns.

Both groups contained officers from Army H.Q. and the political section, almost all of them Communists. And they stopped the Germans from breaking through to the landing-stage, providing cover for the first ferries bringing across the 13th Guards Division.

At 2 p.m. the Commander of the 13th Guards Infantry Division, Major-General Alexander Ilyich Rodimtsev, Hero of the Soviet Union, arrived, covered in dust and mud. In getting from the Volga to our command post he had several

---

[1]Built to house engineering specialists.

times had to take cover in bomb craters and hide in ruins from enemy dive-bombers.

Major-General Rodimtsev reported to me that the Division was pretty well up to strength, with about 10,000 men. But it was badly in need of weapons and ammunition. More than a thousand of his soldiers had no rifles. The Front Military Council had instructed the Front Deputy Commander, Lieutenant-General Golikov, to see to it that the weapons the Division needed were delivered to the Krasnaya Sloboda area by the evening of September 14. There was no guarantee, however, that they would arrive in time. I immediately ordered my deputy in charge of the Army's rear, General Lobov, who was on the left bank of the Volga, to collect guns among the Army's rear units and hand them over to the guardsmen.

General Rodimtsev already knew the position at the front. The Army Chief of Staff, Krylov, knew how to put people quickly in the picture, and rapidly showed General Rodimtsev how things stood. He was given the task of ferrying the division across to the right bank of the Volga during that night. The division's artillery, except for the anti-tank artillery took up firing positions on the left bank, so as to support the operations of the infantry units from there. The anti-tank guns and mortars were ferried across to the city.

The division went straight into battle. Two of its infantry regiments were to clear the centre of the city, the specialists' houses and the railway station of German troops; a third regiment was to occupy and defend Mamayev Kurgan. One infantry battalion would be kept in reserve at the Army H.Q. command post.

The division's sector stretched from Mamayev Kurgan and the loop of the railway line on the right, to the River Tsaritsa on the left.

We proposed to Rodimtsev that he should set up his command post on the bank of the Volga, near the landing-stage, where there were dug-outs, trenches and communications already in existence.

At the end of the conversation I asked him how he felt about it.

He replied: 'I am a Communist. I have no intention of abandoning the city.'

I added: 'As soon as the division's units have taken up position, all other troops on your sector will come under your command.'

After a moment's reflection, Rodimtsev said that he would find it embarrassing to be in a command post to the rear of the Army's command post. I reassured him, telling him that as soon as the division had carried out the task allotted to it, he had permission to move his command post forward. I underlined that we could not bank on the enemy's remaining passive. The enemy had decided to annihilate us and take the city at any price. We could therefore not merely remain on the defensive, but should exploit every favourable opportunity for a counter-attack, impose our will on the enemy and upset his plans with our active operations.

'I understand,' was Rodimtsev's brief answer, and we parted.

It was about 4 p.m. There were nearly five hours to go before dusk. Could we, with the units we had available, splintered and broken as they were, hold out for another ten to twelve hours in the central area? This was worrying me more than anything else. Would our troops be able to carry out the seemingly superhuman tasks facing them? If they could not carry them out, then the newly-arrived 13th Guards Infantry Division would watch the end of the tragedy as spectators on the left bank.

News then came in that the composite regiment had lost many of its officers and was without leaders. The regiment's commander had been missing since morning. If he had been killed, then all honour to his memory. But we feared the worst—had he abandoned the regiment? We had no reserves. Our last reserve, the H.Q. guard and the H.Q. staff, were out fighting. Through the roof of the dug-out we could hear the drone of the Luftwaffe's engines and the explosion of bombs.

In my search for reserves of one kind or another, I called in Divisional Commander Colonel Sarayev. He had been appointed commander of the garrison, and his division was occupying centres of resistance and strongpoints in the city. Colonel Sarayev, in Krylov's words, considered himself indispensable and did not particularly like carrying out the Army's orders.

When he arrived, he reported in detail on the division's

situation, on the defensive positions occupied by his troops, and on the position in the city and the workers' settlements.

It became clear from his report that the defence structure consisted for the most part of small blockhouses, 25-30 per cent of them completed, but of course not strong enough. Some of the defensive positions, in particular the barricades, I had seen myself: they were really no help at all in the fight against the enemy.

I asked Colonel Sarayev whether he understood that his division had been incorporated into the 62nd Army, and that he had to accept the authority of the Army Military Council without demur. I asked him whether there was any need for me to telephone the Front Military Council to clarify the position, which was in fact already clear? Sarayev replied that he was a soldier of the 62nd Army.

While talking to him I realized clearly that I could not count on any of his units as a reserve with which to ward off the enemy's attacks: they could not be taken away from their strongpoints. But Sarayev had at his disposal a number of formations of armed factory and local guards. These units, consisting of city militia, firemen and workers, totalled some 1,500 men. They were in need of weapons.

I ordered Sarayev to pick out some solid buildings, particularly in the centre of the city, place fifty to one hundred men in each one, under a Communist commander, to fortify these strongpoints and hold out in them to the bitter end. Remembering that the division could obtain weapons and stores through the Army's supplies section, I proposed that Sarayev should keep in constant contact with my command post.

On my map of the city he there and then marked some particularly important strongpoints. I agreed with his proposals.

Krylov listened to my conversation with Sarayev, and when it was over he took him aside to organize regular communication and administration.

Communication with the Army's units was frequently interrupted, and Gurov and I left the bunker a number of times, by the Pushkin Street exit, to find out what was happening, by listening to the sound of the fighting going on 400-500 yards away.

Historians maintain that in great battles outstanding generals would often have won a decisive victory if they had only had another battalion. During these days of fighting, it seems to me, Paulus had more than enough battalions with which to split the 62nd Army and reach the Volga. But the German efforts were frustrated by the courage of our troops.

Before dusk the commander of the armoured brigade, Major S. N. Khopko, came to see me and reported that his last solitary tank had been put out of action at the railway crossing near the station. He asked me what he should do.

The tank, I discovered, had been put out of action, but was still capable of firing. The brigade, in addition, had about a hundred men, armed with tommy-guns and pistols.

'Go to the tank,' I instructed him, 'collect all your men and hold the crossing until units of the 13th Guards Division arrive. If not . . .'

He understood and ran to carry out the order. As we later discovered, Khopko carried out his task with honour.

Dusk fell; the battle began to subside. Fewer German aeroplanes appeared overhead. I spent a lot of time at the telephone, finding out where the 13th Division's units were and what they were doing, and what means of ferrying them across were being prepared. Then, together with the H.Q. staff, I set about drawing some conclusions from the day's fighting.

The sum result was depressing. The enemy had advanced right up to Mamayev Kurgan and the railway line, and had crossed the city as far as the Central Railway Station, which was still in our hands. German machine-gunners had occupied many buildings in the centre of the city, after breaking through our depleted units.

Of our units in the Army's centre there was almost nothing left. The Army's observation post on Mamayev Kurgan had been destroyed by bombing and artillery fire.

It was reported from the left flank that although the enemy's attacks had been beaten off, everything went to show that the German troops were massing, carrying out reconnaissance and preparing for a fresh assault.

The Army H.Q. staff did not close their eyes the whole of that night: some of them were helping to reinforce the units in the front line; others were fighting at the specialists' houses and the station, helping to ensure that Rodimtsev's men could cross the river in safety; yet others were at the central landing-stage, meeting in the battalions as they were ferried across and leading them up to the front line through the ruined streets.

During the night only the 34th and 39th Regiments and one battalion of the 42nd Regiment were ferried across. Dawn and the appearance of enemy aircraft prevented any further crossings.

The regiments that had arrived occupied a sector in the centre of the city from Krutoy Gully to the station; the 1st Battalion of the 42nd Regiment was sent to the station. Mamayev Kurgan was being defended by a battalion of Sarayev's division. To the left, that is to the south-west, of the station, the remnants of the armoured brigade, the composite regiment and Batrakov's 42nd Infantry Brigade were defending. On the remaining sectors there was no change.

On the morning of September 15 the enemy began to attack in two places: at the Army's centre, German 295th, 76th and 71st Infantry Division units supported by tanks attacked the station and Mamayev Kurgan; on the left flank, in the suburbs of Minina and Kuporosnoye, units of the 24th and 14th Panzer and 94th Infantry Division were attacking. On the right flank things were relatively quiet. The enemy attack was preceded by a colossal air raid, after which the enemy's aeroplanes circled over the heads of our units.

The battle immediately became extremely difficult for us. Rodimtsev's units, having arrived during the night, had not been able to get their bearings and consolidate their positions, and were attacked straight away by superior enemy forces. The Luftwaffe literally hammered anything they saw in the streets into the ground.

Particularly fierce fighting went on at the station and in Minina suburb. The station changed hands four times during the day, and was ours at nightfall. The specialists' houses, under attack from the 34th Regiment of Rodimtsev's division plus tanks of the heavy armoured brigade, remained in German hands. Colonel Batrakov's infantry brigade, together with units of Sarayev's division, having suffered heavy losses, was pressed back to the forestry station. Dubyanski's Guards

Infantry Division plus a number of other small units, also having suffered heavy losses, withdrew to the western outskirts of the city, south of the River Tsaritsa.

Towards evening on September 15 it was difficult to say whose hands Mamayev Kurgan was in—contradictory information was coming in. Enemy machine-gunners had infiltrated along the Tsaritsa towards the railway bridge and were firing at our command post. The Army H.Q. guard again went into action. Wounded began to be brought in to the command post. In addition, in spite of our guard and check-points at our entrances, lots of people flooded into the corridors of our bunker at nightfall to shelter from the incessant bombing and machine-gunning. Finally, officers and men from signals units and the guard battalion, drivers and others came in on 'immediate and urgent business' and stayed. But as the bunker had no ventilation, the oppressive heat and closeness of the atmosphere, particularly at night-time, made those of us who were working at the command post faint. Our bodies were covered with cold sweat and our ears rang. We took it in turns to go out for some fresh air. South of the River Tsaritsa parts of the city were still ablaze. It was as bright as day. German machine-gun bullets whistled over our heads and round our feet. But nothing would keep us inside the oppressive underground bunker.

That night we were all concerned about the fate of Mamayev Kurgan. If the enemy took it he could command the whole city and the Volga.

I ordered Yelin's 42nd Regiment, which was still at the other side of the Volga, to be ferried across during that night at all costs, and to be sent to Mamayev Kurgan, so that it could take up defence positions there by dawn and hold the summit at any price.

To administer the whole Army from the bunker was becoming very difficult, so I ordered General Pozharski, with a group of officers from the operations section and artillery staff at H.Q. to organize an auxiliary administration post on the bank of the Volga, near the landing-stage, opposite the south bank of Zaitsevski Island. This auxiliary administration post, under Pozharski, was an intermediary between the Army H.Q. and the units on the right flank. In the fighting on September 15 the enemy lost over two thousand men in killed alone. There are always three to four times as many men wounded as killed. During the fighting on September 14-15 the enemy had lost a total of eight to ten thousand men and fifty-four tanks. Our units had also suffered heavy losses in men and material, and had fallen back. When I say 'suffered heavy losses and had fallen back' I do not mean that they did so under orders, in an organized way, from one line of defence to another. It means that our soldiers (even small units) crawled out from under German tanks, more often than not wounded, to another position, where they were received, incorporated into another unit, provided with equipment, usually ammunition, and then they went back into battle.

The Germans quickly realized that they were not going to be able to rush in and take the city, that they had bitten off more than they could easily chew. They later began to act more circumspectly: they prepared their attacks carefully and went into battle without mouth-organs, and without singing and dancing . . . They were going to certain death.

'The land of the Volga has become slippery with blood, and the Germans have found it a slippery slope to death,' said our soldiers defending the city.

Our officers and men all knew that there was nowhere to retreat to, that there could be no retreat. The most important thing was that they knew that the enemy could be defeated, that he was not bullet-proof. Our anti-tank men were not afraid to let the German tanks come up to within fifty to one hundred yards, so as not to miss them.

On September 16 and 17 the fighting grew more and more fierce. Throwing in fresh reserves, the enemy kept up a non-stop attack in the centre against the units of the 13th Guards Division and Batrakov's infantry brigade. Particularly fierce fighting was going on near Mamayev Kurgan and the station.

On the morning of September 16 Yelin's 42nd Regiment took Mamayev Kurgan. Close engagements, or rather skirmishes to the death, began, and continued on Mamayev Kurgan until the end of January 1943.

The enemy also realized that mastery of Mamayev Kurgan would enable him to dominate the city, the workers' settlements and the Volga. To achieve this aim, he spared neither men nor material. We decided that we would hold on to Mamayev Kurgan whatever happened. Many of the enemy's panzer and infantry divisions were destroyed here, and our less-than-a-division withstood the fiercest battles, battles to the death, unparalleled in history in their stubbornness and ferocity.

In these conditions it was hand-to-hand fighting with bayonet and grenade that was most important and effective, and the real means of waging battle.

Mamayev Kurgan, even in the period of heaviest snow, remained black: the snow rapidly melted under artillery fire.

The fighting for the specialists' houses would die down, then flare up again with renewed vigour. As soon as our attacks or fire slackened off, the enemy would start firing on the central Volga landing-stage. This meant that we had to keep up the attack the whole time, in order to pin down the enemy troops who had occupied and consolidated their positions in the specialists' houses.

Near the station the fighting was going on with changing fortunes. The station and neighbouring buildings would change hands four or five times a day. Every attack would cost both sides tens or hundreds of lives. The men's strength began to ebb, the units grew depleted. The enemy, like us, had to bring up fresh reserves.

The firm resistance of our troops in the centre of the city upset Paulus's plans and calculations. Finally he brought up the whole of the 2nd Shock Group from the area of Voroponovo, Peschanka and Sadovaya and threw it into the battle.

Two panzer, one motorized and one infantry division launched a determined attack on the Army's left. The attack was not unexpected, but we had no forces with which to repulse it. But although the enemy was at least twelve to fifteen time as strong as we were, he paid dearly for every step forward.

In military history the height of tenacity in battle is considered to be those occasions when an object of attack—a town or village—changes hands a number of times. This was precisely our situation. On the southern outskirts of the city is an enormous building—the grain elevator. From September 17-20 fighting went on there day and night. Not only the elevator as a whole, but individual storeys and storehouses changed hands repeatedly. Colonel Dubyanski, Guards Infantry Division Commander, reported to me by telephone: 'The situation has changed. Before, we occupied the upper part of the elevator and the Germans the lower part. Now we have driven them out of the lower part, but German troops have penetrated upstairs and fighting is now going on in the upper part.'

There were dozens, hundreds of places defended as stubbornly as this in the city; inside them fighting went on 'with varying fortunes' for weeks on end for every room, every stair.

On the morning of September 16 I reported to the Front Military Council that we had no further reserves, while the enemy was throwing fresh ones into the battle all the time; another few days of such bloody fighting and the Army would disintegrate, would be bled to death. I asked for the Army to be immediately reinforced by two or three fresh divisions.

The Front Command obviously knew the position in the city clearly. On the evening of September 16 it placed one brigade of marine infantry and one armoured brigade at the Army's disposal. The marine infantry brigade was pretty well up to strength, and the men, from the North Sea fleet, were exceptional. It was given the job of defending a position along the railway line, between the River Tsaritsa to the north and the triangle described by the railways to the south.

The armoured brigade contained only light tanks with 45-mm. guns. Its defence line formed an arc in the vicinity of the loop of the railway a third of a mile east of Mamayev Kurgan; it had to prevent the enemy from getting through to the Volga.

The fighting in the southern outskirts of the city round the grain elevator deserves special mention, because of the tenacity shown there by our men. I hope that the reader will forgive me for leaving the main area of the fighting for a moment, and quoting from a letter written by someone who took part in the battle for the elevator, the officer in charge of a machine-gun platoon of the marine infantry brigade, Andrey Khozyayonov, who now lives in Orel.

He writes to me as follows:

I recently heard some chapters from your book, *The Army of Mass Heroism*, on the radio.

I was sitting with my family listening to your account of the heroic exploits of the units and men of the 62nd Army. When you recalled the exploits of the sailors and soldiers of the North Sea brigade I was very moved, and my ten-year-old son noticed the fact. 'Daddy, why are you so excited?' he asked me. 'Because I shall never forget those September days,' I answered.

I remember that we were met at Nizhnyaya Akhtuba by a representative from 62nd Army H.Q. Our brigade was ferried over the Volga during the night of September 16 and at dawn on the 17th it was already in action.

I remember that on the night of the 17th, after fierce fighting, I was called to the battalion command post and given the order to take a platoon of machine-gunners to the grain elevator and, together with the men already in action there, to hold it come what may. We arrived that night and presented ourselves to the garrison commander. At that time the elevator was being defended by a battalion of not more than thirty to thirty-five guardsmen, together with the wounded, some slightly, some seriously, whom they had not yet been able to send back to the rear.

The guardsmen were very pleased to see us arrive, and immediately began pouring out jokes and witticisms. Eighteen well-armed men had arrived in our platoon. We had two medium machine-guns and one light machine-gun, two anti-tank rifles, three tommy-guns and radio equipment.

At dawn a German tank carrying a white flag approached from the south. We wondered what could have happened. Two men emerged from the tank, a Nazi officer and an interpreter. Through the interpreter the officer tried to persuade us to surrender to the 'heroic German army', as defence was useless and we would not be able to hold our position any longer. 'Better to surrender the elevator,' affirmed the German officer. 'If you refuse you will be dealt with without mercy. In an hours time we will bomb you out of existence.'

What impudence, we thought, and gave the Nazi

lieutenant a brief answer: 'Tell all your Nazis to go to hell! ... You can go back, but only on foot.'

The German tank tried to beat a retreat, but a salvo from our two anti-tank rifles stopped it.

Enemy tanks and infantry, approximately ten times our numbers, soon launched an attack from south and west. After the first attack was beaten back, a second began, then a third, while a reconnaissance 'pilot' plane circled over us. It corrected the fire and reported our position. In all, ten attacks were beaten off on September 18.

We economized on ammunition, as it was a long way, and difficult, to bring up more.

In the elevator the grain was on fire, the water in the machine-guns evaporated, the wounded were thirsty, but there was no water nearby. This was how we defended ourselves twenty-four hours a day for three days. Heat, smoke, thirst—all our lips were cracked. During the day many of us climbed up to the highest points in the elevator and from there fired on the Germans; at night we came down and made a defensive ring round the building. Our radio equipment had been put out of action on the very first day. We had no contact with our units.

September 20 arrived. At noon twelve enemy tanks came up from the south and west. We had already run out of ammunition for our anti-tank rifles, and we had no grenades left. The tanks approached the elevator from two sides and began to fire at our garrison at point-blank range. But no one flinched. Our machine-guns and tommy-guns continued to fire at the enemy's infantry, preventing them from entering the elevator. Then a Maxim, together with a gunner, was blown up by a shell, and the casing of the second Maxim was hit by shrapnel, bending the barrel. We were left with one light machine-gun.

The explosions were shattering the concrete; the grain was in flames. We could not see one another for dust and smoke, but we cheered one another with shouts.

German tommy-gunners appeared from behind the

tanks. There were about 150-200 of them. They attacked very cautiously, throwing grenades in front of them. We were able to catch some of the grenades and throw them back.

On the west side of the elevator the Germans managed to enter the building, but we immediately turned our guns on the parts they had occupied.

Fighting flared up inside the building. We sensed and heard the enemy soldiers' breath and footsteps, but we could not see them in the smoke. We fired at sounds.

At night, during a short lull, we counted our ammunition. There did not seem to be much left: one and a half drums for the machine-gun, twenty to twenty-five rounds for each tommy-gun, and eight to ten rounds for each rifle.

To defend ourselves with that amount of ammunition was impossible. We were surrounded. We decided to break out to the south, to the area of Beketovka, as there were enemy tanks to the north and east of the elevator.

During the night of the 20th, covered by our one tommy-gun, we set off. To begin with all went well; the Germans were not expecting us here. We passed through the gully and crossed the railway line, then stumbled on an enemy mortar battery which had only just taken up position under cover of darkness.

We overturned the three mortars and a truck-load of bombs. The Germans scattered, leaving behind seven dead, abandoning not only their weapons, but their bread and water. And we were fainting with thirst. 'Something to drink! Something to drink!' was all we could think about. We drank our fill in the darkness. We then ate the bread we had captured from the Germans and went on. But alas, what then happened to my comrades I don't know, because the next thing I remember was opening my eyes on September 25 or 26. I was in a dark, damp cellar, feeling as though I were covered with some kind of oil. I had no tunic on and no shoe on my right foot. My hands and legs would not obey me at all; my head was singing.

A door opened, and in the bright sunlight I could see a tommy-gunner in a black uniform. On his left sleeve was a skull. I had fallen into the hands of the enemy ...

This letter from the marine tells us something of the nature of the fighting, of the tenacity of the Soviet troops in the battle for Stalingrad.

On September 17, I learned that the Stalingrad Front, occupying positions between the Don and the Volga (under the command of Colonel-General Yeremenko, with Gordov as deputy), was to go over to the offensive southward on the sector between Akatovka and Kuzmichi. The aim of the attacking armies was to destroy the enemy group and join up with the troops of the South-Eastern Front (which was also under Yeremenko's command) south-west of the city. I was cheered by this news: the whole Front was going over to the offensive! The Army Military Council immediately started to think of ways to help the attacking armies. For the 62nd Army, sandwiched between the enemy and the Volga, it was utterly impossible to join up with its neighbours on either flank, and we therefore decided, in spite of the difficulty involved, to continue our active defence in the Army's central sector, and on the right flank to launch an attack, using two infantry brigades and one regiment of Sarayev's division, thereby hastening a link-up with the armies operating north of the city.

The same evening I was warned by Colonel-General Yeremenko that the attack would take place very shortly. We were to support our neighbour on our right flank by attacking towards the south-west from the vicinity of the Krasny Oktyabr workers' settlement and Mamayev Kurgan, cutting off and destroying the enemy in the western part of the city. To reinforce the Army's right flank Gorishny's infantry division was attached to us; it assembled near the ferry towards evening on September 18.

Our command post was under constant enemy fire; we were therefore given permission to leave the bunker in the valley of the River Tsaritsa and move to a point just over half a mile north of Krasny Oktyabr landing-stage.

At evening on September 17 the Army's front stretched, on the right flank, from Rynok to Mamayev Kurgan (there had been no change here—all the enemy's attacks on this sector over the past five days had been beaten off); in the centre the Army's line had been broken (Mamayev Kurgan and Central Station were in our hands; the specialists' houses were occupied by enemy troops, who were machine-gunning the central ferry); the left flank ran from the River Tsaritsa along the railway line to the pump-house on the Volga.

With the arrival of fresh units, the remnants of the composite regiment were incorporated into Batrakov's infantry brigade; all the remaining units on the southern flank, which had also suffered substantial losses, were incorporated into Dubyanski's guards division. The headquarters staffs made redundant by this were sent across the Volga for regrouping.

On the Army's left flank, there were now two infantry brigades and Dubyanski's division. This number of units was easier to administer.

On the night of September 17 the Army H.Q. moved its command post. Signals staff, service personnel and some individual staff officers began to move across in the evening. The Military Council, the Chief of Staff and the operations staff moved across later. To take documents through streets in which there were enemy tommy-gunners and even tanks was an extremely risky business. We decided, therefore, that the main body of headquarters staff officers and the Military Council would be taken by boat. A complicated manœuvre had to be made—from the mouth of the Tsaritsa to Krasnaya Sloboda on the other bank of the Volga, then by road northward to Ferry '62', and then by armoured boat back to the right bank, direct to the new command post.

The crossing in boats from the mouth of the Tsaritsa to the opposite bank was to be carried out by Colonel G. I. Vitkov and his assistants. At midnight, carrying documents and personal belongings, we left the bunker and under cover of darkness assembled without mishap at the point from which the boats were to leave. Shells occasionally flew over our heads.

Having crossed the Volga, we meandered round Bokaldy and Krasnaya Sloboda for an hour or so, looking for our vehicles. We finally found them and got in. At that moment Gurov came up to me and proposed that we should call in at the nursery gardens about three miles from Krasnaya Sloboda, where Army Supplies had its H.Q.; we could have something to eat, have a wash and then go on to the new command post. I agreed.

We asked Krylov to take the H.Q. column on to the new command post, promising to bring him something to eat.

Gurov, our aides and myself then set off for the nurseries. We were greeted as though we were ghosts. After a hot bath we were given clean linen, ate our fill and were given warm soldiers' sweaters. As we ate, and then over a cup of tea, the time flew. The windows were blacked out and we did not notice dawn beginning to break; when we did notice we were horror-stricken: the ferries were now working only at night-time. We were in danger of being late. What would the H.Q. staff and Krylov think of us if we did not arrive at the new command post that day?

We jumped into our vehicles and rushed off towards Ferry '62'. I did not know the road, so Gurov led the way. But he took a wrong turning and we found ourselves back in Krasnaya Sloboda. When we realized our mistake we turned and raced back again.

As we approached the landing-stage I could see a single boat moored there; it looked as though it was about to move off, and then, as ill luck had it, our vehicles went into some sand and skidded. The thought leaped into my mind that the last boat was leaving and that we would have to spend the whole day on the left bank of the river. What might happen to the Army, to the city, during that day? ... My hair stood on end. I rushed to the landing-stage. The boat had already begun to move away. Summoning every ounce of energy I leaped straight for the boat. It worked. I was on the boat. Gurov was running towards the landing-stage. I shouted to the man at the wheel to turn back.

He slowly turned his head and asked:

'And who are you, then?'

'Commander of the 62nd Army.'

The helmsman (who was the Captain) turned the boat back to the landing-stage, and Gurov and the aide clambered aboard. The boat then set off at full steam for the right bank.

The Captain apologized for not having recognized me. Ten

115

minutes later we were at the right bank and I was shaking his hand and thanking him whole-heartedly.

For a long time the sailors waved their hats to us. The boat disappeared behind Zaitsevski Island, on its way back to the left bank.

From the landing-stage we went to our new command post, where we were met by Krylov, Vitkov and the others. We were in good spirits: we were back together again.

In the evening we reckoned up our 'losses'. I had no artillery, engineering and anti-tank deputies.

We assumed that those who had left us to go to the left bank of the Volga would not come back to us. But we were not sorry, and said: 'The air will be purer without them.' Immediately on arrival at the command post, therefore, I appointed some new deputies: for artillery—Major-General N. M. Pozharski; for the armoured units—Lieutenant-Colonel M. G. Weinrub. The post of deputy in command of engineering remained vacant, as I could not find a replacement. I reported this to the Front Military Council, and Major-General Kosenko soon arrived to act as my deputy in charge of army engineering until Lieutenant-Colonel Tkachenko arrived several weeks later.

CHAPTER V

THERE IS NO LAND ACROSS THE VOLGA

AT THE new command post there were no dug-outs or any kind of shelters to protect us even from bullets or shrapnel. Above us, on the bare hillside were oil-tanks and a concrete reservoir for black oil. Piled up on a spit of sand were lathes, motors and other factory equipment, which had been got ready to be carried across the Volga, but which had been left behind. A number of half-destroyed barges lay by the river bank.

The Army H.Q. staff established themselves on the barges or purely and simply in the open. The Military Council and the Army Chief of Staff were accommodated in hastily-dug trenches, open to the sky.

Sappers got to work straight away making dug-outs, taking someone's word for it that the oil-tanks above us were empty. Later on we would pay for that trust.

September 18 began as usual. Dawn had scarcely broken when the enemy's aeroplanes appeared and began bombing our units. The principal air attack was made on the station and Mamayev Kurgan. Immediately after the aeroplanes, the enemy's artillery and mortars opened fire. Our own artillery replied. The fighting grew more and more fierce. Suddenly, at 8 a.m., the sky over the city cleared of German bombers. We knew that the Stalingrad Front armies, operating north of the city, had begun active operations. A probing attack had been launched. At 2 p.m. it was clear that the attack was over: hundreds of Junkers had reappeared. They continued their attack on the 62nd Army's units even more strongly than in the morning. This meant that the attack from the north had been either stopped or suspended.

The Luftwaffe reacted sensitively to any sign of activity by our units, especially to the north. From its behaviour we could guess the state of affairs on other sectors of our front. We were grateful to our neighbours, because the six-hour breathing-space between bombing attacks enabled us to improve our positions.

Our troops on the right flank, who had been on the offensive since morning, had won some slight success: Colonel Gorokhov's infantry brigade seized some high ground and a regiment of Sarayev's division took a hill. On the armoured formation's sector the 38th Motorized Infantry Brigade of Colonel Burmakov won complete control of the orchards south-west of the Krasny Oktyabr workers' settlement.

The remains of Sologub's 112th Division and Yelin's regiment were waging a bitter battle on Mamayev Kurgan. During the day they gained some 100-150 yards of ground and firmly consolidated their positions at the crest of the hill. In the city centre and on the Army's left flank the fighting was going on as bitterly as before. In spite of his enormous numerical superiority, the enemy was unsuccessful. Our units held their positions, with the exception of the station, which, in five days of bloody fighting had changed hands fifteen times, and which was taken by the enemy only on the evening of September 18.

We had no troops with which to launch a counter-attack and try to take the station. General Rodimtsev's 13th Division was exhausted. They had gone into battle immediately upon being ferried across the Volga, and had borne the main brunt of the German attack, aimed at taking the city quickly. The guardsmen had inflicted heavy losses on the enemy. It was true that they had had to relinquish some sections of Stalingrad to the enemy. But this had been neither a withdrawal nor a retreat. No one was prepared to retreat. The guardsmen fought to the death; the only ones who left were the seriously wounded, who crawled away one by one. The stories told by the wounded made it clear that the German forces which had seized the station were suffering heavy losses. When they were cut off from the division, the guardsmen singly or in groups of two or three, consolidated positions in pill-boxes, in the basements of station buildings, behind station platforms and under railway carriages, from where they would continue, alone, to carry out the job they had been given—to attack the enemy from the rear and flanks and destroy them night and day. In this way they forced the enemy into street fighting, which compelled the German officers to keep their companies and battalions on the alert right round the clock, to throw in more and more troops in different places, in order to surround and overcome the 'one-man fortresses' created by Soviet soldiers who had decided to fight to the last breath. Now I began to think more clearly about something which had been in my mind since my first days at the front: how to answer the enemy's well-thought-out but stereotyped tactics?

In the forefront of my reflections was the individual soldier. He is the main hero of war. More than anyone else it is he who has to meet the enemy face to face. Sometimes he knows more about the psychology of the enemy troops than the generals in their observation posts. He is also a student of the character of the enemy. I underline this point that he studies the enemy, because the soldier has a mind, a heart, an ability to think and not merely to understand the orders of his commander; he can weigh up the situation and the enemy's intentions. Of course, he knows less about the enemy's armies than the staff officers do; he does not see the field of battle in as broad a perspective as we do from our observation posts, but as a result of seeing the behaviour of the enemy in battle, facing him in attack and counter-attack, he knows the enemy's morale more fully and acutely than other people do. He knows the enemy's morale not in a general way, but directly, encountering it in battle—and in the final analysis this is a decisive factor in any battle.

A well-trained soldier who knows the state of the enemy's morale is not afraid of the enemy's numerical superiority, even in the fiercest of fighting. This is why our soldiers, even when wounded, did not quit the battle; they went on to hit at the enemy's vulnerable points.

The Communist Party had inculcated among our soldiers a love of and devotion to their country. The political organs of the Army, the Party and Komsomol organizations, under the direction of the Party's Central Committee, had educated every soldier to believe in our cause; on the basis of precise examples from military life and the exploits of our heroes, they had developed an attitude of great responsibility on the part of the soldiers towards their country, and had raised their morale. All these factors taken together made it possible for me to believe in the tenacity of our soldiers, and on that basis, to give serious thought to the problem of revising the tactics of our units in conditions of street fighting.

What was needed was for us to act so that every house in which we had even one soldier became a fortress against the enemy. All would be well if every soldier fighting in a basement or under the stairs, knowing the general task facing the army, stood his ground alone and accomplished that task on his own. In street fighting a soldier is on occasion his own general. He needed to be given correct guidance and, so to speak, the trust of the generals.

You cannot be a commander if you do not believe in the soldier's abilities. During the fighting for the station, after consultations with the Member of the Military Council, K. A. Gurov, and the Chief of Staff, N. I. Krylov, we decided to change our tactics. We were going to break down the formations that existed in the Army: alongside platoons and sec-

119

tions in our companies and battalions appeared new tactical units—small storm groups.[1]

How this was done and what results were obtained, I shall go into later.

On September 18 an order was received from the H.Q. of South-Eastern Front, of which the 62nd Army at that time was a part. This document read as follows:

EXTRACT FROM MILITARY ORDER NO. 00122

South-Eastern Front H.Q. 18.9.42. 18.00

Under attack from the formations of the Stalingrad Front, which has gone over to a general southward offensive, the enemy is suffering heavy losses along the Kuzmichi, Sukhaya Mechetka, Akatovka line. In order to resist the offensive of our northern group the enemy is withdrawing a number of units and formations from the area of Stalingrad and Voroponovo and is transferring them to the north through Gumrak.

With the aim of wiping out the enemy's Stalingrad group, by combined operations with the Stalingrad Front, I order:

1. The 62nd Army Command, after creating a shock force of not less than three infantry divisions and one armoured brigade in the vicinity of Mamayev Kurgan, to launch an attack towards the north-west outskirts of Stalingrad, with the aim of destroying the enemy in this area. The immediate task is to destroy the enemy in the city, firmly securing a line through Rynok, Orlovka, Hills 128.0 and 98.9, and the north-west and western outskirts of Stalingrad.

The Front Artillery Commander to cover the 62nd Army's attack with a powerful artillery bombardment from Gorodishche and Gumrak on the right to the River Tsaritsa on the left.

Gorishny's infantry division, as from 19.00 on 18.9.42, to become a part of the 62nd Army. The 62nd Army Command to ferry the majority of the division

---

[1] Reinforced assault groups, described in detail p. 326 ff.

across to Stalingrad via the northern crossings in the Krasny Oktyabr area by 05.00 on 19.9.42 and to use this division for an attack from the vicinity of Hill 102.0 towards the north-west outskirts of the city.

The first paragraph of this order states that the enemy was withdrawing a number of units and formations from the city. I must categorically reject this statement. Not a single enemy unit, apart from aircraft, was transferred from the city to meet the attacking units of the Stalingrad Front.

As can be seen from the order, we had twelve to eighteen hours in which to ferry Gorishny's division across the Volga, occupy positions from which to counter-attack and make all the necessary preparations for the battle. This was obviously not enough, but the situation was such that schedules had to go by the board.

Executing this order, I issued my own order at 23.50. It read as follows:

MILITARY ORDER NO. 151

62nd Army H. Q. 18.9.42. 23.50

1. The enemy, throwing reserves into the battle and occupying Central Station, is trying to reach the Volga and split the Army.

2. Carrying out its main task—to defend the city—the Army will throw part of its forces into a counter-attack on 19.9.42 with the aim of wiping out the enemy troops which have broken through into the city.

3. On the Army's right, the left flank of the Stalingrad Front will launch an attack with the aim of destroying the enemy group in the region of Rynok and Kuzmichi and joining up with units of the 62nd Army.

On the Army's left, units of the 64th Army will carry out offensive action in the area of Kuporosnoye.

4. I have decided that an attack will be made from Hill 102.0 (Mamayev Kurgan) in the general direction of the station, so as to cut off and destroy the enemy troops which have penetrated into the center of the city.

I therefore issue the following orders:

1. The armoured formation:

(*a*) The motorized infantry brigade will attack in the direction of Hill 126.8 with the aim of wiping out the enemy in the area of the attack, protecting the flank of the group attacking from the north-west.

Boundary on the left—Hill 107.5 the waggon-sheds and the forestry station.

(*b*) The armoured brigade will attack from the area on the south-western outskirts of the Krasny Oktyabr settlement in the direction of the waggon-sheds; its aim will be to wipe out the enemy on the western slopes of Hill 102.0 and by nightfall to occupy Hill 112.5.

Boundary on the left—Hill 102.0 and the machine and tractor station.

2. Gorishny's division will attack from Hill 102.0 towards the machine and tractor station, with the aim of wiping out the enemy in the area of attack, and by nightfall occupying the south-western part of the city.

Boundary on the left—Krasny Oklyabr landing-stage and the western pump-house on the Volga.

3. The 39th Guards Regiment will attack along the railway line towards the station (Stalingrad No. 1), with the aim of wiping out the enemy, joining up with units of the 13th Division, and cutting off the enemy's retreat to the west.

4. The 13th Guards Division will continue to carry out its previous task, and by nightfall will have cleared the city centre of enemy troops.

Boundary on the left—the River Tsaritsa.

5. Sologub's 112th Division will by 11.00 on 19.9 reach the railway line in the sector of the bridges across Dolgi and Krutoy Gullies, and will protect the western and southern slopes of Hill 102.0.

6. Colonel Gorokhov's brigade will continue to attack, and together with the left flank of the Stalingrad Front will wipe out the enemy in the Rynok area.

7. All other units will continue to carry out their previously allocated tasks.

8. The Army's Artillery Commander will create two artillery groups to give support to the attacking units. Night and day, together with groups of the rocket artil-

lery regiments, he will organize the planned destruction of the enemy in the area of the gullies south of Hill 102.0, and along the railway line from the River Tsaritsa. He will pay particular attention to the neighbourhood of the forestry station.

9. The infantry attack will begin at 12.00 on 19.9.42.

10. Army H.Q. command post will be in the gully half a mile north of Krasny Oktabr landing-stage.

My first order set a task for the 'armoured formation', but in strength the formation was equivalent to a regiment and had only thirty-five tanks, the majority of which had been put out of action and could not move. We used them as stationary firing positions, capable purely of defensive action. They did that job very well.

Unfortunately our efforts on this occasion did not yield the results we hoped for: the counter-attack by troops of the Stalingrad Front through Akatovka and Kuzmichi was unsuccessful. Our hopes of linking up with the armies operating north of the city were not fulfilled, and on this score something needs to be said.

The main reason for the failure was the haste with which the decision was taken, the poor preparation of units of all kind for a swift, decisive counter-attack, and the dispersion of our forces.

This attack was intended to play a crucial role in smashing the enemy, who had concentrated masses of men and material near the city. But where and when should an attack be delivered? This is an extremely important question. For comparison let us take one of the episodes in the historical film *Alexander Nevski,* and we will see what the selection of the right moment means. Nevski decides to strike at the rear of the Teutonic swordsmen only when they have cut deep into the Russian armies.

Or take another example—the battle on the field of Kulikovo. Carrying out his plan to destroy the armies of Mamay, Dmitri Donskoy even allowed his main troops partially to retreat, and lured the Tartars so deep into the Russian positions that the army of Prince Andrey, lying in ambush, appeared in the enemy's rear. Prince Andrey then had purely to attack the rear of Mamay's main forces and victory was assured. That is what it means to select the right moment.

Had the main German armies been brought into the battle on the bank of the Volga in September 1942?

There can be only one answer—no. The only enemy forces involved at this time were those which were trying to take the city quickly. On September 12 they had come close to the city, but had been repulsed and halted. Paulus needed this pause in order to rebuild his battle formations and deploy his main forces.

To bring up and deploy his main forces, and particularly reinforcements, to organize combined operations of infantry, tanks, artillery and aircraft, the enemy needed not less than five to seven days. Our counter-attack, scheduled to begin on September 19, was therefore at the wrong time, because at this moment the main forces of Paulus's army had only just been deployed at their starting positions. Our attack was, in fact, launched not against enemy troops weakened by the fighting in the city, but against his main forces, ready for battle.

During these days two of the enemy's armies, which had advanced separately from two directions (the 6th Army from Kalach and the 4th Panzer Army from Kotelnikovo) had joined up and were preparing to advance from the line of Orlovka, Gumrak and Voroponovo.

Our counter-attack, finally, was made along a broad front (from Akatovka to Kuzmichi)—a fifteen-mile frontal attack, and not at the enemy's weak point, not against satellite troops, not against the flank and rear, but against the head of a powerful battering-ram, consisting of four army corps.

It is also impossible to understand why this and subsequent counter-attacks were launched in the daytime (when we had no way of neutralizing or compensating for the enemy's superiority in the air), and not at night (when the Luftwaffe did not operate with any strength).

All this means that the Front Command, having made a wrong assessment of the situation, made mistakes in the selection of both the time and the starting points for the counter-attack.

At exactly 12 noon on September 19 the main forces

launched their attack from north to south. It could have completely changed the situation in our favour. But this did not happen. General Gordov, as Yeremenko's deputy in charge of the Stalingrad Front, had failed to organize the attack as it needed to be. The attack by the main forces of the Front petered out on the first day.

We could again tell what was happening by the behaviour of the enemy's air force: from noon there were only a few dozen enemy planes in the sky above the city, but by 5 p.m. there were already as many as three hundred. The attack by the 62nd Army's shock group took the form of a head-on clash with the enemy both on the Army's centre and on the left flank. Only on the right flank was the enemy comparatively passive.

The battle in the vicinity of Mamayev Kurgan went on all day on September 19 with different degrees of success. The motorized infantry brigade took Hill 126.3; the regiment from Sarayev's division reached a line on the northern ridge of Dolgi Gully, and had well-organized communications with the motorized infantry brigade. Two battalions of Gorishny's division had been ferried across on the night of September 18 and immediately went into battle. Without having had any chance to prepare positions and get their bearings, they crossed the ridge of Mamayev Kurgan and clashed head-on with attacking enemy infantry and tanks. Sologub's infantry division repulsed powerful enemy attacks from the early morning and at nightfall occupied a line along the railway from Mamayev Kurgan to a fork in Dolgi Gully, the road bridge across Krutoy Gully and Artemovskaya Street.

Rodimtsev's 13th Guards Division, severely depleted in the previous fighting, was engaged in fierce street fighting in the centre of the city. One could sense that the enemy had decided to overrun this division at all costs and reach the Volga near the central landing-stage, thus cutting the 62nd Army in two.

Two infantry brigades, with the remains of Dubyanski's 35th Guards Division and Bubnov's armoured brigade, were engaged in street fighting from the River Tsaritsa to Valdayskaya Street and further to the south-east as far as the Volga.

In the area of Mamayev Kurgan our forces were approximately equal to the enemy's, but on the sector occupied by the 13th Guards Infantry Division and further south the enemy had clear, numerical superiority.

The day's fighting on September 19 had shown the enemy was not particularly afraid of an attack by Soviet troops from the north, that he was not thinking of withdrawing units northward from the city, and was trying harder and harder to untie his hands on the bank of the Volga, that is, to destroy the 62nd Army.

During these days of fighting the German generals did everything they could to prevent any fresh Soviet forces being ferried across to the city. From dawn till dusk enemy dive-bombers circled over the Volga, and artillery opened up at night. The moorings and approaches to them were under fire day and night from enemy guns and six-barrelled mortars. The job of ferrying men and goods across the river for the 62nd Army therefore became as difficult as it could possibly be.

Small units ferried across during the night to the right bank had to be deployed and established in positions straight away, during the night, and supplies had to be distributed to the troops, otherwise they would have been bombed and destroyed. We had neither horses nor trucks on the right bank of the Volga, as there was nowhere to hide them from bullets, bombs and shells. Everything that was brought across the Volga, therefore, had to be distributed to the troops' positions on the shoulders of our men: during the day they fought off fierce enemy assaults, and at night, without sleep and rest, they had to carry ammunition, provisions and engineering equipment. The result was exhaustion, and, of course, lower fighting efficiency. This went on not for a day, or a week, but as long as the fighting lasted.

From the beginning to the end of the fighting in the city, the artillery distribution posts at the landing-stages were under the command of Lieutenant-Colonel Sokolov, and provisions distribution was under Lieutenant-Colonel Spasov and Major Zinoviev. These officers spent the whole time on piles of rockets and shells, which could have been blown up at any moment.

On September 19, Batyuk's 284th Infantry Division was

brought across to the right bank, and incorporated into the 62nd Army. We had awaited its arrival impatiently, as an extremely difficult situation had developed that day in the centre of the city, where regiments of Rodimtsev's division were fighting. But the central ferry was already completely paralysed and not a single group of soldiers was able to use it.

That evening we learned that the Stalingrad Front was again going to attack the enemy from the north on September 20, and I therefore decided to counter-attack from the vicinity of Mamayev Kurgan to the south-west. After the first failure of the counter-attack on September 19, we did not believe that further attacks would be successful. Nonetheless, we could not sit and fold our hands and wait, when someone was approaching from north or south to try to link up with us.

The units of the 62nd Army were given orders during the night to continue to counter-attack with all the forces they could muster on September 20. In this order the Army Military Council called on the troops to carry out the tasks that had not been accomplished the previous day.

We knew how difficult was the position of Rodimtsev's division, but we had not a single battalion to send to his aid. The only way to help him was to return to him the 42nd Regiment, which had been fighting under Yelin's command on Mamayev Kurgan up to September 19, detached from its own division.

The remains of the 35th Guards Division, under Dubyanski's command, had for a week been in non-stop battle with numerically manifold superior forces, and had been so weakened that we decided to hand over the remaining men and material to the infantry brigades and send their headquarters staffs across the Volga to be regrouped.

At this time we had a serious quarrel with the Front Artillery Commander. The root of it lay in the fact that he instructed the artillery units, sent with their divisions to reinforce the 62nd Army, to cross over to the right bank of the Volga, to the city, but the Army Military Council categorically opposed this. We left the artillery regiments of the infantry divisions at the other side of the Volga, and brought observation posts across the city bank, from where they could direct the fire of the guns and batteries on a broad front. We allowed only the mortars and anti-tank artillery to be ferried across with their units.

The Front Artillery Commander could not understand that for ground artillery (cannon and howitzers) no suitable positions could possibly be found in the city. To leave them standing in the streets amid the ruins would deprive us of manœuvrability in our fire, as the buildings would be in the way.

In addition, in the city we had neither horses nor mechanical transport for the artillery: we had nowhere to hide tractors, vehicles or horses from enemy fire. We would therefore not be able to move our artillery. To move cannon and howitzers by hand through the ruins of buildings and down streets pitted with bomb and shell craters was impossible. And finally, in the second half of September it became extremely difficult, sometimes completely impossible, to get shells for artillery across the Volga and into the city. By day the enemy watched for any approach to the Volga from the east. From September, when he reached positions near the central landing-stage, he was able to direct accurate fire on any boat. To count on carrying ammunition across by night was also risky: the enemy knew where our ferries crossed and throughout the night lit up the Volga by dropping flares suspended from parachutes. It was much easier to bring ammunition fifty miles to the Volga than to carry it across the half-mile of water.

There were obviously other people who shared the Front Artillery Commander's views, and we had to turn for help to the Member of the Front Military Council, N. S. Khrushchev. He understood the cause of the quarrel, looked into it, and with his co-operation the question was settled in the way we had asked.

The decision to leave the divisional artillery on the left bank played a positive role in our defensive and offensive operations in the city.

With the cannon and howitzer regiments at the other side of the Volga, every divisional or brigade commander could call on his artillery to bombard any sector of the front, and the Army's Artillery Commander, General Pozharski, could

128

at any time concentrate the fire of the brigade and divisional batteries at the other side of the Volga to any one point.

Later, the artillery group of the Front was organized on the same principle, which strengthened the defences still further.

Beating off dozens of enemy attacks along the whole of the Army's front day by day, we could see that there was a new and more powerful German group involved and we massed our men and material to resist it.

As from September 20 I held a meeting every day at 5 p.m. with Generals Krylov, Pozharski and Gurov and our chief of reconnaissance, Colonel Herman. On the basis of information from reconnaissance, we marked the places where the Germans had built up strength in preparation for an attack. Towards dawn we would open up sudden artillery fire on these points and send in 'katyushi' rocket salvos. In these conditions every shell or rocket sent into an enemy concentration was more useful than in defensive fire along the enemy lines. In this way our accurate fire wiped out enemy troops and lowered the Germans' morale. After such night attacks the Germans went into the attack with their morale already undermined, knowing that we were waiting for them to attack and preparing to meet them.

Holding action continued on our right flank (Rynok, Orlovka, Razgulyayevka), but in the area of Mamayev Kurgan regiments of the 95th Division were under attack from freshly-arrived enemy forces.

At noon the commander of this division, Colonel Gorishny, reported to me on the situation:

'Apart from some insignificant fluctuations in the front, amounting to a hundred yards or so in one direction or the other, the situation on Mamayev Kurgan is unchanged.'

'Remember,' I warned him, 'that a fluctuation of even a hundred yards could lead to the loss of the hill . . .'

'I shall die rather than abandon the hill!' replied Gorishny, after a pause. And I knew that he correctly understood the importance of Mamayev Kurgan, and saw his task clearly.

The divisional commander, Colonel Vasili Akimovich Gorishny, and his deputy in the political section, Ivan Alexandrovich Vlasenko, thought deeply and correctly about the progress of the fighting, and on that basis a strong friendship developed between them. They seemed complementary to each other: the former was not just a commander, but also a Communist, paying great attention to the political education of the men, and the latter, in charge of the Party's political work, understood the details of the military operations and could hold his own in discussion with any specialist commander.

Listening to them on the telephone, reporting on the situation on the division's sector, I had no doubt of the reliability and objectivity of the appraisal of the facts, regardless of whether it was Gorishny or Vlasenko who was reporting to me. Both of them were well-informed about the operational situation and were clearly familiar with the enemy's habits.

Gorishny's division had arrived in the city immediately after Rodimtsev's. Also, immediately on arrival from the ferry, without a moment's delay, it went straight into the battle for Mamayev Kurgan, and then in the area of the Tractor and Barrikady plants. The regiments of this division, or, to be more accurate, the regimental staffs, took it in turns to make a short visit to the other bank of the Volga, where they could have a brief rest, replenish their companies, and then return to the battle.

Gorishny and Vlasenko remained at their observation post throughout the battle, calmly and surely leading attack and counter-attack.

To get through to them at their command post was no easy matter, even from the Volga bank. The gully between the Barrikady and Krasny Oktyabr plants was under fire from enemy snipers. Many of our soldiers were killed there in the early days, and it became known as 'the gully of death'. To avoid losses, we had to build a stone wall across the gully, and only by crouching close up to the wall could one reach Gorishny's command post alive.

V. A. Gorishny subsequently became a lieutenant-general. I. A. Vlasenko is a retired major-general and lives in Kiev. I saw him not long ago. He complained about his heart:

'The motor is starting to misfire,' he said.

He was a good, intelligent political worker, and went through a great deal on the banks of the Volga and on other fronts, and, of course, all this could not but leave its mark on his heart.

On the sector occupied by Rodimtsev's 13th Guards Division the situation was becoming extremely difficult for us. At noon on September 20, enemy tommy-gunners got through to the area of the central ferry. The division's command post came under fire. A unit of the 42nd Guards Regiment was half-encircled, and communications were working with long interruptions. Army H.Q. signals officers sent to Rodimtsev's H.Q. were killed trying to get there. Yelin's regiment was sent towards the central landing-stage, but was delayed: it was spotted by enemy aircraft on the way and came under constant air attack.

The only help the Army could give to this division was artillery backing from the left bank, but this was obviously not enough.

Fierce fighting was going on the whole time to the left of Rodimtsev's division, in the sector being defended by battalions of Batrakov's 42nd Infantry Brigade and a regiment of Sarayev's division. Contact with them was frequently interrupted, and it was difficult for us to establish what the position was on this sector; one thing, however, was clear—the enemy had brought up fresh forces and was trying, regardless of the cost, to break through to the Volga in the centre of our defences and particularly on the southern flank. We therefore had to continue to counter-attack in the vicinity of Mamayev Kurgan. If we allowed our attacks to slacken off here, the enemy's hands would be untied and he would throw everything he had against our left flank, smashing our units engaged in defensive operations in the centre of the city.

On the night of September 20 one infantry regiment of Batyuk's 284th Division was ferried across to the city, and sent east of Mamayev Kurgan as a reserve.

At about 2 a.m. I was called to the telephone by the Front Commander, Colonel-General Yeremenko. He reported that one armoured brigade of the Stalingrad Front had broken through the enemy's positions from the north and should be on the point of joining up with us in the vicinity of Orlovka. I got everybody out of bed and sat by the telephone all night waiting to find out what was happening, and to see who would be the first to bring the glad news of a link-up between the troops of the Stalingrad Front and the 62nd Army. But we received no such report. A few days later we learned that the brigade concerned had not achieved its aim. The link-up was not to take place until considerably later—on 26 January 1943.

September 21 and 22 were critical days for the 62nd Army. At the price of great losses, the enemy for the first time cut the Army in two: on the sector of the 13th Guards Infantry Division enemy troops reached 2nd Naberezhnaya (Quay) Street, and forward units reached the central landing-stage.

At nightfall on September 21, the 13th Division occupied a line running through Krutoy Gully, 2nd Naberezhnaya Street, 9th January Square, Solnechnaya, Kommunisticheskaya, Kurskaya, Orlovskaya, Proletarskaya and Gogol Streets, as far as the River Tsaritsa.

Some small units of this division were encircled and fought to the last round. But we had no detailed information, particularly about the fate of the 1st Battalion of Yelin's regiment. That is why in all communiqués, and then in the press and in books about the Battle of Stalingrad, it has been assumed that the battalion, fighting for the station, was wiped out on 21 September 1942, and that the only survivor from the battalion was Second Lieutenant Koleganov . . .

I must say frankly that I never believed that this battalion was destroyed on September 21, because even at the time one could sense from the behaviour of the enemy that our forces were active at and to the left of the station, and that the Germans were suffering heavy losses. But who was fighting and how—none of us knew, and the fate of these men lay like a load on my conscience. But after my notes *The Army of Mass Heroism* were published and extracts from them were broadcast on the radio, I received many letters, including one from Anton Kuzmich Dragan, who was disabled in the war. This ex-serviceman wrote, saying that he could explain what had happened to the battalion after the Germans occupied the station. I was excited about the letter. At last, fifteen years after the event, it was going to be possible to elucidate what had happened to the men about whom I had thought so often. I did not believe that the men who had fought the enemy so stubbornly for seven days in the area of the station could have been wiped out in one night or have laid down their arms.

And I had not been mistaken. In the summer of 1958, whilst on leave, I went to visit the writer of this letter. He lives near the Chernigovshchina River, in the village of Likovitsa, in the Prilugski district. When we met, we recognized each other almost immediately, from the first glance and the first words.

He remembered me as soon as we greeted each other; he remembered where it was we had met the first time.

'It was on the evening of September 15, near the church on Pushkinskaya Street. You saw me and asked me: "Lieutenant, where are your men? ... Ah, here, well there's a job for you. The Germans need to be cleared out of the station. Is that clear? ..." '

'Yes, I remember,' I replied. In front of me I could again see the destroyed house, the smoking hillside, where men were moving with rifles and tommy-guns. I could see the lively, small, red-eyed lieutenant, hung round with grenades. Anton Kuzmich Dragan had at that time been in command of the 1st Company of the 1st Battalion of the 42nd Infantry Regiment of Rodimtsev's division. Having received the order, he quickly deployed his company, and going off with it in the direction of the station, was hidden in the smoke and the darkness that was falling. A few minutes later the sound of frequent firing could be heard from that direction—the company had gone into battle. What happened to the company which I had sent towards the station I had never found out.

'I'll tell you everything in the order it happened,' he proposed, when we were sitting down at the table.

This was his story.

'When I had set off with the company towards the station, and was exchanging fire with the Germans, the Battalion Commander Chervyakov, came and found me. Wiping his glasses he told me: "We need to cut them off—the Germans that is—and hold them. Hang on here as long as you can. Get in a stock of grenades."

'I collected the company and in the darkness moved off to surround the station.

'By now it was night, and the sounds of battle rolled around us. Small groups of our men consolidated positions in

133

half-destroyed houses, and with great difficulty beat back the enemy onslaught. I could tell that the station buildings were in the enemy's hands. We cut across the railway line to the left of it. At the crossing stood our stationary tank with a dozen men by it. We massed near the station building and moved in ready for hand-to-hand fighting.

'A sudden attack, the throw of a grenade, a soldier after it. The Germans ran away, firing chaotically into the dark.

'In this way the company occupied the station. By the time the Germans recovered and realized that there was only one company of us, we had already established strong defence positions, and although they came in to attack us from three sides several times before dawn, they could not regain the station . . .

'Day dawned imperceptibly, and another hard Stalingrad morning began. From daybreak German dive-bombers began dropping hundreds of bombs on the station. After the bombing—an artillery bombardment. The station buildings were on fire, the walls burst apart, the iron buckled, but the men went on fighting . . .

'At nightfall the Germans had failed to occupy the station building, and finally, realizing, that no attack would overcome us, moved to encircle us. We then switched the battle to the square outside the station. A fierce skirmish took place near the fountain and along the railway line.

'I remember the Germans coming round to our rear and massing in a corner building on the station square; for identification sake, we called the building "the nail factory", because the men we sent out on reconnaissance reported that there was a storehouse full of nails there. From here the enemy was preparing to attack us from behind, but we guessed what he was going to do and launched a counter-attack against this position. We were supported by mortar fire from a company under Lieutenant Zavodun, which had now approached the station. We did not manage to take the whole of "the nail factory"; we drove the Germans out of one of the workshops, but they remained in the neighbouring one.

'Fighting now broke out inside the building. Our company's strength was fast coming to an end. Not only our company, but the whole battalion, was in an extremely difficult position. Then Battalion Commander, Lieutenant Chervyakov, was wounded and evacuated across the Volga. Lieutenant Fedoseyev took over command of the battalion.

'The Germans were pressing the battalion back on three sides. The position with ammunition was serious, and there was no question of food or sleep. The worst part was the thirst. In our search for water, in the first instance for the machine-guns, we fired at drain-pipes to see if any water dripped out.

'The fighting in "the nail factory" would die down and then flare up anew. In short skirmishes we used knives, spades and the butts of our rifles. Towards dawn the Germans brought up fresh reserves and threw company after company against us. To hold off such an onslaught became extremely difficult. I sent an urgent report on the situation to Lieutenant Fedoseyev. The 3rd Infantry Company, under Second Lieutenant Koleganov, was then sent to our assistance. On the way this company was under a torrent of fire and was attacked a number of times. Tall, lean Koleganov, in a greatcoat covered with brickdust, nevertheless got through with his company, and reported simply:

' "My company, with twenty men, has arrived."

'In his report to Battalion H.Q. Koleganov noted that he had arrived at "the nail factory", that the position was difficult, but that as long as he lived the scum would not get through. Fierce fighting went on into the night. Small groups of German tommy-gunners and snipers began to penetrate to our rear. They hid in garrets, in the ruins and in sewer-pipes, and proceeded to fire at us.

'Battalion Commander Fedoseyev ordered me to prepare a group of tommy-gunners to be sent through to the enemy's rear. I carried out his order, and this is what I wrote about it in my diary . . .'

Anton Kuzmich handed me a sheet of paper to read, on which the following was written:

18 *September*. A group of volunteer tommy-gunners not long ago slipped away silently into the dark. They went, knowing clearly how difficult and complicated their task was—to reach the enemy's rear and operate there on their own.

Each of them received a five-day ration of ammunition and food and detailed instructions on how to act behind the enemy lines.

The German defences were soon alarmed. The Germans could obviously not understand who had blown up the lorry which had just brought up ammunition for them, or who had put their machine-gun team and artillery detachment out of action.

From morning till noon clusters of German planes hung in the sky over the city. Some of them would break away from their formations, dive and riddle the streets and ruins of houses with bullets from ground level; others would fly over the city with sirens wailing, in an attempt to sow panic. They dropped high explosives and incendiaries. The city was in flames. At night the Germans blew up the wall separating our workshop from the rest of the building and began throwing grenades at us.

The guardsmen could only just manage to throw grenades back through the window frames. Lieutenant Koleganov was severely wounded by a bursting grenade. Our men fell one by one.

With great difficulty two of our men carried Koleganov out of range of the firing, towards the Volga. I do not know what has happened to him.

'Then what happened?' I asked, after reading this.

'For another twenty-four hours or more we continued to fight in "the nail factory",' continued Anton Kuzmich. 'The men of Lieutenant Zavodun's mortar company then came to our aid. They had long ago run out of bombs, and the men were acting as infantrymen. They got down behind barricades in the street, and consolidated their position while putting up a strong barrage of fire. Towards evening—this was September 20—our observers reported that the enemy was actively regrouping his forces, and was bringing up artillery and tanks towards the station. The battalion was ordered to prepare to beat off a tank attack.

I detached a number of groups from the company, armed with anti-tank rifles and grenades and bottles of incendiary mixture. But the enemy's tank attack did not materialize that day.

At night, risking her life, a woman who lived nearby came across from enemy-held territory to tell us that the Germans were preparing a tank attack. She gave us a lot of valuable information about the disposition of the German units. I remember her name—Maria Vadeneyeva. I ought to add that local inhabitants often helped us with information and water. Unfortunately the names of these courageous patriots have remained unknown . . .

So, September 21 dawned. This was to be the darkest day for the 1st Battalion. From daybreak the Germans, with the aid of tanks and artillery, launched a frantic attack. The strength of the enemy's fire and the ferocity of his soldiers were beyond all our expectations. The Germans threw all their resources, all their reserves on this sector, into the battle, in order to break our resistance in the area of the station. But they advanced only at the cost of heavy losses. Only in the latter part of the day did they manage to cut our battalion in two.

A part of the battalion, including the Battalion H.Q., were cut off in the vicinity of the Universal Stores. The Germans surrounded this group and attacked them from all sides. Hand-to-hand fighting broke out inside the Stores. The Battalion H.Q. staff, led by Lieutenant Fedoseyev, waged an unequal battle. The small group of courageous men sold their lives dearly. We sent in four groups to their aid, but the Germans managed to bring up tanks and lambasted everything that moved. That was how the Commander of the 1st Battalion, Fedoseyev, and his courageous assistants, died.

After his death I took over command of what remained of the units, and we began to concentrate our forces in the vicinity of "the nail factory". I wrote a report on the position to the Regimental Commander, Colonel Yelin, and sent it off with one of the signallers, who did not return. From that moment our battalion lost contact with the regiment and acted on its own.

The Germans had cut us off from our neighbours. The supply of ammunition had been cut off; every bullet was worth its weight in gold. I gave the order to economize on ammunition, to collect the cartridge-pouches of the dead and all captured weapons. In the evening the enemy again tried to break our resistance, coming up close to our positions. As our numbers grew smaller, we shortened our line of defence. We began to move back slowly towards the Volga, drawing the enemy after us, and the ground we occupied was invariably too small for the Germans to be able easily to use artillery and aircraft.

We moved back, occupying one building after another, turning them into strongholds. A soldier would crawl out of an occupied position only when the ground was on fire under him and his clothes were smouldering. During the day the Germans managed to occupy only two blocks.

At the crossroads of Krasnopiterskaya and Komsomolskaya Streets we occupied a three-storey building on the corner. This was a good position from which to fire on all comers and it became our last defence. I ordered all entrances to be barricaded, and windows and embrasures to be adapted so that we could fire through them with all our remaining weapons.

At a narrow window of the semi-basement we placed the heavy machine-gun with our emergency supply of ammunition—the last belt of cartridges. I had decided to use it at the most critical moment.

Two groups, six in each, went up to the third floor and the garret. Their job was to break down walls, and prepare lumps of stone and beams to throw at the Germans when they came up close. A place for the seriously wounded was set aside in the basement. Our garrison consisted of forty men. Difficult days began. Attack after attack broke unendingly like waves against us. After each attack was beaten off we felt it was impossible to hold off the onslaught any longer, but when the Germans launched a fresh attack, we managed to find means and strength. This lasted five days and nights.

The basement was full of wounded; only twelve men were still able to fight. There was no water. All we had left in the way of food was a few pounds of scorched grain; the Germans decided to beat us with starvation.

Their attacks stopped, but they kept up the fire from their heavy-calibre machine-guns all the time.

We did not think about escape, but only about how to sell our lives most dearly—we had no other way out. And then a coward appeared among us. I don't want to talk about this, but the truth is the truth, and cowards must bear their shame. In the face of certain, inescapable death, Lieutenant Stavrovski wavered, and decided to abandon us and get across the Volga during the night. Did he understand that he was committing a vile act of treachery? Yes, he understood. He induced one of the privates, as spineless and cowardly as himself, to join with him in his crime, and during the night they slipped out unnoticed and headed for the Volga, made a raft of logs and pushed off into the river. When they were not far from the bank they were shot at by the Germans. The soldier was killed, but Stavrovski reached the administrative platoon of our battalion on the other bank, and reported that the battalion had been wiped out.

'And I personally buried Dragan near the Volga,' he asserted.

All this became clear a week later. But, as you see, Stavrovski was not very successful in burying me before my time . . .

The Germans attacked again. I ran upstairs with my men and could see their thin, blackened and strained faces, the bandages on their wounds, dirty and clotted with blood, their guns held firmly in their hands. There was no fear in their eyes. Lyuba Nesteranko, a nurse, was dying, with blood flowing from a wound in her chest. She had a bandage in her hand. Before she died she wanted to help bind someone's wound, but she failed . . .

The German attack was beaten off. In the silence that gathered around us we could hear the bitter fighting going on for Mamayev Kurgan and in the factory area of the city.

How could we help the men defending the city? How could we divert from over there even a part of the enemy forces, which had stopped attacking our building?

We decided to raise a red flag over the building, so

that the Nazis would not think we had given up. But we had no red material. Understanding what we wanted to do, one of the men who was severely wounded took off his bloody vest and, after wiping the blood off his wound with it, handed it over to me.

The Germans shouted thorugh a megaphone: "Russians! Surrender! You'll die just the same!"

At that moment, a red flag rose over our building.

'Bark, you dogs! We've still got a long time to live!' shouted my orderly, Kozhushko.

We beat off the next attack with stones, firing occasionally and throwing our last grenades. Suddenly from behind a blank wall, from the rear, came the grind of a tank's caterpillar tracks. We had no anti-tank grenades. All we had left was one anti-tank rifle with three rounds. I handed this rifle to an anti-tank man. Berdyshev, and sent him out through the back to fire at the tank point-blank. But before he could get into position he was captured by German tommy-gunners. What Berdyshev told the Germans I don't know, but I can guess that he led them up the garden path, because an hour later they started to attack at precisely that point where I had my machine-gun with its emergency belt of cartridges.

This time, reckoning that we had run out of ammunition, they came impudently out of their shelter, standing up and shouting. They came down the street in a column.

I put the last belt in the heavy machine-gun at the semi-basement window and sent the whole of the 250 bullets into the yelling, dirty-grey Nazi mob. I was wounded in the hand but did not leave go of the machine-gun. Heaps of bodies littered the ground. The Germans still alive ran for cover in panic. An hour later they led our anti-tank rifleman on to a heap of ruins and shot him in front of our eyes, for having shown them the way to my machine-gun.

There were no more attacks. An avalanche of shells fell on the building. The Germans stormed at us with every possible kind of weapon. We couldn't raise our heads.

Again we heard the ominous sound of tanks. From behind a neighbouring block stocky German tanks began

to crawl out. This, clearly, was the end. The guardsmen said good-bye to one another. With a dagger my
orderly scratched on a brick wall: 'Rodimtsev's guardsmen fought and died for their country here.' The battalion's documents and a map case containing the Party
and Komsomol cards of the defenders of the building
had been put in a hole in the corner of the basement.
The first salvo shattered the silence. There were a series
of blows, and the building rocked and collapsed. How
much later it was when I opened my eyes, I don't
know. It was dark. The air was full of acrid brickdust.
I could hear muffled groans around me. Kozhushko,
the orderly, was pulling at me.

'You're alive . . .'

On the floor of the basement lay a number of other
stunned and injured soldiers. We had been buried alive
under the ruins of the three-storey building. We could
scarcely breathe. We had no thought for food or water
—it was air that had become most important for sur-
vival. I spoke to the soldiers:

'Men! We did not flinch in battle, we fought even
when resistance seemed impossible, and we have to get
out of this tomb so that we can live and avenge the
death of our comrades!'

Even in pitch darkness you can see somebody else's
face, feel other people close to you.

With great difficulty we began to pick our way out of
the tomb. We worked in silence, our bodies covered
with cold, clammy sweat, our badly-bound wounds ached,
our teeth were covered with brickdust, it became more
and more difficult to breathe, but there were no groans or
complaints.

A few hours later, through the hole we had made, we
could see the stars and breathe the fresh September air.

Utterly exhausted, the men crowded round the hole,
greedily gulping in the autumn air. Soon the opening
was wide enough for a man to crawl through. Kozhushko, being only relatively slightly injured, went off
to reconnoitre. An hour later he came back and reported:

'Comrade Lieutenant, there are Germans all around us;

along the Volga they are mining the bank; there are German patrols nearby . . .

We took the decision to fight our way through to our lines.

Our first attempt to get through the enemy's rear was unsuccessful; we came up against a strong detachment of German tommy-gunners and got away from them only with difficulty, returned to our basement and waited for clouds to cover the moon. Finally the sky grew dark. We crept out of our shelter and set off cautiously towards the Volga. We supported each other as we went, gritting our teeth so as not to let out a groan with the pain from our wounds. There were six of us left. All of us were wounded. Kozhushko walked ahead—he was now our guard and main source of strength.

The city was covered in smoke, buildings were smouldering. By the Volga oil-tanks were in flames, railway carriages were on fire, and on our left was the unflagging thunder of bitter battle, the roar of explosions, and the multi-coloured fireworks of tracer bullets; the air was full of the smell of cordite. Over there the fate of the city was being decided. In front of us, by the Volga, by the light of flares we could see German patrols.

We crawled up closer and pin-pointed a place where we would break through. The important thing was silently to get rid of a patrol. We noticed that one of the Germans from time to time came close to a truck standing by itself and therefore easy to approach. With a dagger in his teeth Kozhushko crawled up to the truck . . . We saw the German approach . . . A quick blow and the German fell without being able to let out a cry.

Kozhushko took off the German's greatcoat, put it on and slowly walked to meet the next one. The second German, with no suspicion, came up to him. Kozhushko dealt with him also. As quickly as our wounds would let us we cut across the railway track. Walking in file we successfully negotiated the minefield, and there we were—at the Volga. We fell at the water's edge. The water was so cold it cracked our lips, we drank and drank. A wave of lead descended on the bank, bringing us a stern greeting. With difficulty we made a small raft of logs and bits and pieces we fished out of the river, and clinging to it, we floated with the current. We had nothing to row with, and simply used our hands, pulling closer to the main current. Towards dawn we were thrown on to a sandy spit, where there was some of our artillery. In amazement they looked at our rags and unshaven, sunken faces; they could scarcely recognize us as fellow soldiers. They fed us with incredibly tasty crusts of bread and fish soup (I have never tasted anything better!) It was the first food we had had in three days.

The same day the artillery men sent us to the medical battalion ...

Here Anton Kuzmich Dragan finished his story of what happened to the battalion after September 21. Now we know what happened to the 1st Battalion of the 42nd Regiment of the 13th Guards Division. The story is further testimony to the heroism of our troops. Alone, isolated, in small groups, they fought for every building, fought to the last round of ammunition, inflicting enormous losses on the enemy.

A large group of enemy tommy-gunners with tanks broke through to the central landing-stage round about the same time, cutting off two infantry brigades and one regiment of Sarayev's division, which were fighting in the area of Kurskaya, Kavkazskaya and Krasnopolskaya Streets. On September 21, however, Paulus could not consider that he was in full possession of the southern part of the city and the central ferry. Bitter fighting went on here for a long time to come.

On the evening of September 21 our observers spotted a large concentration of enemy infantry and tanks in the area of the Dar Hills. Under cover of a heavy artillery and mortar barrage these forces threw themselves into the attack. They tried to make a quick break-through to the left bank of the River Tsaritsa, but they were met by the shells of our batteries across the Volga. Some of the infantry and tanks returned to where they had come from, and the remainder were dealt with by the men of the brigade belonging to Colonel Batrakov, Hero of the Soviet Union, most of them seamen. This is a description of events written by Lieutenant B. Zhukov, who was in charge of a group of seventeen seamen in this fighting:

The tanks and machine-gunners who had broken through were met with bursts of well-aimed fire from the men in Petty Officer Borisoglebski's squad. The squad commander himself put the first tank out of action with an accurate shot from an anti-tank rifle. He then aimed at a second tank and put it out of action also. But the remaining tanks, firing non-stop, continued to move forward towards our seamen's positions. Petty Officer Borisoglebski put yet another tank out of action. Unable to stand up to the accurate fire, the Germans moved off to take cover. But soon came another attack. Seaman Balatsin now took over from Borisoglebski, and calmly waited for the right moment when he could be sure of hitting the target. The moment came. A tank turned broadside towards us. Balatsin fired. Snakes of flame curled over the enemy tank. Two more shots and another tank was out of action. Seaman Kudrevaty mowed down the advancing enemy infantry with his machine-gun. He let the Germans come within sixty yards before he opened fire.

They beat off six attacks in this way. There were seventeen of our men. But on this sector the enemy lost eight tanks and approaching three hundred men. The Soviet marines did not retreat an inch from the line they occupied.

The following day, in the city centre, the enemy tried to cut off Rodimtsev's division from the Army's main forces. Hour by hour the enemy kept up his attacks on the positions held by Rodimtsev's guardsmen. Only towards evening, when the enemy threw in more tanks, infantry and aircraft, did he succeed in slightly pressing back the guardsmen. His forward units reached Moskovskaya Street near the bank of the Volga. At the same time, an enemy infantry regiment, advancing along Kievskaya and Kurskaya Street, came out in the vicinity of the specialists' houses.

Nonetheless, in spite of his numerical superiority, particularly in tanks, the Germans failed to cut off Rodimtsev's division from the Army. The guardsmen withdrew only slightly to the north of the central ferry, but they held out in the centre of the city. On September 22 alone, they beat off twelve enemy attacks, putting thirty-two enemy tanks out of action. In spite of the ferocity of the enemy's attacks on this sector, he failed to advance a step.

Units of Gorishny's division, which had won a slight success the previous day, on September 21 reached the northern end of Dolgi Gully, adjoining the right flank of the armoured formation. But on September 22, after repeated enemy attacks, they were driven out of their positions and took up defence positions on the south-western slopes of Mamayev Kurgan. This meant that Sologub's division, which had taken up defence positions along Sovnarkomovskaya and Vilenskaya Streets between Dolgi and Krutoy Gullies (at the junction point of Gorishny's and Batyuk's divisions) as a second line of defence, became the front line and went into battle.

This was how our two bitter days of fighting ended.

Since the enemy, in reaching the central landing-stage, was now able to overlook almost the whole of the Army's rear and the Volga, where our supplies were coming across, I ordered my deputy in charge of the rear to organize three landing-stages and three sets of communications across the river. The first was in the vicinity of Verkhnyaya Akhtuba, the second of Skudri and the third of Tumak. On ships of the Volga Fleet and other boats, supplies were ferried across by night to the landing-stages at the Krasny Oktyabr factory and at the Spartanovka settlement.

From the Barrikady factory to Zaitsevski Island a footbridge was made on iron casks, and a ferry was organized between the island and the left bank of the Volga. Strict stock was taken of all boats in the Army's sector, and they were distributed among divisions and brigades. Each division organized its own ferry, under the strict command and control of the commander itself. The infantry brigades operating south of the River Tsaritsa obtained their own supplies via Golodny Island with the help of boats.

It was clear that, having reached the Volga, the enemy

would attack along the river bank to north and south, in order to cut off our units from the river, from the ferries. In order to forestall the enemy, on the morning of September 23 the Army Military Council decided, without suspending the counter-attack from the vicinity of Mamayev Kurgan, to throw Batyuk's division into the battle (it had been completely ferried across the river the previous night). The regiments of this division were given the task of wiping out the enemy in the area of the central landing-stage and firmly straddling the valley of the River Tsaritsa. Their boundary on the right would be Khalturin, Ostrovski and Gogol Streets.

In setting the division this task, I advised the Commander, Batyuk, to bear in mind the experience of street fighting with small groups. At first I felt that he did not understand the importance of the storm groups and their activities. Was it easy to abandon traditional ideas of military company and squad formation, when you taught the art of warfare precisely on that basis? But Batyuk, still a Colonel at this time, a lively, smart officer, looked me in the eyes and said:

'Comrade Commander, I have come to fight the Nazis, not for a parade. I have Siberians in my regiments . . .'

Apparently, while still on the other side of the Volga, he had heard from our officers that new tactical methods were being worked out in the 62nd Army, and had ordered the commanders of regiments and battalions to study the experience of battle in the city, and soldiers to carry a double supply of ammunition and grenades.

After a short conversation I believed Batyuk, when he said that his division would put up a hard fight and was on this side of the Volga to stay. Within an hour Batyuk's division was thrown into a counter-attack along the bank of the Volga southward towards the central landing-stage, in order to help Rodimtsev's division. At the same time Rodimtsev was sent reinforcements—about two thousand men. By this counter-attack we hoped not only to stop the enemy's advance from the south, but, after wiping out his units which had broken through to the Volga, to restore contact with the brigades in the southern part of the city. The counter-attack began at 10 a.m. on September 23.

Fierce fighting broke out and continued for two days.

In this fighting, which frequently turned into hand-to-hand

skirmishes, the enemy's northward advance from the vicinity of the central landing-stage was halted. But we failed to wipe out the enemy forces which had broken through to the Volga, and did not link up with the infantry brigades at the other side of the River Tsaritsa.

At the cost of enormous losses the enemy won only a partial success. Paulus's plan—to reach the Volga and then strike at the flank and rear of the Army by an attack along the Volga—was frustrated. This plan collapsed when his forces came up against the tenacious action of Rodimtsev's, Batyuk's and Gorishny's divisions, Batrakov's brigade, and other units.

For the 62nd Army the crisis was over; it had shown no fear and had not faltered when the enemy made his first break-through to the Volga. We still held Mamayev Kurgan. Not one of our units had been completely wiped out. Counter-attacks by Batyuk's Siberian division had halted the enemy's advance in the city. The Germans were wallowing in their own blood; the streets were littered with dozens of burnt-out German tanks and thousands of the Germans' dead.

From the evening of September 24 the fighting in the city centre began to die down. The radio was telling the world that the Volga stronghold was holding out, that the city was in flames, and that it had turned into a veritable volcano, devouring many thousands of German soldiers. And that really was the truth.

The soldiers of the 62nd Army had learned to fight in flame and smoke, and were staunchly defending every inch of their native soil. All this was reported in the evening communiqués on the radio, and then the following day, taking its revenge, the German Command unleashed thousands of bombers on the city, and bombarded us with tens of thousands of shells. To be frank, we were sometimes very angry with our radio for taunting the enemy with not being able to take the city. It only meant that the next day in his anger he would launch another attack with fresh forces—tanks, infantry . . . We did not then know that the stern, dry communiqués put out by the Soviet Information Bureau at that time were intended to restrain a number of powers who were preparing to attack us.

Hitler would not and could not have any peace until his troops occupied the last vestiges of soil on the bank of the Volga. Apart from hatred of the Soviet Union, his operations were undoubtedly governed also by arrangements with other capitalist powers, whose entry into the war against the Soviet Union was conditional upon the fall of Stalingrad. Not only the German Foreign Minister, von Ribbentrop, but also Goebbels and Hitler himself were trying to persuade the ambassadors of Japan and Turkey, and through them the governments of those countries, to make an armed attack on the U.S.S.R.

Addressing the Reichstag at the end of September, Hitler boastfully declared: 'We are storming Stalingrad and will take it—on that you can rely. If we have taken something we stay there.'

At the same time, in a conversation with some Turkish newspaper men, Goebbels said: 'I always weigh my words when I speak, and I can tell you with conviction that by Christmas the Russian army will no longer be dangerous to Germany. In saying this I am sure that, as always, events will not disappoint me. I ask you to remember this in a few months' time.' Our soldiers did remember this on 2 May 1945, when they found the body of Goebbels in Berlin.

We know that the Kuomintang War Minister, saying good-bye to representatives of Nazi Germany in Chungking, agreed that German and Chiang Kai-shek forces would meet in Alma-Ata.

In 1942 Stalingrad was not only an important strategic centre for Hitler, it was also a political centre, a factor between Germany and some of the countries which were neutral towards the Soviet Union. That is why Hitler threw more and more divisions into the battle to win Stalingrad: he did not spare the blood of Germany's soldiers.

Generals in the Nazi army, like Hans Doerr, saw with their own eyes what price they had to pay for every yard of soil on the bank of the Volga.

The battle for the industrial area of Stalingrad, which began in the middle of September, can be described as 'trench' or 'fortress' warfare. The time for conducting large-scale operations was gone for ever; from the wide expanses of steppe-land, the war moved into the jagged gullies of the Volga hills with their copses and ravines, into the factory area of Stalingrad, spread out over uneven, pitted, rugged country, covered with iron, concrete and stone buildings. The mile, as a measure of distance, was replaced by the yard. G.H.Q.'s map was the map of the city.

For every house, workshop, water-tower, railway embankment, wall, cellar and every pile of ruins, a bitter battle was waged, without equal even in the first world war with its vast expenditure of munitions. The distance between the enemy's army and ours was as small as it could possibly be. Despite the concentrated activity of aircraft and artillery, it was impossible to break out of the area of close fighting. The Russians surpassed the Germans in their use of the terrain and in camouflage and were more experienced in barricade warfare for individual buildings; they defended firmly.

The catastrophe which followed has made these weeks of 'siege' fade from sight. Their history would be a list of heroic exploits by small units, storm groups, and many unknown soldiers.[1]

From the captured diary of operations of the German 29th Motorized Divisions it appears that on September 17 the Divisional Commander reported to the Commander of the 6th Army, Paulus: '... Both of the division's motorized regiments have been almost completely wiped out; of 220 tanks we have 42 left.'

In September, a German lance-corporal, Walter, wrote to his mother: 'Stalingrad is hell on earth. It is Verdun, bloody Verdun, with new weapons. We attack every day. If we capture twenty yards in the morning the Russians throw us back again in the evening.'

This was the appraisal of our forces made by German

---

[1]Doerr, Major-General Hans, *Der Feldzug Nach Stalingrad* (*Campaign to Stalingrad*), Dormstadt, 1955.

generals and men who took part in the fighting for Stalingrad.

On September 23 reconnaissance of all kinds showed us that the enemy, while fighting in the city, was at the same time concentrating large forces in the area of Gorodishche and Aleksandrovka. This new enemy group would obviously strike at the north side of Mamayev Kurgan, against the workers' settlements, against the Tractor and Barrikady plants.

In order to repulse enemy attacks from this direction we hurriedly prepared an anti-tank line in the rear, running from the mouth of the River Mechetka, along the southern bank of the river to the beginning of Vishnevaya Gully, along the western border of a wood and then along the north spur of Dolgi Gully to the Volga. Our sapper units were given orders to lay a continuous anti-tank minefield and to dig scarps and counterscarps. The divisional and brigade commanders were instructed to equip an anti-tank line in their sector and to take the anti-tank minefields under their wing, detaching special units and part of their fire-power to cover them. In the event of enemy tanks breaking through to the rear of the line, they were to have groups of sappers available with stores of mines, with which they could at any moment close all roads and parks in the area of the break-through.

On the evening of September 24, when the fighting began to die down in the city centre, we received confirmation of the build-up of fresh forces in the area of Razgulyayevka and Gorodishche. We decided to partially regroup the Army's units during the night, in order to strengthen and consolidate our formations on the River Mechetka sector and in the area of Mamayev Kurgan. The order to regroup was issued on September 25. The following is the order in full:

MILITARY ORDER NO. 164

62nd Army H.Q. 25.9.42   23.00

1. From the Gorodishche and Alexsandrovka area, the enemy is preparing an attack in the general direction of Gorodische-Barrikady.

2. The Army will continue to hold the line it occupies

and will carry on street fighting with part of its forces in order to destroy the enemy in the city.

I issue the following orders:

1. The 112th Division (Sologub's) with two attached mortar companies and with the support of the 186th Anti-Tank Artillery Regiment will occupy and consolidate a second line of defence along Vishnevaya Gully by 04.00 on 26.9.42.

Boundary on the right—the corner of the gardens 1,000 yards west of Dizelnaya, the bridge across the Mechetka (700 yards north of the Barrikady workers' settlement). Boundary on the left—the east side of Vishnevaya Gully as far as the railway line, and then along the railway to the outskirts of the Krasny Oktyabr settlement.

The aim will be (*a*) to prevent the enemy reaching the Barrikady and Krasny Oktyabr workers' settlements, and (*b*) to prevent any advance by the enemy towards the Tractor workers' settlement.

2. Three garrisons, each consisting of a platoon of tommy-gunners, will be prepared, ready to go into action in the settlements.

One platoon will defend School No. 32 buildings and the stone building on Zherdevskaya Street.

The second platoon will occupy the nursery buildings and shop on Kolpakovskaya Street in the Barrikady settlement.

The third platoon will occupy School No. 20 buildings and the bath-house at the crossroads of Kazachya and Dublinskaya Streets.

Forward line—the east side of Vishnevaya Gully.

An anti-tank line will be equipped on the sector along the River Mechetka and the railway line, with a continuous anti-tank minefield.

The division's command post will be in the gully near the crossroads of Kazachya and Dublinskaya Streets.

3. The 284th Division (Batyuk's) will take over the defences along the north side of Dolgi Gully from the 112th Division, and will prepare them as an anti-tank line of defence, detaching not less than two battalions to carry out reliable defence operations. The remaining forces of

the division will consolidate firm positions along the line through Sovnarkomovskaya and Khoperskaya Streets, then along Krutoy Gully to the Volga.

Under no circumstances will the enemy be allowed to reach Artileriski Street and the bank of the Volga. The division will be prepared to continue to carry out the task of clearing the city.

4. The 95th Division (Gorishny's) will consolidate firm positions along the southern border of the wood (along Kolodeznaya Street) and prepare a stronghold with all-round defences on the slopes of Hill 102.0 itself, with a garrison of one infantry battalion. Under no circumstances must the enemy be allowed to take the stronghold on Hill 102.0. The division will be prepared to continue to carry out the task of clearing the city.

5. The 13th Division (Rodimtsev's) will continue to destroy the enemy in the centre of the city and in the vicinity of the central landing-stage.

6. All the Army's troops will be ready by dawn on 26.9.42 to repel possible enemy attacks, particularly in the direction Gorodische-Barrikady.

This regrouping took place while in direct, close contact with the enemy, under his very nose, with a small depth in front. There were no through or trunk roads. The terrain abounded in deep gullies, destroyed buildings, obstructions, bomb and shell craters.

The slightest miscalculation in timing or failure to carry out proper camouflage threatened to wreck our regrouping operation and bring about heavy losses from enemy fire. All the Army H.Q. commanders were again sent out among the troops as guides and organizers of the troop manœuvre by night.

I ought at this point to say something about the position on September 25.

From documents on German dead and prisoners we ascertained that the 62nd Army was faced by eleven enemy divisions: three panzer (14th, 24th and 16th), two mechanized (29th and 60th), and six infantry (71st, 76th, 94th, 100th, 295th and 389th). They were distributed over the following sectors.

The right flank, from Latashanka to Hill 145.0, was occupied by the 16th Panzer Division and battalions of the 501st Infantry Regiment; this group was under constant, strong pressure from the armies of the Stalingrad Front to the north.

From point 145.1 to point 129.1 was the 100th Infantry Division; it had become severely depleted in the previous fighting and was 50 per cent below strength.

In the area of Gorodishche and Razgulyayevka, facing eastward, was the 389th Infantry Division, which had arrived at the beginning of September, completely up to strength, from the reserve.

In the area of Mamayev Kurgan and the northern part of the city was the 295th Infantry Division, reinforced by tanks and artillery; from September 12–24 this division suffered heavy losses—companies contained twenty to thirty men instead of 180.

In the area of the station and the central landing-stage were the 71st and 76th Infantry Divisions with large reinforcements; after the fighting from September 12–24 both divisions had lost two-thirds of their men.

In the area of Sadovaya and Minina suburb were the 14th and 24th Panzer, the 29th Mechanized and the 94th Infantry Divisions. All four divisions had been utterly worn down in the fighting from September 12–24.

By September 25, according to our reconnaissance, the enemy had 150 of his 500 tanks left.

The Luftwaffe had also somewhat spent its strength. In the last days of the fighting, groups of ten to twenty aeroplanes had been flying in, one after the other, instead of the forty to fifty in the earlier period. The Germans were obviously building up their strength and resources in the air for a future battle.

Our reconnaissance constantly reported the approach of columns of the enemy from the west, bringing up more men and material. The enemy divisions which had suffered heavy losses were being made up with draft battalions and equipment, accompanied by teams of instructors.

We could not, therefore, count on a long breathing-space; we were waiting for strong attacks from the west, from Gorodishche and Razgulyayevka. Our forecasts were soon confirmed.

Where and how the 62nd Army's units were distributed at this moment is clear from the Army Order given above. All I need to add is that on the Army's northern flank Gorokhov's group, consisting of three brigades and one regiment of Sarayev's division, had taken up position. Left of Gorokhov's group, on the sector from the River Mechetka to the northern spur of Dolgi Gully, the defence was in the hands of an armoured formation which had fifty-six tanks, thirty-six medium and twenty light.

On the western border of the wood, near point 112.0, in the second line of defence, was an armoured unit with seven T-34 and six T-60 tanks. Almost all of these tanks were out of action and were being used as stationary firing posts.

One regiment of Sarayev's division had been surrounded and was waging a battle in the park, near Central Station. Contact with it was intermittent. The regiment had very few men left.

Two infantry brigades, cut off from the Army, were fighting south of the River Tsaritsa. Officers of Army H.Q. sent to these brigades did not return and were presumably killed. The only contact with the brigades was by radio. As from September 23 the reports from these brigades began to raise doubts in our minds. We felt that something was wrong, and I decided to inspect the left bank of the Volga, find someone from the combined staffs of these brigades and find out the real state of affairs. Our suspicions were fully confirmed. On the morning of September 25 it was reported to me that the commander and H.Q. of the combined brigades, abandoning their units, had left the city, been ferried across to Golodny Island and from there were sending false reports about the progress of the fighting.

On September 26, on the Army's left flank, south of the River Tsaritsa, what we must now expect actually happened: under attack from two enemy divisions (the 94th Infantry and the 29th Motorized) the officers and men of one of the brigades which had been abandoned by their headquarters, streamed to the Volga and crossed to the left bank. As a result, we had to withdraw the second brigade (the 42nd) across the Volga and then ferry it across to the factory district.

Having freed his hands on our left flank, the enemy began

to transfer his units from there to Mamayev Kurgan. A new attack threatened our troops in the area of Mamayev Kurgan and to the north.

The Germans, with their superiority in the air, did not deploy their troops particularly carefully, and badly camouflaged attacks they were preparing against us. They acted impudently, cheekily. This was particularly true of new units which had not yet been in battle.

German soldiers in the evening or during the night would often shout:

'Russians! Tomorrow bang-bang!'

On these occasions we knew unerringly that the following day we would be attacked in strength in precisely that area.

With every powerful new attack the Germans were obviously convinced that they would be fully successful, and their shouts were obviously intended to prey on our soldiers' minds.

In the fighting against such devil-may-care ruffians we worked out our own tactics and methods. We studied and learned ways to hit and smash the attackers and shatter their morale. We anticipated their attacks with counter-attacks and counter-preparations, and left them no peace, night or day.

We paid particular attention to the development of a snipers' movement among our troops. The Army Military Council supported this move. The Army's newspaper *In Our Country's Defence* published daily figures of the number of the enemy killed by our snipers, and published photographs of outstandingly accurate marksmen.

The snipers' movement was led by the political sections, the Party and Komsomol organizations: at Party and Komsomol meetings questions were discussed and measures worked out to improve their work with relation to the good marksmen. The Front Commander, A. I. Yeremenko, and the Member of the Military Council, N. S. Khrushchev, constantly called for a wider development of the snipers' movement. And woe to the gaping Nazis. Hundreds, thousands, of them were killed by our 'hunters of two-legged animals'.

I met many of the well-known snipers, like Vasili Zaitsev, Anatoli Chekhov and Viktor Medvedev; I talked to them, helped them as far as I could and frequently consulted them.

These well-known soldiers were not distinguished in any

particular way from the others. Quite the reverse. When I first met Zaitsev and Medvedev, I was struck by their modesty, the leisurely way they moved, their particularly placid temperament, the attentive way they looked at things; they could look at the same object for a long time without blinking. They had strong hands: when they shook hands with you they had a grip like a vice.

The snipers went out 'hunting' early in the morning to previously selected and prepared places, carefully camouflaged themselves and waited patiently for targets to appear. They knew that the slightest negligence or haste would lead to certain death: the enemy kept a careful watch for our snipers. They used very few bullets, but every shot from a sniper meant death or a wound for any German caught in his sights.

Vasili Zaitsev was wounded in the eyes. A German sniper obviously took a lot of pains to track down the Russian 'hunter' who had about three hundred German deaths to his credit. But Zaitsev continued to be an enthusiast of 'sniperism'. When he came back to active service after his injury he went on selecting and training snipers, his 'young hares'.

Every well-known sniper, as a rule, handed on his experience, taught young marksmen the art of sharp-shooting. Our soldiers used to say, therefore:

'Zaitsev trains his young hares, and Medvedev his young bears.[1] They all kill Germans and never miss . . .'

Viktor Medvedev went right to Berlin with us. He shot more Germans than Zaitsev, his teacher.

The activities of our snipers caused the German generals a lot of disquiet, and they decided to turn this military craft against us as well.

This happened at the end of September. One night our scouts brought in an identification prisoner, who told us that the head of the German school of snipers, Major Konings, had been flown in from Berlin and given the task, primarily, of killing the leading Soviet sniper.

The Divisional Commander, Colonel N. F. Batyuk, called in the snipers and told them the position:

---

[1]The name 'Zaitsev' comes from the Russian word for 'hare' and 'Medvedev' from the word for bear.

'I think that the German super-sniper from Berlin will be easy meat for our snipers. Is that right, Zaitsev?'

'That's right, Comrade Colonel,' answered Zaitsev.

'Now, this super-sniper will have to be got rid of,' said the Commander. 'Only you'll have to be very careful.'

'Right, we'll get rid of him!' the snipers agreed.

By this time our rapidly expanding group of snipers had killed over a thousand Germans. This feat was written about in the papers and in leaflets. Some of the leaflets fell into enemy hands and the enemy studied our snipers' methods and took active measures to fight them. This is a thing of the past, so I say quite frankly that at that time there should have been less haste in publicizing our experience. No sooner did our snipers kill one or two enemy officers than artillery and mortars lying in ambush would start firing. Our men would hastily have to change position in order to get out of a tight corner. Vasili Zaitsev gives us this account:

The arrival of the Nazi sniper set us a new task: we had to find him, study his habits and methods, and patiently await the right moment for one, and only one, well-aimed shot.

In our dug-out at nights we had furious arguments about the forthcoming duel. Every sniper put forward his speculations and guesses arising from his day's observation of the enemy's forward positions. All sorts of different proposals and 'baits' were discussed. But the art of the sniper is distinguished by the fact that whatever experience a lot of people may have the outcome of an engagement is decided by one sniper. He meets the enemy face to face, and every time he has to create, to invent, to operate differently.

There can be no blue-print for a sniper; a blue-print would be suicide.

Just the same, where was the sniper from Berlin?—we asked ourselves. I knew the style of the Nazi snipers by their fire and camouflage and without any difficulty could tell the experienced snipers from the novices, the cowards from the stubborn, determined enemies. But the character of the head of the school was still a mystery for me. Our day-by-day observations told us nothing definite.

It was difficult to decide on which sector he was operating. He presumably altered his position frequently and was looking for me as carefully as I for him. Then something happened. My friend Morozov was killed, and Sheykin wounded, by a rifle with telescopic sights. Morozov and Sheykin were considered experienced snipers; they had often emerged victorious from the most difficult skirmishes with the enemy. Now there was no doubt. They had come up against the Nazi 'super-sniper' I was looking for. At dawn I went out with Nikolay Kulikov to the same positions as our comrades had occupied the previous day. Inspecting the enemy's forward positions, which we had spent many days studying and knew well, I found nothing new. The day was drawing to a close. Then above a German entrenchment unexpectedly appeared a helmet, moving slowly along a trench. Should I shoot? No! It was a trick: the helmet somehow or other moved unevenly and was presumably being held up by someone helping the sniper, while he waited for me to fire.

'Where can he be hiding?' asked Kulikov, when we left the ambush under cover of darkness. By the patience which the enemy had shown during the day I guessed that the sniper from Berlin was here. Special vigilance was needed.

A second day passed. Whose nerves would be stronger? Who would outwit whom?

Nikolay Kulikov, a true comrade, was also fascinated by this duel. He had no doubt that the enemy was there in front of us, and he was anxious that we should succeed. On the third day, the political instructor, Danilov, also came with us to the ambush. The day dawned as usual: the light increased and minute by minute the enemy's positions could be distinguished more clearly. Battle started close by, shells hissed over us, but, glued to our telescopic sights, we kept our eyes on what was happening ahead of us.

'There he is! I'll point him out to you!' suddenly said the political instructor, excitedly. He barely, literally for one second, but carelessly, raised himself above the parapet, but that was enough for the German to hit and wound him. That sort of firing, of course, could only come from an experienced sniper.

For a long time I examined the enemy positions, but could not detect his hiding place. From the speed with which he had fired I came to the conclusion that the sniper was somewhere directly ahead of us. I continued to watch. To the left was a tank, out of action, and on the right was a pill-box. Where was he? In the tank? No, an experienced sniper would not take up position there. In the pill-box, perhaps? Not there either—the embrasure was closed. Between the tank and the pill-box, on a stretch of level ground, lay a sheet of iron and a small pile of broken bricks. It had been lying there a long time and we had grown accustomed to its being there. I put myself in the enemy's position and thought—where better for a sniper? One had only to make a firing slit under the sheet of metal, and then creep up to it during the night.

Yes, he was certainly there, under the sheet of metal in no-man's-land. I thought I would make sure. I put a mitten on the end of a small plank and raised it. The Nazi fell for it. I carefully let the plank down in the same position as I had raised it and examined the bullet-hole. It had gone straight through from the front; that meant that the Nazi was under the sheet of metal.

'There's our viper!' came the quiet voice of Nikolay Kulikov from his hide-out next to mine.

Now came the question of luring even a part of his head into my sights. It was useless trying to do this straight away. Time was needed. But I had been able to study the German's temperament. He was not going to leave the successful position he had found. We were therefore going to have to change our position.

We worked by night. We were in position by dawn. The Germans were firing on the Volga ferries. It grew light quickly and with daybreak the battle developed with new intensity. But neither the rumble of guns nor the bursting of shells and bombs nor anything else could distract us from the job in hand.

The sun rose. Kulikov took a blind shot: we had to rouse the sniper's curiosity. We had decided to spend the morning waiting, as we might have been given away by the sun on our telescopic sights. After lunch our rifles were in the shade and the sun was shining directly on to the German's position. At the edge of the sheet of metal something was glittering: an odd bit of glass or telescopic sights? Kulikov carefully, as only the most experienced can do, began to raise his helmet. The German fired. For a fraction of a second Kulikov rose and screamed. The German believed that he had finally got the Soviet sniper he had been hunting for four days, and half raised his head from beneath the sheet of metal. That was what I had been banking on. I took careful aim. The German's head fell back, and the telescopic sights of his rifle lay motionless, glistening in the sun, until night fell . . .

That was the kind of snipers we had in the 62nd Army.

City fighting is a special kind of fighting. Things are settled here not by strength, but by skill, resourcefulness and swiftness. The buildings in a city are like breakwaters. They broke up the advancing enemy formations and made their forces go along the streets. We therefore held on firmly to strong buildings, and established small garrisons in them, capable of all-round fire if they were encircled. Particularly stout buildings enabled us to create strong defensive positions, from which our men could mow down advancing Germans with machine-guns and tommy-guns.

In our counter-attacks we abandoned attacks by entire units and even sections of units. Towards the end of September storm groups appeared in all regiments; these were small but strong groups, as wily as a snake and irrepressible in action. When the Germans occupied an object, it was quickly subjected to attack by storm groups. The Germans rarely stood up against an attack by bullet and grenade, backed up by bayonet and dagger. Fighting went on for buildings and in buildings—for a cellar, for a room, for every corner in a corridor. Streets and squares were empty.

Our commanders and men learned to crawl right up to enemy positions during enemy bombardments and bombing, and by doing so avoid being killed. German airmen and artillerymen would not risk attacking our units, for fear of hitting their own troops. We deliberately fought as close as possible.

The Germans did not like, or rather were no good at, close fighting. Their morale would not stand it; they did not have the spirit to look an armed Soviet soldier in the eyes. You could locate an enemy soldier in a forward post from a long way off, especially by night: he would constantly, every five to ten minutes, give a burst on his tommy-gun, obviously to boost his morale. Our soldiers could easily find such 'warriors', creep up and polish them off with bullet or bayonet.

The troops defending the city learned to allow German tanks to come right on top of them—under the guns of our anti-tank artillery and anti-tank riflemen; in this way they invariably cut off the infantry from the tanks and destroyed the enemy's organized battle formation. The infantry and the tanks which had broken through were destroyed separately: the tanks were unable to do very much without infantry and, without achieving anything, they would turn back after suffering big losses.

Night and night-fighting were natural elements to us. The enemy could not fight at night, but we had learned to do so out of bitter necessity: by day the enemy's planes hung over our troops, preventing them from raising their heads. At night we need have no fear of the Luftwaffe. More often than not in the daytime we were on the defensive and beat off German attacks, which very rarely took place without tank and air support. The storm groups literally clung to buildings and to the earth, waiting for the enemy to come up within grenade-throwing distance.

We used every possible means of killing the enemy. For example, we knew that not all Germans were on the lookout; the majority of them were resting behind shelter. In order to bring them out from behind their shelter, at night-time our Russian 'Hurrah!'[1] rang out and our grenades exploded. The Germans would rush in alarm to their windows and loopholes to beat off an attack. And at that moment our artillery and machine-guns would open up at them.

---

[1] A cry used by soldiers when attacking; the word is also used, therefore, to describe a quick, decisive attack.

Particularly effective were the salvos from our 'katyushi' rocket-launchers into concentrations of infantry and tanks which we detected before enemy attacks were due to begin. I shall never forget the 'katyushi' regiment under Colonel Yerokhin. This regiment spent practically the whole time under the steep bank of the Volga, clinging to the very precipice. Before they opened fire, the lorries carrying the rocket-launchers would reverse about ten yards from the precipice, leaving the wheels in the air. From here they would fire bursts of rockets. Their salvos claimed hundreds of German victims.

It would be impossible to enumerate all the new methods our troops worked out: in the most bitter days of fighting on the Volga we grew, learned, matured—everyone, from the private soldier to the commander.

Later, towards the end of the battle, from diaries taken from German dead and prisoners we learned how hard our new methods of battle had hit the Nazis. They never knew where, how and with what we were going to strike on any given day. We shattered their nerves so thoroughly at night-time that they went into battle in the morning exhausted from lack of sleep.

As soon as we knew that the enemy was levelling an attack against sectors where we had been inactive the previous evening, or where our units were weak, we would hurriedly reinforce our troops there, organize a barrage of fire and lay minefields.

Our reconnaissance in Stalingrad worked well. We knew about the enemy's weak points and his concentration areas, and we did not miss a favourable opportunity for making an effective attack.

At the end of a day or of a whole battle we would make an attack, though not always a strong one. But for a weakened enemy even a weak attack was frightening. We kept the enemy in an almost permanent state of strain and fear of an unexpected attack.

I have related all this so that the reader can see clearly what activities the Army H.Q. staff and Army political workers were engaged in among the units, in the forefront of battle; what our units were doing and how they were preparing to beat off new attacks by the enemy on Stalingrad's factories and workers' settlements. These were the days when our troops defending the city, foreseeing the bitter battle which will be described below, used to say:

'For us, there is no land across the Volga! . . .'

CHAPTER VI

THE VALOUR OF THE GUARDS

ON SEPTEMBER 26 it became clear that the main attack in the enemy's new offensive was being prepared from the direction of Gorodishche and Razgulyayevka.

Without stopping our artillery bombardment of concentrations of enemy infantry and tanks, we decided to meet this attack thoroughly with units of the armoured formation and Sologub's infantry division. In addition, we had now acquired a division under Major-General Smekhotvorov, with which we intended to strengthen the sector occupied by the armoured formation.

We were all extremely worried about Mamayev Kurgan, on the crest of which defensive action was being waged by Gorishny's division. The southern and western slopes of the hill were occupied by the enemy. The Germans had only to gain another hundred yards and this key tactical point in the defence of the city and the factory areas could fall into their hands. In order to prevent this and to frustrate the enemy's preparations for his planned attack on the factory areas, we decided to counter-attack again.

Order No. 166 was issued, containing the following instructions:

1. The armoured formation will attack with its left flank in the direction of Hill 112.0 and Rzhevskaya Street. The most immediate aim is to occupy the bank between Rzhevskaya and Batakhovskaya Streets. The next aim will be to occupy the cemetery south of Rzhevskaya Street.

Boundary on the left—the crossroads with the path

500 yards south of Banny Gully, the farm 200 yards west of Kashirskaya, Irtyshskaya and Chervlenaya Streets.

Support will be given by the 397th Anti-Tank Artillery Regiment.

2. Gorishny's division will attack in the direction of the park, Chapayevskaya and Donetskaya Streets. The most immediate task will be to occupy the southern spur of Dolgi Gully, and then to reach the park.

Support will be given by the 651st Anti-Tank Artillery Regiment and the 101st Mortar Regiment.

3. Batyuk's division will attack with its right flank towards Khoperskaya Street and the station. Its immediate task will be to occupy a line along Krutoy Gully, and then to reach the area of the station.

Boundary on the left—the Volga.

Support will be given by the 2nd Battery of the 457th Artillery Regiment.

4. The 13th Division will continue to carry out its previous task of wiping out the enemy in the centre of the city. Its immediate aim will be to occupy the area of the central landing-stage, and then to clear the area as far as the railway station.

5. The Army Artillery Commander will use all the Army's artillery and rocket artillery regiments in support of the offensive by the 95th Division. The aim will be:

(*a*) to destroy the enemy's pill-boxes on the southern slopes of Hill 102.0;

(*b*) to destroy the enemy's mortar batteries at the ends of Dolgi Gully and in the vicinity of the cemetery;

(*c*) to prevent reserves from being brought up from the north-west along the road from Gumrak to Stalingrad.

6. The artillery barrage will begin at 5.00 on 27.9.42.

The infantry attack will begin at 6.00 on 27.9.42.

7. I again warn the commanders of all units and formations not to carry out operations in battle by whole units like companies and battalions. The offensive should be organized chiefly on the basis of small groups, with tommy-guns, hand-grenades, bottles of incendiary

mixture and anti-tank rifles. Regimental and battalion artillery should be used to support attacking groups by firing point-blank into windows, embrasures and garrets.

As can be seen from the last paragraph of this order, not all of our forces were being sent in to counter-attack, but only a part of them; not on a continuous front but in storm groups. Our main forces were remaining in prepared positions to repulse a German attack from the direction of Gorodishche.

The order to counter-attack was issued at 7.40 p.m. on September 26, but preliminary instructions had been sent out twenty-four hours previously. Observation of the enemy and reconnaissance of the weak points in his battle formations were being carried out by all our units, along all the front, all the time.

Everybody knew, felt and could see that the enemy was preparing for new active operations. To sit back and wait for the attack to begin was tantamount to suicide. The area occupied by the 62nd Army on the right bank of the Volga was as narrow as could be—there was no room for retreat.

How fully and well the officers and men in our units understood the position at this time can be seen from the following example.

Ammunition and provisions, as we have seen, were unloaded and distributed from the landing-stage to firing positions and trenches by hand. This was heavy, exhausting work. But whereas a week ago units had had to be reminded that ammunition had arrived and that they had to collect it immediately, now whole units sent their tally-men and porters to the moorings without any prompting. They appeared when darkness fell, and the boat had no sooner arrived than they rapidly unloaded it and carried the material away to the front line.

It should be noted that in the delivery of material from the left bank the Army was rendered an incalculable service by the sailors of the Volga Fleet, under the command of Rear Admiral D. D. Rogachev. Every trip across the Volga involved a tremendous risk, but no boat or steamer ever lingered with its cargo on the other bank.

About the role of the sailors of the fleet and their exploits,

I would say briefly that had it not been for them the 62nd Army might have perished without ammunition and rations, and could not have carried out its task.

Infantrymen and artillerymen, tank crews and sailors—all those defending the city were preparing to resist an attack on the factories and the workers' settlements. We began our counter-attack at 6 a.m. on September 27.

To begin with we had some success, but at 8 a.m. hundreds of dive-bombers swooped on our formations. The attacking troops took cover.

At 10.30 a.m. the enemy counter-attacked. His fresh 100th and replenished 389th Infantry Divisions, reinforced by the 24th Panzer Division, launched an attack aimed at occupying the Krasny Oktyabr workers' settlement and Mamayev Kurgan.

The Luftwaffe bombed and strafed our units from our forward positions right to the Volga. The strongpoint organized by the troops of Gorishny's division at the top of Mamayev Kurgan was utterly destroyed by aircraft and artillery. The Army H.Q. command post was under attack from the air the whole time. The oil-tanks nearby were on fire. Enemy tanks which had advanced from the vicinity of Gorodishche went straight through the minefields. Infantry crawled forward in waves behind the tanks. Towards noon telephone communication with the troops began to function erratically, and radio links were put out of action . . .

Being out of regular communication with our units, we were unable to stay doing nothing at the command post. Although it was no more than a mile and a quarter from the forward positions, we still did not know exactly what was happening at the front and had to go up even closer if we wanted to have any influence on the progress of the fighting.

Taking signals officers with him, Gurov went out to the front occupied by the armoured formation, I went to Batyuk's division, and Krylov went to Gorishny's command post.

Even in direct touch with our units, however, we were still unable to clarify the general picture: we were hampered by the constant smoke. When we returned to our command post in the evening we found that many of our Army staff officers were missing.

Only well into the night were we able to get an exact picture of the position. It was very serious: after crossing the minefield and our forward positions, and in spite of heavy losses, the enemy had in some sectors managed to advance eastward a mile or two. 'One more battle like that and we'll be in the Volga,' I thought.

The armoured formation and the left flank of Sologub's division, which had borne the main brunt of the attack, had suffered heavy losses and at nightfall on September 27 occupied a front from the bridge over the Mechetka, a mile and a half west of the Barrikady settlement, the south-west part of the settlement, and the western outskirts of the Krasny Oktyabr suburb as far as Banny Gully. The Germans had occupied Shakhtinskaya and Zherdevskaya Streets and Hill 107.5.

Gorishny's division had been driven back from the summit of Mamayev Kurgan. The division, severely depleted, held the north-east slopes.

On the remaining sectors the enemy had been beaten back.

In the day's fighting the enemy had lost no less than two thousand killed and more than fifty tanks. We had also suffered heavy losses, especially in the armoured formation and Gorishny's infantry regiments.

That evening N. S. Khrushchev telephoned the Army's command post. His first question was: 'How are spirits?'

I gave him an unvarnished account of the extremely difficult situation at the front. In spite of all our efforts, the enemy, with his superiority in men and material, was gaining the upper hand. I also reported that the Military Council was in the process of working out and preparing measures for destroying the large concentration of enemy troops which was battering its way forward from the direction of Razgulyayevka. Nikita Khrushchev endorsed our plans and said that he knew the position and the progress of the fighting; he advised us to use the maximum cunning and surprise in our operations. He then asked what help we needed. I replied:

'I make no complaint about our air force, which is fighting heroically, but the enemy has mastery in the air. His air force is his unbeatable trump card in attack. I therefore ask for increased help in this sphere—to give us cover from the air, if only for a few hours a day.'

'You will understand, Comrade Chuikov,' he answered, 'that we are giving you all the help we can; nonetheless I will pass on your request and I will press for increased air cover for the city.'

Wishing us success, he again advised us to act with the maximum use of the surprise factor, ensuring that the enemy 'knew and saw nothing that was happening on our side.' He then asked to speak to Gurov, with whom he had a similar conversation, advising him to mobilize the political sections, Party and Komsomol members better, 'so that there are no deficiencies in this field'.

That night the Military Council asked all commanders and political workers to go out to the front line, into the dug-outs and trenches, to bring all sub-units up to fighting trim and to fight to the last round of ammunition.

Is there any need to explain how important it is for senior commanders and political workers to chat with the troops in the front line? I know from my own experience that when you talk to soldiers in a dug-out, share their grief and happiness, smoke each other's cigarettes, weigh up the situation together and ask their advice about our operations—then the soldier will inevitably feel: 'If the general was here that means we need to hold firm!' The soldier will not retreat without being ordered to do so, and will throw everything in his power into the fight against the enemy.

It is important for every soldier to feel that his exploit will not pass unnoticed. One can then rest assured that orders will be carried out. Of course, there is no need for, let us say, a divisional commander to spend all his time in the forward trenches—his place is at the command post, from which he has to direct the fighting. I stress, however, that in the face of danger the commander must be near the front line, as close to his men as possible. In that situation the soldiers will not disappoint you, will do the job you call on them to do.

I learned this at the school of the Battle of Stalingrad. This was why the Military Council called on all commanders and political workers, including the H.Q. staff, to be in the front line. They needed to explain to all that there could be no retreat.

During the night of September 27–28 two regiments of General Smekhotvorov's infantry division were ferried across to the city and were immediately sent into battle on the western outskirts of the Krasny Oktyabr settlement. A counter-attack was organized against Mamayev Kurgan, using what was left of an infantry regiment of Gorishny's division, supported by units of Batyuk's division. The Army Artillery Commander was ordered to shell Mamayev Kurgan non-stop throughout the night with artillery and mortars, so as to prevent the enemy from consolidating his position on the hill.

At daybreak on September 28 the enemy launched fierce infantry and tank attacks. The Luftwaffe kept up a constant, concentrated air attack on our troops, on the ferries and on the Army H.Q. command post. The German aeroplanes dropped not only bombs, but also pieces of metal, ploughs, tractor wheels, harrows and empty metal casks, which whistled about the heads of our troops.

Of six cargo boats operating on the Volga only one had not been knocked out of action. At H.Q. command post the heat and smoke were suffocating. Flames from the burning oil-tanks had spread to the Military Council's dug-out. Every air raid by dive-bombers put radios out of action, took its toll of lives.

Even the cook, Glinka, who had established himself and his kitchen in a shell-hole, was injured.

Nevertheless, in spite of this state of affairs, we felt that the enemy attacks were losing their punch. They were uncoordinated, not as rapid and well-organized as they had been. Enemy battalions, supported by tanks, were thrown into battle at different points, and not very confidently. This enabled us to mass our fire and beat off attacks in turn, and then go on to the counter-attack ourselves. I would then ask the Air Force Commander, Khryukin, for help, and he did not refuse—he gave us everything he had.

During the biggest air attack we had yet made, a counter-attack by the regiment of Gorishny's division and the two battalions of Batyuk's division was organized. By a determined thrust they recaptured the trigonometrical point on Mamayev Kurgan, but they failed to reach the actual summit. The summit was now in no one's hands, with artillery keeping up a constant barrage from both sides.

In the day's fighting on September 28 we had to all intents

and purposes held our positions. The enemy had not been able to press home his attack and advance any further. He was unable to overcome tenacious action by men who were determined to die rather than retreat. On that day the enemy lost at least 1,500 dead, and more than thirty of his tanks were burnt out. Nearly 500 German dead littered the slopes of Mamayev Kurgan alone.

Our losses were also heavy. The armoured formation had lost 626 men dead and wounded, and Batyuk's division had lost about 300 men. Gorishny's division had few men left, but it continued to fight.

With the loss of ships on the Volga the ferrying across of men and ammunition had become more difficult. On the right bank there was an accumulation of wounded whom it had not been possible to take across the river during the night. Our reconnaissance reported at the same time that fresh enemy infantry and tanks were being brought up from the area of Gorodishche. They were moving towards the Krasny Oktyabr settlement. It was clear that the battle for the factories and the workers' settlement had only just begun.

We decided to put up a stiff defence, using every obstacle our sappers could possibly devise. At 7.30 p.m. on September 28, Order No. 171 was issued, indicating the lines our units had to defend, and including the following:

I ask commanders of all units to act with all possible haste in carrying out the engineering work to strengthen their positions, in building anti-tank and anti-infantry obstacles at the front line and in depth, and in preparing buildings for defence action in the event of street fighting.

In building obstacles all resources available on the spot should be used, even by dismantling buildings and taking up tramlines, bringing in the civilian population to help in the work through the local organizations.

The main work should be carried out by the units themselves. The work should be carried on night and day.

The initial work (mainly the anti-tank obstacles) must be completed by morning on 29.9.42, making the defences of the city and its industrial centres impregnable. Every obstacle should be given constant fire-cover.

It must be explained to every soldier that the Army is fighting on its last line of defence) there can be no further retreat. It is the duty of every soldier and commander to defend his trench, his position—not a step back! The enemy must be wiped out whatever happens!

Reading this, you may well ask—thousands of bombs and hundreds of thousands of shells were being dropped on the city every day, so what civilian population and local organizations could exist?

The local authorities and thousands of inhabitants in the factory areas were giving the 62nd Army every help they could. For example, at the Tractor factory, right up to the last minute, until October 14 that is, our tank crews were repairing tanks with the help of the workers, and at the Barrikady works the workers and our artillerymen together were repairing guns.

Some of the workers were in detachments defending their factories. City and regional Party committees were working amid the roar of explosions, and were helping the Army's political organizations and commanders in establishing strongpoints in the city and the workers' settlements.

I shall never forget Comrades Piksin and Vdovin, secretaries of the Party's city committee. The leaders of the regional organizations also kept in touch with the Army. The inhabitants, the workers in the factories, the Party organizations, the Communists in the city, were with us. We were fighting side by side, were suffocating in the heat from the flames together, were defending the city together.

How could one ever forget the late V. A. Malyshev, representative of the Council of People's Commissars and later Deputy Chairman of the Council of Ministers of the U.S.S.R.? In the bitterest days of the fighting in Stalingrad, at the Tractor factory, he was there carrying out the instructions of the Party and the government.

These men are not usually written about as heroes, but we have nothing but respect for the heroic exploits which, without noticing it, they performed day by day. Only the Soviet people, devoted to their country and their Communist Party, are capable of such feats and such modesty.

The Communists, led by the Party organizations and political bodies, were the life-blood of the defence of the city.

I can only repeat and repeat how harmoniously the Army Military Council worked. It worked collectively on the principle of all for one and one for all in the fight for victory. We were always united, were always together, and never had any disagreements. Woe betide anyone who might try to cast the shadow of mistrust or suspicion amongst us!

We were united in aim, Party spirit and friendship. I cannot but remember the leaders of the political organizations, such Communists as Brigade Commissar Vasiliev, Colonels Vavilov, Chernyshev and Vlasenko, Lieutenant-Colonels Tkachenko and Ovcharenko, and others. By their loyalty, intelligence and authority they led the troops into performing feats of heroism and won victories where victory seemed impossible. They always quickly grasped new methods of waging battle, new methods of street fighting, for example, and the experience of the best snipers and the sappers who constructed the best obstacles. Close military co-ordination on a Party basis among commanders, commissars and leaders of political organizations strengthened all the soldiers in their belief in victory.

Every soldier knew that the Army Military Council was with them, on the right bank of the river. The Party's continuous political work produced a high level of morale among the men defending the city and increased the fighting efficiency of every unit.

In spite of heavy losses, the Party and Komsomol organizations grew in numbers and strength. Dozens, hundreds of soldiers, who had not had a moment's rest from the heat of battle, submitted applications to join the Party. They all wanted to fight, and if necessary die, as members of the Party or Komsomol.

The name of Sergeant Jacob Pavlov has become a legend. For more than fifty days, without sleep and rest, a handful of courageous men led by Pavlov held out in the centre of the city in a house which was extremely important to the defence positions held by Rodimtsev's division. The Germans unleashed a torrent of bombs and shells on to the house, but could not break the stubborn defence of its heroic garrison. 'Pavlov's House' remained impregnable. It was defended by ordinary Soviet people, true sons of many of the nationalities which make up our country: for example, Pavlov (now a Hero of the Soviet Union), Alexandrov and Afanasiev were Russians; Sabgayda and Glushchenko were Ukrainians; Mosiyashvili and Stepanashvili were Georgians; Turganov was an Uzbek, Murzayev a Kazakh, Sukba an Abkhazian, Turdiev Tajik and Ramazanov a Tatar.

Pavlov's small group of men, defending one house, killed more enemy soldiers than the Germans lost in taking Paris.

Or take another example of the whole-hearted loyalty of the Soviet people to their country. Between the Krasny Oktyabr and Barrikady factories runs a gully, westward from the Volga. The Germans picked this gully for a breakthrough. Lieutenant Zaitsev and a platoon of machine-gunners were given the task of holding it and preventing the enemy reaching the Volga.

By day here it was impossible to raise one's head. The Germans fired at every stone, every trench, every square yard of soil. Zaitsev brought up his men during the night. Quietly, not giving away their arrival by any kind of noise, the machine-gunners took up firing positions. The machine-guns were placed so that they covered the whole terrain ahead of them.

In the morning the enemy opened up concentrated artillery and mortar fire on the gully and then launched an attack. Our machine-gunners met them with short bursts. The water inside the gun-casing started to boil with the continuous firing. For a minute one of the guns fell silent: the gunner had been hit. He was replaced by the platoon's Party organizer, Private Yemelyanov. The Lieutenant was also soon lying behind one of the guns. The Germans continued, however, to move forward. Zaitsev was fatally wounded. Sergeant Karasev took over command of the platoon. The battle went on till nightfall. The Germans had been unable to break through our defence or break the resistance of the courageous machine-gunners. The enemy had paid dearly for his attempt to reach the Volga: over 400 enemy dead lay in the gully.

The exploit of Marine Mikhail Panikako also happened in the same factory district.

German tanks were advancing on positions occupied by a battalion of marine infantry. A number of them, with cannon and machine-guns blazing, were approaching Panikako's trench.

Through the firing and bursting of shells the clank of tank tracks could be heard more and more clearly. Panikako had already used up all his grenades. He had only two bottles of incendiary liquid left. He leaned out of the trench and raised his arm, aiming a bottle at the nearest tank. At that instant a bullet smashed the bottle raised over his head. The soldier burst into a living sheet of flame. Despite the terrible pain he did not lose consciousness. He grabbed the second bottle. The tank had come up close. Everyone saw a man in flames leap out of the trench, run right up to the German tank and smash the bottle against the grille of the engine-hatch. A second later an enormous sheet of flame and smoke engulfed both the tank and the hero who had destroyed it.

The commander of an anti-tank gun, Boltenko, showed particular tenacity in a street battle. His gun occupied a position amidst the ruins of a house of which, as the soldiers joked, the only thing left was the address: 'Grishin, 76a Voznaya Street'. Boltenko hid his gun so well among the bricks that not even the most sharp-sighted observer would have spotted it.

By now the gun-crew consisted of only three men: the commander and two shell-bearers. Boltenko was waiting for reinforcements, but prepared for any eventuality and was ready, should the need arise, to act as commander, to aim and load the gun.

An enemy tank emerged from behind a railway embankment to reconnoitre. Boltenko set it on fire with the first round. The Germans who jumped out of the tank were promptly destroyed by short bursts from carbines.

Half an hour later eight tanks appeared from behind the embankment. They headed straight for Boltenko's gun, but were firing in a different direction. The German crews did not suspect that they were being carefully watched from the ruins by three pairs of eyes. With three rounds Boltenko put the first tank out of action. Another tank approached the first. A few shots, and the second one stood rooted to the spot. But Boltenko saw the tank's turret slowly start to turn towards him. The shot he fired hit the target, piercing the turret. The remaining six tanks raced for cover behind the embankment. But barely ten minutes later fifteen German tanks lumbered into sight. Infantry came running after them.

One of the bearers suggested wheeling the gun back into the gully.

'We can't compete with that sort of strength, Comrade Commander,' said the soldier. 'Better withdraw.'

'I've had no such order!' Boltenko exclaimed sternly.

Fifteen tanks—that means fifteen cannon and fifteen machine-guns. Boltenko had only one gun and two carbines. The first skirmish with the enemy had also been unequal, but the Soviet artilleryman had had the advantage of surprise on his side. He had this advantage no longer: their firing position had now been detected by the enemy.

Bullets drummed against the gun-shield. But this did not deter Boltenko either. With his gun, hidden in the ruins of the house, he fought single-handed against fifteen tanks and emerged the victor. The anti-tank gun sent two tanks up in flames and forced the others to turn back.

That is how the soldiers of the 62nd Army fought. It was as if the very earth, soaked in the blood of heroic Soviet soldiers, had called forth courage and steadfastness. Stalingrad had become a symbol of resistance unparalleled in human history.

On the right flank, in the region of Orlovka, the fighting was not particularly fierce until September 28. We and the enemy both carried out small-scale attacks resulting in minor fluctuations in the front line, amounting to not more than 100–200 yards.

The enemy's divisions which bordered on this flank, after beating off the attacks by the troops of the Stalingrad Front, were presumably being reorganized and reinforced. Apart from limited counter-attacks, we did not and could not wage active operations, because we had no forces with which to do so.

Andryusenko's brigade and the regiments of Sologub's division (almost on its last legs, with no more than 250 able-bodied infantrymen left) were defending the tactically important position of the so-called 'Orlovka salient'. They had the task, come what may, of holding this salient, hanging like the sword of Damocles over the head of the main enemy group, concentrated in the area of Gorodishche. When the troops of the neighbouring front went into action this salient could have an important role to play. If even one unit advancing from the north linked up with the units in the salient, then the substantial enemy forces which had reached the Volga at Latashanka would be cut off and the left flank of the main enemy group would be encircled.

But Paulus, reading our thoughts, organized an offensive against the salient. In an effort to wipe out our troops in the Orlovka area as rapidly as possible, he threw several regiments of the 16th Panzer, the 60th Motorized Infantry and the 389th and 100th Infantry Divisions into the battle.

He was able to manœuvre with forces of this size because our neighbouring Front, trying several times to develop a counter-attack against the enemy formation from the north and link up with troops of the 62nd Army, had been completely unsuccessful. It had been unable to make any headway southward, and from that moment on Paulus was not afraid of the attacks being repeated.

I should add that I believe it would have been much better and more useful if the forces north of the city had been deployed on the front between Kachalinskaya and Kotluban. They would then have been on the enemy's flank, threatening the rear of his main group which had torn through into the city, and then, after proper preparation, our forces could have struck southward along the Don. In that case, in my view, the German Command, having failed to take the city quickly, would have had to pay close heed to the operations of our armies to the north. The Stalingrad Front Group, purely by its presence on the Kachalinskaya–Kotluban front, would have drawn more German forces away from the city than by its unsuccessful counter-attack on the front between Akatovka and Kuzmichi.

But as this did not happen, Paulus was able, on the morning of September 29, to set about destroying the Orlovka salient.

The attack against the salient was made from three sides.

Approximately one battalion of infantry with eighteen tanks attacked southward across Hill 135.4, and about a battalion of infantry with fifteen tanks across Hill 147.6 towards the south-east.

Nearly two battalions of infantry with sixteen tanks attacked east-ward from Uvarovka, aiming to wheel round the south of Orlovka.

At the same time the Germans launched fierce attacks against units of Sologub's infantry division.

The units under attack fought with exceptional tenacity. The enemy suffered heavy losses, but his units were being continually brought up to strength with reserves.

At 3 p.m. some fifty tanks, together with tommy-gunners, attacked Hills 109.4 and 108.9 from Gorodishche, and after over-running units of the 2nd Battalion of Andryusenko's infantry brigade, approached Orlovka from the south.

At the same time, enemy tanks and infantry, attacking Orlovka from the north, smashed the 1st Battalion of the same brigade. The battalion suffered heavy losses and withdrew to the northern outskirts. A threat of encirclement developed for the units fighting west of Orlovka.

On September 29 enemy attacks on other sectors of the Army's front were also extremely bitter and caused us heavy losses.

Sologub's division, which had been fighting non-stop from the Don to the Volga, had to withdraw to the Silicate factory. Its regiments contained only a few dozen soldiers each.

On the sector occupied by Smekhotvorov's division, which was defending the western outskirts of the Krasny Oktyabr settlement, the Germans succeeded in driving a wedge into our positions. Three of the division's regimental commanders and three battalion commanders were killed in the one day of fighting.

After heavy fighting the armoured formation virtually ceased to have any real fighting power—it was left with only seventeen tanks, all of which were out of action, and 150 soldiers; the latter were handed over to infantry units, and the H.Q. staff were ferried across the river for regrouping.

The battle on Mamayev Kurgan was going on the whole

time. German attacks were met with counter-attacks by our troops. Every square yard of earth was fought for.

On September 30 the Germans began their attacks at 1 p.m. Their main efforts were concentrated on destroying the units of Andryusenko's brigade, defending in the Orlovka region. The enemy's attack began on this occasion after a two-hour air and artillery barrage. The 1st and 2nd Battalions of the brigade suffered extremely heavy losses, but continued to hold the northern and southern parts of the settlement. The enemy's pincers were close to joining east of Orlovka. The way was opening to the enemy along Orlovka Gully to the Tractor factory and Spartanovka.

On the same day our reconnaissance established that there was a heavy concentration of infantry and tanks in Vishnevaya Gully, in the vicinity of the Krasny Oktyabr cemetery, in Dolgi and Krutoy Gullies. Units of the 14th Panzer and 94th Infantry Divisions, brought back up to strength after the losses they had suffered, had been brought up from the southern outskirts of the city. The enemy's intention was clear: he was preparing a fresh attack on the Tractor and Barrikady factories.

The Front Command asked me what measures were being taken to hold the Orlovka salient and support the units fighting there.

What answer could I give? The best assistance would undoubtedly have been for the Stalingrad Front to launch an attack towards Orlovka from the north, striking at the rear of the enemy's 16th Panzer and 60th Motorized Infantry Divisions. But nobody had planned such an attack.

I had no reserves left. Faced with an undoubted threat of a strong enemy attack on the Tractor and Barrikady factories, I could not offer any real assistance to the Orlovka salient. In these conditions we decided, after strengthening the 1st and 2nd Battalions of Andryusenko's infantry brigade with one anti-tank regiment and two companies of Colonel Gorokhov's infantry brigade, to prepare and launch (on October 2) a short counter-attack in the vicinity of the Barrikady settlement.

After nightfall on September 30 the 39th Guards Infantry

Division began to be ferried across the Volga. It was only half up to strength: its companies contained forty to fifty men each. They were all ready for battle, however, and the majority of them consisted of commandos, Communist Party and Komsomol members. The division was under the command of energetic Major-General Stepan Savelievich Guriev, who had had experience of battle right from the beginning of the war. He was short, stocky and robust—a man whom, as they say, the enemy would not find it easy to budge. This was the impression he left me with at our first meeting. 'He very likely trains his subordinates in the same spirit,' I thought at the time, and soon discovered I was not mistaken: the 39th Guards Infantry Division defended the Krasny Oktyabr factory for many long days. His men did not know the meaning of the word retreat. Guriev himself did not leave his command post even when the grenades of German tommy-gunners were bursting at the entrance. This happened on more than one occasion. Following the example of the Divisional Commander, the Regimental Commanders fought equally stubbornly and courageously.

The Communists and Komsomol members of this division were always in their place—in the forefront, in the most dangerous positions. Chernyshev, the Commissar, and later Deputy Commander of the division, organizing the political work in the units, spent a large percentage of his time right in the front line. He was wounded in the leg, but stayed at his post. I can see him now—holding a crutch, standing alongside an artillery battery firing at point-blank range.

The 39th Guards Division distinguished itself in fighting elsewhere than on the Volga too. It played an active part right through to the end of the war in the defeat of the Germans, and ended its military road in Berlin. There are five military honours on its guards' banner.

On the day this division arrived in the city it was decided to place its regiments along a line of defence from the Silicate factory on the right to Zuevskaya Street on the left, with the aim of preparing a counter-attack against the Barrikady settlement. But in the fighting on October 1, I had to alter this decision, as on the sector occupied by Smekhotvorov's division the enemy drove a deep wedge into our lines and there was a danger he would occupy the

179

Krasny Oktyabr factory. On that day General Guriev's division was deployed as a second line of defence behind Smekhotvorov's division, along the railway line west of the factory, along a front from Kazachya Street to Banny Gully. The division was instructed to consolidate itself firmly in the workshops of the Krasny Oktyabr factory, turning them into powerful strongpoints.

For the counter-attack against the Barrikady settlement we earmarked the 308th Infantry Division of Colonel L. N. Gurtiev, whose regiments had already arrived on the east bank of the Volga and were getting ready to be ferried across to us.

The 308th Infantry Division was involved in the defence of the city for the shortest period of all the divisions, but in its operations, in the number of attacks it repulsed and its tenacity in battle, it did not fall behind the other divisions of the 62nd Army. In the bitterest fighting in the factory area it was in the main path of the German army's offensive, and fought off not less than a hundred ferocious attacks.

The Commander of this division, Colonel Gurtiev, his deputies—the regimental commanders, the whole Party organization and all the soldiers, for the most part Siberians, were models of courage. They clearly understood the task allotted to them—not to retreat a step, and carried it out with great self-sacrifice.

The mass heroism of the troops of the 308th Division was crowned, as it were, by the unparalleled courage of Gurtiev himself, whom the soldiers often saw in counter-attacks or in the front-line trenches. Tall and slim, he did not like to stoop to German shells and bombs. (This courageous commander, by then already a general, died a hero's death after the Battle of Stalingrad, in 1943, in the region of Orel. A monument was erected to him there. I feel that it would be correct, however, for the monument to be in Volgograd[1] where he defended to the death, and defeated death.)

On October 1 the enemy launched a number of large-scale attacks along the whole of the Army's front. In the area of Orlovka the enemy's pincers met. The 3rd Battalion of An-

---

[1]Stalingrad was renamed Volgograd in 1961.

dryusenko's infantry brigade, one artillery battery (which had 380 rounds) and one 82-mm. mortar (with 350 rounds), were surrounded. There were about 200 rounds for each rifle, and enough rations for two days.

East of Orlovka, facing west, the 1st and 2nd Battalions of this brigade, again reinforced, were consolidating themselves. Strengthened by two fresh companies and an anti-tank regiment, they had the job of advancing towards Orlovka and joining up with the units that had been cut off.

On the same day the enemy again exerted strong pressure on Smekhotvorov's division, and at nightfall it was occupying a line through Zhmerinskaya and Ugolnaya to Karuselnaya Street, and then through Ayvazovskaya Street as far as Banny Gully. On the sectors occupied by Batyuk's and Rodimtsev's divisions the German units attacked along Dolgi and Krutoy Gullies, trying to reach the Volga and again split the 62nd Army. But they were unsuccessful. They left about 500 dead behind them in the gullies.

Day and night the enemy's artillery and aeroplanes directed withering attacks on our barges and ferries. The process of ferrying the units of Gurtiev's division across dragged on. By morning on October 2 only two infantry regiments had been landed on the right bank.

Without waiting for the arrival of all the units of this division, the 1st and 2nd Battalions of Andryusenko's brigade were ordered to continue the counter-attack, to try to join up with the third, surrounded, battalion. The units of Gurtiev's division which had been brought across were given the task of launching a short counter-attack against the Barrikady settlement, throwing out the enemy and consolidating positions there.

Smekhotvorov's division was instructed to clear the enemy out of the western part of the Krasny Oktyabr settlement and seize Hill 107.5. With concentrated fire the Army's artillery was to provide support for the counter-attack against the Barrikady settlement.

The fighting in these areas went on non-stop day and night for several days. Only in a few sectors were there short pauses in the fighting.

The encircled units of Andryusenko's infantry brigade, numbering nearly 500 men, fought against superior enemy forces from October 2-7. On the night of October 7 this group, having used up all its ammunition, made a successful attack by night and broke out of the ring and reached the northern outskirts of the Tractor workers' settlement. There were only 120 men left alive.

Paulus had had to pay dearly for his plan to destroy the salient with one blow: the depleted forces of Andryusenko's brigade had kept the 60th Motorized Division, about 100 tanks of the 16th Panzer Division, and regiments of the enemy's 389th and 100th Infantry Divisions tied up on the Orlovka sector for ten days.

On October 9 the northern group, consisting of the 124th, 143rd and the remains of the 115th Infantry Brigades, held a line through Rynok, Spartanovka, the wood west of Spartanovka and the Tractor workers' settlement along the River Mechetka.

The regiment of Sarayev's division was held in reserve.

The battle on the Army's central sector, in the area of the Barrikady and Krasny Oktyabr settlements, was becoming increasingly fierce. The counter-attack by Gurtiev's division against the Barrikady settlement at noon on October 2 was stopped by a head-on attack by the enemy. Nonetheless, by nightfall the division had cleared part of the Silicate works and occupied the north-western outskirts of the Barrikady settlement. It was unable, however, to develop the attack any further.

Smekhotvorov's division, each regiment of which contained 200 men, was waging an unequal battle against enemy infantry and tanks attacking along Bibliotechnaya and Karuselnaya Streets. After fierce fighting, including bayonet skirmishes, in the evening the enemy managed to reach Tsekhovaya and Bibleyskaya Streets.

At the junction point of Batyuk's and Rodimtsev's divisions, a battalion of German soldiers, disguised as Red Army men, penetrated through our lines to Krutoy Gully and headed for the Volga. Reserve companies of Batyuk's division counter-attacked and completely wiped out the German detachment. The German ruse failed.

At night on October 2 we decided to regroup some of our forces:

—to move Sologub's divison to the left flank of Gorokhov's

northern group, to occupy a line of defence from the railway bridge, across the stream about 800 yards south of Hill 75.9, to point 97.7 and then along the gully to the southeast as far as the River Mechetka;

—to move Gurtiev's 308th Division to a line of defence from the orchards north of the Barrikady settlement to the Silicate factory, Makeyevskaya Street and as far as the gully;

—to establish Guriev's division in defence positions along Tsekhovaya, Bibleyskaya and Severnaya Streets, relieving units of Smekhotvorov's division and thereby strengthening the latter and creating partial reserves.

The Army's command post, as I have already said, was near some oil-tanks, just below a big open reservoir. The black oil in the reservoir caught fire and for more than a week clouds of thick black smoke hung over us. Flakes of ash and soot descended on us all the time, so that everything at the command post turned black and looked burnt. On the other hand, the enemy's planes stopped bombing us—the Germans could not imagine that the Army H.Q. might be in such an inferno. By and large, we had a successful camouflage. We were already used to this kind of situation and were quite unmoved. Two or three times a day the Military Council met in the dining-room—Gurov's dug-out. Sitting round the table and waiting for food to arrive we would listen to the jokes which Krylov could tell so well.

We often had to wait a long time for our food. Our kitchen was not far from Gurov's dug-out—in the control-well of the drainage pipes from the Barrikady factory. But bringing the food from there was not easy. The cook and the waitress had a complicated journey to make: like acrobats, they climbed out of the well, then up on to a footbridge hanging over the well, and, balancing along narrow planks, brought us the mess-tins and plates, in which, with the soup, we often found splinters of shells. In any case, we were quite used to such condiments, though our cook, Glinka, could not reconcile himself to them. Just before our command post was moved again, he was wounded. It was a serious wound and I did not think I would ever meet him again ... But not long ago we met again in Volgograd. I immediately recognized him. We embraced. For a long time, in tears, he could not say a word. Nor could I.

And when we had dried our tears we could see each other again under fire on the banks of the Volga. Fumes, smoke—we could not breathe. Shells and bombs bursting all round us. So much noise that however loud you shouted no one would hear you. And Glinka, oblivious to everything, pottering about in his kitchen, getting a meal ready, then carrying it through the fire and smoke to the dining-room, where the smell of tasty soup mingled with the smell of burning; and the second course—'seasoned' with sand from the dug-out roof, wrenched by a bomb explosion.

On October 2 the Germans, probably having spotted our command post, launched a heavy air and artillery bombardment against it. Bombs dropped all over the bank, blowing up the oil-tanks full of oil, and a burning mass gushed across our dug-outs towards the Volga. The command post was in the middle of a sea of flames.

The streams of flame burned everything in their path. Reaching the bank of the Volga, the burning oil poured on to the barges standing near the command post. The burning oil floated down with the current. The Volga itself seemed to be bursting into flame.

Telephone lines also went up in flame. Communication could be maintained only by radio, which worked with interruptions. We were imprisoned by fire, descending on us from all directions, and we stood in the gully alongside our smoking dug-outs. On everyone's face was the same question—what were we going to do?

Krylov, the Chief of Staff, gave an order:

'Everyone stay where they are! Let's get to work in the dug-outs still intact! ... Let's establish and maintain contact with the troops by radio!'

He then came up to me and in a whisper asked:

'What do you think? Will we be able to stand it?'

I answered:

'Yes, of course! But in case of need, let's clean our pistols.'

'Good,' he said, and again we had understood each other.

To be quite frank, at the beginning of the fires, when I jumped out of the dug-out I was blinded, bewildered. But

General Krylov's loud command was for everyone, including me, like a 'Hurrah!' in an attack, jolting us into action. Surrounded by fire, we stayed where we were and continued administering the Army.

The fire lasted several days, but we had no emergency command post—all our units, including the sappers, were out fighting; we decided, therefore, to carry on working in dug-outs, trenches and shell-holes, under fire. We did not sleep for several days.

General Krylov and I were constantly being called to the radio for discussions with the Front Chief of Staff, General G. F. Zakharov. Talking to him was torture. He wanted precise information about the situation at the front, information which we ourselves did not always know very accurately, and the divisional headquarters themselves did not know it either, because communications were being constantly interrupted and knocked out of action.

To talk on the radio, to filter words through a secret code, when bombs and shells were bursting overhead, was both unpleasant and difficult. Many a time the radio operator would be killed with the microphone in his hands.

'Where are you?' Front H.Q. kept asking us.

We realized that Front H.Q. was trying to make sure whether we were alive and whether there was still an H.Q. to administer the troops in the city.

Krylov and I, without prearranging it, both answered:

'We're where the most flames and smoke are.'

The enemy launched new attacks at dawn on October 3. Sologub's infantry division, without having occupied and consolidated its sector, was attacked by an infantry regiment and twenty tanks. After heavy fighting the division withdrew eastward to the clearing half a mile east of point 97.7.

Until 6 p.m. Gurtiev's division held off the German attacks, but at nightfall, under attack from both flanks, it withdrew to the railway south of Nizhneudinskaya Street, and its left flank to Vinnitskaya Street. Regimental Commander Major Markelov was seriously wounded.

Smekhotvorov's division fought the whole day for the bath-house and the kitchens. The bath-house changed hands several times, but finally remained in ours. The regiments in the division now contained 100-150 men each.

A five-year-old boy, Gena, was found in the vicinity of the bath-house. He was looked after and loved like a son by Colonel G. I. Vitkov. We all loved the boy. He knew all the staff officers and generals by name. He is now a student at one of the institutes in Kharkov.

Guriev's division beat off all German attacks on the Krasny Oktyabr factory. Gorishny's, Batyuk's and Rodimtsev's divisions consolidated their positions, beating off all attacks.

On October 3 Front H.Q. handed over Major-General Zholudev's 37th Guards Infantry Division to the 62nd Army.

During the fighting on these days we felt that the enemy had decided to take the Tractor factory at all costs. His forces in this area were growing the whole time, and by October 4 we had established that from the River Mechetka to Hill 107.5, along a front of about three miles, three enemy infantry and two panzer divisions were operating. The fighting in the area of Orlovka had been intended not only to liquidate the salient, but also to distract our attention from the main attack being prepared against the factories. We decided to ferry Zholudev's division across the river as rapidly as possible and place it in positions on the right flank of Gurtiev's division, to defend the Tractor factory.

On the night of October 3 Sologub's division withdrew across the Mechetka. By reaching Shchelkovskaya Street the enemy had established a jumping-off ground for a final thrust to the Volga bank. Gurtiev's division, throwing all its reserves into the battle, fought off furious enemy attacks against the Silicate factory, and was thrown back to Mytishchi, Aviatornaya and Petrozavodskaya Streets.

The 37th Guards Division was ferried across the same night, but without anti-tank artillery, for which we did not have enough boats. The division's H.Q. was also left behind. We had to issue instructions directly to the regiments. We sent out almost all the officers from our command post to these regiments to take them to their defensive positions.

As soon as these regiments had taken up position they

went into action against enemy infantry and tanks, which had broken through units of Sologub's and Gurtiev's divisions.

The Army needed a breathing-space, if only for a day. We needed to pull our units into shape, bring up artillery and ammunition and bring units back up to strength, so as to be able to launch counter-attacks to throw the Germans out of the Tractor and Barrikady settlements. The Front Commander ordered us to start a counter-attack on the morning of October 5. But the Army was in no position to do so: we were running out of ammunition.

On the night of October 4 the ferrying across of the 84th Armoured Brigade began. But only light tanks could be brought across; they were immediately sent to Zholudev's and Gurtiev's divisions. They were used as firing points, because to throw them into a counter-attack against German tanks would have been pointless.

On October 5, in the city's factory area alone, about 2,000 enemy sorties were counted. At daybreak all troop movements came to a standstill, because anything that moved was hammered by the Luftwaffe. The wounded did not leave their dug-outs or trenches until nightfall, and crawled to the evacuation points on the bank of the Volga under cover of darkness.

In the evening, the Member of the Military Council, Gurov, returned from the other side of the Volga. He was clean, had had a shave, and looked about ten years younger: he had been able to have a hot bath and change his clothes. Knowing that I also had not had a wash for a month, he tried to persuade me to go for a short trip across the Volga. The temptation was very great, but I refused. What would the soldiers think, seeing the Army Commander going across to the left bank at such a difficult moment? Would my country forgive me if something dreadful happened to the Army while I was across having a bath? Of course not. The trip to the left bank had to be postponed.

The same evening the Deputy Commander of the Front, General F. I. Golikov, visited us. Things had quietened down a little when he came. The oil had already burnt out, but a shell-hole above our dug-out still contained smoking oil. But communications were even worse. They were being interrupted every minute as before. The German mortars, obviously, had discovered precisely where our command post was. Mortar bombs were exploding at the very entrance to my dug-out. The number of wounded and killed at the command post was increasing with every hour. In other words, it had become impossible to keep the command post here. F. I. Golikov stayed with us about twenty-four hours, and having seen the picture of what was happening, advised us to move elsewhere.

But where? We discussed the question and decided to move to the dug-outs of Sarayev's divisional H.Q., which was being sent back for regrouping. We had to move along the Volga bank about 500 yards nearer to the Tractor factory. We moved during the night. Gurov and I went first, and Golikov came with us. The Army Chief of Staff, N. I. Krylov, stayed at the old post until dawn, that is, until communication had been established with the troops from the new command post.

We had all had no sleep for several days and were utterly exhausted. On arrival at the new command post I felt that I could go on no longer. Asking F. I. Golikov and K. A. Gurov to watch over the establishment of communications, I collapsed on the floor and slept like the dead.

I woke up at dawn and learned that Krylov was still under fire at the old command post. Communications were now working and I proposed to Krylov that he should come straight across to the less dangerous command post. He appeared two hours later, covered in dust, pale and exhausted. He came into the dug-out and fell fast asleep.

We were all delighted to be back together again.

From daybreak on October 5, the Germans continued to press home their attack, delivering their main attack from the Barrikady settlement towards the Tractor settlement. They were obviously not expecting to find General Zholudev's 37th Division in the path of their main attack. Extremely fierce fighting started.

Zholudev's division really was a guards division. The men were all young, tall and healthy; many of them were dressed as commandos, with knives in their belts. They fought heroically. With a bayonet-thrust they could fling a German over their shoulder like a bag of straw. They attacked in groups. Having broken into a house they would use their knives. They had no thought of retreat, and when encircled fought to their last breath, and died singing or with shouts of 'For our country!' or 'No retreat, no surrender!'

The division counted seven hundred sorties by enemy planes against its units on that one day. Nevertheless, the Germans could not advance a step. The 1st Guards Regiment even managed to make a little ground and occupied a line of defence from the cemetery through Bazovaya Street and along the gully to Tipografskaya Street. The division was supported by the 499th Anti-Tank Artillery and the 11th Artillery Regiments, and a battery of the 85th Guards Howitzer Regiment.

On the remaining sectors, with the exception of the Or-lovka area, all German attacks were beaten off.

At night, the 84th Armoured Brigade reached the sector being defended by Zholudev's and Gurtiev's divisions. All the Army's units were now busy digging themselves in and preparing defence positions and obstacles. Everyone was getting ready for big developments on the front. Our reconnaissance had reported new German concentrations in the Barrikady settlement. October 6 passed without any particular enemy infantry and tank activity, from early morning to late evening enemy aeroplanes bombed our formations. The entire 339th Infantry Regiment H.Q. staff, including the Commander and the Commissar, were killed in a bomb explosion.

The relative quiet of October 6 was obviously taken by Front H. Q. to be a sign of the enemy's exhaustion; they therefore pressed us strongly to counter-attack again with the 37th Division. We spent the whole day in discussions with the Front Command. In the evening, under great pressure, I had to agree to launch a counter-attack, using part of Zholudev's and Gurtiev's divisions. We decided to launch the attack during the afternoon of October 7, reckoning that the enemy would not have time to parry our blow before nightfall, and would not be able to bring in his aircraft.

I signed the order to counter-attack at 4 a.m., but we were unable to implement it. At 11.20 a.m. the enemy launched a new, powerful attack. We met the attackers with fire from previously prepared and well-camouflaged positions.

It was a full-scale attack. From the vicinity of Verkhneud-inskaya Street they threw in two divisions and more than 500 tanks. The first attacks were thrown back. The units of Zholudev's division inflicted heavy losses on the enemy. The Germans brought up reserves and repeated their attack several times. After bitter fighting they managed to penetrate our lines in the evening, seize a block of the Tractor workers' settlement and approach close to the stadium. Prospect Stakhanovtsev and Sculpturny Park remained in our hands.

At 6 p.m. a reinforced battalion of enemy infantry attacked west of the railway bridge across the River Mechetka. An accurate 'katyushi' salvo destroyed the battalion almost completely. On the sector occupied by Smekhotvorov's division fighting went on the whole day for the bath-house in the Krasny Oktyabr settlement. It changed hands not less than five times, and at nightfall it was difficult to say in whose hands it was. Attacks in all other sectors were beaten off.

Approximately four enemy battalions and sixteen tanks were destroyed in the day's fighting.

After such losses the enemy could not continue his offensive the following day. The appearance of the 37th Guards Division in the path of his main attack had upset Paulus's calculations. He had been unable to strike a lightning blow and break through our front. We had not failed to locate his main group.

Preparations for decisive battles began on October 8. We learned that Hitler had promised his vassals he would be master of Stalingrad in the next few days. German soldiers shouted from their trenches: 'Russians! Soon bang-bang on the Volga.'

Aeroplanes dropped leaflets on the city. They contained drawings of our Army, surrounded on all sides by tanks and artillery. They taunted the Stalingrad Front with having failed to link up with us from the north and with retreating.

The activity of Goebbels's propagandists only annoyed our men. Our Party and Komsomol organizations were working untiringly among our troops, showing the impudence and falsity of the enemy's propaganda. The Army Military Council awarded decorations to outstanding soldiers and commanders, had short discussions with them, and through them communicated its determination to hold the city, come what may.

Our troops clearly understood our decision.

The following document is from the records of one of the Komsomol organizations.

The Conduct of Komsomol Members in Battle

Motion: It is better to die in the trenches than to retreat in shame. Not only not retreat oneself, but to act so that one's neighbour does not retreat either.

Question to Speaker: Are there any extenuating causes for withdrawing from a firing position?

Answer: The only extenuating cause is death.

When this meeting was taking place, the Germans were beginning their twelfth attack that day on the line held by Guriev's guardsmen.

The company commander summed up this meeting. This is what he said:

I would like to clarify what the Komsomol organizer said. He said a lot about death, and said that our country demands that we should die for victory. Of course, he did not express himself clearly. Our country demands victory, but not death. Yes, some will not return from the field of battle—but that is war. The hero is the one who dies wisely and courageously, bringing victory nearer. But doubly heroic is the one who can defeat the enemy, and live! . . .

General Gurov described at this time:

I have a young soldier called Alexey Popov. When the Germans approached, on one side he placed a tommy-gun, on the other a machine-gun, and in his hands he held his rifle. He put his grenades round him in a circle. If a lot of Germans approached he got down behind the machine-gun; if one German approached he used his rifle. If the Germans came up any closer he threw grenades. That is how one man can do the work of five . . .

The strength of our guardsmen lay in the fact that they fought intelligently and prudently, trying to use their weapons with maximum effect. In those days thousands of soldiers like Popov were matchless examples of courage and resourcefulness in battle, showing how well they had mastered every type of weapon.

A song entitled 'To the Hero City' soon grew popular in the 62nd Army. It was written by Sergeant N. Panov. The words of the song were simple and it did not lay claim to any great poetic standard. But there was one thing about it that our soldiers liked—it was true to the life they were leading.

> The streets were shaking with explosions,
> The terrible roar of engines filled the sky,
> But our regiments stood fast like granite
> To defend the Volga, or to die.
>
> A comrade spoke as he lay dying:
> 'The enemy must always know
> That never will the Sixty-Second
> Retreat a single step before the foe'.

That was the law of the troops in the 62nd Army: not to retreat but only attack, to win back their native land yard by yard.

In front of me I have some small leaflets, yellow with age, which were distributed in the front line.

Here is one of them:

TODAY'S HEROIC FIGHTERS

Kozlov, Andrey Yefimovich—machine-gunner, member of the Komsomol. Since the war began Comrade Kozlov has killed 50 Germans, not counting those killed by his machine-gun team. Since October 7, 1942, Comrade Kozlov has killed 17 of the enemy. Kozlov's machine-gun team is the best in the battalion. Comrade Kozlov took part in the battles of Leningrad and Kharkov. He has been wounded twice. He has been decorated twice. Emulate Kozlov.

Marshal Vasili Ivanovich Chuikov

Imperial War Museum

A Soviet "Hedge-hog" force in action.

Camera Press

Red Army charging from a bomb-damaged

Some 330,000 Germans died during the Stalingrad battle.
United Press International

factory in the Stalingrad district.

German forces on the attack.

Armed with light machine guns, Soviet troops attack German forces in the vicinity of the Red October plant in Stalingrad.

Camera Press

Transporting supplies across the frozen Volga.
Camera Press

62nd Army fortresses on the Volga.
Camera Press

Soviet artillery.

Camera Press

Winter camouflage in the Karpovka district.

Camera Press

The Germans in attack and in defeat.

Associated Press

And here is another one:

A TOLL OF SEVEN TANKS

Red Army men, Jacob Shcherbina and Ivan Nikitan, both wounded, did not leave their posts. As true sons of their country they fought until the last enemy attack was beaten off. In a half an hour or so these two courageous anti-tank men put seven enemy tanks out of action.

There are lots of these extremely short leaflets. But how convincingly, how clearly, they tell of the men who, defying death, forged our victory.

And what exceptional men there were on the ferries across the Volga!

The men who worked there were face to face with death every hour. Nerves of steel and unparalleled courage really were needed to cross the Volga backwards and forwards under fire. But our boat crews, our seamen of the Volga fleet, made such journeys night and day, bringing ammunition and provisions to the city.

The same courage was shown by our infantrymen and tommy-gunners, sappers and artillerymen in the fighting for the factory districts. They destroyed the Germans who had occupied the attics of miraculously standing houses, they rooted them out from under the stairs of destroyed buildings, out of dug-outs and basements, from everywhere that the sharp eyes of a Stalingrad defender could see. Our troops put all their knowledge and experience into the defence of the city, regardless of their own lives.

In the fighting for the factory district the soldiers of Zholudev's, Gorishny's, Andryusenko's and Gorokhov's divisions distinguished themselves. It was they who stopped the enemy on October 7 at the walls of the Tractor factory, and in the Krasny Oktyabr and Barrikady settlements, and by doing so made it possible for the Army to regroup its forces and prepare for the battles ahead.

CHAPTER VII

THE DARKEST DAYS

THE LULL lasted four days. But it was not, and could not be, a lull in the proper sense of the word, because our positions were only a grenade-throw from the German positions.

The distance from our front line to the Volga was not more than two miles. By a properly-organized attack the enemy could have covered such a distance in an hour and a half to two hours, as we later did through the German defences. The situation forced us to be extremely vigilant, to conduct constant reconnaissance. If we missed anything, it would mean disaster.

We considered the best form of vigilance and military preparedness to be active operations. Our snipers and storm groups gave the enemy no peace. Any foolish German who poked his head out of a trench or any other kind of cover, was immediately given a dose of lead.

Keeping an eye on the enemy concentrations in the areas of the Barrikady settlement and Vishnevaya Gully, our artillery and 'katyushi' hit them hard. Our aeroplanes flew over the enemy positions at night, bombing and machine-gunning.

The Commander of the 'katyushi' regiment, Colonel Yerokhin, and other artillerymen, headed by the Army Artillery Commander, General Pozharski, came to me every day for their orders as to where and when to fire, as counter-preparations, on the enemy during the night.

Diaries and letters taken from the German dead told us what losses and what a terrifying effect our counter-preparations had on the enemy. 'Stalingrad is hell . . .', 'Stalingrad is a mass grave . . .', 'Stalingrad belches out death . . .', wrote the Germans.

The enemy also, having pressed us back towards the Volga, gave us no rest. His aircraft carried out constant reconnaissance over our troops, bombing them and the ferries, and his artillery and mortars pounded our positions.

Firing never died down on the Army's front, day or night.

Rockets and tracer bullets split the darkness.

Staff officers and political workers were out among the troops all the time. After regrouping our forces and establishing lines of defence in greater depth in the probable path of the enemy's main attack, we tried to consolidate ourselves better, and turn every house into a strongpoint. We considerably strengthened the defences in the factory area.

Gorishny's division, for example, now held the junction point between Zholudev's and Gurtiev's divisions, as a second line of defence in depth for our forward units. One regiment (the 117th) of Guriev's division was moved to the vicinity of Zhitomirskaya Street on October 12, in order to provide defence in depth and strengthen the junction point between Zholudev's and Gorishny's divisions.

Detachments of workers and militia were organized at the Tractor factory, and also at the Barrikady and Krasny Oktyabr works. They were well-armed and prepared to fight to the last round.

On October 12, the 524th Infantry Regiment of the 112th Division, which had previously been on the left bank of the Volga, being reinforced by men from the rear, was ferried across to the right bank and deployed as a second line of defence along a sector near the northern stadium.

We reviewed all our rear units, leaving a minimum number behind, armed the remainder and distributed them among our companies and batteries. We felt that the enemy, carrying out limited attacks on different sectors of the front, was making preparations for a powerful attack on the Tractor factory. Our reconnaissance, under Colonel Herman, brought in more and more information to confirm the fact. We would have to put up a full-scale defence against this attack.

On October 12, in accordance with an order from Front Command, Zholudev's division, together with one regiment of Gorishny's division, launched a counter-attack against the western outskirts of the Tractor settlement. The aim was to upset the enemy's preparations for a new offensive.

We did not expect any great results from this counter-attack, but we felt that on this occasion the Commander of the Front was not asking the 62nd Army to carry out active operations to no purpose: the plan received from the Front artillery staff for the delivery of ammunition during October put the Army on short supplies—which meant that our armies were preparing a powerful counter-attack somewhere or other. The city into which Hitler had thrown his all and spared nothing was being turned into a bait for the German aggressors.

We delivered our counter-attack against the enemy's main group, reckoning that we could upset his preparations for a new offensive only by a counter-attack. To force the enemy to go on to the attack before he had intended was better for us than sitting and waiting for him to throw all his strength into an attack when he was fully prepared.

We were taking a risk, but as I have already said, we had established a defence structure in depth, and we were only using part of our forces for the counter-attack. It began on the morning of October 12. The Germans put up fierce resistance. As a result of the day's fighting Zholudev's left flank and centre moved forward some three hundred yards westward and were fighting in the nameless settlement north of the southern stadium. Units of Gorishny's division also moved forward some two hundred yards.

The fighting on October 12 showed us that the enemy was not expecting a counter-attack, but that his formations were so strong that our units could throw them back no further.

On October 13, continuing our counter-attack, we tried to throw the enemy back from Mytishchinski Gully. A head-on battle was fought throughout the day.

October 14 dawned—a day which saw the beginning of fighting of unprecedented ferocity. Three of the enemy's infantry divisions and two panzer divisions, deployed on a three-mile front, were thrown against our units.

Those of us who had already been through a great deal will remember this enemy attack all our lives.

We recorded some 3,000 sorties by enemy aircraft on that day! German aeroplanes bombed and machine-gunned our troops without stop. The enemy's artillery and mortars bombarded the whole battlefield from morning to night. It was a sunny day, but the smoke and dust cut visibility down to a hundred yards. Our dug-outs shook and caved in like houses of cards.

The enemy's main attack was levelled against units of Zholudev's 37th, Gorishny's 95th and Gurtiev's 308th Divisions and the 84th Armoured Brigade in the general direction of the Tractor and Barrikady factories. At 11:30 a.m. some 180 tanks broke through the lines of Zholudev's division.

One section of the tanks, with tommy-gunners, headed for the Tractor factory, and the other along Co-operativnaya Street towards the River Mechetka, in the rear of Sologub's division. On Gorishny's sector the enemy overran our positions at the junction point of two regiments. The Commander of the 117th Regiment of the 39th Guards Infantry Division, Andreyev, was killed.

At 4 p.m., Sologub's and Zholudev's divisions and the right flank of Gurtiev's division, cut off by the tanks, were fighting in a position of encirclement.

The regimental command posts did not move, and fought to the last round. The Commander of the 37th Division, General Zholudev, was buried in his dug-out by a bomb explosion. Soldiers from the Army H.Q. guard dug him out and brought him to my dug-out. The Army H.Q. staff took over the administration of the units of his division.

Conflicting information was coming in from the troops, and it became more and more difficult to get a precise picture. Regimental command and observation posts were being blown up by shell and bomb. Many commanders had been killed. Thirty men had been killed at the Army command post. The Army H.Q. guard was unable to dig people out of destroyed dug-outs. The administration of the troops was being carried on for the most part by radio: an emergency radio service had been brought into action in the morning, operated from the left bank. We sent our orders by radio, and it retransmitted them across the Volga to the units on the right bank.

Fighting was going on continuously night and day. Encircled and cut-off units continued to fight, reporting on their positions by radio: 'We will die for our country, but we will not surrender!'

By midnight on October 14 it had become clear that enemy forces had surrounded the Tractor factory on three sides and were fighting in the workshops. Preliminary accounts put the number of German tanks destroyed at forty. Nearly 3,000 German dead lay at the walls of the factory.

We also suffered great losses, particularly from the bombing. On the night of October 14, 3,500 of our wounded were ferried across to the left bank of the Volga. This was a record figure for the whole period of fighting in the city.

General Hans Doerr describes the attack on the Tractor factory in the following words:

On October 14 began the biggest operation so far: an attack by several divisions (including the 14th Panzer, 305th and 389th Infantry) on the Dzerzhinski Tractor factory, on the eastern outskirts of which was the Russian 62nd Army H.Q.[1] From all ends of the front, even from the army's flanks on the Don and in the Kalmyk steppe, engineering and anti-tank units were brought up as reinforcements, though they were needed just as much where they had been brought from. Five engineering battalions were brought into the fighting area from Germany by plane. The attack was supported by the entire 8th Air Corps.

The troops which attacked advanced 1¼ miles, but could not overcome the resistance of the three Russian divisions defending the factory and occupying the sheer bank of the Volga. During the day our troops did succeed at some points in reaching the bank, but at night they were forced to retreat, as the Russians in the gullies were cutting them off from the rear.

This was how the enemy saw the tenacity of our troops.

It is also important that we did not make a mistake, and correctly guessed the intentions of the German Command. But we had not waited for the German attack to be at its most powerful.

It would be true to say that October 14 was our most critical day. After surviving it and the next three days we knew that the enemy would not be able to repeat an attack

---

[1] This is a mistake. 62nd Army H.Q. was at the eastern outskirts of the Barrikady factory. (*Author's note.*)

of this kind, that even though our Army had been split for a second time its regiments were, and would remain, on the right bank of the Volga.

In the tense hours of the evening of October 14, N. S. Khrushchev telephoned us. He asked me:

'What can the 62nd Army do to prevent the enemy from taking the Tractor factory?'

I replied that if the following day I threw the whole of the Army's forces into the defence of the Tractor factory this would only play into the enemy's hands: we would not hold the factory and would be surrendering the city.

He agreed with me.

I realized that in asking this question he was looking for confirmation of his own analysis of the situation. He went on to remind me that Stalingrad now had not only strategic, but even more important, political significance. Whatever happened, we must hold it.

'What is your major need at the moment?' he asked.

'More ammunition. Without it the Army could perish without completing its task.' I answered, and complained about the difficulty of administering the Army, as telephone lines were going up in flames and radio equipment was being destroyed together with the command posts.

'I understand. We'll send you more ammunition,' he replied.

It was clear from the conversation that G.H.Q. was also worried about the position in the city, and was obviously asking the Front Military Council, and Nikita Khrushchev in particular, to clarify the situation.

On October 15 the enemy threw fresh forces (the 305th Infantry Division) into the battle, and continued to press his attack northward and southward along the Volga. His artillery pounded our positions and the Luftwaffe continued to drop thousands of bombs on the city.

But the Army, now split in two, continued to fight. The northern group (the 124th, 115th and 149th Infantry Brigades and what remained of Sologub's division), under the command of Colonel Gorokhov, was fighting in encirclement against the enemy's superior numbers, attacking from Lata-shanka in the north, along the valley of the River Mechetka from the west, and from the Tractor factory. Communication with this group was constantly being broken.

Zholudev's division, which had taken the main brunt of the attack, was split into several sections, fighting as separate garrisons in the Tractor settlement, and in the vicinity of Minusinskaya Street. Gorishny's division had also suffered heavy losses and was fighting in defence positions along Tramvaynaya and Sculpturnaya Streets. The enemy, moving southward, was threatening to emerge in the rear of Gorishny's division and reach the Army command post. Enemy tommy-gunners infiltrated through breaches between our units. The Army H.Q. guard went into action.

During these hours of fighting Paulus did not have a single fresh battalion he could throw in to make a dash across the three hundred yards left to reach the Army command post. Only three hundred yards, but we had no thought of withdrawing. Fighting was going on all the time ...

The desperate situation at the front called for incredible efforts from every soldier, requiring him to do the fighting of five, of ten men. Everyone was aware of the fact. Many of our men, therefore, acted in turns as infantryman, tommy-gunner, machine-gunner and anti-tank rifleman, using the weapons of their dead comrades.

Telephone wires were being blown up and in flames not only on the right, but also on the left bank of the Volga, where we had our emergency command post. This caused us particular anxiety, because the bulk of the Army's and the entire Front artillery were on the left bank. I asked the Front Command for permission to send several sections of the Army H.Q. to the emergency command post on the left bank, on condition that the entire Military Council stayed in the city. We wanted to be able to administer the 62nd Army from the left bank, in case the Army command post was destroyed.

'We will not give permission,' was the answer I received.

The Military Council's dug-outs, what is more, were becoming more and more crowded. People were arriving from the destroyed headquarters of Zholudev's division and the 84th Armoured Brigade. This was the only place where they could find shelter from the bombing and find any way of administering their units.

On my own responsibility I proposed to the Army's

Artillery Commander, General Pozharski, that he should go across to the left bank and from there take charge of the artillery. Almost with tears in his eyes he said:

'I will not go . . . I'm staying with you. We'll die together . . .'

And he did not go. I would find it difficult to say, however, that his presence on the right bank continued to be of use. It is possible that from the left bank he might have been better able to administer the artillery and destroy more of the enemy. The Commander of the Army's armoured units, Weinrub, spent all these days with the tanks of the 84th Brigade, putting them into the positions of best vantage, organizing ambushes and combined operations by tank, infantry and artillery men. Everyone in the Army understood the seriousness of the situation, but no one had any thought for himself.

Alarming information was coming in. Many units were asking for help, wanting to know what to do, and how. It is probable that divisional and regimental commanders were making these approaches in order to find out whether the 62nd Army Command still existed. We gave a short, clear-cut answer to all these questions:

'Fight with everything you've got, but stay put!'

Our losses were extremely heavy. On October 15 Zholudev's and Gorishny's divisions lost about 75 per cent of their personnel, but the enemy had been unable to advance: his attacks had been beaten back. The enemy had lost thirty-three tanks and nearly three battalions of infantry.

On the night of the 15th a regiment of Ivan Ilyich Lyudnikov's division was brought across to the right bank of the Volga, and we immediately sent it into action north of the Barrikady factory.

During that night one enemy infantry division (the 389th) and one panzer division (the 16th), reinforced with motorized regiments, renewed the attack. They were aiming to wipe out the encircled northern group, defending Rynok and Spartanovka. On the morning of October 16, three infantry divisions (the 305th, 100th and 94th) and two panzer divisions (the 14th and 24th) attacked northward and southward along the Volga, trying to smash our formations from the flanks and rear.

The utterly exhausted units of Zholudev's and Gorishny's

divisions and one regiment of Lyudnikov's division, together with the 84th Armoured Brigade, waged an unequal battle against five divisions, with substantial air and artillery support. Our units would have been overwhelmed if the Germans had not suffered heavy casualties from the fire of our infantry, our dive-bombers (which, with heavy losses, reached the city through masses of German aircraft), and our artillery, including the artillery of the Volga fleet.

The Germans were bold at the beginning of an attack, freely pursued a retreating enemy, but were helpless in battle against even the remnants of a group of soldiers determined to die rather than let the enemy pass.

During the fighting for the Tractor and Barrikady factories our reconnaissance had spotted a powerful enemy group preparing to attack the Krasny Oktyabr factory from the vicinity of Shakhtinskaya Street and Hill 107.5. We captured documents and prisoners from enemy engineering units which had been flown in here from Kerch, Millerovo and even Germany.

We watched this sector of the front very carefully, constantly pressing Smekhotvorov's, Guriev's, Batyuk's and Rodimtsev's divisions to consolidate their positions more firmly and carry out active reconnaissance and operations by storm groups to destroy the enemy.

Paulus's tactics were clear: he was trying to lure our main forces to the factory area and, paralysing them there, at the same time surreptitiously prepare an attack on a new sector. He failed to lull our vigilance, however. His plans were being constantly revealed by our reconnaissance, and every enemy attack came up against prepared defences.

For example, on October 16, masses of enemy infantry, supported by tanks, swooped along the road from the Tractor factory to the Barrikady factory. This large-scale, determined attack came up against the 84th Brigade's tanks, which had been dug in. At and to the west of Tramvaynaya Street our tank crews met an enemy attack with concentrated fire from a distance of 100–200 yards. Ten or more enemy tanks immediately went up in flames. The German attack petered out. At that moment our artillery on the left bank opened up blistering fire on the enemy's halted infantry and tanks.

Being a long way away from the field of battle, and not seeing what was happening on the sector of the main attack, the German generals sent up more and more fresh units, which rolled up to our lines in waves. Here they were stopped and were pulverized by powerful salvos from our 'katyushi'. The German tanks, coming under heavy fire from our well-camouflaged T-34's and anti-tank guns, turned back and abandoned the infantry.

My deputy in charge of armoured units, M. G. Weinrub, and the Commander of the 84th Armoured Brigade, D. N. Bely, had done their preparatory work well. On October 16 they gave the Germans a sound thrashing. Only in the latter part of the day did the German Command realize what was happening and what their main attack had come up against. They threw their air force into this sector. On other sectors of the front, the Army also beat off the attacks. We gained a whole day, preventing the enemy from moving a step forward.

During the night of October 16 the remaining two regiments of Lyudnikov's division were ferried across to our bank. We sent them straight into action. They joined up with units of Zholudev's and Gorishny's divisions along a line from Volkhovstroyevskaya Street to the Barrikady factory and Sculpturny Park. Lyudnikov's H.Q. also established itself in the dug-out of the Army Military Council. There was nowhere else.

The same night I was warned that the Commander of the Front, Colonel-General Yeremenko, and his deputy, Lieutenant-General Popov, were coming to see us.

Gurov, the Member of the Military Council, and I went to the landing-stage to meet them. Everything round us was exploding, the noise was deafening; German six-barrelled mortars were keeping the Volga under incessant attack. Hundreds of wounded were crawling towards the landing-stage and the ferry. We often had to step over bodies.

Not knowing where the boat with the Front Commander would land, we walked up and down the bank, then returned to the dugout ... To our surprise, Generals Yeremenko and Popov were already at the command post.

It was a wretched picture that they had found. The command post dug-outs had been turned into craters with logs sticking out of the ground. Everything on the bank was covered in ash and dust.

When we said good-bye at dawn I asked the Front Commander to let us have more men, not divisions, but small draft units, and more ammunition.

'You will have what you want,' he said, and, as he left, recommended that with the arrival of the 138th Division we should move our Army command post further south along the bank of the Volga.

A day later we received the plan, confirmed by the Front Commander, for deliveries of ammunition to the Army. We were scheduled to be sent as much ammunition for the month as we could use in one day of fierce fighting. We could not but protest, and we managed to obtain a little more than the amount set out in the plan.

October 17 was spent in fierce defensive fighting. Gorokhov's northern group continued to fight in encirclement. Twenty or more German tanks with tommy-gunners broke through to the southern outskirts of Spartanovka settlement. Here our men were fighting to the death. The slightest weakness or confusion on the part of the commanders could have brought catastrophe to the whole group.

We received a telegram from the commanders of the 124th and 115th Brigades with a request for permission to allow them to cross to Sporny Island. I replied that if they left the right bank I would consider their act as desertion from the battlefield. After the telegram, I sent Colonel Kamynin, officer in charge of operations, to the northern group to find out more detailed information about the position on this sector.

At the same time the enemy was continuing his southward attack from the Tractor factory towards the Barrikady factory. Hundreds of dive-bombers and assault aircraft bombed and machine-gunned our sector, where tanks of the 84th Brigade were dug in. Buildings were burning, the earth was burning and the tanks were burning. Our anti-aircraft artillery was unable to give our troops any real cover.

On that day individual groups of enemy infantry and tanks

broke through to the north-western part of the Barrikady factory.

The armed detachment of factory workers went into action.

The remaining troops of Gorishny's division were grouped into one regiment, the 161st, which was waging a defensive battle in the vicinity of Sormovskaya Street. We sent the divisional H.Q. and the staffs of two regiments to the left bank for reinforcements.

Gurtiev's division spent the day beating off enemy infantry and tank attacks in the area of the stadium.

Smekhotvorov's units were beating off similar attacks in the vicinity of Kazachya Street.

Gurtiev's division was in a difficult position, with both of its flanks under attack.

In the evening a German battalion penetrated as far as Severnaya Street. On the sector occupied by Guriev's and Batyuk's divisions, all attacks were beaten off. In the day's fighting on October 17, forty tanks were put out of action and nearly 2,000 enemy infantry were killed.

On the evening of October 17 the Member of the Military Council, Gurov, reported to me that Comrade Manuilski wanted to come to the city to visit us, and that he, Gurov, had given his agreement. I categorically protested and pressed Gurov to withdraw his permission. Gurov would not give way. Then I said:

'Manuilski is too valuable a person to risk his life. He cannot help us by coming here.'

Gurov agreed.

How Comrade Manuilski found out about this I do not know, but it came up in 1947. Manuilski was on his way back from America to Moscow via Berlin. We met at the aerodrome, or more precisely at a dinner we arranged for him. Sitting next to me at the table he reproached me for a long time for not letting him visit my command post on the right bank of the Volga.

I answered:

'If I had let you visit us in 1942, I doubt whether we would have had the opportunity for this conversation today.'

Bitter fighting for the Krasny Oktyabr factory lay ahead. Our reconnaissance told us so. With the agreement of Front

H.Q. we decided to transfer our command post to Banny Gully, near the railway bridge.

On the night of October 17 the Army staff officers together with the Army Military Council left their dug-outs, laden with documents and the equipment they needed to be able to continue their administrative work. On reaching Banny Gully we spent a long time searching for a place for the command post, and several times came under fire from enemy machine-gunners. It was obvious that there was nowhere here suitable for the command post, and we had to go some half a mile further south and set to work on the bank of the Volga itself, in the open. We were barely half a mile from Mamayev Kurgan, our front line. Had Paulus known this he would certainly not have hesitated to send in two or three dozen dive-bombers to wipe us off the face of the earth.

This was our last command post; we did not leave it until the Battle of Stalingrad was over.

Colonel Kamynin, whom I had sent to the northern group, sent us some information on October 18. The position there was difficult but not hopeless. The enemy troops which had broken through into Spartanovka had been destroyed. Gorokhov's group was defending positions on the northern outskirts of Rynok, on the western and southern outskirts of Spartanovka, including the landing-stage near the mouth of the River Mechetka. This information reassured us somewhat: we were not so alarmed about the Army's right flank.

The main fighting on the 18th continued to be for the Barrikady factory, and was spreading southward towards the Krasny Oktyabr factory. Lyudnikov's, Zholudev's and Gurtiev's units were beating off attacks night and day on the Barrikady factory and Sculpturny Park from the north. At 3 p.m. the enemy broke through our lines south of Derevenskaya Street and reached the Volga. The 650th Infantry Regiment counter-attacked, destroyed the Germans who had broken through, and restored the position.

In the evening enemy infantry and tanks, attacking along Tramvaynaya Street, broke through our lines and reached the railway west of the Barrikady factory. The workers' detachment in the factory fought bitterly, and continued to do so for several days. At the end of the fighting only five men in the detachment remained alive.

206

From daybreak Smekhotvorov's units repulsed German infantry and tank attacks from the west. At 11.30 a.m. the division's right flank was overrun. Gurtiev's units in the vicinity of Sculpturny Park were obviously threatened with encirclement. In order to prevent this, for the first time in the entire fighting for the city I had to order the withdrawal of some of my own troops, in this case for some 200–300 yards, towards the Volga. By doing this we straightened out the front and strengthened our positions.

There was no reference to withdrawal in the order. It said: 'At 4.00 on October 19 Gurtiev's division will occupy defence positions along the sector Sormovskaya Street, Tupikovskaya Street . . .', which meant moving back from Sculpturny Park. In our orders we could not and must not use such words as 'withdrawal' or 'retreat', so that the other commanders would not think that they could withdraw to new positions with the approval of Army or Front H.Q.

I remember with what bitterness I signed this order, how dear every yard of earth west of the Volga was to us.

In the fighting on October 18 the enemy lost eighteen tanks and nearly three battalions of infantry.

We felt not only that our own ranks were thinning and our strength ebbing, but that the enemy could not go indefinitely launching his insane attacks. They were being drowned in their own blood. The enemy's material resources were also being exhausted. The Luftwaffe's sorties had dropped from three thousand to one thousand a day.

Nevertheless, despite his tremendous losses, Paulus did not give up the idea of taking the city. Some inexplicable force drove the enemy to go on attacking. Fresh infantry and panzer units appeared and, regardless of losses, they rolled forward towards the Volga. It seemed as though Hitler was prepared to destroy the whole of Germany for the sake of this one city.

But the Germans were no longer what they had been. Even the fresh units and reinforcements now knew the meaning of battle by the Volga. The following extract is from the diary of a non-commissioned officer in the 226th Regiment of the 79th Infantry Division, Josef Schaffstein:

Gorodishche, near Stalingrad. This is real hell! . . . I

saw the Volga for the first time today. Our attacks are having no success; we began our attack successfully, then retreated . . . Heavy bombing at night. I thought our end had come . . . Our next attack again unsuccessful. Bitter fighting. The enemy is firing from all sides, from every hole. You must not let yourself be seen . . . At night there is no peace from Russian aircraft, artillery and 'katyushi'. Heavy losses.

It is clear from these notes that the German soldiers had begun to understand that they had not been sent here on a pleasure trip.

The fighting at Stalingrad showed the Herculean strength of the Soviet citizen and soldier. The more the enemy raged, the more tenaciously and courageously did our soldiers fight. The soldier who survived strove to defend himself and his sector of the front; he was taking revenge for himself and his dead comrades. There were many cases when lightly-wounded soldiers were ashamed not only to be evacuated across the Volga, but even to go to the nearest dressing-station to have a wound attended to.

On October 19 and 20 the Army beat off attacks on Spartanovka, and on the Barrikady and Krasny Oktyabr factories. These two days and nights of fighting produced no real results for the enemy.

But we knew and saw that in the area of the Barrikady settlement and Hill 107.5 the enemy was building up strength. He was getting ready to strike another blow with fresh forces. We had to calculate our strength very carefully, so that we could beat off the constant enemy attacks and economize or build up forces to repulse a new major attack.

We had to make up our losses at the expense of our Army's and divisions' rear units. Groups of Army H.Q. officers went to the rear. They left one man in charge of every five to seven horses and cut down the workshop and stores staff. They formed draft companies of tailors, cobblers and other craftsmen and sent them across to the right bank. These men, with little or no training, on arrival in the city, soon became 'craftsmen' in street fighting.

'Approaching the right bank is terrifying,' they would say.

'But as soon as you set foot on it, the terror goes. We knew only one thing—there was no land beyond the Volga for us, and to stay alive we had to destroy the enemy.'

Fresh German units appeared on October 21 and 22, and they were thrown against Smekhotvorov's and Guriev's divisions along Communalnaya and Tsentralnaya Streets. From this time on the fighting for the Barrikady and Krasny Oktyabr factories and our ferry across the Volga began to grow more and more fierce.

Enemy aircraft again stepped up their sorties to 2,000 a day.

On these two days the enemy lost fifteen tanks and more than a thousand infantry. The German positions came so close to ours that we began to use flame-throwers, which, throwing a jet of flame for a hundred yards, burnt everything they hit.

On October 23 the enemy threw into the battle the reinforced 79th Infantry Division together with heavy tanks. They began an attack under mass cover from the air. The main attack was along Tsentralnaya and Karuselnaya Streets towards the Krasny Oktyabr factory. The centre of gravity of the fighting now moved to the sector from the Barrikady factory to Banny Gully.

In the evening, at the cost of heavy losses, the enemy managed to break through to Stalnaya Street (near the mechanical bakery) and advance along the factory's railway, piled up with broken trucks. A group of enemy tommy-gunners, nearly a company strong, got through to the north-west of the Krasny Oktyabr factory.

At dusk our artillery made a heavy attack on enemy tanks and infantry which had concentrated at the approaches to the factory.

The enemy's first attacks on the morning of October 24 were beaten back with heavy losses for him. The Germans then threw in their second line and their reserves. At 4:30 p.m. they succeeded in overrunning the central and south-west parts of the Barrikady factory.

At 6 p.m. enemy infantry and tanks reached the command

post of the 895th Infantry Regiment. The Regimental Commander, Major Ustinov, got in touch with us by radio, and asked for our 'katyushi' to fire a salvo at his command post. 'There is no other way out,' were the final words of his request.

The 'katyushi' regiment fired an immediate salvo on the enemy concentration round Ustinov's command post. Ustinov himself remained unhurt.

Some two enemy infantry battalions and seventeen tanks approached along Krasnopresnenskaya Street towards the north-west gates of the Krasny Oktyabr factory. The 117th Regiment of Guriev's division waged a bitter battle with them, but small groups of German tommy-gunners managed to get through into the factory workshops.

At the end of the day we were told that the command post of the 1045th Regiment had been destroyed by a direct hit from a bomb. The Commander of the regiment, Lieutenant-Colonel Timoshin, had been killed.

From the information that came in to us and from the course of the fighting, it was clear that both the enemy's and our own strength was running out. In ten days of fighting the Germans had again split our Army, inflicted heavy losses on us and taken the Tractor factory, but had been unable to wipe out the northern group and the Army's main forces.

The enemy did not have the men and resources to do this. He had had to bring up reserves. The Army was face to face with not only fresh German divisions, but also individual regiments and battalions hurriedly brought up by air. But even that was not enough.

Paulus could not repeat an attack on the scale of the one on October 14. To do that he would have had to have a lengthy breathing-space of ten to fifteen days in order to bring up large quantities of shells, bombs and tanks. We knew, however, that in the region of Gumrak and Voroponovo there were two enemy reserve divisions which could be brought into action. We reckoned that it would take between three and five days for these divisions also to spend themselves, and Paulus would have to relax his pressure. We would then be able to pull ourselves together, regroup our forces and consolidate our positions. But how were we going to survive those three to five days, when we had such small forces at our disposal? The 37th, 308th and 193rd Divisions existed in reality only as numbers—they had only a few hundred infantrymen left between them. After holding off the enemy's most powerful attack we were so weak that we doubted whether we would be able to beat off attacks by fresh enemy reserves, but everyone, as before, was prepared to fight to the last man and the last round. Our fighting spirit was higher than ever. If anyone had ordered us for some reason or other to leave the city, all of us, soldiers, officers, generals, would have treated the order as a fake or as a betrayal and would not have crossed the Volga.

From October 24 the Germans resorted less frequently to night attacks, obviously feeling that the results did not justify them; they decided to use the night for rest and preparations for the next day's fighting. We decided, on the other hand, that we would continue to operate at night, using our storm groups and surprise attacks by air and artillery. This would upset the enemy's preparations and keep them on the go. We felt at home in the dark.

On October 25 the enemy renewed his attacks along the whole of our front, throwing in substantial forces. His attack on the Spartanovka settlement, using an infantry division with tanks, created a difficult position on the front occupied by the northern group.

Backed up from the air, the enemy's tanks and infantry pushed back units of the 149th Brigade and occupied an area south of the Gumrak-Vladimirovka railway and the centre of Spartanovka settlement. Gorokhov's northern group was helped by ships of the Volga fleet, whose artillery caused the enemy heavy losses.

Repeated attacks by the enemy on the 26th and 27th brought him no success. The northern group, with the artillery support of the vessels of the Volga fleet, threw the enemy out of the Spartanovka settlement.

On October 27, Major Kachmarov, Chief of Staff of the 149th Brigade, was killed by a direct hit from a shell.

Units of Lyudnikov's and Gurtiev's divisions, on the Army's central sector, were fighting bitterly in defence of the Barrikady factory. The Germans' freshly-brought-up regiments were obviously incapable of close fighting. Even though we had only a handful of men in the workshops of the factory, the enemy, with five times as many, could make no progress on the sector occupied by our storm groups.

Paulus was throwing fresh reserves into the battle the whole time. We had none.

On October 27 the left flank of Lyudnikov's division and a regiment of Gurtiev's division were overrun by the enemy. Enemy tommy-gunners occupied Mezenskaya and Tuvinskaya Streets and began to fire on the area of our last ferry. At the same time units of Smekhotvorov's and Guriev's divisions were beating off attacks by the German 79th Infantry Division, whose main thrust was towards the Krasny Oktyabr factory.

German tommy-gunners infiltrated through these depleted units. They reached the 39th Division's H.Q. and hand-grenades were thrown into Guriev's dug-out. When I heard this I rushed a company of the Army's H.Q. guard to Guriev's aid. With a rapid attack they pushed the tommy-gunners back from the divisional H.Q. and, following them, reached the Krasny Oktyabr factory, where they remained. We incorporated them into Guriev's division.

The enemy continued to attack the ferry and Krasny Oktyabr. The attacks were successfully beaten back until 3 p.m., when the Germans managed to occupy Mashinnaya Street.

On the sector between the Barrikady and Krasny Oktyabr factories, German tommy-gunners were only about 400 yards from the Volga. Our last ferry, therefore, was under enemy machine-gun fire. The gullies running westward from the Volga were under enemy machine-gun and artillery fire. To move along the bank you now had to get down on knees and elbows. This did not suit us. Our sappers soon managed to construct a double wooden fence across the gullies, filling up the holes with stones, to stop the bullets.

After nightfall on October 26 regiments of Sokolov's 45th Infantry Division began to reach the east bank of the Volga, sent by Front Command to join the 62nd Army. During that night we managed to ferry across only two battalions of the division; to avoid unnecessary losses, we turned the remainder back to Akhtuba.

I put the battalions which had been ferried across under the Commander of the 193rd Division. They took up positions between the Barrikady and Krasny Oktyabr factories. They were given the task of stopping the enemy from reaching the Volga and the ferry.

Presumably having found out that fresh forces had arrived in the factory area, the enemy spent virtually the whole day bombing the sector between the factories. Bombs of up to a ton were dropped on the battalions. Then, as always, after the air attack came enemy infantry, with thirty-five tanks. After the first attack failed, the enemy tried a second attack, then a third . . .

In the day's fighting the battalions lost half their men, but kept the enemy away from the Volga. In the evening, however, the enemy managed to press the left flank of these battalions, together with isolated groups of the 193rd Division's infantry, back to a position only 300 yards from the Volga.

In the evening the enemy also succeeded in occupying the northwest part of the Krasny Oktyabr factory. Stubborn fighting was going on here, and it continued for many days and weeks.

The forces of the 62nd Army had become so weak in the fighting from October 14–27 that we were unable to move a single detachment from the front line. Every soldier was doing the jobs of three, if not five, men. We knew that the enemy's losses were heavier than ours, and that his reserves were running out, but the initiative was still in his hands, and he still had broad room for manœuvre.

Paulus could still take troops from passive sectors of the front and throw them into battle against us. But we had no reserves whatsoever. The Army H.Q. virtually had no guard at all. There was not a man left in the Army's reserve regiment. I had kept back the sole training battalion of this regiment (which trained sergeants for the Army) till the last minute, but it was now fighting in the factory district.

The ferrying across the regiments of Sokolov's 45th Division was going slowly, very slowly. The 62nd Army's landing-stages had been blown up or gone up in flames. The regiments embarked on to the ferries away from the city (in the Akhtuba channel of the river, near Tumak), and set off into the Volga only at night and at great risk (at points under the very noses of enemy troops which had broken through to the Volga) in order to reach the Army's defence sector.

We would have to hold out for two or three days before Sokolov's 45th Division arrived in full. But where were we going to find forces with which to do so? Again we set about cutting down our staff in the various sections and services. We collected about a dozen men and put them together with thirty soldiers discharged from the medical centres by the bank of the Volga. And—oh joy!—we had found, or rather had dragged from the battlefield, three broken-down tanks— two light tanks and one with a flame-thrower. We had had them rapidly repaired, and I decided to give the enemy a 'shock'—to send the three tanks and fifty infantrymen into an attack. The area of the attack was to be the junction point between Smekhotvorov's and Guriev's divisions along Smarkandskaya Street, where the enemy had almost reached the Volga.

Weinrub, my deputy in charge of armoured units, spent the whole night taking these tanks up and down the steep bank, trying to find a good base from which to launch the attack. The counter-attack began in the early morning, before dawn. It was supported by artillery from the left bank, and by Yerokhin's 'katyushi' regiment. We did not manage to advance very far, but the results were impressive. The tank with the flame-thrower sent three German tanks up in flames, and our two light tanks overwhelmed the enemy in two trenches, in which our infantrymen immediately took up position.

We know that the enemy's eyes grew wide with fear. The Germans talked their heads off about Russian tanks on the radio. They went on about our tanks all day, obviously in an attempt to pacify the Supreme Command. In this way, we gained a whole day on this sector. On the remaining sectors of the Army's front no great changes took place in these two days. In the Barrikady factory area, after repeated attacks, the enemy managed to advance to Novoselskaya Street. Here isolated groups of German tommy-gunners managed to reach the Volga, but were destroyed in hand-to-hand fighting on the bank.

Units of Lyudnikov's and Gurtiev's divisions beat off seven attacks in these two days.

Batyuk's division and the 13th Guards Division beat off hourly attacks on and to the south of Mamayev Kurgan. We used our flamethrowers.

On the evening of October 29 the battle began to die down, and on October 30 there were only exchanges of fire: the enemy was utterly exhausted.

We knew that the Soviet troops were winning the battle.

Paulus was no longer capable of repeating an attack on the scale of the one we had just withstood, and in which we had at times been within a hair's breadth of catastrophe.

The anniversary of the October Revolution approached. We expected Hitler would try to cast a shadow over our celebrations by a new offensive against the city: he still had reserves at Gumrak and Voroponovo Stations. But this no longer frightened us. We knew that to renew his offensive the enemy would need time and strength, and time was on our side. No one told us of the new events that were taking shape on the front. But I have already mentioned how in wartime even in the most isolated and cut-off units there are signals which nobody organizes, a grapevine. By one channel and another it brought news to us of big troop movements towards the Volga, of the arrival of Comrades Vasilievski, Voronov and other representatives of G.H.Q. at the front.

It was quite clear that they did not come and go just for the sake of admiring the Volga. We felt that a powerful counter-attack was being prepared, but none of us knew where or when.

We could not sit with our arms folded, waiting for some unspecified event to take place—our last ferry was under enemy machine-gun fire, and we were holding on to our positions by the skin of our teeth. We had to protect our landing-stage in the vicinity of the Krasny Oktyabr factory from enemy machine-gun and tommy-gun fire, so that ships of the Volga fleet could be moored and unloaded, if only at night. After the 45th Infantry Division had been brought across, therefore, the Army Military Council decided to counter-attack. The order stated that the main attack would be delivered by the 45th Infantry Division in the strip between the Barrikady and Krasny Oktyabr factories.

The aim was as follows: after a thirty-minute artillery preparation, the first line of attacking troops, keeping up close to the barrage, and not lingering over individual enemy firing positions and small groups, was to reach the railway line. Remaining pockets of enemy troops were to be mopped up by regimental and divisional reserves.

Guriev's division was ordered to attack at the ends of the strip it was defending and also reach the railway line.

All attacking units were asked to advance boldly and rapidly.

How on earth, the unwitting reader may ask, could the 62nd Army Command be considering on one day that it was within a hair's breadth of catastrophe, and then on the next day decide to counter-attack?

Yes, that is how things are in war, and particularly in the kind of situation we were in.

Imagine the 62nd Army, defending a narrow strip of land along the bank of the Volga. If it did not use the opportunity to hit the enemy, now exhausted, and push him back even 100–200 yards away from the bank, the Army might find itself in the river. Could we really sit dangling our legs in the Volga and wait for the enemy to recover? Could we really let the enemy see that we were capable only of defending and spinning round on the same spot, like a tethered animal, while the hunter reloaded his gun? For us it would have been lunacy to wait and see what the enemy was going to do, and not to try to alter the position at least a fraction in our favour.

Our counter-attack took place on October 31, and in my view was a great success. In some places we advanced a hundred or so yards, occupied the left side of Novoselskaya Street and the western fringe of the park, and in the Krasny Oktyabr factory won back the open-hearth, calibration and profiling shops and finished products warehouse. But the most important thing was that we had shown the enemy that we could not only defend ourselves, but attack and win back what we had lost. And finally, the last blow, at the end of the fighting from October 14–31, was delivered by us, not by the enemy. This was the moral victory which the 45th Division brought us. Its success was no accident. The regiments of this division had rich traditions. The division bore the name of its first commander, a hero of the Civil War, Nikolay Shchors, who commanded its regiments in the days of the famous marches to liberate the Ukraine.

At the time of the Battle of Stalingrad the Shchors division was commanded by Vasili Pavlovich Sokolov, a young lieutenant-colonel, later a general. He and his closest deputies—Mozheyko, Bakanov, Serov and others—quickly mastered the conditions and needs of street fighting, and created small storm groups. It is true that this division took little part in the defence of the city, but on the other hand it gained valuable experience of offensive fighting in the city. The division went right through to Berlin. The experience of battle here at the Volga helped it to tackle successfully the task of storming such cities as Zaporozhe, Odessa, Lublin, Lodz, Poznan and Berlin. The division's storm groups were irresistible in city fighting. They could smash any defence and emerged victorious from the most difficult situations.

CHAPTER VIII

PAULUS'S LAST OFFENSIVE

PAULUS had presumably begun preparations for his next offensive before November 1, but in the thick of the fierce fighting we had not noticed the fact. Now, however, when the fighting had died down, and when our reconnaissance planes were able to penetrate as far as the enemy's rear formations, it became clear that the battle for the city was not yet over. Hitler obviously could not reconcile himself to the collapse of his entire strategic plan for 1942 and would insist on Stalingrad being taken, in spite of everything.

What was it that drove the Germans towards the Volga deep into the autumn of 1942? There can be only one answer. Hitler was afraid to lose his military and political authority with the Axis powers, and he therefore acted on the premise of better late than never. To boost Nazi Germany's undermined prestige—that was his aim. The German generals, therefore, like bulls, put their horns up against the ruins by the Volga, and tried with idiotic stubbornness to carry out the Führer's orders. They did not notice that we had already set a trap for the German armies.

The Front Commander, Colonel-General Yeremenko, in a telephone conversation I had with him, said that the Germans were planning to discontinue the offensive against the 62nd Army, that they had already started withdrawing forces from the Army's front to the rear and flanks. We understood this to mean that G.H.Q., whose plans Yeremenko of course knew about, in preparing its counter-attack, had decided at any price, principally by active operations in the city, to pin down the enemy group at the Volga. An attack by one corps of the 64th Army southward from the area of Beketovka, ostensibly with the aim of helping the city's defenders, was calculated purely to attract the enemy's attention.

German General Hans Doerr, in his book *Campaign to Stalingrad*, describes this period in the fighting as follows:

> The Supreme Command (Hitler), however, wanted to 'finish off the battle for Stalingrad, clearing the enemy from the remaining areas of the city', as the orders of the Army High Command put it.
>
> The importance of this task was now tactical. The propaganda of both sides attached strategic importance to it. As long as Russians were fighting west of the Volga Stalin could talk about the heroic defence of his city. Hitler could not rest until his troops seized the last patch of earth called Stalingrad. Politics, prestige, propaganda and emotions had the upper hand over the sober analysis of the generals.

Herr Doerr, of course, is exaggerating.

By blaming Hitler (a fashionable pursuit of late among a whole galaxy of West Germans bent on revenge), he is trying to exonerate himself and his colleagues, who, not seeing the threat hanging over them, not only did not think of withdrawing their forces from the bank of the Volga, but

218

even brought up fresh reserves from the rear for a new offensive against the city. This happened at the very moment when the 62nd Army's artillery on the left bank was gradually being removed. This one sign alone—weaker fire from our batteries at the other side of the Volga—should have shown them that our attack was being prepared elsewhere. But in their malicious and wild hatred of the defenders of the city the Germans could see nothing but the walls of the factory district towering above them. In the meantime, correctly understanding the intentions of Front Command and G.H.Q., we prepared for the battle ahead, so as to entice as many enemy divisions to the city as we could.

It is true that with the forces at the 62nd Army's disposal, after the extremely bitter fighting in the factory district, it was impossible to launch immediate offensive operations on a large scale. However, launching active operations in the opening days of November, we began to increase the area we occupied on the right bank of the Volga.

I must mention the fact that some of our responsible Army H.Q. staff believed that on the anniversary of the October Revolution the German Command would repeat its attack and try once again to throw us into the Volga. They felt, therefore, that we should not undertake active operations and dissipate our strength. The Army Military Council rejected these analyses by the operations staff. We did, of course, expect the enemy to attack, but not on the same scale as on October 14. We were convinced that active operations on our part, even using our last energeies, would lure German armies into the city and do what our Supreme Command needed.

We used all our experience, ability and cheek. Our storm groups gave the enemy no rest by night or day. They seized individual houses and whole areas, and forced the enemy to use up his strength and bring up reserves. The Germans sat in the houses they occupied as if on powder-barrels, expecting to be attacked and blown up at any minute.

We engaged the enemy in battle night and day along the Army's entire front. General Krylov, the Army Chief of Staff, with the agreement of the Military Council, of course, pressed Generals Rodimtsev and Batyuk, whose sector was

219

the quietest, to organize constant reconnaissance, attacks with storm groups and sorties to capture prisoners.

We were preparing at the same time to beat off the new enemy offensive. Our reconnaissance kept systematic watch on the approach and concentration of German forces in the vicinity of the Barrikady and Krasny Oktyabr factories. The increasingly cold weather seemed to drive the Germans towards the city, where the 62nd Army was still operating; they wanted to settle accounts with it as rapidly as possible and shelter peacefully in the warm cellars. On November 4 I wrote in my diary: 'In the next few days the enemy will continue his fierce attacks. He will use fresh forces—up to two divisions. It is obvious, however, that he is making his last efforts.'

Carrying out active operations with small storm groups, the Army managed to build up some reserves. On the left bank of the Volga we had two infantry regiments and the H.Q. staff of Gorishny's division (having been sent there to be brought back up to strength) and the 92nd Infantry Brigade, which had been reinforced with seamen arrived from the Far East.

When we had ferried these units across the city we decided we would regroup our forces. We decided to put Gorishny's two regiments along the front between Lyudnikov's and Sokolov's divisions, south of the Barrikady factory (in fact we did only half of this, managing to ferry across only one of the regiments); to incorporate the whole rank and file and junior officers of Zholudev's division into the 118th Regiment, which we would leave in its present positions under the operational charge of Lyudnikov; to transfer the whole rank and file and junior officers of Gurtiev's division to Lyudnikov as reinforcements; to send Zholudev's and Gurtiev's divisional and regimental H.Q. staffs across to the left bank, and put our artillery on the left bank directly under the Army's Artillery Commander; to disband the Army H.Q. guard (formerly the Army's emergency training regiment), and transfer the personnel and weapons of this battalion to Guriev's infantry division as reinforcements; and to move Smekhotvorov's division back into a second line of defence, to protect the ferry.

All the divisions had the general task of conducting limited operations to expand the bridgehead occupied by the Army, to advance westward by not less than 80—100 yards a day, so as to clear the Barrikady and Krasny Oktyabr factories of the enemy by November 6. Every advance, however, insignificant, was to be slowly, surely and reliably consolidated.

In the special order issued in this connection there is mention of two companies of tanks. They appeared as a result of the self-sacrificing labour of the repair mechanics who, in spite of being shot at and bombed, were bringing broken-down tanks back into action.

On the days preceding the anniversary, the Luftwaffe noticeably increased its activity. For days the enemy's reconnaissance aircraft hung over the heads of our troops, and after tracking down important targets (such as command posts and infantry concentrations) called in the bombers, which made their attacks in groups of forty to fifty. The Commander of the 149th Infantry Brigade, Colonel Bolvinov, a man of iron will and initiative, was fatally wounded. He was buried in the Krasnaya Sloboda area. His name will always live in the memories and hearts of the men of the 62nd Army. He was a soldier at heart, lived in a dug-out like a soldier, and died a hero's death. On November 5 a direct hit from a bomb killed the H.Q. staff of the 895th Regiment, including the Regimental Commander, Ustinov. Our answer was to increase the night activities of our storm groups. The Siberians of Batyuk's division distinguished themselves particularly. They waited till darkness fell, set off, captured dug-outs and pill-boxes, wiped out the garrisons inside them, and so, step by step, gradually extended our territory.

Some people might be wondering what Rodimtsev's 13th Guards Division was doing. Why have I not been saying anything about it? The reason is that our press, describing the progress of the fighting by the Volga, most of the time wrote primarily about Rodimtsev's division.

I want in no way to play down the part played by Rodimtsev's division, which from September 14—25 bore the main brunt of the German attack. For ten days it fought with unsurpassed tenacity. Let me say frankly that had it not been for Rodimtsev's division the city would have fallen completely into enemy hands approximately in the middle of September.

But on September 26 Paulus's army moved its main attack northward, to Mamayev Kurgan, the factories and workers' settlements. Other, new divisions went into action on our side: those of Gorishny, Batyuk, Guriev, Smekhotvorov, Gurtiev, Zholudev, Lyudnikov and Sokolov, Gorokhov's brigade, and others. Rodimtsev's division was then not involved in the fighting on the main sector; the sector it was on remained passive until the end of the battle.

To Rodimtsev's quiet sector rushed correspondents, photographers, writers and journalists. They could not get through to other sectors because fierce fighting was going on there, and we would not have allowed them there anyway. The majority of newspaper men therefore could only visit the 13th Division's sector and use its now somewhat out-of-date military material. That is why readers were sometimes made familiar only with the operations of Rodimtsev's division.

I hope Vasili Grossman will not be offended if I reveal a secret. He wrote an extraordinarily interesting reportage[1] entitled *The Line of the Main Drive,* about the fighting in the factory district during October, but he collected the facts about the operations of Gurtiev's 308th Division when that division was already back on the left bank of the Volga.

I hope Nikolay Virta will not be offended. He writes that he lived for about a month on the right bank of the Volga, in the city itself. This is true. But I would like to explain more precisely that he did so in December and January, when the enemy was already encircled and Virta could walk freely up and down the Volga bank, collecting the material that interested him about the battle that had been fought out there.

I must be true to history and, as the former commander of the 62nd Army, I have no wish to belittle the importance of any division or unit which took part in the battle by the Volga. Do the men of Sologub's infantry division, which fought throughout the battle in the city in the direction of the enemy's main attack, and was attacked hundreds of times by the enemy's numerically superior forces, really not deserve

---

[1] For extensive extracts see Werth, A., *The Year of Stalingrad,* London, 1946, pp. 277-281.

the same glory and honour as others? Was General Smekhotvorov's infantry division, which was utterly smashed and mutilated, but courageously went on fighting against superior German numbers, not heroic? I do not exaggerate when I say that in the 62nd Army we had no bad divisions, there were no units with a poor fighting spirit, because in the blazing city we did not suffer cowards, we had no room for them.

The temperature dropped sharply. The local inhabitants told us about conditions on the Volga: in November appears 'sludge,' small pieces of ice, which then turn into large pieces, floating down the river. In the period of floating ice communications across the Volga are halted, as shipping cannot get through it.

Those of us who live in the north of Russia can imagine floating ice on small rivers in the spring, when the spring waters break up the ice. This usually happens at the end of March, sometimes in April, when the rooks fly in; everyone is waiting for the warm weather, the flowers, the beginning of work in the fields. In autumn or at the beginning of winter, all the rivers I had known up to 1942 usually somehow or other acquired a coating of ice unnoticed, as if they were falling asleep under the thicker and thicker cover lying over them. Sometimes in the evening you see the quietly flowing water of a river, and in the morning you find it is ice-bound.

I used to see this on the River Oka and other rivers in the Moscow and Tula districts where I spent my short childhood.

What happens on the Volga in autumn is quite different: it takes weeks, months, to ice over. The temperature of the air drops to 10 degrees centigrade below zero, but the Volga is still free of ice, steam rises from it. The temperature drops to 12 degrees below, and small pieces of ice appear. Finally, when the temperature is 15 degrees below, the small pieces of ice begin to be replaced by large ice-floes, and then a solid mass of ice moves and moves without end, without stop. At this stage not even armoured boats can cross the Volga, and only individual bold spirits with boat-hooks in their hands, jumping from floe to floe, can cross over to the opposite bank without a boat. But this was something that only our desperate and courageous spirits who were natives of the Volga region could manage. Others, however courageous and strong they might be, even the seamen from the Far East, could not do it.

Paulus was possibly waiting for precisely this moment to begin his new offensive. Our reconnaissance brought in documents from dead officers and men of the 44th Infantry Division, which had previously been in the Voroponovo area, as a reserve for the main forces of the 6th Field Army. This meant that fresh forces for the new offensive were already in position. We were going to have to fight on two fronts— against the enemy and the Volga.

Foreseeing possible complications, the Army Military Council had previously given our rear headquarters a strict time-table for deliveries to the units operating in the city, and had asked primarily for large-scale reinforcements of men and material to be brought up, because without them the Army would perish; the second priority was to be food, and the third priority warm clothing. We were deliberately going on hunger strike and were prepared to put up with the frost, but, aware of the attack that the enemy had prepared, we could not do without men and ammunition. Shortage of ammunition in this situation meant certain death.

For some reason or other the Army and Front bodies in charge of supplies could not understand this. Our main need was also under-estimated by the Deputy Chief of Staff of the Red Army's rear, General Vasili Ivanovich Vinogradov. He arrived at the left bank to help the Army overcome its imminent difficulties, but his intervention in the job of supplying our Army was more of a hindrance than a help. Having firmly decided that unless the Army had a store of provisions and winter clothing it could not carry out its military tasks, General Vinogradov obviously could not get to grips with our real difficulties. 'In defence, the important thing is grub,' soldiers say in jest. Vinogradov, as we saw, took them seriously.

We needed a lot of ammunition, the more the better in fact, because knowing the enemy's intention to wipe out the troops defending the city as rapidly as possible, we could not, and had no right to, tell the men to use ammunition sparingly in battle. Our soldiers made sure they always had a proper store of grenades, mortar bombs, bullets and shells. They said

224

quite openly that they were prepared to tolerate hunger and cold, as long as they were not left without ammunition.

But General Vinogradov made the 62nd Army's rear units send us warm clothing, felt boots and provisions instead of ammunition. Surplus clothing therefore began to accumulate in the stores of the 62nd Army's units.

Such 'help' boded no good. Through the Chief of Staff of the 62nd Army's rear I sent General Vinogradov several telegrams with a categorical demand to stop interfering with the Army's supplies. But there was no stopping him: jerseys, caps with ear-flaps and felt boots were sent to us as priority cargoes. I had to turn to the Front Military Council . . . Only N. S. Khrushchev's intervention stopped the flood of ear-flaps and felt boots. Vinogradov soon went away and we breathed a sigh of relief.

I put Spasov, Sokolov and Zinoviev in charge of stocktaking, distribution and accumulation of ammunition. They spent the whole time in the city and reported to me personally every day on the arrival of cargoes. The decision as to how much to distribute and how much to hold in reserve was submitted to the Army Military Council for endorsement.

Our soldiers, as we have seen, had to carry the supplies by hand, as we had no horses or vehicles; now they would have carried the boats themselves to the firing line if necessary.

In addition, our unit and formation commanders did not count on 'centralized' supplies, and accumulated stocks of ammunition by other means: they selected officers and men who had formerly been fishermen or sailors, who made their own rafts and boats, and obtaining grenades and shells from the Army and Front stores, ferried them across to the right bank.

Of course, all this was not without risk. Very often in the darkness boats did not land at the right place or struck an ice-floe and met with disaster.

There were many cases when an ice-bound boat would come under fire from enemy machine-gunners, who fired frantically at helpless targets. We had to organize rescue teams. They were on duty at the bank at nights in boats, with barge-poles, cables and ropes, and as soon as a distress signal went up they would rush out to help.

So, for several days before the period of heavy drifting ice and the beginning of the new enemy offensive, the Army laid in ammunition. In the same way we laid in reasonable supplies of provisions, and on the anniversary of the October Revolution we treated the soldiers to Siberian meat dumplings. I also had my own secret store. Colonel Spasov was in charge of it. In it was the Army's emergency stores—about twelve tons of chocolate. I reckoned that in a difficult moment, by giving out half a bar per man at a time, we could survive a week or two, until the Volga had frozen over and regular supplies could be delivered.

On November 11, at 6:30 a.m., after air and artillery preparation, the enemy launched his offensive. Taking part in it were five enemy infantry divisions (the 389th, 305th, 79th, 100th and 44th) and two panzer divisions (the 24th and 14th), reinforced by individual units of the 294th Infantry Division brought in by plane from Rossosh, and by units of the 161st Infantry Division, also brought in by plane from Millerovo.

The three-mile front along which the offensive was launched ran from Volkhovstroyevskaya Street to Banny Gully. Although the majority of these German divisions were not up to strength (they had been given a sound thrashing in the recent fighting), the strength of the enemy's formations was astonishing.

Paulus was obviously intending to crush Lyudnikov's, Gorishny's, Sokolov's, Guriev's and Batyuk's divisions with one blow, and reach the Volga.

Exceptionally stubborn fighting went on all day for every yard of ground, for every brick and stone. Fighting with hand grenades and bayonets went on for several hours. At the same time our northern group under Colonel Gorokhov counter-attacked from the railway bridge at the mouth of the Mechetka, southward towards the Tractor factory.

On Mamayev Kurgan Batyuk's division clashed head-on with the attacking enemy forces.

The factory chimneys were tumbling down under air bombing and artillery fire. The enemy's main attack was clearly being made at the junction point of Lyudnikov's and Gorishny's infantry divisions. The 118th Guards Infantry

Regiment, which the previous day had had 250 infantrymen, by noon had only six left. The Regimental Commander was seriously wounded.

At 11.30 a.m. the Germans threw in their reserves, and their infantry and tanks overran our lines on the right flank of the 241st Infantry Regiment of Gorishny's division, and reached the Volga along a front of about 550-650 yards. The Army had been split for a third time, and Lyudnikov's division was cut off from the main body of the Army.

But the Army held its positions on the other sectors. Paulus had been unable to capitalize on his superior strength, and had not achieved what he intended. He had not thrown the 62nd Army into the icy Volga.

The enemy's new offensive, as we had reason to expect, coincided with the appearance of heavy floating ice on the Volga. Boats of the Volga fleet could not reach us by day or night from Akhtuba or Tumak. We were finally and for a long time cut off from the left bank. In spite of the difficulty of the position, spirits were not low in the Army. The enemy's long-awaited attack had not caught us unawares, and the first day of the battle had not brought Paulus any decisive results.

We could tell from documents taken from dead enemy soldiers that the Germans would not be able to keep up their attack for long, that they would be exhausted in two or three days. We felt that we were accomplishing our task properly: the enemy was not only not abandoning the city, but, bringing up fresh forces, was again crawling into the trap which, we sensed, would soon be sprung.

From telephone conversations I had with Front Command I knew that they were satisfied with our tenacious resistance. However, the 62nd Army still had trials of no small order to endure: on the morning of November 12 the enemy regrouped his forces and brought up more reserves, which meant that another attack was on its way. And the attack came at noon that day. Fighting flared up along the whole of the Army's front. German soldiers, drunk or mad, came on and on. The Far East seamen who had come to reinforce Gorishny's infantry division, showed the enemy what was what and how the famous Red Navy men could fight. The petrol tanks on Tuvinskaya Street changed hands several times. In the heat of battle the Red Navy men threw off their greatcoats and in their singlets and hats beat off the attacks and then went on to the offensive themselves. The fighting in the Krasny Oktyabr and Barrikady factories and on Mamayev Kurgan was no less fierce. We now felt that our men had become warriors that no force could defeat.

In the afternoon telephone communication with Batyuk's divisional command post on Mamayev Kurgan was broken. A signaller, called Titayev, went out to repair the line. After a short while the line was working again, the break had been repaired, but Titayev himself did not return. He was lying motionless on the edge of a shell-hole, with the two ends of the wire pressed together in his teeth. The signallers who found him described how his teeth were tightly clamped together. Death had not prevented this courageous signaller from carrying out his instructions. It was as if, dead, he continued to fight the Germans. A song was soon written about him, embodying the feelings and experiences of the troops. The words, as later became known, were written by the correspondent of *Komsomolskaya Pravda* at the front, A. Gutorovykh. Though many of the lines are imperfect, I reproduce it in full, as it was sung at the time by Titayev's comrades:

SONG OF TITAYEV

The Major sent for the signallers
One frosty night. 'My lads,' said he,
'There's an urgent job that has to be done
To help to smash the enemy.

The line is broken. For our regiments' sake,
Through blizzards howl, it must be repaired.
Someone must crawl near the enemy lines,
And to battle with death must be prepared'.

'We've already had forty lives, here goes!'
Said Vasili Titayev, and shouldered his pack.
The Komsomol lad said farewell to his friends.
Behind him the blizzard covered his track.

A shell had cut the wire. He took
The ends in his teeth; fate was kind.
Then machine-guns fired from a nearby hill,
And another shell blew up behind.

It seemed to him he could hear the cranes.
His eyes looked far, far away—
Over the bodies blizzards raged,
Under snow and blood his Russia lay.

The snow was deep; he kneeled; the wires
Between his teeth in blood were pressed;
The skeleton paws of death walked by.
He fell with his head towards the west.

The Commander gave the order, 'Attack!'
Through Titayev's body. If only he
Could have seen our men take house after house,
And pursue the fleeing enemy!

Our assessment of the fighting, of the enemy's strength and
resources, was fully borne out. The Germans' desperate attack came to a halt on the evening of November 12. The
Germans' attacks on that day had been beaten off on all
sectors occupied by the Army. German losses in these two
days of fighting were colossal, running into thousands.

We sent Front H.Q. a whole sack full of documents
belonging to German officers and men killed in the fighting.

General Hans Doerr describes the fighting in November as
follows:

At the beginning of November, after receiving reinforcements, the Russian troops launched limited counter-attacks on various sectors. Although they brought no tan-
gible results, the very fact that they attacked showed that
the prospects of 'taking Stalingrad once and for all' had
not improved.

Nevertheless, Hitler ordered the offensive to continue
'with growing strength'. On November 10, the 51st Army
Corps launched an attack on the Lazur chemical works
(it was nicknamed "The Tennis Racquet because of the

shape of the railway round it) east of Mamayev Kurgan. The factory had already changed hands many times (many of our engineering troops took part in this attack). The Corps also attacked the Krasny Oktyabr engineering factory. The workers' settlement was occupied and scouting groups also managed to get into the workshops. On the second day, however, the offensive petered out. The attack was halted, and the bulk of the factory remained in Russian hands.

The overall results of these two months of fighting had been insignificant from the operational point of view, and inadequate from the tactical point of view. Apart from the strip along the bank of the river north of Stalingrad at Rynok, the 62nd Army occupied positions only north and south of the Barrikady works and on the southern outskirts of Stalingrad. But the most important sector, the landing-stage for the ferries between Krasnaya Sloboda and the city, continued to be held by the Russians.

The 6th Army's losses in men and material were the heaviest since the summer campaign began. The possibility of its operational use had grown significantly less.

There were a number of critical moments for the defending Russian troops during these weeks: October 14 and November 11 were particularly difficult days for them. Pressed back to a narrow strip of territory, having the Volga behind them, they had no choice but to surrender the city or stubbornly defend every inch of land west of the river. The 62nd Army could have received reinforcements if there had been more favourable conditions for communication with the opposite bank, but conditions grew better only after the beginning of the Russian counter-attack on December 16, when the Volga had frozen over; previously all communications with the rear had been by boat and ferry. The Russian Command tried to keep their strength for a counter-attack, setting themselves the task of using as few forces as possible to pin down as many German forces as possible in Stalingrad.

After such an appraisal of the situation, we can but say

that the Germans were right, but that they became wise only after the event!

Crack units of the German army, equipped with the most up-to-date weapons, took part in the fighting by the Volga. But our men fought to the death, and several times forced the enemy to withdraw his divisions from the front line so as to bring them back up to strength in men and material. But even the new divisions lasted only for three to five days in battle. In the fire of the Battle of Stalingrad they melted away like wax. Enemy units arriving from other fronts at Stalingrad were met with bombs, 'katyushi' salvos and the fire of our storm groups.

The Luftwaffe, which in October was flying up to three thousand sorties a day, by the beginning of November could not manage more than a thousand even on the days of the fiercest fighting. The Luftwaffe suffered enormous losses both in air battle and in particular on the ground at their aerodromes. The wreckage of hundreds of burnt-out and shattered enemy aircraft littered the steppe between the Volga and the Don.

On November 15, on the fourth day of the offensive, from Rynok in the north to Kuporosnoye in the south, the 62nd Army was faced by fifteen enemy divisions: the 14th, 16th and 24th Panzer, the 3rd, 29th and 60th Motorized, and the 94th, 389th, 305th, 79th, 100th, 295th, 71st, 371st and 297th Infantry Divisions. The basic task of all of them was to take the city.

All this powerful enemy group, supported by the 4th Air Force, had been fighting right by the Volga almost non-stop since August 23. And when, on November 11, eight days before the beginning of our general counter-offensive, Paulus threw all his forces into a last attack, along a three-mile front (from Volkhovstroyevskaya Street to Banny Gully) seven infantry divisions (the 389th, 305th, 79th, 100th, 44th, 294th and 161st) and two panzer divisions (the 14th and 24th) were involved. The remaining enemy divisions had been smashed by the troops of the Stalingrad Front. It was not for nothing that Hitler and his generals concentrated the units of nine divisions, one of which (the 294th) had been brought up by plane from Rossosh, and one (the 161st) from Millerovo, on a three-mile front.

But in November the German armies were no longer what they had been in August and September, and Paulus's shock force which went into action on November 11 and 12, was again smashed. The attack petered out on the second day, and could not be renewed—there was nowhere to bring up reinforcements from.

Having beaten off the enemy attack on November 11, in spite of the fact that the enemy had reached the Volga and split the Army a third time, all the defenders of the city, from the Members of the Army Military Council to the rank-and-file soldier, knew that this was the enemy's last offensive. We were convinced that he would not now be able to reorganize his forces quickly or obtain new material, particularly tanks, ammunition and fuel. Without them, especially without fresh equipment, he had no terror for us.

Everyone was convinced that the next attack, a powerful and irresistible one, would be made by our armies. The progress of the fighting since the second half of July had created all the conditions necessary for this.

Of course, after November 12, Paulus did not stop active operations; there was, and could be, no lull at the front. The German Supreme Command could not believe that the offensive had petered out. And the fighting which had begun several months ago continued as it were under its own momentum on all sectors of the front. But until the enemy had laid down his arms, the defenders of the city considered it their sacred duty to destroy him, understanding that there was no other way of defending themselves and their compatriots. The Russian people have always been known for their peaceful disposition. But the enemy had come to our land with his sword bared; he had forced us draw our own swords, and that was the beginning of the end for him. Defending himself, his country and its socialist achievements, the Soviet soldier had to destroy the invader without mercy.

Fighting continued on all sectors after November 12.

We now had the task of trying to help Lyudnikov's division, cut off from the main army. Its position had become extremely serious: it was under enemy pressure from the north, the west and the south, and on the east was cut off by the Volga, with its non-stop floating ice.

The delivery of ammunition and provisions, and the evacuation of wounded, were erratic, with gaps of two or three days. Ice continued to drift down the Volga.

We had to find, or rather to squeeze out, some resources or other among our units on the right bank. The Army Military Council decided primarily to incorporate all the units of Smekhotvorov's division into one regiment, the 685th, and, concentrating it on the right flank of Gorishny's division, to counter-attack northward along the Volga to join up with Lyudnikov's division.

In all Smekhotvorov's units we managed to collect only 250 able-bodied men. With this composite regiment and the right flank of Gorishny's division, which was gradually being reinforced with soldiers and small groups of soldiers coming over from the left bank, we counter-attacked northward continuously until November 20, aiming to link up with Lyudnikov's men.

Our counter-attacks, it is true, did not restore the position, but neither was the enemy able to wipe out Lyudnikov's division.

I cannot omit to mention the courage of the encircled division's commanders, led by Colonel Ivan Ilyich Lyudnikov. In spite of the extraordinarily difficult situation, they remained calm and confident. Telephone links, of course, had been broken. Our only communication was by radio. I several times had a personal, uncoded conversation with Lyudnikov over the radio. We recognized each other's voices and did not call each other by name. I had no hesitation in telling him that help would be forthcoming, and that we would soon be joining up with him. I hoped he would understand why I was talking openly to him, and that our troops could in fact give him no help. He also said he hoped we would be meeting soon. In this way we tried to mislead the enemy.

On the night of November 15 our night-flying aircraft dropped four bales of provisions and four of ammunition to Lyudnikov. On the night of November 19 four armoured boats finally reached the Denezhnaya Volozhka channel of the river, and then reached the bank where the division was defending. The boats delivered ammunition and medical supplies, and took off 150 wounded.

The work of the crews of the steamboats *Pugachev*, *Spartak* and *Panfilov*, and armoured boats 11, 12, 13, 61 and 63, deserves special mention. During these days and nights they performed truly heroic feats.

I myself watched these boats at night forcing a path through the ice-floes from Tumak northward along the Volga to the bank where the 62nd Army's positions were.

There were times when these boats were unable to return during the hours of darkness, and to move along the bank occupied by the enemy was tantamount to suicide. In that case they stayed on our bank, camouflaged with parachutes, white sheets and sacks, the colour of snow or ice.

We finally felt that the days of the Germans were numbered. But we were concerned about the fate of Lyudnikov's division. We had to come to their rescue. Using their every last ounce of energy, our units began to counter-attack day after day, round the clock, against the enemy who had occupied the Volga bank between Lyudnikov's division and the Army's main forces.

At the same time our storm groups were step by step winning back buildings and dug-outs on other sectors of the Army's front, or to be more precise, along the whole of the front. Colonel Gorokhov's group attacked towards the Tractor factory from the north; Sokolov's and Guriev's divisions attacked the Krasny Oktyabr factory; Colonel Batyuk's division attacked Mamayev Kurgan, and Rodimtsev's division stormed individual buildings in the city.

Our attack developed slowly, but continuously, day by day. Our storm groups began to seize equipment and prisoners.

On the evening of November 18 Comrades Gurov, Krylov, Pozharski, Weinrub, Vasiliev and myself met in my dug-out. We were discussing possibilities of further active operations: our strength was ebbing, and our request for draft reinforcements for the Army had not been met. The telephone rang and Front H.Q. told us to stand by to receive an order that would shortly be coming through. We all glanced at one another. 'What can the order be?' was in all our minds.

Suddenly Gurov struck himself on the forehead and said:

'I know! It's the order for the big counter-offensive!'

At midnight it finally came through.

The order said that on the morning of November 19 the armies of the South-Western and Don fronts would launch an offensive from the region of Kletskaya and Ilovlinskaya in the general direction of Kalach; the armies on the Stalingrad front would go over to the offensive a day later, on November 20, from the region of Raygorod, in the general direction of the village of Sovietski, and then further to Kalach. The aim was to break through the enemy's front, encircle and destroy him.

Now we realized what an important part our regiments and divisions had played, in fighting continuously for three months against the enemy's superior numbers by the very bank of the Volga.

In order to inform every soldier in good time of the order, we collected a group of officers from the H.Q. and political section, warned divisional headquarters also to have a group of officers ready, and during the night, without waiting for dawn, we took the news of the order out to the units.

We could imagine the joy of our troops who, since November 7, had been waiting for the words, 'There will be a holiday in our street too'[1] to come true. Now that day had come.

On November 19 the armies of the South-Western and Don fronts attacked, and on November 20 the armies of the Stalingrad front did likewise. With bated breath we watched the progress of the gigantic battle. At the same time the troops of the 62nd Army counter-attacked even more vigorously, with the aim of pinning down the enemy forces in the city, giving him no room for manœuvre, or opportunity to transfer troops to other sectors of the front where the main attacks were being delivered.

I am convinced that the Germans did not expect to be attacked simultaneously on three fronts; they had failed to notice the concentration of our shock groups. Beginning their last offensive against the 62nd Army on November 11, the Germans themselves had crawled into the trap which shut behind them on November 23 in the region of Kalach. On

---

[1] Stalin issued an Order of the Day on November 7, 'in which a great counteroffensive was cautiously foreshadowed, and which ended with the words of the Russian popular saying: "There will be a holiday in our street too," meaning, "It'll be our turn to rejoice".' (Werth, A., ibid., p. 305).

November 24, the 62nd Army's isolated northern group under Colonel Gorokhov joined up with the 99th Infantry Division of the Don Front. Our joy knew no bounds.

'We'll soon be back with the rest of the world,' said the officers and men of the 62nd Army.

And although the Volga raged behind us, cutting us off from the world, all of us—from the private to the general—felt proud to be sons of the Soviet people, felt the pride of the unconquered!

When the world was told about the 62nd Army having beaten off every attack on the enemy's main path of advance, every soldier in the Army realized the part he had played in these months of battle for the fortress on the Volga. The slogans 'Not a step back!' and 'For us, there is no land beyond the Volga!' now took on a different meaning.

'Not a step back!' now meant go forward. 'For us, there is no land beyond the Volga!' now meant we had to advance to the west!

CHAPTER IX

THE ROUT

THE FORTRESS on the Volga had held out, and the news ran round the world: twenty-two of Hitler's divisions were encircled in the great cauldron of Stalingrad.

As we know, the Germans always tried to encircle the enemy facing them. And as they had been successful in doing this, the German generals considered themselves unrivalled practitioners of the encirclement manœuvre. Now they themselves were inside an iron ring of Soviet troops. This was the first time it had happened to the German Wehrmacht, and it had not happened somewhere in the West, but on the territory of Soviet Russia, which they believed to be broken and almost under their heel. It happened by the Russian River Volga, some 1,250 miles from Germany. And when, with some delay, the German population found out about it, to judge only by the newspapers of the period, many Germans realized that something irreparable had happened to Nazi strategy.

The German General Staff and Ministry of Propaganda deliberately curtailed the stream of black-bordered letters, but murder will out. Crippled soldiers soon began to arrive back in Germany. They could not keep quiet about what was happening on the banks of the Volga. At the request of their comrades left behind at the front, they wrote and told of what fate awaited those whom Hitler had sent to the east, particularly those he had sent to the Volga.

It was not long before news of the encirclement of Paulus's 300,000-strong army shattered the morale of the German nation.

For three years the Germans had been used to reading in the newspapers and hearing on the radio about the victories of the German army, about the bombing of Warsaw, London and other European cities. Now, however, judging by documents of the German General Staff and letters written by German officers, the Nazis began to think about the reckoning that awaited them for their crimes in the east. A sudden change had taken place in the mood of the invaders: more and more they began to talk about their failures. True, they tried to explain these failures by the fact that Russia had been saved by some miracle. But as everyone knows, there are no such things as miracles.

Fighting almost alone for a year and a half against the Germans, for whom the industry of the whole of Europe was working, the Soviet people had dealt the Nazi war machine a crushing blow and shattered the enemy's plans. This turning point in the war had been prepared by the battle-hardened Communist Party, around which all the patriotic forces of the country had united. The Soviet people had spared no sacrifice to save their socialist country—neither material resources, nor their strength, nor their very lives. The mass heroism of the troops at the front had inspired millions and millions of workers and collective farmers to heroic efforts in their work. At the height of the battle by the Volga a Saratov collective farmer, Ferapont Golovaty, gave all his savings towards the purchase of an aeroplane for the Stalingrad front. At the call of the Party ('Everything for the front!') a movement spread throughout the country to collect funds to help in the country's defence. The whole of this tremendous exploit at the front and in the factory culminated in the sudden change of fortunes, to the advantage of the Soviet armed forces and socialism.

From letters and anecdotes told us by comrades who came to visit us from all parts of the country, it was clear how delighted the Soviet people had been to learn of the encirclement of the German troops by the Volga. Engineering workers in the Urals wrote to us: 'Having learned of the encirclement of the Germans at Stalingrad, we are prepared to put up with even greater hardships for the sake of victory, for the sake of our country. Now we know that our labour will not have been in vain.'

The workers in the districts and republics for the moment occupied by the Germans also learned of the encirclement of the German armies and saw in it the beginning of the final collapse of Nazism. The partisans of the Ukraine, Belorussia and other areas, even more ardently pursued their raids on German headquarters, blew up bridges, wiped out German officials and dealt with traitors.

The soldiers of the 62nd Army, obviously, greeted the news of the encirclement of the German armies with tremendous satisfaction and delight. Our efforts had not been in vain. It would be no exaggeration to say that every soldier believed, before the encirclement took place, that the German invaders would not go very far from the banks of the Volga, that they would either die or be taken prisoner here.

Without any false modesty I would say that during these days we felt a constant pride, knowing that in all corners of the Soviet Union the soldiers of Stalingrad, their unyielding resistance and tenacity were being talked about. We knew that the road from the Volga to Berlin was still long and hard, but we already believed that the defeat of Hitler Germany was now inevitable.

The success of our 62nd Army was to a large extent conditioned by the fact that we were fighting in close combination with the troops of neighbouring armies and fronts, and with constant attention from the G.H.Q. of Supreme Command and from the Front Command. It is no exaggeration to say that Stalingrad was being defended by the whole country, the whole Soviet people. It is enough to point out that during the defensive fighting in the city the 62nd Army was sent some of the best forces available to G.H.Q. and Front H.Q.—seven infantry divisions, one infantry brigade and one armoured brigade. Large air forces and the Front's artillery group were brought in to work with our Army.

One cannot but express gratitude for the help given to the 62nd Army by the counter-attacks launched by the Don Front from the Kletskaya-Yerzovka line, and the stubborn defence by the troops of the 64th Army in the southern part of the city. Their operations drew off considerable enemy forces and prevented the German Command from using the whole of its shock group against the 62nd Army. They held Paulus back by the ears.

Thinking back to the battle on the banks of the Volga, I must dwell for a moment on one important question which has, in my opinion, not been given enough attention in literature about the war, and is sometimes, without justification, ignored in attempts to draw conclusions from our experience in it. I am thinking about the part played in the war by women, who played a tremendous role not only at the rear, but at the front also. They bore all the burdens of military life on the same footing as men, and went right through to Berlin with the men.

There have been many women in military history, from the 'marketantki' in the times of Peter the Great and Suvorov, to the women partisans in the War of 1812, and the sisters of mercy at the defence of Sevastopol and at the siege of Port Arthur, and also during the first world war, who are remembered as devoted and courageous Russian patriots. But in no previous war have women played such an important part as they played in the Soviet-German war of 1941–45.

Whereas in the past many women have served in the forces and at the front on their own initiative, our Soviet women went to the front at the call of the Party and the Komsomol, deeply aware of their duty in defending the interests of their socialist country. They had been prepared for this by our Communist Party, because at this time our state was the only one in the world where women enjoyed, as laid down in the Constitution, equal rights with men.

The deliberate mass entry of women, particularly girls,

into active service in the army was not always clearly understood by everyone. There are some who probably still do not understand that they did so as equal builders of socialism and equal defenders of the interests of the workers. This is why, in the war against the Nazi invaders, we saw our Soviet women acting as orderlies, carrying tens and hundreds of wounded from the firing line, as doctors, carrying out operations under air and artillery attack, or as telephonists and radio operators, handling operational conversations and administration in battle. We saw them working at headquarters and in political organizations, where they did army administration work and educated the troops in a spirit of military tenacity. Anyone who visited the front would see women acting as gunners in anti-artillery units, as pilots of aeroplanes doing battle with the German air aces, as captains of armoured boats, in the Volga fleet, for example, carrying cargoes from the left bank to the right and back again in unbelievably difficult conditions.

It is no exaggeration to say that women fought alongside men everywhere in the war.

It must also be remembered that in the second half of 1942, when our armies had retreated to a line running through Leningrad, Mozhaysk, Voronezh, Stalingrad and Mozdok, leaving densely populated areas of the country in enemy hands, new recruits were needed. Women volunteered for the army *en masse*, and this made it possible for us to bring our units and establishments back up to full efficiency.

We had whole units (such as anti-aircraft batteries and night-flying PO-2 bomber regiments) in which the majority of gun-teams and crews were women. And it must be said that these units did their jobs as well as the units in which men predominated. We can take two types of work involved in defence operations—anti-aircraft defence and signals—as examples.

The majority of gun crews in the Stalingrad anti-aircraft defence corps, in both anti-aircraft batteries and on searchlights, consisted of women. But the efficiency of these crews and batteries was not the slightest inferior to the anti-aircraft units we saw on the Don and in other parts of the front, where the majority of the crews were men. In terms of tenacity and self-sacrifice, in the battle with the German dive-bombers the women anti-aircraft gun crews on the banks of the Volga were models of courage. They would stick to their guns and go on firing when bombs were exploding all round them, when it seemed impossible not merely to fire accurately, but even to stay with the guns. In the fire and smoke, amid bursting bombs, seemingly unaware of the columns of earth exploding into the air all about them, they stood their ground to the last. The Luftwaffe's raids on the city, therefore, in spite of heavy losses among the anti-aircraft personnel, were always met by concentrated fire, which as a rule took a heavy toll among the attacking aircraft. Our women anti-aircraft gunners shot down dozens of enemy planes over the blazing city.

The troops of the 62nd Army will never forget how the women anti-aircraft gunners stood their ground on the narrow strip of land by the Volga and fought the enemy planes to the last round.

In October 1942 I met a gun crew containing five quite young, but battle-hardened and courageous girls. I shall never forget the sadness on the face of one blonde girl who, after firing a formation of nine enemy aircraft, and shooting one of them down, was told by one of her friends that in her opinion it should have been possible to shoot down two or three.

The girls of the anti-aircraft units in the city did not shut their eyes to danger, duck their heads or run for cover, even in the days when enemy sorties of two thousand a day were being recorded.

I am sure that there were no soldiers in the 62nd Army who had anything with which to reproach the women who, alongside them, were defending their native land.

The 62nd Army's signals units were staffed mainly by women, who carried out instructions devotedly. If they were sent to an auxiliary signals post you could be sure that communication would be assured. Artillery and mortars could fire at the post, planes could drop their bombs on it, and the enemy's troops could surround it—but unless they were ordered to do so the women would not leave their post, not even when faced with death.

I know of a case when only one girl signaller was left at a signals post near Basargino Station, a girl called Nadya

Klimenko. When all her friends had been either killed or wounded, she stuck to her post and up to the last minute went on reporting on what was happening on the field of battle. This is her last report to the Army's signals centre: 'There is no one left near the post. I am alone. Shells are bursting all round ... To the right I can see tanks moving with crosses painted on them, and there are infantrymen behind them ... It's already too late for me to leave. I should care if they shoot! I'll go on reporting just the same. Listen! ... There's a tank coming up to my post. Two men are getting out of it ... They are looking around—I think they're officers. They're coming towards me. My heart's stopped beating with fear of what's going to happen ...' That was the end. What happened to Nadya Klimenko no one knows.

Not long ago I met a woman signaller who was in the 62nd Army and is now Secretary of the Zlatopol district committee of the Party, Comrade Razumeyeva. I met her for the first time on 13 September 1942 on Mamayev Kurgan. The signals centre had been destroyed by German bombs and shells, but she continued to sit by the telephone and put through calls to unit commanders.

I met her at an electors' meeting on the eve of elections to the Supreme Council of the U.S.S.R. and we chatted for a long time. Again and again we remembered incidents in the fighting, which was now a long time ago, but which we shall never forget.

Razumeyeva was born in 1921, of a peasant family in the village of Krasny Yar, in the Kirov region. In 1941 she answered the call of the Komsomol and volunteered for the Red Army. Like many other girls who served in the forces, Razumeyeva did a month's course as a signaller, and was sent to a signals company of the army in the field. In the summer of 1942 she arrived in Stalingrad.

Razumeyeva joined the army of her own accord, from conviction, and devoted all her strength and knowledge to the defence of her country. In 1943 she was accepted as a Communist Party member. After demobilization she worked as a teacher, and transferred to Party work in 1949.

Talking to her, I found her to be modest and serious. She spoke about her friends, but only spoke about herself when I put direct questions to her and asked for more details about what she had done herself.

'Myself? . . .' she shrugged her shoulders in surprise. 'All right, I'll talk about myself as well. With me on Mamayev Kurgan was Maria Gulyayeva, a small girl from Kamyshin, and later Shura Sheshenya; we were on duty at the switchboard. In the city, but at different places, there were also Taya Vdovina, Lyuba Stukalova, Klavdia Shtonda, Lena Peretolchina and others. I remember Maria particularly well. It was with her and Taya that I was on duty on Mamayev Kurgan on September 13. On that day both Maria and Taya were seriously wounded. The limewashed walls collapsed on top of me. Maria was wounded by a fragment of the bomb or shell—I don't know what it was. When they dragged me out Maria was unconscious. We bandaged her legs and did not notice straight away that she was wounded in the chest. Hard though it was we carried her to the nearest dressing-station, thinking she was still alive. We laid her down, and I was shattered when I heard them say: "But she's dead! . . ." '

When the meeting was over, Razumeyeva continued to reminisce about life at the front.

'A moment's lull at the front . . . Earth, trees, sky—just like before the war. And one tried to forget, tried not to think that a war was going on, that blood was flowing, people dying, dying not only in the front line, but far into the rear, from enemy bombing.

'Thoughts about days of peace, about blue skies and silence (such a rare visitor at the front) for one moment dispersed the hateful drone of enemy aeroplanes in the blue sky.

'It was not fear that tormented, though the danger of being killed or wounded was always with us. Everyone at the front was used to that. It was hatred, burning hatred for the accursed enemy. But how could we express our anger, our hatred for the enemy? And even in the moments of greatest danger we carried out our military task to the letter.

'I remember August 31, 1942. It was in Yablonovaya Gully. Fanya Raznik, small, with dark complexion and hardly a curl in her chestnut hair, was sitting with her comrade at the transmitter in a tent, which had been pitched on some ground that was bare, but for a little ditch alongside the tent.

'The girls could hear the sound of approaching bombers,

but stayed where they were: they had to relay information rapidly about an enemy advance and a break-through by enemy tanks to the rear of one of our units. And neither Fanya, who was relaying the information, nor her friend, sitting alongside her, left their places. Girls in signals behaved like that—they wouldn't leave a friend, whatever danger threatened.

'Keeping an eye on the aeroplanes, and listening to the whistle of the bombs, the girls guessed approximately where the bombs would burst. The aeroplanes made a first, then a second run. The girls continued to transmit ... But the aeroplanes came in a third time, and where the tent had been a crater appeared.

'The signallers left Yablonovaya Gully with heavy hearts, leaving their comrades, Fanya Raznik and her friend, behind.

'Events happened so swiftly in these days that we did not even manage to bury our comrades. And so they stayed there for ever in Yablonovaya Gully, inconspicuous rank and file soldiers of the Soviet army, who died, but did their duty . . .'

The same evening Razumeyeva told me about her good friend, Shura Sheshenya.

'Before the war she worked in a children's home. When it was known that the recruiting office had called up several girls, members of the Komsomol, who had expressed their wish to join the Soviet army, Shura went straight to the director of the children's home and told him she wanted to go to the front.

'Shura understood that she was doing important work, that the education of children had been entrusted to her, but her wish to go to the front was so strong that any work in the rear seemed to her minor and insignificant.

'The director of the children's home, with which Shura had been evacuated from the Ukraine to Astrakhan, could not let all his teachers go. Nevertheless Shura lived in hopes that she would manage to go and serve with the army in the field.

'And that day came. At the end of April 1942, together with five other girls, all Komsomol members, Shura, already a candidate-member of the Party, set off for the recruiting office.

'The formalities were all completed in a day, and on May 2 the girls were in the army. After a month's training in

244

Astrakhan on a course for telephonists, Shura joined a signals company and began to work on a switchboard. This was in July 1942 on the Don. From then on, even in the most difficult circumstances, she remained at her post.

'Shura grew up an orphan. Her father and mother were killed in the Civil War and she didn't remember them. She was brought up in a children's home, which taught her to love her country and hate her country's enemies.

'She did anything she was given to do with a kind of special care. She always tried to do more than she was asked . . .

'On September 13, 1942, telephone communication was established between the commander of one of the units and General Pozharski. There was not a moment's lull on this sector that day. Artillery and mortar fire was raging the whole time. It was difficult to maintain communication, of course, but maintained it was.

'About 3 p.m. there was not a single linesman left at the signals centre—they were all out mending the line.

'When there was no one left to go out, Shura said to the Company Commander:

' "Let me go, they can manage without me on the switch-board."

' "There's such heavy fire you won't even get through to the place where the line's broken."

' "I'll manage, Comrade Lieutenant, you just let me go," Shura insisted.

'He agreed, and Shura, pinching the girl who sat at the switchboard (as a sign of farewell), climbed out of the dug-out.

'The Company Commander soon regretted that he had let her go, as he knew that she would not get through under such a barrage. None of the men who had gone out to the line had come back, and they had not even once switched in on the line. But what could he do? . . .

'Shura did switch in on the line several times, and the few people who were on Mamayev Kurgan that day and stayed alive remember how the line was broken again at noon on September 14 and they never heard Shura's voice again . . .

'And what signaller of the 140th Mortar Regiment of the Reserve High Command does not remember the courageous and always gay and resourceful Lena Peretolchina and her friend, shy Klavdia Shtonda? They got to know each other and became friends on the bank of the Volga, and together travelled the hard but glorious road from the great Russian river to Berlin.'

In the most difficult days, in the days of mortal danger, our soldiers believed that the Soviet people would win through to victory.

You judge people by their deeds, by how they behave at difficult moments in their lives.

In the early morning and late in the evening, when shells were not bursting all around and the whistle of bullets had stopped, the defenders of the city liked to dream about the future.

I have in front of me a letter written by Lena Peretolchina, which was given to me by her friend, Razumeyeva. After the war Lena completed her middle-school education in the evenings, then went to a teacher training college and is now working in Odessa.

Her letter contains a girl's thoughts about happiness, and I should like to reproduce it in full:

Happiness is a relative concept. Everyone interprets it in their own way. No one will dispute the fact that different sections of society, people in different classes in different periods, have interpreted it differently. People's existence determines their consciousness, including their view of happiness. Can we compare what, for example, a nineteenth-century daughter of a nobleman thought about happiness with what a Soviet girl thinks about it? Even two equally good, clever, nice, gay seventeen-year-old girls in the Komsomol in our day see happiness differently. And I, twice as old as those girls, cannot find a cogent answer to the question: what is happiness? On the other hand, I do know what a 'happy day' is, or rather a happy evening . . .

I have had a lot of pleasant evenings in my life, but I have remembered one, though it was more than fifteen years ago. Never before or since have I felt such really complete happiness.

In itself, it was an evening like any other. Even the silence, so rare at the front, was not a novelty that week.

From the distance, it is true, came the sound of guns—sometimes monotonous, like the hollow wail of a siren, sometimes intermittent, like the roll of a drum . . . Perhaps I'm not expressing myself in good literary style? Too bad, I'm afraid the only relation between literature and me is that I love it . . .

Sleet began to fall, and the air seemed to be full of a dull dampness . . .

Such days were dreary in the front line. In our dug-out, the radio operators' dug-out, it was so warm and cosy! Three of the girls were asleep. My friend, Klavdia Shtonda, and I were sitting at the radio equipment: I was on duty. Klavdia, for friendship's sake, was keeping me company. I had just been in touch with H.Q. There were no radiograms.

In silence we thought over the events of the past weeks, months . . .

We had been retreating all summer, withdrawing into the depths of the country, to the bank of the Volga. Anyone who went through this will remember the heavy heart of the retreating soldier. We went on, tired, depressed, thinking about the last battle . . . Another inhabited area had fallen into the hands of the enemy, and us? We went on and on . . . German aeroplanes circled overhead bombing and machine-gunning us. Along the sides of the roads lay shattered vehicles, guns, smouldering ruins with smoke-blackened stove chimneys. The sad spectacle of war . . .

But what picture could have been more awful than the one that awaited us in the city itself? The roofless skeletons of houses, with gaping holes where windows had been, streets in ruins, and all around smoke, the smell of burning . . . And after a routine air-raid—bodies of old men, women, children . . . Then the fighting for Mamayev Kurgan, for the Meat Combine, for the Pioneers' Palace. Tired and weak, we retreated to the bank of the Volga itself.

And then we were on the other side of the Volga. For some strategical reason our already reinforced unit was not left in the city but stationed in the area of Sredne-Pogromnoye. About 7½ miles from it, on the bank of the river, the battalion to which they had attached our unit, was in defensive positions . . .

And what was happening there on the right bank? What lay ahead of us? What was going to happen? What? . . . I had only one thought in my head: why did we go on retreating, retreating, retreating? . . . I wanted to shout aloud: 'Enough! No more!' When were we, instead of they, going finally to advance? When?

For the first time in many long months I felt sick at heart . . . I sat thinking, feeling my cheeks grow damp, with a choking sensation in my throat. Klavdia also sat looking miserable, and, as if she was following my thoughts, said:

'Where do we go now, then? The Urals . . .'

I winced. I felt I had to protest. Not against Klavdia, but against my own faint-heartedness.

'No, no!' I answered in a whisper, almost inaudibly. 'We . . . we'll win just the same!' and my voice became firmer. 'We are Russians, we are Soviet citizens . . . Remember your history.'

'I remember it,' she answered in a toneless voice.

'Have you forgotten where Napoleon got to, and what happened to him? Have you forgotten the Civil War? . . .'

'Do you really think I don't know that?' she interrupted. 'I know it all. But that's only with my mind. Here in my heart . . .' and she burst into tears, her head on my shoulder.

We sat feeling dull and paralysed, perhaps for an hour, perhaps just for a few minutes. I was the first to pull myself together. Wasn't it time to switch on the radio? I looked up at the clock, an ordinary wall clock we had picked up in some destroyed village, so that we could make our radio contact at the right time. It was 10.35 p.m. And I have not forgotten what time it was then for the rest of my life!

'Klavdia, we must switch on Moscow. We're five minutes late.'

'Switch on,' she answered indifferently. 'Let's listen to what some captured lance-corporal has to say . . .'

It was true that recent communiqués had not been very informative. But we had to get the information just the same: in the morning the battalion commander always wanted to know it. I took a sheet of paper, a pencil, switched on the radio, and began to tune in to Moscow.

Moscow, Moccow, when will we hear any joy in your voice? When will you tell us of victory? When? . . .

Then suddenly . . . What's this? Whose voice is this— a firm, proud and confident voice on the Moscow wavelength? . . .

'Klavdia, what's this?'

'That's our voice,' she whispered. 'That's a Soviet voice . . .'

We did not understand what the announcer was saying, we only heard the pride of the victor. Gradually words crept through to our consciousness: Kalach . . . Krivomuzginskaya . . . Abganerovo . . . All names we knew very, very well. They were places near here, near us, near the Volga. They were places we had fought for and retreated from.

I looked at Klavdia and my head was filled with a kind of fog. Again the voice of the announcer quoted figures, the number of weapons captured—large, no, huge numbers! My heart seemed to have stopped beating. And then the final words of the communiqué: 'The offensive by our Russian troops is continuing', spoken proudly by the voice alongside us. And there we had been, sitting and not knowing what was going on thirty-five to fifty miles away from us.

We remembered our sleeping colleagues. We must wake them up . . . But all three of them were sitting and excitedly looking at the radio. The announcer's voice had woken them up.

I felt my cheeks grow wet again. But they were tears of pleasure, tears of happiness. And I was not ashamed of the fact that I was crying.

I ran out of the dug-out to tell people what we had heard; I had been unable to write down a word. I ran to the command post, stumbled, and the H.Q. sentry stopped me, asked me for the password. In my excitement I said: 'Victory' . . . Someone came out of H.Q. People came out of other dug-outs, surrounded me, asked me questions, but all I could utter was 'Victory'.

'Where? What has happened?' I already had a crowd round me. 'Is Hitler dead?' . . . 'Have they finally opened a second front?'

'No, not that, not that at all,' I finally managed to say. 'Victory here, near here, do you understand, near the Volga . . .'

'Where?' . . . 'How?'

A radio operator ran up with a written communiqué and began to read it to the assembled crowd.

'Do you hear? They've advanced over forty miles!'

'Thirty thousand prisoners! Well done! Bravo!'

And like a little girl, I sobbed my heart out. I was crying for joy. I wanted to embrace the whole country, all of our people . . .

I believed that light would triumph over darkness. Perhaps I would not live to see the day—it was a long way yet from the Volga to the frontier.[1] But others would live to see it! And spring would come back for them again.

I believed that the day would come, the still very distant day, that we call the Day of Victory . . .

That was how Komsomol girl-soldiers thought about the future, about happiness. Whatever hardships they had to go through, they believed that the day of victory would come.

I often remember the conditions our women signallers had to live and work in. In the fighting in the city no one made them dug-outs and shelters; they themselves, alone or together, dug trenches and over them put a thin covering of anything they could lay their hands on, and for months on end they huddled together in such trenches. Very often they were buried where they worked.

In October, when the enemy destroyed all the H.Q. dug-outs, the conditions in which women on the right bank worked and lived became even more difficult. They worked in stuffy, cramped shelters, rested in the open, ate whatever they could get hold of and for months on end never saw hot water.

---

[1] At this time many people thought that the war would come to an end when our armies reached the country's frontiers. (*Author's note*.)

However you look at it, it was hard and difficult for our women at the front. But they did not shirk the difficulties and carried out their military tasks with integrity and self-sacrifice.

In Batyuk's division there was a woman orderly called Tamara Shmakova. I knew her personally. She earned fame by her activities in carrying seriously-wounded soldiers from the firing line, when it seemed impossible to lift a finger above the ground.

She would crawl up to the wounded man on all fours, would lie down next to him and bind his wounds. Having discovered how badly wounded he was, she would then decide what to do with him. If the man was too badly wounded to be left on the battlefield, she would take steps to evacuate him straight away. To remove a man from the battlefield two men, with or without stretchers, are normally needed. But more often than not Tamara coped alone. What she did was to crawl under the wounded man, and straining every muscle, would carry on her back a living load sometimes one and a half times or twice her own weight. But when a wounded man could not be lifted, she would spread out her ground-sheet, roll the wounded man on to it and, again on all fours, drag the heavy burden behind her.

Tamara Shmakova saved many lives. Many men alive today owe their lives to her. Soldiers who had been rescued from death often could not even find out the name of the girl who had saved them. She is now working as a doctor in the Tomsk district.

There were many heroines like Tamara in the 62nd Army. There were more than a thousand women in the 62nd Army who won decorations. They included Maria Ulyanova, who was engaged in the defence of Sergeant Pavlov's house from start to finish, Valia Pakhomova, who carried more than a hundred wounded from the battlefield, Nadia Koltsova, twice awarded the Red Banner, Dr Maria Velyamidova, who dressed the wounds of hundreds of soldiers under fire in forward firing positions, and many others. Was Lyuba Nesterenko not a heroine, when, in Lieutenant Dragan's besieged building, she bound the wounds of dozens of wounded guardsmen and, bleeding profusely, died with a bandage in her hand alongside a wounded comrade?

I remember the women doctors who worked in the divisional medical battalions and at the evacuation points by the ferries across the Volga; each of them during one night would dress the wounds of and treat a hundred or more wounded. There were times when the medical personnel at an evacuation point would send two or three thousand wounded across the Volga in a single night. And they did all this under incessant bombing and fire from every kind of artillery weapon.

In the second half of October the situation grew considerably worse, and the distance between the front line and the Volga grew so short that the Army Military Council had to ferry some units and establishments across to the left bank, so as to avoid unnecessary losses. First and foremost it was decided to send the women across to the left bank. Commanders and chiefs of staff were ordered to propose to women soldiers that they should temporarily go across to the left bank, so as to rest and return to us in a few days.

The Military Council took this decision on October 17. On the morning of October 18 a deputation of women signallers came to see me. The deputation was led by Valya Tokareva, a native of Kamyshin. She put a point-blank question to me:

'Comrade Commander, why are you sending us packing out of the city? We want to die or win alongside the rest of the Army. Why are you making a distinction between women soldiers and men? Do we really work any worse? As you like, but we're not going across the Volga . . .'

As this conversation took place on October 18, the day we transferred to our new command post, I told them that at our new command post we could not use all kinds of equipment; circumstances compelled us to use smaller signalling equipment, like portable radios, and this was our only reason for sending them across to the other bank, temporarily, until we had organized enough room for heavier types of equipment.

The women's deputation agreed to carry out the Military Council's order, but asked me to give my word of honour that as soon as conditions were ready for them to resume work, we would bring them back across to the right bank.

They crossed the Volga on October 18, and as from October 20, as soon as Krylov, Gurov or I telephoned the left bank, the operators gave us no peace. 'We've had a rest,' they would say. 'When are you going to bring us back to the city?' or 'Comrade Commander, when are you going to keep your word?'

We kept our word. At the end of October, together with signalling equipment, we brought them back to dug-outs we had had prepared. They were extremely pleased.

That was the kind of woman we had at the front.

After throwing back the German armies in the main line of attack, from November 19, the 62nd Army's formations were not more than about half a mile in depth. Behind them was the Volga, in front the enemy. Between the two was a narrow strip of ruins, in which our units had consolidated themselves.

On the right flank of the Army's main forces was Lyudnikov's division. It had been encircled and pressed back to the Volga, and was defending an area of not more than a third of a square mile.

On the left flank, the 13th Guards Infantry Division occupied a narrow strip along the bank. Its defence positions were not more than some two hundred yards deep. The Army H.Q. was at the junction point of the 13th Guards and 284th Infantry Divisions, a hundred yards from the front line, but my command post was even nearer, on the railway track skirting Mamayev Kurgan to the east, under the enemy's very nose.

The front occupied by the Army (about eleven miles long) could be covered by enemy artillery fire from either flank, and our positions could be covered in depth by enemy machine-gun fire. Life in this narrow bridgehead was made even more difficult by the fact that Mamayev Kurgan, or more particularly the water-tanks on it, and Hill 107.5, both of which dominated the city, were in enemy hands. From them the enemy could see anything approaching the Volga from the east, which meant that ammunition, equipment and provisions coming into the city were targets for enemy artillery fire.

We could not, of course, reconcile ourselves to this situation, and the Army set itself two paramount tasks—to link up with Lyudnikov's division by destroying the enemy forces which had broken through to the Volga, and occupy Mamayev Kurgan and Hill 107.5, so that by widening the bridgehead to a depth of nearly three miles, we could deprive the enemy of the observation posts from which he was keeping an eye on our units and anything approaching the Volga.

To carry out these tasks we needed men and ammunition, and tanks.

I must here point out that the 62nd Army was constantly short of men and tanks. In the days of the bitterest fighting in the city we were refused almost nothing, though it had not always been possible to ferry what we needed across the Volga. Now that the Germans were encircled, however, we were put on short rations: we were given neither men nor tanks, and we received only limited supplies of shells, mortar bombs and small arms ammunition.

This was correct policy, of course, and in the general interest of the war, but from the Army's point of view, shot at as it was from all directions, and with every soldier wanting with all his heart and soul to broaden the bridgehead so as to breathe more freely, such economies seemed unjustified cruelty.

But so as not to mark time, we had to mobilize all our resources, and reman our units for the most part with wounded soldiers who were now convalescent, and who were trying as hard as they could to return to their units, to their city. The 62nd Army's fame had spread, and like a magnet it drew its veterans back to it.

As far as supplies of ammunition or tank reinforcements were concerned—these were something we could only dream about. The ferrying of cargoes across the Volga continued to be terribly difficult. The period of floating ice on the Volga lasted from November 12 to December 17. For days at a stretch not an armoured boat or steamer was able to cross the river.

The following are a few extracts from the 62nd Army's reports to Front H.Q.:

November 14. No ships arrived at all. The plan of deliveries has fallen through for three days running. The intended reinforcements have not been ferried across, and our units are feeling an acute shortage of ammunition and rations. The boats which set off from Tumak on the left bank with men of the 90th Infantry Regiment could not get through and turned back. The drifting ice has completely cut communications with the left bank . . .

November 27. The channel of the Volga to the east of Golodny and Sarpinski Islands has been completely blocked by dense ice, as a result of which the Tumak ferry has been out of action, and not one armoured boat or steamer has arrived. No ammunition has been delivered and no wounded evacuated . . .

December 10. There is continuous drifting ice on the Volga. Bringing boats through the ice is attended with great difficulties. During the day 20 tons of ammunition and 27 tons of provisions were brought across to the right bank.

As a result of this situation Front Command organized ammunition, and particularly food, deliveries across the Volga by PO-2 planes. But there was not much they could do, as a load had to be dropped within a strip about a hundred yards wide. The slightest miscalculation and the load would fall either in the Volga or behind the enemy's lines.

Ammunition and food deliveries fell off day by day, and the drifting ice went on and on. It seemed as if it would never end. The ice-floes piled up and formed obstructions, and made a disgusting crunching noise which made our flesh creep and sent shudders up our spines, as if someone were sawing into our vertebrae.

Finally, on December 16, at about 4 o'clock in the afternoon, everyone's attention was drawn by the extraordinary noise of crashing ice-floes near the bank of the river. At the time the members of the Military Council were having a meal in the dug-out which had been made into a dining-room. Hearing this unusual noise, we all ran out of the dug-out and saw an enormous quantity of ice coming down from behind Zaitsevski Island. Smashing everything in its path, it crushed and pulverized small and large ice-floes alike, and broke the logs frozen into the ice like matchwood. It was an amazing spectacle. Across the whole span of the Volga this mass of ice was slowing down. We waited with great excitement to see whether or not it would stop. Were we going to have a real bridge across the river, or would we go on having boats, cries on the river, calls for help from men being buried or crushed in ice? . . .

And then, to everyone's indescribable joy, the cumbersome mass of ice came to a halt opposite our dug-outs. We could hardly believe that it had happened.

I immediately telephoned our engineering officers and instructed them to arrange two or three groups of men with barge-poles and ropes and send them across to the left bank.

They had the simple job of crossing the ice, there and back. The sappers set off. Darkness had now fallen. Everyone was impatient. Everybody went down to the bank several times to listen for any sound of moving ice.

At 9 p.m. the first party of sappers returned, having crossed the ice successfully in both directions. Everyone felt as though a weight had been taken off their shoulders. We had links with the rest of the world again!

The next day, December 17, in our report to Front H.Q. appeared the postscript: 'On the morning of 17.12, rows of planks were laid across the Volga on the ice, for people crossing on foot'.

The difficult situation on the Volga had hampered us in carrying out the tasks facing the Army. Nonetheless, almost every day, using every appropriate opportunity or slip on the part of the enemy, we attacked him, and won back our land yard by yard.

But we could not destroy the enemy who had reached the Volga in the area of the Barrikady factory merely by attacks with our infantry regiments: we had neither tanks nor reserves.

What were we to do? How could we help Lyudnikov's division?

The artillery we had installed on the left bank of the Volga now came to our aid. To use this artillery we did not have to ferry ammunition across the Volga. We decided to wipe out the enemy by artillery fire. But to do this also involved difficulties, which seemed insuperable: we needed to organize absolutely accurate fire on every enemy position, we needed artillery and mortar marksmen. We had such marksmen, but to correct their fire from the right bank was difficult—

telephone links were being continually broken by the ice, and radio communication was weak and unreliable. Studying all these factors, we worked out and started to implement the following method of destroying the enemy who had broken through to the Volga.

We marked out the area occupied by the enemy from north and south and from the Volga to the farthest point in the front line, indicating landmarks which were clearly visible from the left bank. This gave us a 650-850-yard corridor occupied by the Germans. Our artillerymen, seeing this corridor clearly, could fire accurately at the enemy's firing positions.

Spotters on the right bank watched the firing. They indicated and watched the targets, and errors in the gunners' aim. All this was communicated to the artillery observation posts, and then in turn transmitted to the firing positions.

Lyudnikov's and Gorishny's small infantry units, watching the withering fire from our artillery, would come up within a grenade's throw of the enemy. When a light signal was given, our artillery would cease fire, and the infantry units, mostly storm groups, with short grenade throws would attack and catch the enemy in their pill-boxes and basements.

Operating in this way, our units began to advance. It was a long and stubborn battle.

To show the kind of fighting this was, I will quote some extracts from the Army's reports:

December 21. Since 5 a.m. Lyudnikov's division has continued its attack in a south-westerly direction. In spite of strong enemy opposition, our units have occupied four buildings, and on the right flank advanced between 100–125 yards. Three enemy counter-attacks have been beaten off. Five heavy machine-guns and two prisoners of the 578th Infantry Regiment of the 305th Division, have been captured.

Since 5 a.m. Gorishny's division has been attacking in a northwesterly direction. Overcoming stiff enemy resistance, they have surrounded and wiped out individual enemy garrisons. After hand-to-hand fighting (with extensive use of hand-grenades) units occupied a transforming station which the enemy had turned into a pill-box.

One building, six dug-outs and two blockhouses have been captured. Fighting is continuing. The enemy is trying to restore the position, launching counter-attacks, which have been successfully repulsed.

Equipment captured: machine-guns 3, tommy-guns 6, rifles 35, grenades 380; blockhouses destroyed 4. In the captured dug-outs the enemy had left behind 40 dead . . .

December 23. Lyudnikov's division has continued its south-westerly attack. The enemy has put up stiff resistance, and counter-attacked twice at a strength of over two companies. The enemy suffered heavy losses and his attacks were beaten off.

Two buildings were captured, in one of which the enemy had left behind 30 dead. Other storm groups are continuing their attack to gain possession of the big rectangular building on the bank of the Volga.

Gorishny's division has continued its north-westerly attack. In spite of strong enemy resistance, our units have slowly advanced. Direct communication with Lyudnikov's division has now been established.

This victory was won by a stubborn battle fought against the enemy and the Volga.

On the following day, December 24, by order of G.H.Q., Sologub's, Smekhotvorov's and Zholudev's divisions, and two infantry brigades, all of which had been particularly worn down in the nonstop fighting, were transferred from the Army to the reserve and sent away to be re-formed.

As a rule, commanders of divisions, brigades and even regiments, before they left for the opposite bank of the Volga, came to the Army's command post, simply, following the Russian custom, to say good-bye.

To part from friends, particularly those alongside whom one has done battle, was extremely hard. As we said good-bye our minds went back over what we had been through, we re-lived every battle, every counter-attack.

The departure from the Army of commanders with whom I had lived through many difficult days, called up many sad memories. When I said good-bye to a commander, in my mind's eye I could see his units as they had arrived in the city—vigorous, proud of the dangerous job that had been given to them, courageous and determined. No sooner had they arrived by the Volga than they went into battle.

Every day, or rather every morning, the Military Council received a report of how many wounded had been ferried across the Volga, and from which units they had come, so that we knew how many infantrymen, machine-gunners, mortar and artillery men, tank and signals men, the Army had lost. The Army's numbers had fallen all the time, suffering heavy losses as it did, but that did not mean that its military efficiency had also fallen. The Army's morale, in fact, had grown stronger; after every enemy attack had been beaten off, our soldiers' faith in the power of their weapons grew. We gained experience in battle with the enemy, and such experience, if I may put it this way, compensated for our physical losses. Of course, the loss of men is a bitter thing—but war is war.

It was therefore, I repeat, hard to part from the commanders and political workers I was seeing off. In the days of stress for the whole Army, particularly when we had suffered partial defeats, when every man and every inch of ground had had a special value, it had been very hard listening to reports by commanders and political workers on how the enemy had taken some block or other, or even some house, which was important for our defence. Sometimes it had appeared as if the commander who was reporting had not conducted the battle properly, had made a blunder, had not used all the possibilities open to him. Sometimes such reports and conversations had led to voices being raised. Then, some time later, it had become clear that the commander and the whole unit could not have done more, and that without prompting and urging they had in fact done a great deal.

I recall Sologub's division, which began to do battle with the Germans before the Germans crossed the Don, on the River Chir. Fighting then as part of the 64th Army, the division beat off an offensive by the 51st Army Corps, which was thrown in by Paulus against the flank and rear of the 62nd Army. This division also fought valiantly on the banks of the Don, where, in one of the battles, the Divisional Commander, Ivan Petrovich Sologub, died a hero's death.

I can still see this tall, slim commander, a true son of the

Soviet people, a man who did not bow his head to German shells.

I remember the end of July 1942. It was a hot, sunny day. Sologub and I were on Hill 116.0, north of the village of Rychkovski, on the right bank of the Don. I was giving the division some instructions. Suddenly the enemy, who must have spotted us, opened fire on the hill with 150-mm. guns. The distance between the bursting shells narrowed, and the explosions came closer to us. The shells would clearly soon be bursting right on the top of the hill. I then proposed to Ivan Petrovich that he should return to H.Q. He looked at me and said:

'And you? Can I really retreat from this hill before you?'

I reassured him, saying that it was not a retreat, but a return to our units from reconnaissance, so that we could lead our units forward.

Moving down the steppe, as smooth as a table top, under heavy enemy fire, was not exactly a pleasant occupation. But, watching Sologub's tall figure, I could not but admire the even, unhurried step with which he went on ahead.

An officer from divisional H.Q. with him was wounded by a shell that burst close to them. Sologub calmly went up to him, took his arm and started down the hill with him. I caught up with them in a gully, where Sologub was dressing the officer's wounds, and I noticed how the Divisional Commander's calm, confident manner had a marked effect on the wounded officer.

That was the kind of man who commanded the 112th Division. In Colonel Sologub you could sense the power of a commander and a leader.

My next contact with the 112th Division was on September 12, on the banks of the Volga. The division was now under the command of Colonel Yermolkin. The division was during manœuvres in the city: from Mamayev Kurgan to Vishnevaya Gully, at the Tractor factory and in other places where the enemy was about to attack us. It was in a hundred or so battles, including at least ten on the enemy's main line of advance.

The division was particularly expert at manœuvring, which does credit to its commander and H.Q. staff. It was never behindhand, and corageously beat off attacks by the enemy's numerically superior forces.

I had had contact with Smekhotvorov's division since I was with the first reserve army in May 1942, when it was still in the process of formation. I had also since then known General Fedor Nikandrovich Smekhotvorov. In the tactical exercises we carried out in the Tula area, Smekhotvorov showed his knowledge of modern warfare, the sharpness of his mind and his ability to do everything at the right time.

On its arrival in Stalingrad, this division was given the task of defending the Krasny Oktyabr settlement. The division did little manœuvring, but beat off dozens of attacks by enemy forces many times greater than its own. The soldiers of this division, following the example of their commanders and political workers, never looked behind them. If the Germans managed to capture two or three streets in a week, they did so at the cost of heavy losses. The men of this division did not retreat. The Germans advanced on this sector only by filling the dug-outs and trenches with their dead. Even in the bitterest fighting Smekhotvorov never showed the slightest trace of faint-heartedness or confusion. I can still hear his calm, measured voice today. In the days when hundreds of bombers and dive-bombers were over his division, when shells were bursting in their thousands on the sector defended by units of his division and there was nothing but bomb and shell explosions to be heard, and when in a telephone conversation with him you could hear the wail of German dive-bomber sirens, Smekhotvorov, it seemed, was even calmer. He did his administrative work only a few hundred yards from the firing line.

The division commanded by Smekhotvorov fought to the death, smashing German regiments and divisions; it would not retreat, and he left the city only when the enemy was encircled, when he was no longer attacking, but defending.

I also said good-bye to General Victor Grigorievich Zholudev. His 37th Guards Infantry Division had been in the city a shorter time than the others, but had earned no less credit.

The Germans broke through Zholudev's division and seized the Tractor factory, but they paid so dearly for this breakthrough, and lost so many men and so much material, that

261

they were unable to develop the attack any further. It was not one, not two, but five whole enemy divisions, including two panzer divisions, that broke through the regiments of the 37th Guards Division to the Tractor factory.

I remember V. G. Zholudev arriving at the Army's command post with his deputies early on the morning of October 4. Crossing the Volga in boats, they had come under heavy artillery and mortar fire.

Gurov, Krylov, and I welcomed him. We were all bundled in together—there were no separate 'offices'. As he came in, Zholudev banged his head on the door post. He was dressed in a commando's fur jacket. His powerful figure and sprawling gait bespoke a man born to fight in open spaces, with unbounded room for manœuvre.

After being given the job of defending the approaches to the Tractor factory, Zholudev began to ask each of us questions, trying to understand what city fighting was all about. We tried to explain the particular features of this kind of fighting to him as comprehensively as we could. When N.I. Krylov told him that the 37th Division's command post was ready on the bank of the Volga, not far from the Barrikady factory, Zholudev asked persistently for the command post to be moved to the area of the stadium in the Tractor factory settlement.

'We can't,' I told him. 'The area round the stadium is under artillery and mortar fire and we have no right to risk the life of the Divisional Commander . . .'

He left after a quick breakfast with us, as the enemy had begun artillery and bombing preparations.

When General Zholudev was buried in his dug-out by a German bomb which caught the command post, an Army H.Q. rescue squad went to his aid. When it was reported to me that air was getting through to the dug-out and the people inside were still alive, I ordered that they should all be brought to the Army command post.

An hour and a half later a man came into the Military Council covered in dust and sweat. He could hardly walk. It was General Zholudev. He seemed to have grown shorter.

'Comrades of the Military Council,' he reported, 'the 37th Guards Division has not retreated, what remains of it is continuing to fight heroically . . .'

Having said this, he sat down on a bank of earth and buried his face in his hands.

No words were needed to tell us what this man of steel was going through.

On December 24 units of Guriev's 39th Guards Division, operating in the grounds of the Krasny Oktyabr factory, began to storm the workshops where the Germans were ensconced.

At nightfall storm groups had cleared the Germans out of the calibration, central sorting and machine shops, then reached the western outskirts of the factory, thereby surrounding the Germans left in the factory. The enemy put up exceptional resistance, not wishing to retreat eastward from the factory to the destroyed houses and into the open.

During the night of the 24th, after a short breathing-space, the guardsmen continued to storm the factory.

Hand-to-hand fighting and close fighting with hand-grenades, continued till morning. In close fighting the Germans could not stand up against the quick-acting resourcefulness and pressure of our storm groups, and by morning the factory was completely cleared.

The Germans managed to hold out only in the main office building, which they had turned into a powerful stronghold of defence. A few days later, however, they were surrounded and finished off by storm groups of Sokolov's 45th Division.

Now that the Army had joined up with Lyudnikov's division and occupied the Krasny Oktyabr factory, and with the Volga frozen over and peaceful behind it, it could manœuvre more freely and plan more decisive attacks on the enemy.

To replace the units withdrawn to G.H.Q. Reserve, we were sent some reinforcements, consisting of an administrative unit and a number of small units with strong fire-power. They were not suited for offensive action, but were good in defence. To begin with we put these units on islands in the Volga—Sporny, Zaitsevski and Golodny—then they relieved some of Lyudnikov's and Rodimtsev's units.

These units were given the task of preventing the enemy from reaching the Volga if he tried to break out of encirclement eastward across the river.

The Army Military Council now decided to seize and

firmly hold Mamayev Kurgan, then to send in strong forces to take Hill 107.5, and thereby cut off the enemy's detachments in the city from those in the workers' settlements, so as later to wipe them out unit by unit.

To take Mamayev Kurgan the Army could draw on Batyuk's division, and for the attack on Hill 107.5— Sokolov's and Guriev's divisions and Shtrigol's Marine Infantry Brigade.

Gorishny's division was attacking the Barrikady settlement and had to cover the attack from the north.

Rodimtsev's division, by active operations in the central area of the city, would cover the Army's left flank.

Lyudnikov's division was withdrawn behind the Army's main line, as it needed to reorganize itself.

Colonel Gorokhov's group was given the job of advancing from the area of Rynok and Spartanovka and seizing the Tractor factory, and at the same time pinning down the enemy in the north of the workers' settlements.

For the accomplishment of this task, Army H.Q. drew up separate orders. This was the order for the main attacking force:

1. The encircled enemy, with limited forces, is putting up stiff resistance, trying to hold the positions he occupies.

2. On the morning of 28.12.42 the Army will continue the consistent destruction of the enemy, its main attack being directed towards Hill 107.5.

3. Sokolov's division will attack in the area of Tsentralnaya Street, seize Promyshlennaya Street and then reach the western outskirts of Zherdevsk . . .

4. Guriev's division, with an attached company of T-34 tanks, the 457th Artillery Regiment, one 203-mm. and two 152-mm. batteries, will attack at Karuselnaya Street, occupy Pinskaya Street and then seize Hill 107.5 . . .

5. Shtrigol's brigade, with one 203-mm. and three 152-mm. attached batteries, covered by one battalion from Ovrazhnaya Street, will occupy Narodnaya Street, then reach the eastern side of the gully west of Narodnaya Street . . .

6. Batyuk's division, holding the position it has occupied, will cover the attack by Shtrigol's brigade, neutralize the enemy's firing positions in the area of Mamayev Kurgan and not allow the enemy to counter-attack from the Tirov area.

7. The officer in charge of the Army's chemical department will prepare a smoke-screen on the right flank of Batyuk's division, so as to blind the enemy's firing positions.

During the attack and the destruction of the enemy's fortifications, flame-throwers will be used.

8. The chief of staff of Army engineering will:

(a) ensure that groups of tanks are accompanied by groups of sappers with mine-clearing equipment;

(b) provide men and material for the immediate consolidation and equipping of buildings captured west of the railway line as blockhouses.

9. The tasks of the three regiments of the Army artillery group will be:

(a) the destruction of the enemy's artillery batteries;

(b) the destruction and neutralization of firing positions in the enemy's front line and behind the lines;

(c) to cover the attacking troops;

(d) at the beginning of the infantry attack to blind the enemy's observation posts.

Units will be prepared by 20.00 on December 27. The time for the beginning of the attack will be the subject of a separate order.

We knew that the encircled enemy forces amounted to not less than twenty divisions. In fact, there were twenty-two of them, in all about 300,000 men. This powerful group was encircled and held in an iron ring by seven armies, those under A. S. Zhadov, I. V. Galanin, P. I. Batov, I. M. Chistyakov, F. I. Tolbukhin, M. S. Shumilov, and the 62nd Army.

Of the twenty-two enemy divisions facing the seven armies of the Don Front, six divisions remained against the 62nd Army (the 79th, 94th, 100th, 295th, 305th and 389th Infantry Divisions). These divisions had been reinforced with five engineering battalions (the 50th, 162nd, 294th, 366th and 672nd), which Hitler had sent in to storm the city in October.

It is difficult to explain why Paulus kept a third of his total forces facing the 62nd Army, weakened and exhausted by five months of non-stop battle, but that is the fact. When he found himself surrounded, he did not forget the 62nd Army and kept a powerful force in the field against it. Our attacks against Mamayev Kurgan and through the Krasny Oktyabr settlement towards Hill 107.5, therefore, came up against not only stubborn resistance, but also counter-attacks.

In addition, having learned from bitter experience that in city conditions it is tactically impossible not only to attack but also to defend on a continuous front in trenches, the enemy made the best use of the stoutest buildings and the basements of dwelling-houses as strongpoints, which we found it extremely difficult to take.

For example, to destroy the enemy strongpoint in the main office building of the Krasny Oktyabr factory, the storm group of Sokolov's division had to smash through a main wall. They did so with the help of a 122-mm. howitzer, which was pulled into the occupied section of the factory piecemeal. There it was assembled and put into action. After several rounds at point-blank range a breach was made in the wall, and the German garrison in the factory ceased to exist.

As before, the streets and squares were empty. Neither the enemy nor ourselves could operate in the open. Anyone who lifted his head carelessly or ran across the street was overtaken by a bullet from a sniper or a burst from a tommy-gun.

To begin with, the surrounded German soldiers put up stubborn resistance. The generals and officers obviously carefully kept back from them the news that the ring of Soviet armies had been closed at Kalach. But when, nevertheless, the German soldiers found out about their situation, they were reassured by the fact that a powerful panzer group under von Manstein was coming to the rescue. And so, until the end of December, they lived in hopes and defended themselves desperately, often to the last round. There were virtually no prisoners.

Only after von Manstein's group was defeated, and our armies had driven the Germans back to Kharkov, Lugansk and Rostov-on-Don, did the morale of the encircled troops become noticeably worse. Not only the rank and file, but also the officers and generals, stopped believing in a break-through and release from encirclement.

Soon our men began to take even officers as prisoners, which showed the steep drop in the morale and strength of Paulus's army.

In the demoralization of the enemy's encircled troops no small role was played by the work of our political organs, which put out special radio broadcasts for the German soldiers, describing what awaited them in the very near future. The German soldiers soon realized that food for more than 300,000 men could only be brought by air. But, as our broadcasts said, to cover the transport planes intending to deliver food, ammunition and fuel and evacuate the wounded on the return flight, a large number of fighter planes would be needed, planes which Hitler now had to have on other sectors of the front. 'German officers and men, your daily ration will therefore soon be down to 3½ ozs of bread and a third of an ounce of cold sausage.'

Such broadcasts had their effect on the minds of the encircled men, because they were correct: the German soldiers were already beginning to feel the pangs of hunger.

Many German officers and men at the front kept diaries. Why they did so, I do not know, but from the diaries which fell into our hands one can see how the morale of the German armies, which reached its peak in July and August, began to fall, until in January 1943 it had virtually disappeared altogether.

I have in front of me the diary of Wilhelm Hoffman. The notes show that Hoffman served in a company and then in a battalion office of the 267th Regiment of the 94th Infantry Division. The diary begins in May 1942. It looks impressive, with stout binding. I have the diary in my personal files. My quotations from the diary begin with the first mention of the word 'Stalingrad'.

July 27. After long marches across the Don steppe, we finally reached the Don and took the big village of Tsim-lyanskaya almost without a battle. Hot, extremely hot, and how pleased we all were when we saw the Don. How pleasant it was to bathe in the fresh Don water and wash our sweat-soaked clothes.

They say that first-class wine is made in this village. I'll have to send ten bottles home to father—a present from Willi. How pleased he'll be . . .

Today, after we'd had a bath, the company commander told us that if our future operations are as successful, we'll soon reach the Volga, take Stalingrad and then the war will inevitably soon be over. Perhaps we'll be home by Christmas.

July 29. We have been resting for two days. The neighbouring regiment, the 264th, this morning crossed the river. We can hear fighting going on. The company commander says the Russian troops are completely broken, and cannot hold out any longer. To reach the Volga and take Stalingrad is not so difficult for us. The Führer knows where the Russians' weak point is. Victory is not far away.

August 1. Our regiment has crossed the Don and is advancing eastward . . . We are advancing almost without battle. The heat is terrible, the steppe is bare, waterless. For the first time in my life I saw a mirage with my own eyes. It's such a miracle of nature that it's difficult to explain it. There was what looked like a wood and a lake ahead. They invited you to go and rest there. The wood and the lake get further away or vanish like mist when you start going towards them. They are a mirage! . . .

August 2. We occupied some station or other, came to the River Sal. The River Sal is not the Don, its water is warm, hardly makes you feel any fresher . . .

What great spaces the Soviets occupy, what rich fields there are to be had here after the war's over! Only let's get it over with quickly. I believe that the Führer will carry the thing through to a successful end.

August 7. After light fighting we have reached the River Aksay—which is muddy, hardly moves at all and in places has dried up. The one cheering thing is that the Volga and Stalingrad are near, and then—the end of the war. Our company is tearing ahead. Today I wrote to Elsa: 'We shall soon see each other. All of us feel that the end, victory, is near.'

August 10. Our regiment is advancing on Abganerovo. The Führer's orders were read out to us. He expects victory of us. We are all convinced that they can't stop us.

August 12. We are advancing towards Stalingrad along the railway line. Yesterday Russian 'katyushi' and then tanks halted our regiment. 'The Russians are throwing in their last forces,' Captain Werner explained to me. Large-scale help is coming up for us, and the Russians will be beaten.

This morning outstanding soldiers were presented with decorations for the fighting near Kantemirovka. Will I really go back to Elsa without a decoration? I believe that for Stalingrad the Führer will decorate even me.

August 17. The last few days our regiment has been in battle all the time. The Russians are resisting. With heavy losses we have reached Tinguta. The Russian air force has started being cheeky, especially at night. This week our company has lost nineteen men. The heat and the constant fighting are utterly exhausting. But we are all ready to advance quickly to the Volga. They say Stalingrad is now twenty-five miles away . . .

August 23. Splendid news—north of Stalingrad our troops have reached the Volga and captured part of the city. The Russians have two alternatives, either to flee across the Volga or give themselves up. Our company's interpreter has interrogated a captured Russian officer. He was wounded, but asserted that the Russians would fight for Stalingrad to the last round. Something incomprehensible is, in fact, going on. In the north our troops capture a part of Stalingrad and reach the Volga, but in the south the doomed divisions are continuing to resist bitterly. Fanaticism . . .

August 27. A continuous cannonade on all sides. We are slowly advancing. Less than twenty miles to go to Stalingrad. In the daytime we can see the smoke of fires, at night-time the bright glow. They say that the city is on fire; on the Führer's orders our Luftwaffe has sent it up in flames. That's what the Russians need, to stop them from resisting . . .

We are being sent to another sector . . .

September 1. The Russians are retreating towards the Volga. Are they really going to fight on the very bank of the Volga? It's madness. Last night the Russian air force never left us in peace, circling overhead and bombing us all the time. We have been putting up strong anti-aircraft fire. It's a mystery where the local Russian population has disappeared to. You don't even see any old men or children . . .

September 4. We are being sent northward along the front towards Stalingrad. We marched all night and by dawn had reached Voroponovo Station. We can already see the smoking town. It's a happy thought that the end of the war is getting nearer. That's what everyone is saying. If only the days and nights would pass more quickly . . .

September 5. Our regiment has been ordered to attack Sadovaya Station—that's nearly in Stalingrad. Are the Russians really thinking of holding out in the city itself? We had no peace all night from the Russian artillery and aeroplanes. Lots of wounded are being brought by. God protect me. . .

September 8. Two days of non-stop fighting. The Russians are defending themselves with insane stubbornness. Our regiment has lost many men from the 'katyushi', which belch out terrible fire. I have been sent to work at battalion H.Q. It must be mother's prayers that have taken me away from the company's trenches . . .

September 11. Our battalion is fighting in the suburbs of Stalingrad. We can already see the Volga; firing is going on all the time. Wherever you look is fire and flames . . . Russian cannon and machine-guns are firing out of the burning city. Fanatics . . .

September 13. An unlucky number. This morning 'katyushi' attacks caused the company heavy losses: twenty-seven dead and fifty wounded. The Russians are fighting desperately like wild beasts, don't give themselves up, but come up close and then throw grenades. Lieutenant Kraus was killed yesterday, and there is no company commander.

September 16. Our battalion, plus tanks, is attacking

the elevator, from which smoke is pouring—the grain in it is burning, the Russians seem to have set light to it themselves. Barbarism. The battalion is suffering heavy losses. There are not more than sixty men left in each company. The elevator is occupied not by men but by devils that no flames or bullets can destroy.

September 18. Fighting is going on inside the elevator. The Russians inside are condemned men; the battalion commander says: 'The commissars have ordered those men to die in the elevator'.

If all the buildings of Stalingrad are defended like this then none of our soldiers will get back to Germany. I had a letter from Elsa today. She's expecting me home when victory's won.

September 20. The battle for the elevator is still going on. The Russians are firing on all sides. We stay in our cellar; you can't go out into the street. Sergeant-Major Nuschke was killed today running across the street. Poor fellow, he's got three children.

September 22. Russian resistance in the elevator has been broken. Our troops are advancing towards the Volga. We found about forty Russian dead in the elevator building. Half of them were wearing naval uniform—sea devils. One prisoner was captured, seriously wounded, who can't speak, or is shamming.

The whole of our battalion has as many men as a regular company. Our old soldiers have never experienced such bitter fighting before.

September 26. Our regiment is involved in constant heavy fighting. After the elevator was taken the Russians continued to defend themselves just as stubbornly. You don't see them at all, they have established themselves in houses and cellars and are firing on all sides, including from our rear—barbarians, they use gangster methods.

In the blocks captured two days ago Russian soldiers appeared from somewhere or other and fighting has flared up with fresh vigour. Our men are being killed not only in the firing line, but in the rear, in buildings we have already occupied.

The Russians have stopped surrendering at all. If we take any prisoners it's because they are hopelessly wounded, and can't move by themselves. Stalingrad is hell. Those who are merely wounded are lucky; they will doubtless be at home and celebrate victory with their families. (He still believes in victory. v.c.)

September 28. Our regiment, and the whole division, are today celebrating victory. Together with our tank crews we have taken the southern part of the city and reached the Volga. We paid dearly for our victory. In three weeks we have occupied about five and a half square miles. The commander has congratulated us on our victory . . .

Regimental H.Q. has telephoned to say that the division is being withdrawn for a rest and to be brought back up to strength. Some companies have only a few men left.

When on earth is the war going to finish? When will the Russian forces in Stalingrad be exhausted? Will this blood-bath be over by Christmas?

October 2. The number of men in our battalion had dropped to between eighty and ninety. We are under orders to move somewhere northward during the night. Our battalion will be the first to attack.

Yesterday I wrote to Elsa; there was no good or happy news I could give her, and I couldn't lie. In Stalingrad anyone can die at any moment.

October 3. After marching through the night we have established ourselves in a shrub-covered gully. We are apparently going to attack the factories, the chimneys of which we can see clearly. Behind them is the Volga. We have entered a new area. It was night but we saw many crosses with our helmets on top. Have we really lost so many men? Damn this Stalingrad!

October 4. Our regiment is attacking the Barrikady settlement. A lot of Russian tommy-gunners have appeared. Where are they bringing them from?

October 5. Our battalion has gone into the attack four times, and got stopped each time. Russian snipers hit anyone who shows himself carelessly from behind shelter.

October 10. The Russians are so close to us that our planes cannot bomb them. We are preparing for a decisive attack. The Führer has ordered the whole of Stalingrad to be taken as rapidly as possible.

October 14. It has been fantastic since morning: our aeroplanes and artillery have been hammering the Russian positions for hours on end; everything in sight is being blotted from the face of the earth ...

October 17. Fighting has been going on continuously for four days, with unprecedented ferocity. During this time our regiment has advanced barely half a mile. The Russian firing is causing us heavy losses. Men and officers alike have become bitter and silent.

October 22. Our regiment has failed to break into the factory. We have lost many men; every time you move you have to jump over bodies. You can scarcely breathe in the daytime: there is nowhere and no one to remove the bodies, so they are left there to rot. Who would have thought three months ago that instead of the joy of victory we would have to endure such sacrifice and torture, the end of which is nowhere in sight? ...

The soldiers are calling Stalingrad the mass grave of the Wehrmacht. There are very few men left in the companies. We have been told we are soon going to be withdrawn to be brought back up to strength.

October 27. Our troops have captured the whole of the Barrikady factory, but we cannot break through to the Volga. The Russians are not men, but some kind of cast-iron creatures; they never get tired and are not afraid of fire. We are absolutely exhausted; our regiment now has barely the strength of a company. The Russian artillery at the other side of the Volga won't let you lift your head ...

October 28. Every soldier sees himself as a condemned man. The only hope is to be wounded and taken back to the rear.

Have just had the news that our regiment is to be withdrawn to the rear for reinforcements. This is the third time this autumn.

October 30. We have had no rest. Our battalion was given a few transport drivers and sent to another part of the front, on the northern outskirts of Stalingrad. You can scarcely do battle with a complement of this size. Everyone is depressed. Stalingrad has turned us into beings without feelings—we are tired, exhausted, bitter.

If our relatives and families could see us now they would be horrified.

November 3. In the last few days our battalion has several times tried to attack the Russian positions in the Spartanovka settlement, to no avail. On this sector also the Russians won't let you lift your head. There have been a number of cases of self-inflicted wounds and malingering among the men. Every day I write two or three reports about them.

November 10. A letter from Elsa today. Everyone expects us home for Christmas. In Germany everyone believes we already hold Stalingrad. How wrong they are. If they could only see what Stalingrad has done to our army.

November 18. Our attack with tanks yesterday had no success. After our attack the field was littered with dead.

November 21. The Russians have gone over to the offensive along the whole front. Fierce fighting is going on. So, there it is—the Volga, victory and soon home to our families! We shall obviously be seeing them next in the other world.

November 29. We are encircled. It was announced this morning that the Führer has said: 'The army can trust me to do everything necessary to ensure supplies and rapidly break the encirclement'.

December 3. We are on hunger rations and waiting for the rescue that the Führer promised.

I send letters home, but there is no reply.

December 7. Rations have been cut to such an extent that the soldiers are suffering terribly from hunger; they are issuing one loaf of stale bread for five men.

December 11. Three questions are obsessing every soldier and officer: When will the Russians stop firing and let us sleep in peace, if only for one night? How and with what are we going to fill our empty stomachs, which, apart from 3½–7 ozs of bread, receive virtually nothing at all? And when will Hitler take any decisive steps to free our armies from encirclement?

December 14. Everybody is racked with hunger. Frozen potatoes are the best meal, but to get them out of the ice-covered ground under fire from Russian bullets is not so easy.

December 18. The officers today told the soldiers to be prepared for action. General Manstein is approaching Stalingrad from the south with strong forces. This news brought hope to the soldiers' hearts. God, let it be!

December 21. We are waiting for the order, but for some reason or other it has been a long time coming. Can it be that it is not true about Manstein? This is worse than any torture.

December 23. Still no orders. It was all a bluff with Manstein. Or has he been defeated at the approaches to Stalingrad?

December 25. The Russian radio has announced the defeat of Manstein. Ahead of us is either death or captivity.

December 26. The horses have already been eaten. I would eat a cat! they say its meat is also tasty. The soldiers look like corpses or lunatics, looking for something to put in their mouths. They no longer take cover from Russian shells; they haven't the strength to walk, run away and hide. A curse on this war! . . .

That was the end of the diary, and presumably of its author.

At the beginning of January we were visited at our command post by the Commander of the Don Front, Lieutenant-General Konstantin Konstantinovich Rokossovski, the Member of the Front Military Council, Major-General Konstantin Fedorovich Telegin, and the Front Artillery Commander, Major-General Vasili Ivanovich Kazakov. They crossed the Volga on the ice.

Leaving their vehicle near the Army H.Q. dug-out, Rokossovski and Telegin asked us questions for a long time, where and in what conditions we spent the period of heavy fighting and the fires, how we breathed when the Germans, during their advance, scattered thousands and thousands of bombs on the city.

Entering the dug-out, and sitting down on the bench of earth at the table of earth, the Front Commander briefly

275

outlined the plan for the destruction of the encircled enemy group, and set the Army its tasks. The crux of the plan was that the main attack would be delivered from the west, by the armies of Generals Batov and Chistyakov, with the aim of splitting the encircled enemy group. A simultaneous attack would be delivered from the north by the armies of Generals Zhadov and Galanin, and from the south by the armies of Generals Shumilov and Tolbukhin. The 62nd Army had the job of 'carrying out active operations from the east, so as to attract more enemy forces in its direction, preventing them from reaching the Volga if they try to break out of encirclement across the frozen Volga'.

The task was clear enough, and I assured the Front Commander that it would be carried out, and that until the main attack was launched by the Front armies, Paulus would not withdraw a single division from the city.

The Front H.Q. officers then asked us several times:

'Will the 62nd Army be able to hold the enemy, if, under attack from our armies from the west, he throws all his forces eastward?'

N. I. Krylov answered this as follows:

'If in the summer and autumn all Paulus's forces were unable to throw us into the Volga, then the hungry and half-frozen Germans won't move even six steps eastward.'

I was asked a similar question by the Front Chief of Staff, General Malinin. I replied that the Germans in 1943 were no longer what they were in 1942. They now sat tied up in the city waiting for us to deal with them. Finally, I said that Paulus's army was not really an army, but a campful of armed prisoners.

Until the beginning of the offensive by all the armies of the Front, that is until January 10, the units of the 62nd Army, carrying out the task set them by the Commander of the Front, attacked the waiting enemy with storm groups. Our positions improved day by day. Every day dozens of strong-points and pill-boxes were destroyed and captured. Six of the enemy's twenty-two divisions and five engineering battalions, therefore, remained pinned down by our Army.

Particularly active operations were carried out during these days by the storm groups of Batyuk's division. In the fighting on Mamayev Kurgan they pinned down a number of regiments, and, capturing the enemy's forward observation posts, deprived the German generals of the opportunity to watch the regrouping of our armies in the city.

Here I must make it clear that while on other sectors of the front our armies could be successful or unsuccessful, advance or fall back half a mile or so during a given day, we could not afford any such luxury on Mamayev Kurgan.

From the second half of September until January 12, nearly four months (112 days to be precise), constant and unrelenting fighting went on around the water-tanks.

How many times the summit of the hill changed hands no one can say; there are no witnesses, no one who kept count, to tell us. They did not survive.

Mamayev Kurgan was fought for by soldiers of Rodimtsev's division, the whole of Gorishny's division, and above all Batyuk's renowned and four-times-decorated guards' division. The regiments of this division arrived on the right bank on September 21, and on the 22nd went into battle at Dolgi Gully. The division then, as it were, grew into Mamayev Kurgan and its ridges, and fought on it to the end, until, on January 26, we linked up with the forces of the Don Front, with General Chistyakov's divisions.

A few words about Divisional Commander Nikolay Filippovich Batyuk. He arrived in the city a lieutenant-colonel and left it, after Paulus's army had been smashed, a general. He combined three invaluable qualities—the tenacity of a commander, courage and Party spirit. He could be strict and just, he was feared and loved. His men saw him frequently. He suffered with his legs, and at times could scarcely walk, but he did not sit comfortably in his dug-out: he went out to the front line, to his observation posts, using a stick, but he returned to his dug-out on his aide-de-camp's shoulders, but only at night, so that no one should see. Batyuk did everything he could to conceal his illness, and I found out about it only in January, when he could virtually not walk at all without assistance. He would not hesitate to tell any chief of staff or subordinate the truth to his face, however bitter it might be. His reports required neither clarification nor verification; they were always correct.

Batyuk's division had distinguished itself before it came to us, near Kastornoye, where it successfully repulsed a mass tank attack. This division trained soldiers known not only to the men of Stalingrad, but also to the whole country: the battery commander and celebrated destroyer of tanks, Shuklin; the commander of a mortar battery, who always hit the target, Bezdidko; the famous snipers—Vasili Zaitsev, Viktor Medvedev, Akhmet Avzalov, and many, many other officers and men, heroes of the Battle of Stalingrad. The division's Party organization developed many fine commanders: Regimental Commander Mitelev, Battalion Commander Mayak, who died on Mamayev Kurgan at the end of the fighting, Company Commander Shumakov, and fine political workers like Tkachenko, Yermakov, Soloviev and Grubrin, and Party organizers Yevdokimov, Krushinski and Ladyzhenko.

The team of commanders and political workers of this division went through Kastornoye, Stalingrad, Zaporozhe and Odessa, through Lublin and Poznan, and ended its military path victoriously in Berlin.

General Batyuk did not accompany us to Berlin. He was killed in the Ukraine, Slavyansk. We buried him on the bank of the northern Donets. It would be just to remove his remains to Volgograd, to Mamayev Kurgan, where the division he commanded fought. This was something he earned, because he was a driving force in the battle for Mamayev Kurgan, for the city on the Volga.

On 10 January 1943, the whole of the Don Front armies simultaneously went on to the offensive, cutting into the encircled German group. The 62nd Army also moved westward towards the advancing armies. Particularly fierce fighting broke out on Mamayev Kurgan. This showed how correctly the enemy had estimated the tactical value of Mamayev Kurgan. The attack by Batyuk's division across Mamayev Kurgan was met the whole time, until January 25, that is, by counter-attacks from the enemy, who had summoned up his final strength to hold his positions here.

On sectors occupied by other Army divisions, the enemy did not retreat, but when he counter-attacked, as on Mamayev Kurgan, he made no progress. He continued to fire back, often to the last round.

On January 23, an officer of Sokolov's division reported the following unusual incident. His units approached the western outskirts of the Krasny Oktyabr settlement and surrounded a strong German defence point. To avoid unnecessary bloodshed, it was proposed to the garrison that they should surrender. After long parleying the Germans asked our soldiers for bread. Our men took pity on the hungry Germans and handed over a number of loaves. Having received the bread, and presumably feeling refreshed, the Germans started firing back again.

After such 'diplomatic negotiations' our men quickly got in touch with the artillery, who drew up a number of guns and began firing at point-blank range at the Germans' strongpoint. When the strongpoint had been captured it was found that it was occupied by a group of bold desperadoes, almost all of whom had several medals pinned to their breasts.

On January 25 we sensed that our armies were approaching from the west, and on reaching the western outskirts of the settlements, the 62nd Army discontinued its advance. Gorishny's, Sokolov's, Lyudnikov's, Guriev's and Rodimtsev's divisions turned northward to wipe out the Germans' northern group in the region of the factories and workers' settlements. Batyuk's division turned southward against the enemy's southern group. January 26 dawned—the day of the long-awaited link-up between troops of the 62nd Army and units of Batov's and Chistyakov's armies, advancing from the west.

This was how the meeting took place.

At dawn it was reported from an observation point that the Germans were rushing about in panic, the roar of engines could be heard, men in Red Army uniforms appeared ... Heavy tanks could be seen coming down a hillside. On the tanks were inscriptions: *Chelyabinsk Collective Farmer, Urals Metal-Worker* ...

Guardsmen of Rodimtsev's division ran forward with a red flag.

This joyous, moving encounter took place at 9.20 a.m. near the Krasny Oktyabr settlement. Captain A. F. Gushchin handed representatives of the units of Batov's army the banner, on the red cloth of which was written: 'A token of our meeting on 26.1.1943'.

The eyes of the hardened soldiers who met were filled with tears of joy.

Guards Captain P. Usenko told General Rodimtsev, who had now arrived, that he had accepted the banner from his renowned guardsmen.

'Tell your commander,' said General Rodimtsev, 'that this is a happy day for us: after five months of heavy and stubborn fighting we have finally met!'

Heavy tanks came up, and the crews, leaning out of the turrets, waved their hands in greeting. The powerful machines rolled on, towards the factories.

Soon other units of the 62nd Army met up with representatives of Batov's, Chistyakov's and Shumilov's armies.

Courageous men, who had lived through many bitter battles, and had passed through the crucible of great ordeals, wept, and did not hide their tears.

The enemy continued to resist, but every day more and more of his soldiers and officers surrendered. A few Soviet soldiers would on occasion round up hundreds of German prisoners.

On January 31, soldiers of the 64th Army took prisoner the Commander of the 6th Army, Field-Marshal von Paulus, and the whole of his H.Q. On that day the Germans' southern group abandoned its resistance. The fighting in the centre of the city was over. On the evening of the same day troops of the 62nd Army took prisoner the H.Q. staff of the 295th Infantry Division, led by its Commander, Major-General Korfes, and also the 4th Army Corps Commander who was with them, Lieutenant-General Pfeffer, the Commander of the 51st Corps—Lieutenant-General von Seydlitz-Kurzbach, the Chief of Staff of the 295th Division—Colonel Dissel, and a number of senior staff officers.

The German generals were made prisoner by three soldiers of the 62nd Army, under an eighteen-year-old Komsomol organizer of a signal regiment, Mikhail Porter, who had been in the fighting at Odessa, Sevastopol and Kerch, before coming to the Volga.

On the evening of January 31, Gurov, Krylov and I talked in my dug-out, now spacious and light, with the captured German generals. Seeing that they were hungry and nervous and anxious about their fate, I ordered tea to be brought and invited them to have a snack. They were all dressed in parade uniform and were wearing their medals. General Otto Korfes, picking up a glass of tea and a sandwich, asked:

'What's this, propaganda?'

I answered: 'If the general thinks that the tea and the sandwiches contain propaganda, we certainly won't insist that he accept our propagandist food . . .'

My reply made the prisoners somewhat brighter, and our conversation lasted for about an hour. General Korfes spoke more than any of the others. Generals Pfeffer and Seydlitz kept silent, saying they did not understand political affairs.

In the discussion General Korfes developed the idea that the position of Germany at that time had much in common with that at the time of Frederick the Great and Bismarck. Considering Hitler's mental stature and deeds to be no less than those of Frederick and Bismarck, Korfes obviously meant that if the latter had had their setbacks and nonetheless emerged to greatness, then Hitler's defeat on the Volga did not mean the end of Hitlerism. Germany, under Hitler's leadership, would survive this defeat and would in the end be victorious. Generals Pfeffer and Seydlitz sat, from time to time uttered the words 'jawohl' or 'nein', and wept copiously.

Finally, Lieutenant-General von Seydlitz-Kurzbach asked:

'What will happen to us?'

I told him the conditions of captivity, adding that they could if they wished wear their decorations and regalia, but could not carry weapons.

'What kind of weapons?' said Pfeffer, looking interested and seeming not to understand. He glanced at Seydlitz.

'Captured generals are not allowed to carry any kind of weapons,' I repeated.

Seydlitz then took a penknife out of his pocket and handed it across to me. Of course, I returned it to him, saying that we did not consider such 'weapons' to be dangerous.

After our conversation with the captured generals, we sent them off to Front H.Q., expressing the hope that they would soon get to know the real situation in the Soviet Union, so as to shake off their mistaken notions and the poison of Nazism.

Running several years ahead for a moment, I met General Otto Korfes again in 1949 in Berlin. He was then working actively for the German-Soviet Friendship Society. We met as old acquaintances. I was working as a representative of the Control Commission and was helping German friends to rebuild their war-shattered economy. Former Major-General Otto Korfes did a lot to strengthen friendship between the German and Soviet nations. Korfes was not the only one. Many German ex-generals, officers and soldiers, when they discovered the truth, began to work for peace and friendship.

After the German southern group had been liquidated, the northern group continued to resist, though it was clear that it would take only a few hours to wipe out the group.

On the morning of 2 February 1943, Gurov and I went to General I. I. Lyudnikov's observation post in the ruins of the Krasny Oktyabr factory offices. Not far away were the observation posts of Divisional Commanders Sokolov and Gorishny. The 62nd Army's final attack was delivered against the Tractor and Barrikady factories and their settlements. The attack was made by Gorishny's, Sokolov's, Batyuk's, Lyudnikov's, Guriev's and Rodimtsev's divisions, and Shtrigol's brigade. The Germans' northern group was attacked simultaneously from the west and north-west by units of neighbouring armies. The attack was launched at noon.

There was a brief preparation by our artillery, firing only at point-blank range and at visible targets. We could distinctly see the Germans rushing about among the ruins. Then our infantry units and tanks went into the attack.

The Germans who were still alive could not resist our final attack. They put their hands up. Their bayonets had scraps of white rag on them.

We watched hundreds of prisoners go by. They were taken to and across the Volga, towards which they had been fighting their way for about six months. Among the prisoners were Italians, Hungarians and Rumanians. All the privates and non-commissioned officers were emaciated, and their clothes were infected with vermin. Most wretched of all were the Rumanian soldiers; they were dressed so badly it was terrible to look at them. Although the temperature was thirty degrees below zero some of them were barefoot. The German officers, on the other hand, were well-fed and had pockets stuffed with cold sausage and other food, obviously left over after the meagre rations had been issued.

At the Army's last observation post, in the shattered offices of the Krasny Oktyabr factory, the Military Council, divisional and some regimental commanders met. We joyfully congratulated one another on the victory, and remembered those who had not lived to see it. In many faces, however, one read the question: What next? On February 2, the front line was a long way away, hundreds of miles from the Volga. Now that the victory here was ours, we had found ourselves deep in the rear.

Hitler, who in November 1942 had promised to rescue the encircled troops, was compelled to announce the disaster and declare three days of national mourning.

The 6th Army, which had been encircled and routed by the Volga, was no ordinary army. It contained twenty-two divisions with reinforcements, more than twice the size of a normal army.

Hitler boasted about its manoeuvrability and its power as a shock-force, its personnel—officers and men. The divisions of this Army were composed entirely of 'pure Aryans'. For example, the 79th Infantry Division was formed in August 1942 almost exclusively of soldiers between twenty and twenty-seven years old. The prisoners themselves told us that one in every five soldiers was a Nazi Party member.

The 6th Army's Commander, Friedrich von Paulus, was a typical German general. When he was storming the fortress on the Volga he was fifty-three years old, having spent thirty-three of them in the German army. In the first world war he was a combatant officer, but by the end of it he had become a general staff officer. After the defeat of the German army in 1918 Paulus did not retire, and spent a long time working in the Ministry of War, and then became chief of the armoured troops' administrative staff, and played an active part in preparations for the second world war.

When Hitler came to power, Paulus was moved to the post of Chief of Staff of the army under the command of Field-Marshal von Reichenau. With this army, in the autumn of 1939, Paulus invaded Poland, and in 1940 took part in the defeat of France. In September 1940 Paulus was appointed Quartermaster General of the General Staff of the Wehrmacht. In January 1941 he was promoted to the rank of general of the armoured forces and at the time of the invasion of the Soviet Union played a prominent part among the German generals.

During the days of the defeat of the 6th Army encircled by the Volga, Hitler decorated Paulus with the oak leaf to the Knight Cross of the Iron Cross, and named him a Field-Marshal.

The 6th Army was given the most crucial operations to carry out. On 10 May 1940, it was the first, on Hitler's orders, treacherously to cross Belgium's frontiers. Overcoming resistance by the Belgian armies at the Albert Canal, this German army swept like a whirlwind through the country, sowing death and destruction. The divisions of the 6th Army went through many European countries. After Brussels and Paris, it took part in the fighting in Yugoslavia and the conquest of Greece.

In 1941 Hitler turned the 6th Army eastward against the Soviet Union. It took part in the fighting in the vicinity of Kharkov and then went on towards the Volga. It was given the task of carrying out the most important part of the plan of campaign for 1942 in the south—the capture of the fortress on the Volga.

Hitler tried to hide the collapse of his strategic plans by creating an artificial halo round the 6th Army, which had already been routed. On 30 January 1943, Hitler's G.H.Q. issued a special communiqué, saying: 'The Russians are calling on the 6th Army men to surrender, but without exception they are continuing to stand and fight'. The following day the G.H.Q. reported: 'A small number of German and allied soldiers have surrendered to the Soviet armies alive'. This small number totalled more than 91,000. About the fate of his 2,500 officers, twenty-four generals and Field-Marshal von Paulus, now in Russian hands, Hitler remained silent.

By the Volga the Soviet army routed one of the strongest army groups Nazi Germany possessed, an army group which had been formed with crack units and absolutely bristling with weapons. Only after this group had been defeated were the 150,000 or so German dead collected and buried. The Volga steppe was covered with graves and crosses, more than a hundred thousand of them. We know that there are normally four or five times as many wounded as there are dead. Even at a conservative estimate, therefore, Stalingrad had cost the German Command not less than one and a half million men in killed, wounded, missing and taken prisoner.

In memory of the destroyed 6th Army, Hitler quickly created a new 6th Army, which was given the name of the '6th Army of Avengers'.

In the spring of 1944, those who had taken part in the defence of Stalingrad, the men of the 62nd Army, had occasion to meet this '6th Army of Avengers' on the fields of the Ukraine. It was under the command of Colonel-General Holidt, who had taken part in the unsuccessful attempt to break the encirclement of Paulus's army. He had seventeen divisions; the 62nd Army had only nine. The battle was bitterly fought. 'The Avengers' counter-attacked a number of times, as if they knew that we had few reserves (our Army had just made a long, fighting advance). They wanted to drive the 62nd Army back to the Volga, but they miscalculated: we had another, more powerful, reserve—experience, gained in the fighting on that very Volga. And the army of 'avengers' was smashed, and what was left of it, together with its Army H.Q., raced through Odessa to the River Dnestr.

On the sunny morning of February 4, a rally was called in the Square of Fallen Warriors. Soldiers and citizens came through the snow-covered, bomb-and shell-scarred streets of the hero city. I can see, as if it were today, the burnt-out trucks on the railway lines, the trams riddled with bullet holes and shell and bomb splinters, the ruins of multi-storey buildings, and the streets, piled with shattered German equipment. In the centre of the city, destroyed by German bombers, were the scorched walls of the Central Universal Store, and the shattered buildings of the Post Office and the Book Store.

On the Square of Fallen Warriors were fresh shell and mortar craters. Fighting had been going on here three days ago against the remnants of the German armies. Meeting here now were the Party and local government leaders of the city and district, soldiers, commanders and political workers, citizens—all those who had taken part in the heroic battle. At the meeting was Nikita Sergeyevich Khrushchev, member of the Politbureau of the Party's Central Committee and

Member of the Military Council for the Stalingrad Front. He was surrounded by military comrades-in-arms and friends. He embraced and kissed K. A. Gurov, A. I. Rodimtsev, M. S. Shumilov, myself and others. Then, to thunderous applause, together with A. S. Chuyanov, I. A. Piksin, D. M. Pigalev, and generals of the 26nd and 64th Armies, he went up on to the platform.

The rally was opened by the Chairman of the City Soviet, Comrade Pigalev, who, on behalf of the workers of the city, warmly thanked those who played a heroic part in the Battle of Stalingrad.

'The days of the bitterest fighting and ordeals are behind us,' he said. 'Eternal glory to the heroes of Stalingrad, with whose blood victory was won! Glory to our courageous soldiers and commanders! Glory to our Communist Party!'

I was asked to speak next. I confess, it was difficult for me to speak at all. Seeing the ranks of soldiers with whom I had spent these hundred and eighty days and nights under fire, I felt extremely moved. I began my speech with the words:

'We swore we would fight to the death and not surrender Stalingrad to the enemy; we held out; we kept our promise to our country . . .'

What I said afterwards I do not remember. I remember only that I wanted to tell those gathered at the rally that the final reckoning with the Nazi invaders still lay ahead of us.

Major-General A. I. Rodimtsev addressed the rally with fiery words:

'The guards withstood the onslaught of a numerically superior enemy. Their stubborn and tenacious resistance was not broken by bombs or shells or furious attacks. In the annals of the great Battle of Stalingrad, the names of the warrior-guardsmen, the staunch defenders of the city, will live for ever. The 13th Guards Division has today been one hundred and forty days on the right bank of the Volga. It is painful to look at this mutilated city, every inch of earth, every stone, of which bears the terrible traces of war. And we swear to our country that we will smash the enemy, in the tradition of the guards, in the tradition of Stalingrad.'

General Shumilov then came to the microphone. The troops of his army had fought the Germans at the southern approaches to the city and prevented them from reaching the Volga.

'On February 2,' he said, 'we heard the last firing in Stalingrad. The capitulation of the enemy's northern group saw the end of an operation unparalleled in history, carried out in accordance with the plan of the Supreme High Command. Our soldiers halted the enemy, kept him from reaching the Volga, and Stalingrad became a tomb for the German invaders.'

After the Secretary of the Stalingrad District Committee of the Party, A. S. Chuyanov, the Member of the Front Military Council, Nikita Sergeyevich Khrushchev, spoke:

'Comrades,' he began, 'we have gathered here on an historic day, when our troops, having completed the rout of the Nazis in the Stalingrad region, are celebrating their glorious victory over the sworn enemy. The enemy failed to leave the Volga, and found he had made a grave for himself here. We have met here today like old friends, after a long separation, to look at one another. All of us would like to and could say a great deal ...'

Speaking about the role of the 62nd Army in defeating the German army group, Comrade Khrushchev said:

'Anyone who was here knows how hard it was for the 62nd Army on the right bank of the Volga.

'The army under General Shumilov also played a great part, and also had to wage bitter battles against the enemy ...

'All our efforts,' he ended, 'must be directed towards perfecting our military skill ... Our cause is just. We shall crush the enemy.'

The whole square answered by bursting into thunderous shouts of 'Hurrah!' in honour of the Party and the Soviet people.

The rally ended, and the soldiers dispersed, to prepare for new battles.

We spent about a month in the villages along the River Akhtuba. During this time the 62nd Army's divisions had a thorough rest, brought their units up to strength, received new weapons and got ready to be loaded into troop trains so as to head westward and catch up with the front, now far away.

Our units and divisions were generously decorated by the country. Almost all the divisions and regiments which had taken part in the defence of Stalingrad were given the title of guards. The 62nd Army was also renamed the 8th Guards Army. The 'guard' badge appeared on the chests of officers and men.

Not long before we set off for the front, we saw off the Member of the Military Council, Kuzma Akimovich Gurov, on his way to a new post. Divisional Commissar, later Lieutenant-General, Gurov, was for all of us first and foremost a comrade-in-arms. Throughout the whole of the fighting he had been on the right bank and shared with us the bitterness of defeat and the joy of victory. Now we were to part ...

We saw him off from the village of Srednyaya Akhtuba. Seeing him off were Krylov, Vasiliev, Pozharski, Weinrub, Tkachenko and I. There were no send-off speeches or toasts, but Gurov was embraced and kissed by all of us. And though all of us had tears in our eyes, it was hardest for Gurov: he was going away, but we were staying ...

K. A. Gurov was a man of strong nerves and icy calm. I remember an occasion when a bomb splinter pierced his fur cap. We were standing on the bank of the Volga. He looked at us, took off his cap, smiled and said:

'It's a bit spoiled, but I can still wear it.'

He was a Leninist Communist, able to combine the word of persuasion with the sternness of Party and military discipline. He was always able to carry out in good time the political tasks involved in military plans and measures, whenever they arose. He could study people, and having chosen someone he would trust him, and not watch over him all the time. He would often say to me: 'Those reports need to be checked, but these are accurate'. And true enough, that was the case. He was by nature a cheerful person, and it was never dull in his company.

After seeing off our friend and comrade-in-arms, we felt deserted, and often reminisced about him. In August of the same year, 1943, we were all shocked by the news of Comrade Gurov's death. He had died a premature death, and did not share the joy of final victory with us. He is someone we shall never forget.

The Army began entraining and setting off westward, to the front. The 62nd Army was being sent to the area of Kupyansk, on the northern Donets. The Army H.Q. was to entrain at Voroponovo Station. During the day I toured all the stations where the divisions which comprised the Army were being loaded into troop trains, and I arrived at Voroponovo before evening.

The engine gave a whistle, there was a jolt, and then the rhythm of the wheels.

'Good-bye, Volga,' was in all our minds. 'Good-bye, mutilated and exhausted city. Shall we sometime, somehow, see you again? Good-bye, comrades-in-arms, who have stayed behind in the earth steeped in our nation's blood. We are going westward, our duty—to avenge you . . .'

CHAPTER X

THE SCHOOL OF EXPERIENCE

BOURGEOIS politicians in the service of imperialism, and former Nazi generals, claiming to be objective historians of the Battle of Stalingrad, try to explain where and how this fundamental turning-point in the second world war came about, and why the German army, which had seized almost the whole of Europe with its mighty military and economic arsenal, in 1942 failed to achieve final victory on the eastern front. They try to explain what happened to the Russian soldier, who, having retreated hundreds of miles to the Volga, suddenly became invincible.

However, try though the reader may to find the truth in these 'objective accounts', he is doomed to disappointment. There is not even a trace of the truth. Such western military authorities as Guderian, or the authors of the voluminous *The World War of 1939–1945* Lieutenant-General Dittmar, Field-Marshal von Rundstedt, Major-General Butler and others, do not reveal, indeed they only obscure, the real state of affairs. By throwing the whole blame on to Hitler, they have so far, what is more, been unable convincingly to explain what brought about the basic change in the course of the second world war. And the whole trouble lies in the fact that, for various reasons, they do not wish openly to admit who dealt the decisive blow against the Wehrmacht. They are unable to say that without the Soviet Union there would have been no real force capable of stopping, and then crushing, the Nazi hordes.

Montgomery, for example, maintains that the turning point in the second world war took place in 1942 in the sands of North Africa, where he commanded an army: as though the sands of Africa were more important to Hitler than the oil, coal, metal and grain of Russia. But Hitler was not as stupid as Montgomery paints him, and the number of troops sent by Hitler in one direction alone—to the Volga—was some ten times more than he had in Africa. It was advantageous to Hitler to divert the Anglo-American forces to Tunisia, and this he succeeded in doing. But the facts show that the turning point in the war came not in Africa, but on the Volga, and then at the Kursk Bulge in the summer of 1943, when Hitler Germany was pushed to the brink of disaster.

The authors of the book *The World War of 1939–1945* have unwittingly let the cat out of the bag and refuted Montgomery. In the chapter entitled 'The War and Russia', Butler, describing the battle on the bank of the Volga, admits: 'The losses on both sides were tremendous. Whether the result obtained was worth such sacrifices could be decided only if it could be consolidated and used for operational purposes'. And then further on: 'A new solution had to be found and, even more difficult, appropriate influence had to be brought to bear on Hitler, so as to take the general leadership out of the blind-alley into which it had gone. What was needed was to go over to tactical defence and end the war in more or less tolerable conditions. Future events were to provide the answer as to whether the new Chief of the General Staff was a man suited to do this, and whether in the situation which had developed a man could be found to lead the German army out of the crisis.'

Why, suddenly, in September 1942, was there a need to lead the German army out of a crisis? Was it not because the great mass of German armies which had been drawn into the battle on the Volga was unable to carry out its task and was suffering incalculable losses?

Having let out the secret, Butler goes on to make a deferential bow to his present patrons. 'This laid the basis,' he writes, 'for the drama which was then enacted under the African sun in Tunisia and on the snow-covered ruins of Stalingrad. The disaster the Germans met with in Africa and at Stalingrad was a serious warning of the turning point that had arrived in the fate of the German nation.'

We can leave this naïve hypocrisy, with its gestures to the German nation and to Montgomery, for Butler's conscience, but it is clear enough from what he says that the Battle of Stalingrad was the turning point of the second world war.

Other, in my view, naïve assertions are made, to the effect that the defence of the fortress on the Volga lost its real significance as soon as the German forces broke into the city. From this moment on, they say, the Volga was no longer a vital transport artery, and the city, now turned into ruins, was no longer a centre of communications; was it, therefore, worth fighting for?

Yes, it was worth it, as the number of German troops drawn into the battle gave the defence of the city at that moment a political and strategic importance. Without the protracted, stubborn and successful defensive battle, it would have been impossible to prepare powerful reserves and begin a counter-offensive.

What were the causes of our victory on the Volga?

THE BINDING FORCE

Considering the beginning of the battle for Stalingrad as the opening of a new stage in the war, the Communist Party mobilized the whole Soviet people to carry out the operation successfully. This was the way, the only way, we saw the development of the battle by the Volga. All mankind owes a debt to the Communist Party and its Central Committee for organizing the defeat of the German armies at Stalingrad, bringing a crucial change in the progress of the second world war.

This answer is inadequate, however, unless we add that the

Communist Party was preparing for this change in unbelievably difficult conditions and long before the beginning of the Battle of Stalingrad.

As we know, in the first year of the war many of our industrial areas were occupied by the enemy. In the shortest possible space of time the factories on defence production, which had been transferred to the east, had to be restarted. What skill, talent and will-power this required from Communists working behind the lines, organizing the assembly of the factories evacuated to almost barren plains, organizing labour for them, obtaining electricity and raw materials and going full speed ahead to produce everything needed for the front!

In addition to overcoming the economic difficulties, the Party had to undertake enormous and complicated work on the strictly military plane, so as to overcome the consequences of the so-called surprise attack. I say 'so-called', because we could not but know of the concentration of Nazi troops at the frontiers of the Soviet Union.

Many military experts of the General Staff and G.H.Q. believed that as Hitler had been unable to win decisive victories in 1941 in conditions of a surprise attack, in 1942, when the front had stabilized itself as a result of the winter operations, and when surprise as a factor had been overcome, victory over Nazism was not far away, was already certain. It turned out, however, that the enemy was still strong; the whole arsenal of Europe was working for him. From the spring of 1942 the war became even more bitter and we continued to wage it alone, as we could not count on a second front that year; it was not in the interests of the British and Americans.

Preparing to seize the oil regions of the Caucasus, the German armies broke through to the Crimea, destroyed our bridgehead at Feodosiya, and then, repulsing a frontal attack by our armies which had advanced to Kharkov (the best units and material, built up during the winter, had been thrown into this attack), launched a determined offensive towards the south-east with all the strength they had available. At the beginning of the summer of 1942, consequently, our armies retreated to the Don and then to the Volga and towards the Caucasus, and the country lost the Donbass, the Krivorozhe engineering industry, the wheat of Rostov and

Stavropol, and much more. By the middle of the summer of 1942 over 40 per cent of the population of the Soviet Union was in the occupied zone.

Such a situation could not but give rise to alarm. Every new retreat by the Soviet armies had a demoralizing effect on the people. The army was faced with the biggest danger of all—losing the trust of the people.

Without hiding this from the Party organizations and the people as a whole, the Central Committee of the Party intervened and put forward the slogan: 'Not a step back!' This slogan was transmitted to the troops in an order from the Supreme Commander.[1] All the leaders of the armed forces were warned that there could be no more retreat, there was now nowhere to retreat to, and that the enemy had to be fought to the death. And when this order was read out to the troops in all units, it was clear to all that in the conditions that prevailed this was the only way to increase fighting efficiency and save the country.

Those were the conditions in which the Communist Party had to prepare the army and the whole nation for a critical battle. And when that battle began to take shape at the approaches to the Volga, the Party sent its best members there. The Front Military Council was headed by a member of the Politbureau of the Communist Party, N. S. Khrushchev. He did not try to hide the fact that the position on all fronts was difficult, and particularly emphasized the fact that we could not surrender the city and could retreat no further. I remember the words he he said to me before I set off for the blazing city.

'The people have entrusted the fate of the country to us, and we have to defeat a strong and perfidious enemy, otherwise a bitter tragedy faces the country.'

The leadership of the political administration and of the most important sections of Front H.Q. was taken in hand by energetic Party workers, members of the Central Committee and secretaries of regional committees, Comrades Chuyanov, Doronin and Serdyuk. Thousands of Communists with extensive experience of Party political work joined the troops at the front. In the 62nd Army alone, of the ten thousand

---

1 Stalin.

Communists summoned from various regions of the country, there were more than five hundred secretaries who had been in charge of departments of, and instructors from, district, regional and city committees, secretaries of collective farm and factory organizations, and other Party workers. To strengthen the Army's political section the Central Committee sent I. V. Kirillov and A. N. Kruglov; a Deputy People's Commissar of the R.S.F.S.R., A. D. Stupov, and others, also came. A strong Party nucleus had been formed in the Army. There was no company without a substantial stratum of Party members, and in the 33rd, 37th and 39th Guards Divisions many battalions consisted exclusively of Communist Party and Komsomol members.

The Party's forces were posted to all the Army's key sectors. On marches, in the trenches and in battle, Communists, by their personal example, showed how to fight to carry out the demand of the Party, of the nation, that there should be 'Not a step back!' Hundreds, thousands, of Communists explained to the men that there could be no further retreat, that the enemy could not only be halted, but could be thrown back. For this, all that was needed was only determination and skill. The example and spirit of self-sacrifice of the Communists were a force that it is impossible to measure; its influence on the minds of every soldier will never be understood by the modern writers of fat volumes published in the west about the last war, or by those who refuse to admit that the decisive blow, the one which brought a turning point in the course of the war, was delivered by the Soviet armed forces.

I must, therefore, take a few examples from the experience of the Party political work of Communists in the 62nd Army.

As I have said, the Party's forces were posted to all the most important sectors, and that means that the political work was not carried out as something separate from the Army's tasks, but in the units themselves, so as to ensure that military orders were carried out.

We are now accustomed to reading articles and reports that the 'soldiers of the 62nd Army fought to the death'. It was not a simple matter, however, to prepare men to resist so tenaciously.

Imagine a soldier marching in a column along a dusty road towards the Volga. He is tired and can hardly keep his eyes open for dust and sweat; on his shoulder he has an anti-tank rifle or a tommy-gun, on his belt a cartridge-pouch with bullets and grenades; on his back he has a knapsack with provisions and bits and pieces given him by his wife or mother for the long road. In addition, somewhere, a long way away, he has left his mother, his wife, his children. He is thinking about them, is hoping to go back to them. But here he is approaching the Volga, and he sees the sky, lit crimson by the fires; he can already hear the thunder of explosions, and again he thinks about his home, his wife, his children. Only this time he thinks something different: 'How will they manage to live without me?' And if at this moment you don't remind him about the mortal danger that hangs over his country, of his sacred duty to his homeland, the weight of his thoughts will make him stop or slow down. But he goes on, he does not stop: along the sides of the road are posters, slogans, eagerly calling him on:

'Comrade! If you don't stop the enemy in Stalingrad, he will enter your home and destroy your village!'

'The enemy must be crushed and destroyed in Stalingrad!'

'Soldier, your country will not forget your exploit.'

Evening falls. He arrives at the ferry. Alongside the landing-stage are smashed-up boats, an armoured boat with holes in its sides. Along the bank, under bushes, under broken-down poplars, in shell-holes and ditches, are men. Hundreds of men, but there is silence: with bated breath they are watching the city across the Volga, the city enveloped in flames. The very stones there seem to be on fire. In places the glow lights up the clouds. Are men really alive and fighting in that inferno? How can they breathe? What is it they are defending—smouldering ruins, heaps of stones? . . . But there is an order to cross to the other side in the ferry, and go straight into battle . . .

Yes, there is such an order, but if you rely on one order, without preparing the morale of men to carry it out, then it will be a slow process getting the men on to the ferry, and as soon as the boat comes under fire the men will abandon it and swim, not to the blazing inferno, not towards the battle, but back, back to the bank they have just set out from. What do you do in this situation? In this case posters and slogans won't help you. Someone has to set an example. In every company, in every platoon, there is a man who will swim, not back, but forward, and will lead the men to the bank of the blazing city ... And there were such men not only in the companies and platoons, but in every squad. They were Communist Party and Komsomol members. Carrying out their commanders' orders, they set a personal example of what to do in the situation, and how to do it.

This is the political work entailed in carrying out battle orders.

This story of political work on the ferry across the Volga is told by a former machine-gunner in Gorishny's division, Petr Belov, now a joiner at the Orekhovo-Zuevo Textile Combine.

Before embarking on the ferry a small, round-faced general with a shaved head came up to us—it was the Front Deputy Commander, Golikov. He had just come back from the opposite bank and said: 'From this side it looks as though everything is on fire and there's nowhere to set down your feet. But whole regiments and divisions are living there, and fighting well. But they need help. They are waiting for you . . .' Then newspapers were handed out and everyone was given a printed leaflet of instructions: 'What a Soldier Needs to Know, and How to Act in City Fighting'.

The ferry arrives. We await the command, and everyone is uneasy—after all, everyone wants to live . . . We watch. The first to go on board, without any command, is a diminutive captain; he has a star on his sleeve, which means he's a senior political instructor. I later discovered he was secretary of a divisional Party committee, Syromyatnikov, a long-standing Party member, since 1918. After him went a whole group of soldiers, and what soldiers! We had amongst us, for example, Stepa Chikarkov. On the day when we detrained, and when the anti-aircraft guns started firing, the poor fellow took to his heels across the fields, and it was with some difficulty that he was caught up with and brought back to his senses. He couldn't hide his terror . . . That was the kind of man that Syromyatnikov had collected, and he led them on to the ferry without a word of command, ahead of everyone. Even Chikarkov was not afraid.

We embarked quickly and cast off. There were a lot of men on the boat—five hundred or so. The Communists were put round the rails as far as possible, to prevent panic.

The boat moves on . . . The water already looks red from the fires. Then, as ill luck would have it, the moon came out from behind the clouds, and then a bright flare appeared right over our heads, so bright that you could have read the paper by it. Explosions roared to the right and to the left—the Nazis were firing from the right bank. One mortar bomb burst on board. Well, I thought, that's it—now we all go down to the bottom. It's deep here in the middle of the Volga. But he, the bearded captain, Syromyatnikov, climbed up on to the boxes of ammunition, sat down where everybody could see him, and starts sorting out letters with the postman. He sorts and the postman points now to one man now to another. Someone lets out a groan, and suddenly everyone is silent, because Syromyatnikov looks in that direction. 'Hold on, comrade,' he says. 'There might be at letter for you too.'

And when our ferry drew out of range of the firing and it became dark (someone had shot down the flare with a rifle), everyone heard a voice:

'Comrades, just in case—the postman and I will be over there, near the burning oil-tanks. That's where battalion H.Q. will be . . .'

You might say that the officer was only being smart. To a soldier a letter is like seeing his family again, and everyone is dying to receive one. But you have to have courage and resourcefulness in a situation like that to sit so calmly in the most dangerous place—on the ammunition—and do a job like that. The Communist, in other words, is the resourceful man . . .

Such examples, which tell of the resourcefulness, self-control, determination and courage of the political workers, their ability to capture the soldiers' attention at the most critical moment, can be quoted galore. That was what the personal example of a Communist in battle meant.

Personal example ... I think the Army's political section was quite right when it asked Party meetings in all units to discuss the question of the conduct of Communists in battle. This demand of the political section was set out in a letter signed by the Member of the Military Council, Gurov, and the chief of the political section, Vasiliev. It talked about the fighting in the streets of the city. Every Party member, said the letter, regardless of his rank and post, in every circumstance should be an example for those around him. Tenacious, resolute action should be standard behaviour for every Communist in battle. If a Communist shows any confusion or faint-heartedness, the Party organs should act towards such a Communist with all the rigour of Party discipline, even to the length of expelling him from the Party.

This letter was discussed not only in company and battalion Party organizations, but also in all H.Q.'s, including Army H.Q., and had a strong influence on all Communists occupying important posts. Every chief of staff, as it were, felt that his conduct was being watched constantly by the rank-and-file Party members, who, in accordance with the constitution of the Party, had the right to demand that decisions of Party meetings should be carried out. That is the law of the Party—the decision of a meeting is binding on all; a breach of internal Party discipline has to be answered for by everyone with the same strictness, regardless of his rank. And I, as Army Commander, welcomed such a demand by Communist Party members.

That is why, in the most difficult days, at the beginning of the street fighting in the centre of the city, the Army Military Council was able quickly and effectively to stop the spreading demoralization caused by the former Commander, who doubted the utility of defending the city. With the help of the Party organization, the Military Council adopted measures against cowards and panic-mongers. I know of no 62nd Army soldier who would not have judged anyone who left the field of battle as a coward—be he private or commander. The true soldier could not suffer men who hid behind his back or betrayed him by their cowardice. That was the attitude of the majority of the city's defenders, and in spite of the extremely difficult situation and the enemy's superiority in men and material, there was no instance of mass panic. This redounds to the credit of the Party organizations of the 62nd Army.

It must be borne in mind that in the conditions of street fighting, when continuously, night and day, for weeks and months at a stretch, the noise of battle roared, the political workers could not, had no opportunity to, hold big meetings and rallies of Red Army men, so as to explain to them the most important Party decisions and the orders from Front Command. There was neither place nor time for long, passionate speeches. The Party agitator or propagandist would often explain Party policy in a short chat with a soldier in a cellar or under a staircase, more often than not while the battle was raging, showing in practice how to use weapons and carry out the commander's instructions. Quite frankly, such a demonstration had a greater effect on the men than a long speech would have done. The political workers of the 62nd Army, therefore, had to be fully conversant with the tactics of street fighting, and be able themselves to make first-class use of weapons, primarily tommy-guns and grenades. And the majority of them coped well with the task.

On September 26, an inspector from the Army's political section, Battalion Commissar A. Kruglov, after visiting the units fighting in the streets of the city, wrote an article summarizing the experience of fighting in a besieged house. The article contained a great deal that was valuable and instructive, was endorsed by the Military Council and distributed to all units. All the Army political section's instructor and inspector staff spent an hour a day by the Volga bank being trained to shoot and throw grenades. Divisional political sections did the same.

But these are only individual examples and anecdotes. It seems to me that the basic service performed by the 62nd Army's Party organizations was that, after clarifying the characteristics of street fighting, the political workers transferred the centre of gravity of their work to the companies, to the platoons, to the storm groups. The basic form of the work of the political instructors, the Party and Komsomol organizers, and the instructors from the political sections became the individual conversation. This was the only way of helping each soldier to understand that he could and must put everything he had into the fight, even in the eventuality of his remaining alone behind enemy lines. He had to make use of the trust placed in him by his commanders, the right to act on his own, intelligently; he had to bear in mind the task that had been set for the whole regiment, division and Army. Trust, trust and more trust—that was what made it possible to raise the creative, fighting efficiency of the mass of the soldiers. This was painstaking, complicated and responsible work, and, as we know, it produced excellent results. We can say without exaggeration that thanks to such activity by the Party organizations, every man defending the city became an insuperable obstacle in the path of the enemy.

The work of the Party organizations to ensure that military orders were carried out was conducted effectively and with a clear purpose. The inspectors and instructors of the Army's political section would go out to the sectors where the most difficult and complicated tasks had to be carried out. They went with the well-defined aim of taking the Army's orders to every soldier, of mobilizing the Party and Komsomol organizations to carry out military orders in all conditions. Conditions, as we know, were complex and different on every sector. And it was very good to see that the political workers selected their form and methods of work with the troops in accordance with the circumstances, did not sit waiting for an appropriate moment, but went straight to the storm group, to the machine-gunners, the infantrymen, the sappers, wherever they might be. No break in carrying out mass political work among the troops—that was what the political sections constantly demanded of their workers.

Sometimes the political workers from the higher organs, visiting a division, would hold a meeting with the regimental political section and Party workers, and they in turn would hold equivalent meetings in the battalions with the Party and Komsomol organizers in the companies, at the battalion command post. This meant that men in the forward trenches and at firing positions always had discussions with the same company agitators and platoon commanders. In the 62nd Army that system was completely changed and simplified. Political workers and commanders at all levels went out to the front line—everyone from the battalion Party organizer to the head of the Army's political section and Member of the Army Military Council. I also had occasion to be with the soldiers in their dug-outs, at their machine-gun posts, and I explained to the men both the most important decisions of the Party and the military duties facing the unit I was in. After such a heart-to-heart talk with the soldiers in the trenches they obviously felt more deeply their responsibility for the job entrusted to them, and understood more clearly how important it was to carry it out.

That is how Party political work was carried out in the 62nd Army.

An Army political section inspector, Battalion Commissar, later Lieutenant-Colonel Ivan Sergeyevich Panchenko, in the days of the fighting in the region of Orlovka fought with the battalion when it was encircled. He broke out with a group of 102 men during the night through the German lines and joined up with the units operating in the factory area.

The Party organizations of Batyuk's 284th Infantry Division worked particularly harmoniously and well. The head of the political section, Tkachenko, and the political workers in the regiments of this division organized the Party and Komsomol work so well that there was not a single case of cowardice or confusion in battle. The tenacious and determined fight put up by the Siberians of Batyuk's division wreaked havoc among the Germans. On Mamayev Kurgan alone, the machine-gun and tommy-gun fire of Batyuk's storm groups killed several thousand of the enemy.

The political machinery of Batyuk's division paid particular attention to the development and publicizing of new methods of fighting the enemy. No sooner did Dmitri Shumakov, an anti-tank rifleman, adapt his rifle for shooting at aeroplanes, than a political worker, S. Nekhoroshev, on the same day, distributed sketches of the adaptation to all units in the division, and in two days the regiment's anti-tank rifles had already shot down six dive-bombers. And when the snipers' movement started (initiated in this division by Vasili Zaitsev), all units, dug-outs and trenches started producing their 'snipers' registers', to keep an account of the number of Germans killed day by day. Every day the divisional newspaper published material about the marksmen. Also widely publicized in Batyuk's division was such important political work as letters to the families of comrades who had been killed. In these letters the soldiers made a vow to revenge their comrade-in-arms. Whole platoons, companies and even battalions appended their signatures to these letters. The man who signed such a vow, of course, did his best to fulfil it.

The influence of the Communists spread to cover all facets of the Army's life. They paid a lot of attention to the problem of ensuring hot meals in the front line, at firing positions; they devoted much attention to organizing proper evacuation of the wounded; in dugouts they equipped rooms for political educational work, where every soldier and N.C.O could read the newspapers, listen to music and have a rest.

The divisional and Army Party committees normally held their meetings in the units themselves. Soldiers who had distinguished themselves in battle were often received into the Party right in the front line.

I had occasion to be present at the handing over of Party cards to distinguished soldiers of the 284th Division, including Vasili Zaitsev. They swore on their Party cards to fight the enemy to the death in the Bolshevik spirit.

That is all far from being a complete picture of the indefatigable activity of the Communists in the 62nd Army, in boosting the morale and ensuring a high level of fighting efficiency among the troops. They played a leading role, acted as a binding force, were to the fore in battle, fought most bitterly in hand-to-hand fighting, were most resolute in attack, were most resourceful in the storm groups and had greatest tenacity and staying-power in defence.

Running the Komsomol was an integral part of the Army Party organization's work.

Komsomol ... I pronounce the word with enthusiasm and pride. What great feats were performed by our young Communists during the war, how firmly and courageously they fought the German invaders!

When bitter fighting was still going on in the streets of the shattered city, I asked the leaders of the Party's city committee, after the city had been rebuilt, to name the finest street Komsomol Street. This was the request of the Army Military Council, because the 62nd Army which fought in the streets of the city was composed primarily of young soldiers. Many

302

companies, battalions and regiments consisted entirely of Komsomol members.

The 37th Guards Division contained more than 8,000 Komsomol commandos. In October they were defending the Tractor factory. On one day, October 5, the enemy flew 700 sorties, and each plane dropped eight to twelve bombs, which meant that on that day the enemy dropped something like 6,000 bombs on this division, and the enemy still failed to advance a step. And the 1st Guards Regiment of this division threw back the Germans and itself advanced to new positions.

Anyone who was in the city in these terrible and difficult days could see what part was being played in the battle by the young Komsomol members, displaying a high level of morale and military skill. And it was gratifying to us older soldiers, who had smelled gunpowder before, to see and acknowledge that our young officers and men, in the difficult fighting, did not fall behind the older men in endurance and courage. We are proud of the fact that our young soldiers not only showed themselves worthy of the heroic traditions of the older generation, but enhanced them.

During the most bitter fighting one of the infantry companies of Rodimtsev's division, occupying the station area, was attacked by enemy tanks. There was confusion in the company. But the secretary of the Komsomol organization, Fedor Yakovlev, did not waver. He took two anti-tank grenades, drew himself up to his full height, and with a shout of 'Not a step back, comrades!' threw a grenade at the leading tank. The tank went up in flames. Yakovlev was about to throw a second grenade, but he was stopped short by an enemy bullet. The soldiers, inspired by Yakovlev's example, drove off the enemy attack with grenades. After the fighting the men found a piece of paper in Yakovlev's handwriting inside his locket. Under the title 'My Vow' were the following simple, but sincere lines:

I am a son of the Party, my country is my mother,
My father—our beloved Lenin.
I will not retreat in battle.
Let my friends and enemies know it.

We remember young Sergeant Jacob Pavlov—the 'owner' of the famous 'Pavlov's house', and young Lieutenant Timofey Semashko, the hero of the fighting on the River Mechetka. The Komsomol members became the spirit of the celebrated and (for the Germans) deadly storm groups.

Bloodstained Komsomol cards found on the battlefield are preserved like holy relics. New generations of young Communists will look with reverence at these cards—a testimony to the great courage of the young defenders of Stalingrad.

I have in front of me card No. 13145761, pierced by a bomb fragment. With this card in his pocket an eighteen-year-old Komsomol member from Saratov, Nikolay Borodushin, went into the attack and died the death of the brave.

Kisym Amanzholov, a Kazakh, cherished his Party card. Hit by an enemy bullet in a street in the factory district, Kisym fell holding his Party card tight in his hand. It was his banner, with it he fought and died...

During the fighting in the city, not dozens or hundreds, but thousands of young soldiers rose to become commanders of regiments, battalions, companies and batteries.

Where did this unprecedented courage and tenacity come from? Soviet youth had learned these high moral qualities from the traditions of the Bolshevik Party. They had been forged in the years of the five-year plans in self-sacrificing work in the construction of the Dnepr hydro-electric power station, of Komsomolsk-na-Amure, of factories on the Volga and in the Urals, in the Ukraine and in Siberia, in the north and the south.

The Communists and Komsomol members of the 62nd Army had one privilege—to be in the forefront, to fight best.

As a result of the carefully thought out, constant Party political work, close, comradely unity was achieved between rank-and-file, officers and generals. The soldiers loved and respected their officers, defended them. The officers were always with the men, fought alongside them. Such front-line friendship strengthened discipline.

You would often go out to an observation post and feel yourself being protected by the men.

General Rodimtsev will certainly remember how he and I one day went out to a forward area on the western outskirts of the Krasny Oktyabr settlement, and how the soldiers and officers persuaded us to come back from a dangerous point, arguing that they could cope with the job they had been given without us.

There are many examples of how the soldiers guarded their commanders, and such examples testify to the great authority our commanders had, and to the fact that their leadership was supported and strengthened by every kind of Party political work.

How, in fact, could our N.C.Os and men not love and respect their officers? They had all emerged from the same background. This is something that bourgeois historians, studying the causes of the defeat of Germany on the eastern front, will never understand.

Cut off from the rest of the world by fire and water, we were bound heart and soul to the Soviet people, and were constantly aware of the care they lavished on us. Not a day passed without their showing us attention of some kind: we received letters, parcels, radiograms, not to mention ammunition and guns. And this attention inspired the 62nd Army to accomplish feats of arms.

In spite of the exceptionally difficult conditions in which it had to manœuvre, the 62nd Army nevertheless managed to manœuvre. The Germans were perplexed: only yesterday there was no one or almost no one here, but this morning there is firm, stubborn resistance, and even a counter-attack.

Bourgeois writers have said that the Russians, defying death as no nation has ever done, seemed not to care about life. They cannot understand that a Soviet citizen, loving life, cannot conceive of it apart from his Soviet country.

The tactics of the Nazi generals and officers in the fighting for the city ended in bankruptcy. In street fighting their pincers were broken, lost their sharpness.

Quantitative superiority in material, particularly in the air, also did not bring the enemy any decisive success in city fighting. His estimate that the Luftwaffe would destroy everything and clear a way for the ground troops, turned out to be mistaken: our storm groups, coming up to within a grenade's throw of the enemy, presented the German airmen with a dilemma—could they bomb the Russians without hitting their own men? And whenever they tried to bomb our storm groups they hit Germans.

Let me take one example. On a sector of the front occupied by General Smekhotvorov's division, where our trenches were extremely close to the Germans', there was a destroyed house. Near this house fighting was going on with grenades. The Luftwaffe was called in to help and began bombing both the German troops and ours, since it was impossible to tell which were their own and which were our trenches. For about twenty minutes they were bobbing up and down, protecting their heads from bombs, splinters and bullets from the dive-bombers. When the bombing was over they began to sort out who was going to take whom prisoner. The result was that we had seventeen German prisoners brought in.

We opposed the Germans with our own tactics of city fighting, not according to any blue-print, but as we worked them out in the course of the battle, perfecting them all the time.

The most important thing that I learned on the banks of the Volga was to be impatient of blue-prints. We constantly looked for new methods of organizing and conducting battle, starting from the precise conditions in which we were fighting.

TACTICS PERFECTED IN BATTLE

Like all the country's peaceful cities, Stalingrad was not prepared for defence, or for a long battle in a state of siege. No defence works had been previously carried out in the streets of the city. They had to be created when street fighting was already in progress. This was one of the features of the conditions in which the 62nd Army was operating, and I ought to say a little more about this in detail.

The Army's basic defence position was the centre of resistance, comprising a number of strongpoints. Buildings, especially good stone and brick buildings, were used as strongpoints. After being adapted for defence purposes, they were linked with other buildings by means of trenches, including communication trenches. The spaces between strongpoints were strengthened by obstructions and covered by fire.

A strongpoint usually consisted of individual buildings or groups of buildings at key points. There was an advantage in using burned-out stone buildings, to which the enemy could not set fire before an attack, thereby smoking out our men. Every strongpoint, depending on its size and importance, was defended by a section, a platoon, a company or even sometimes a battalion. Strongpoints were adapted to permit all-round defence, and could wage battle independently for several days.

The garrisons in the strongpoints, as a rule, had anti-tank rifles and artillery, and whenever possible tanks and self-propelled guns also. I do not need to mention bottles of incendiary liquid and antitank grenades, because we tried to supply every soldier with these. The garrisons also included snipers, sappers, chemical experts, and always a medical worker with a large stock of medical supplies.

A group of strongpoints, with a common firing network, under a single administration and also equipped for all-round defence, constituted a centre of resistance.

The factory workshops, powerfully built of metal and reinforced concrete, with their system of underground works, were a basis for a long and stubborn defence.

To begin with we made little use of the factories' underground works—their sewerage, communications and water-supply system—as we were not familiar with them. But during the fighting, when we were in touch with the factory administration, and also with the Party's area organizations, everything was brought into use for the fight against the enemy.

In order to make it more difficult for the enemy to manœuvre in the city, streets and squares were partitioned off with obstructions of various kinds. The approaches to the obstructions and the obstructions themselves were covered by oblique, serried fire from all kinds of weapons in neighbouring buildings and special points distributed in chess-like order.

The garrisons of the strongpoints and centres of resistance contained representatives of every kind of soldier, excluding airmen. They had tommy-gunners, flame-throwers, sappers, heavy and large-calibre machine-guns, anti-tank guns, individual artillery weapons, mortars and tanks, and were supported by artillery fire from concealed positions.

The commanders of the artillery units involved acted as commandants of the strongpoints or centres of resistance, which also contained observation posts for the concealed artillery.

The weapons used in the defended building were distributed according to the strength of the building and its position in the city. In a multi-storey building, multi-tiered defence was organized: in the semi-basement and lower floors firing positions were prepared for weapons firing along the street, and on the upper floors and in the attics for firing from above at tanks, into the streets, yards and neighbouring buildings and at distant targets. Guns for firing at point-blank range and some of the heavy machine-guns, including short-range machine-guns, were placed on the lower floors. Heavy and large-calibre machine-guns, for long-range firing, were often placed on upper floors. The infantrymen were posted throughout the building. The individual pieces of artillery, used for firing at point-blank range, tanks, heavy machine-guns for defending the approaches to the building from the flanks and gaps between the buildings, were posted outside the building, and were used as a detachment either behind or on the flanks of the building.

The particular features of fighting in the city made it essential for infantry units to have ample automatic weapons, grenades and bottles of incendiary liquid. A network of emergency and temporary firing positions was set up for all types of weapon, with the purpose of being able to manœuvre our fire-power in all directions.

The firing network established in connection with the obstructions had the following aims:

—to prevent the enemy from occupying vantage points for his artillery, tanks, self-propelled weapons and infantry;

—to make it difficult for enemy infantry and tanks to attack, or to repulse such an attack at the approaches to the strongpoint and in the spaces between them;

—to cut off enemy infantry from their tanks;

—to destroy any enemy troops who broke through our units into the strongpoints or into the gaps between them;

—to prevent the enemy from spreading out in depth on any sector where he had broken through;

—to ensure that strongpoints and centres of resistance could be firmly held if surrounded by the enemy;

—to give reliable cover to junction points;

—to create pockets in which to wipe out the enemy by fire or counter-attack;

—to give support to counter-attacks.

In organizing our firing system we allowed for broad use of weapons for short-range firing; this applied not only to infantry weapons, but also artillery. We also allowed for an increased use of mortars, which could hit the enemy behind vertical shelter.

Anti-tank defence inside the city had its own characteristics. The fight against tanks was waged at close range. Particular importance was attached to the anti-tank riflemen, armed with bottles of incendiary liquid, anti-tank rifles and grenades. Tanks could be fired on most advantageously from ambushes, for which holes in fences and walls, and also house doorways, gates, windows, and so on, were used.

All-round anti-tank defence by a strongpoint or centre of resistance was achieved by preparing the position for guns firing point-blank and tanks, so as to beat off enemy tank attacks from all sides, including the rear. In the event of a shortage of artillery, all-round defence was obtained by preparing the necessary quantity of paths and passages for mobile detachments to be able to manœuvre, and by preparing mined obstructions with anti-tank rifles. The firing positions of individual batteries were equipped as anti-tank strongpoints. A number of such points, covering one area vulnerable to tanks, constituted an anti-tank fortification.

All H.Q.'s, command posts, artillery and infantry firing positions were organized as strongpoints. In other words, defence was constructed in depth—from the firing line to the bank of the Volga. All rear and supplies units were made part of active formations and had their own defence sector.

Of particular importance in organizing defence was personal reconnaissance by commanders at all levels. The commander of an infantry regiment, by his personal reconnaissance, could pin-point where forward defensive positions should be, and decide on what scale obstructions should be built in order to provide the defence fortifications necessary in the key areas. He also co-ordinated firing and obstructions ahead of forward positions as an integral part of the defence sector, the protection of junction points between battalions, centres of defence and strongpoints, directed counter-attacks by reserves and decided on measures to cover their operations.

The commanders of infantry battalions and companies, in carrying out reconnaissance personally, organized the defence of strongpoints and centres of resistance and the spaces between them, and directed the operations of garrisons when fighting took place at the approaches to a strongpoint or a centre of resistance, or inside them, established targets and selected firing positions for short-range machine-guns and artillery, decided on areas in which to counter-attack, and prepared paths and passages to give room for manœuvre. They indicated areas in which snipers should operate and gave them their instructions.

Every centre of defence and strongpoint had its plan of defence, which generally contained:

—the tasks of the strongpoint garrison: the establishment of a network of fire, providing all-around defence;

—the tasks of the men and material in the strongpoint, trenches, pill-boxes and areas between the strongpoints;

—the distribution of the garrison's men and material in order to beat off enemy attacks from one direction or more, and also for all-round defence;

—the distribution of weapons in such a way as to keep the enemy from the strongpoint and provide cover for areas between it and neighbouring strongpoints and between it and the enemy, and also combined operations with the weapons of other strongpoints;

—the tasks of supporting artillery;

—area and direction of any counter-attacking manœuvre;

—defence procedure in the event of the loss of several strongpoints, a centre of resistance or individual buildings in them;

—fortification of areas between strongpoints and centres of resistance by night;

—ways of fighting any enemy troops who might break into the strongpoint, and necessities for such a fight inside the strongpoint.

The plan and the organization of the defence were prepared carefully, not necessarily in writing, were improved upon in the course of the fighting, and every lull in the battle was used to decide on and make fortifications, and root them firmly into the ground and buildings.

I should particularly like to underline the active nature of the defence. Whenever the enemy penetrated into our lines he was wiped out by fire or counter-attacks, which, as a rule, were surprise attacks in the enemy's flanks and rear.

Counter-attacks, always caused the enemy heavy losses, frequently forcing him to abandon his attack in a given area and rush up and down the front searching for a weak point in our defences, lose time and lower his rate of advance.

The active nature of the defence was obtained by:

—efficiently organized reconnaissance by troops of all kinds;

—a carefully prepared network of fire by all types of weapons, so as to smash enemy forces concentrated ready for an attack;

—intelligent camouflage of our forces (particularly of counter-attacking groups), of the approaches to our lines and of the actual beginning of counter-attacks;

—the co-ordination of operations by a counter-attacking group and our weapons, given the task of preventing the enemy from bringing up his second line of defence or reserves.

Counter-preparations took place more often than not in the form of a counter-attack, directed against the flank or even the front of an enemy group getting ready to attack. We often had the aim not only of causing the enemy losses, but, by a surprise attack with infantry and tanks, with artillery and air support, to penetrate into the enemy's starting positions, upset his formations, break his attack and gain time.

We could not count on being able to break an enemy attack with defensive fire, though the Front Command strongly recommended that we should do this. They did not take into account at Front H.Q. that the depth of our Army's defences ranged from two hundred yards (on Rodimtsev's sector) to between half a mile and a mile on other sectors. To break through across this distance with one blow the enemy would need from fifteen minutes to an hour. This means that we would have had to keep our artillerymen on the alert, waiting for an enemy attack, the whole time. What is more, we would not have had enough ammunition to put up a defensive barrage of this kind. We could not entrust the defence of the city, and therefore the fate of the Army, to the artillery alone, on the left bank of the Volga.

And we hit at the enemy wherever we detected him, and wherever he was most prepared for an attack. We hit him physically, and we hit his morale.

This scheme of counter-preparations, counter-attacks, artillery and air bombardments, fully justified itself, and there can be no better testimony to this than the enemy's soldiers, who experienced all this for themselves.

This is what Kurt Bäcker, a lance-corporal in the 578th Regiment of the 305th Infantry Division, wrote in his diary:

October 29. Attacking the factory. During the night before the attack the Russians opened fire with artillery on our sector, then Russian planes bombed us just before dawn. Of course, we got no sleep.

November 4. Heavy fighting going on all the time. In a week we have advanced less than half a mile. We can see the Volga, but cannot reach it. By day we advance 100–200 yards, then the Russians throw us back again at night.

November 8. We haven't slept for several nights. The Russian artillery and planes give us no peace. We're worn out, but the main thing is that we can't see any end to it all.

November 11. Our offensive has collapsed. We have lost a lot of men, and the Russians are still firing. We lose men by bombing and shelling by night and day.

If the enemy managed to break through he came up against a defence structure which made it possible, throughout the whole battle, to strike from the rear of our forward lines not only at the advancing enemy's weak points, but also at his flanks, which became exposed as he advanced.

Our troops (infantry, artillery and even tanks hidden in buildings) were not afraid to let the enemy penetrate into our lines, because there, in the second line of defence, there were anti-tank defence points and obstacles. We very often succeeded in cutting off the enemy infantry from the tanks by machine-gun fire, and 'polishing off' the infantry ahead of our

312

lines. Then, in the second line of defence, the German tanks, not seeing our anti-tank riflemen hidden in basements and trenches, would lay themselves open to attacks from the sides, and go up in flames. Sometimes they would find themselves in fire-pockets, stumbling into our anti-tank defences.

Our advantage lay in the fact that we were in secret fortifications, but the enemy remained in the streets and squares as a good target.

Enemy soldiers making a break-through laid themselves open to fire from our snipers, machine-guns and artillery weapons, and often fragments of buildings specially blown up for the purpose.

If the enemy managed to seize a building, he would be driven out again by our second line of defence and reserves, launching a counter-attack and restoring the position.

Our rear defences were situated in strongpoints deep inside the defence belt, intercepting the enemy at points where he might advance, and kept in a state of readiness to counter-attack with all or part of their forces.

Should there not be enough men or material for a counter-attack, our military structure was arranged in such a way that we could have some reserves available, and they were kept in particularly important and stout buildings.

If things worked out badly, our second lines and reserves in the threatened areas went over to defensive action in their pre-prepared strongpoints.

At the same time as preparing defence positions, our rear defences and reserves also prepared for counter-attacks inside their own area and to help neighbours. Such preparations consisted in organizing co-ordinated operations and clearing paths for troop movements, that is, clearing paths and yards of obstructions, making breaches in the walls of buildings, preparing observation posts and artillery firing positions.

Counter-attacks by rear defence units and reserves in city conditions were markedly different from counter-attacks in the open fields.

At the very beginning of the fighting in the central area of the city, it became clear that methods of waging battle adopted in conditions of open country were inapplicable inside the city: the enemy's numerous fortified stone buildings, and the high density of fire, made it more difficult for us to counter-attack and caused us heavy losses.

Both sides exposed their flanks when attacking and counter-attacking; battle formations were broken down by the fortification of separate buildings, and to penetrate an advancing enemy's junction points and rear was not difficult.

Active defence in such a situation meant that counter-attacks by our units, widely used during the early days of the battle, led either to the capture of buildings in which the Germans had established themselves behind our lines, or to attacks ahead of our forward positions against blocks turned into strongpoints by the enemy.

When the battle was under way, it became clear that this job could be successfully coped with by small sub-units, infiltrating between enemy strongpoints and centres of resistance. They would slip into the wings of a building and take it by assault, rapidly converting it for purposes of our own defence.

In the city, infantry sections could not overcome all obstacles and neutralize enemy fire by themselves. Artillery fire from concealed positions was of little effect, and to smash buildings and walls from behind which the enemy was firing, our infantry sections therefore had artillery and tanks attached to them. In order to be able to make breaches in walls, overcome obstacles and smoke the enemy out of strongpoints, small infantry groups had sappers and chemical warfare specialists attached to them. This was the beginning of the battle unit—the storm group, adapted to the needs of battle in the city. It was always formed in accordance with the object under attack and available resources of men and material. The assault of enemy fortifications was planned and organized by the commander and his staff. The storm group normally consisted of an infantry platoon (twenty to fifty men), plus two or three guns, one or two squads of sappers and chemical warfare men. Every man had a tommy-gun and a large number of hand-grenades.

Active counter-attacks by our storm groups were the factor in our defence which kept the enemy in a constant state of tension. Under attack from our groups, the enemy had to abandon not only buildings, but his strongpoints also.

Attacks were frequently made without any preliminary

314

artillery barrage. The time of the attack was fixed in accordance with the enemy's behaviour. Their sleeping and eating habits and their relief times were worked out. After studying all this information we frequently caught whole enemy garrisons in the cellars.

Experience showed that the storm groups and the strongpoints were the most important facets of our defence. The Army beat off enemy attacks, itself attacked, made bold sallies, and took the initiative out of the enemy's hands. The power of our troops lay in the fact that, while defending themselves, they attacked the whole time.

In conclusion I would note that modern city warfare is not street fighting in the literal sense of the word. In the city battle raging in Stalingrad the streets and squares were empty.

The young 62nd Army worked out new methods of conducting battle in the conditions of a big city. Our officers and generals were learning the whole time. Boldly rejecting tactical methods which were unsuited to these conditions, they applied new methods, introducing them in all units. Battalion commanders learned, so did regimental and divisional commanders, everyone learned, including the Army Commander, and their studies bore fruit every day.

The battle on the Volga is an example of active defence. Our troops not only beat off the enemy's furious onslaught, but, by constantly attacking, wore down the enemy, destroyed him.

It became clear in the early stages of the battle for the city that the only way to make the enemy abandon his wild plans was by active defence—to defend by attacking. By this time our garrisons in the strongpoints had already had experience of operating independently, on their own initiative; they had learned to work together with the artillery, mortar, armoured and sapper groups attached to them, and to fire point-blank from short distances with all types of weapons; frequent sallies with the aim of counter-attacking had made it possible to gain experience of manœuvring in conditions of street fighting.

The men of the 62nd Army began to attack and to drive the enemy out of buildings he had occupied and out of sections of the city by sudden, bold attacks by small, well-knit groups. Day and night they kept the enemy in a state of strain, making strong attacks, penetrating behind enemy lines, and firing at point-blank range at anyone who tried to lift a finger above the ground.

Our storm groups played a major role in this development. The character of these groups was governed by the very nature of city battle. City battle, city attack, is an assault on fortified houses, buildings and other objects, turned into strongpoints and centres of resistance by the enemy. Attacks by storm groups, therefore, have to be short, their operations swift and daring.

These needs rule out the possibility of using big units, and the centre of the stage is taken by small infantry groups, individual guns and tanks.

The conditions in which the storm groups operated were different at different periods of the fighting in the city. When the enemy had only just broken into the city and captured a part of it, he had, naturally, not yet been able to fortify buildings and organize strong defences. In that situation a small group can operate, independently, without any organizational link with the unit it belongs to. But when the enemy has been in the city two or three weeks, and he has been able to undertake considerable defence works and has organized an elaborate network of fire, then the chances of success by an independently operating small group become so much smaller, and it acts only as a spearhead of a strong detachment. In this case the group will be carrying out part of an overall plan.

As we shall see, the success of the storming of the Railwaymen's House was won by three storm groups, with six to eight men in each. But eighty-two soldiers of various kinds were working with them. It is quite clear, therefore, that the strength, constitution and character of the operations of a storm group are governed by the situation. When a group is operating independently it can be small in numbers and its constitution more homogeneous; in different circumstances it has to work in combination with other groups, carrying out part of a general battle plan.

For the storming of an object, the 62nd Army's units created assault groups, reinforcement groups and reserve groups. These three groups were designed to carry out one single task, and formed one whole—the storm group.

The strength and constitution of each group depended on the object it was to attack. The commander would gauge them in the process of preparing for the assault, on the basis of reconnaissance information about the nature of the object and the size of its garrison. The special features of the operations of each group were then worked out. These special features were crucial—without clarifying them it was impossible to get to grips with the tactics of the battle for the fortified building.

The basis of the storm group was the assault groups, containing between six and eight men in each. They would first of all swiftly break into the building and wage battle independently inside it. Each group had its own part of the overall task to carry out. These groups were lightly armed, carrying a tommy-gun, grenades, a dagger, and a spade (often used as an axe). The groups were under one commander, who had signal rockets and flares, and sometimes a telephone.

The reinforcement group was normally divided into separate parties, which would enter the building simultaneously from different directions immediately after the assault groups (as soon as the commander gave the signal 'We're in'). After entering the building and seizing the firing positions, they rapidly created their own system of fire against the enemy, to prevent any attempts to come to the assistance of his beleaguered garrison. This group was equipped with heavier arms: heavy machine-guns and tommy-guns, mortars, anti-tank rifles and guns, crow-bars, picks and explosives. Each group contained sappers, snipers and soldiers of various trades, able to operate effectively against the enemy.

The reinforcement group came under the commander of the storm group.

The reserve group was used to supplement and strengthen the assault groups, to stop any possible enemy attack from the flanks, and also (should need be) as a blocking party. The reserve group could be utilized for the rapid creation and use of additional assault groups. That was the structure of the storm group of Guards Lieutenant Sedelnikov, which seized the large and well-fortified 'L-shaped house', a powerful German strongpoint. From it the enemy was covering an extremely important section of the Volga, and observing anything approaching it for a long way.

We became convinced with practice that it was essential to make up the storm groups out of the personnel of one small unit. There was no question of constructing them at company strength. Every platoon, every squad, every soldier, had to be able to carry out an assault.

Timing and surprise were the two most important factors for success in a storm group operation. Let me show what I mean with examples. The Railwaymen's House was attacked at 10 a.m. Commander Yelin's assault groups had three minutes in which to rush the building. Three minutes was the time between the last artillery round and machine-gun burst against the enemy's firing positions and the moment when those firing positions might be expected to be back in action. The men were inside the house before the enemy had recovered from the devastating fire. Thirty minutes later all resistance in the strongpoint had been overcome, the first prisoner had been taken, and the garrison of two companies of infantry and a company of heavy artillery, had been completely wiped out. That is what timing means.

Lieutenant Sedelnikov's men attacked the 'L-shaped house' without any preliminary barrage. One after the other the assault groups broke into the house through the window, throwing grenades into the windows as they ran. The enemy could not fire a shot. Twenty minutes later the assault groups had cleared a third of the six-storey building, which occupied two entire blocks. That is what the factor of surprise means.

Each commander given the task of storming a strongpoint or centre of resistance, had to put the timing and surprise factors to good use. In close fighting, and all the more so in city conditions, this is always of vital importance.

In assault, the soldier's irreplaceable weapon is the grenade. It often predetermines the distance for an assault. The closer the starting point for the attack is to the enemy's position the better. If, from this point of view, one looks at the experience of the storm groups of the 62nd Army's units, it is clear that their success was founded to a very large extent on their ability stealthily to approach close to the enemy. Sedelnikov's group, when defending, was nearly two hundred yards from the 'L-shaped house'; but the group started its attack on the building from a position some thirty yards away. It became a tactical rule to try to achieve such a distance for the launching of an assault.

Experience taught us: get close up to the enemy's positions; move on all fours, making use of craters and ruins; dig your trenches by night, camouflage them by day; make your build-up for the attack stealthily, without any noise; carry your tommy-gun on your shoulder; take ten to twelve grenades. Timing and surprise will then be on your side.

A commander may have a heroic storm group, but if an attack has not been properly prepared he will wait in vain for successful results. The assault has to be carefully prepared, and its details all have to be calculated exactly. There are two basic factors in preparations—a study of the object and the working out of the plan of assault.

In studying the reconnaissance information on the object concerned, the commander has to answer the following questions: the type of building, the thickness of the walls and floors, whether there is a cellar, where the entrances and exits are, the nature of the fortifications, where secret embrasures are situated, where obstacles are and what they consist of, and whether the strongpoint garrison is able, by means of trenches, to communicate with the unit it belongs to. With this information in his possession, the commander can quickly discover the distribution of the enemy's firing positions, their sectors of fire and dead spaces. But the picture of the object to be attacked will be incomplete if reconnaissance does not take into account the behaviour, the daily routine, of the enemy garrison and enemy fire from neighbouring buildings. The complete information, of course, will influence the choice of the most suitable time at which to make the assault.

Commander Yelin, preparing to storm the Railwaymen's House, had all the information, enabling him to work out an exact plan of operations and trick the enemy. Feigning an attack from the south, and having neutralized the enemy's fire, he made his main attack from the east. A careful study of the object under attack made it possible for Lieutenant Sedelnikov to attack that part of the 'L-shaped house' where the enemy's flanking fire could not do any harm, as there were dead spaces on the line of approach.

An assault plan is worked out after a thorough study of the object. This enables the commander to decide on the strength, composition and battle formation of the assault groups and the reinforcement groups, the size of the reserves, the tasks of the groups at different stages in the battle, the degree of artillery support, communication and signals.

Our troops stormed the railway station, 'the nail factory' and 'Pavlov's House'. Their experience taught us: two of you get into the house together—you, and a grenade; both be lightly dressed—you without a knapsack, and the grenade bare; go in grenade first, you after; go through the whole house, again always with a grenade first and you after.

Their experience is completely dependable.

The tactics of the storm group are based on rapid action, a sudden charge, a wide sense of initiative and boldness on the part of every soldier. These groups need to be flexible in tactics, because, after entering a fortified building and the labyrinth of rooms occupied by the enemy, they are faced with a welter of unexpected situations. There is one strict rule now—give yourself elbow room! At every step danger lurks. No matter—a grenade in every corner of the room, then forward! A burst from your tommy-gun around what's left; a bit further—a grenade, then on again. Another room— a grenade! A turning—another grenade! Rake it with your tommy-gun! And get a move on!

Inside the object of attack the enemy may go over to a counter-attack. Don't be afraid! You have already taken the initiative, it is in your hands. Act more ruthlessly with your grenade, your tommy-gun, your dagger and your spade! Fighting inside a building is always frantic. So always be prepared for the unexpected. Look sharp!

In one building the following happened. The commander foresaw that there would be fighting in the basement, but it turned out that a wall through the basement had been broken down across the whole width of the building. To get into the second half of the basement, they had first of all to go through the first, but it was under German fire from some depth. A second unexpected factor was that the enemy had bricked up the entrances to the building, leaving passageways to the firing points only through the basement. A third unexpected factor was that the house was divided by a blank wall, with the enemy concealed behind it.

Then the reinforcement group went into action. Crowbars, picks and explosives were brought into play. Walls were breached, making it possible to use grenades and go on further.

After twenty-six hours of close and fierce fighting in the 'L-shaped house' it was proposed to the remaining German soldiers who had taken cover in the basement that they should surrender. The Germans rejected the ultimatum. The reinforcement group then blew up the whole of the left wing of the building and buried the Germans under the ruins.

The reinforcement groups worked out their own tactical methods, tested many times in practice:

1. Machine-gunners, anti-tank riflemen and mortar gunners enter the building first with their weapons, followed by their assistants carrying enough ammunition and rations for a day's battle.

2. Having entered the building, the men immediately occupy the centre or upper floors of the building, so as to be able to cover the surrounding area and prevent enemy reserves from coming up.

3. After occupying and equipping firing points in the building, the group organizes additional firing points at the approaches to the object—in front and at the flanks (to enable further active operations to take place).

4. After taking possession of the building, the group, without losing any time, must rapidly make communication trenches, adapt blockhouses and build new ones. There is no point in just settling down in the building; you have to persistently try to get closer to the enemy.

It became a rule in the Army that when enemy weapons were concentrated purely inside a building or uninhabitable object, transformed into a strongpoint, the assault was carried out without prior artillery preparation, relying on the surprise factor.

In many cases, however, the use of individual pieces of artillery during an assault was found to be advisable. A small-calibre gun, brought up during the night or under cover of a smoke-screen, and supported by anti-tank rifles, could give the attacking soldiers invaluable help in neutralizing the enemy firing positions. Such a gun, suddenly moved forward to a previously prepared position, can cut off and render impotent any enemy troops trying to help the garrison in the object under attack.

Skilful support for a storm group by individual tanks, firing point-blank into embrasures or wrecking a building, speeds up the assault, makes it more powerful. Other modern means of warfare can also be used to advantage.

Some commanders have asked the question: which is better for camouflaging operations in city battle—darkness or smoke? They are both good. It is important that, acting under cover of darkness or with a smoke-screen, a commander should organize his operation flexibly. A smoke-screen was used when the Railwaymen's House was stormed. The smoke-screen lasts thirteen minutes, and the activities of a number of groups moving up from the south were therefore hidden from three German blockhouses standing on the flanks. The smoke did not interfere with the operation. Darkness did not hamper the organization of the assault of the 'L-shaped house'. The moment chosen for this attack was the break of dawn, but the build-up took place in absolute darkness.

An underground mine attack is also extremely effective. It can be used when to approach the object by any other means could involve heavy losses. The sapper is therefore an important figure in a storm group.

These, basically, are the tactical questions connected with the operations of the storm groups in city battle.

It would be wrong to imagine that city fighting is the same thing as street fighting. When the enemy has established himself strongly in the city, it is houses, buildings, blocks that are being fought for. The fighting takes place, if I may express myself figuratively, on, above and below ground: in rooms, in attics, on roofs, in cellars, in ruins—and least of all in streets and squares.

The soldier in a storm group must have initiative and boldness, must rely on himself alone and believe in his own powers. No one else can carry out his job for him; his comrades have got enough of their own to do. The soldier needs to know exactly where he is going to launch the assault from, by what means he is going to enter the house, where he will go and what he will do next. In an assault he is very often left to his own devices, acts alone, on his own responsibility. Clearly, to wait and look round for one's comrades is letting them down, not helping them. Once you are inside the house it is too late to ask the commander to repeat his explanations of what you have to do.

To inculcate qualities of this kind in the men of the Red Army was not easy. Commander Yelin, before storming the Railwaymen's House, rehearsed the battle in detail below the steep precipice of the Volga bank. He put in a lot of hard work. Lieutenant Sedelnikov also studied the plan of assault with the commanders and carefully prepared every soldier. In both cases the excellent work of the individual soldiers and of the storm group as a whole, testify to the fact that the commanders' work was not in vain: the men fought bravely, showing amazing courage and superhuman endurance.

The first underground mine attack was carried out by two squads under Sergeant Dubovy and Sergeant Makarov. Their attack was directed against a powerful enemy strongpoint, from which the enemy were machine-gunning the Volga.

The tunnel they made led off from a shaft they had dug; it was five yards below ground and was 142 feet long. The hole burrowed underground was thirty-two inches wide and forty inches high.

The sappers underground worked unheard and unseen. For fourteen days oil-lamps flickered in the tunnel. The men underground forgot the light of day, lost the habit of standing upright. Air was short. Their eyes became sunken and their skin yellow. Finally, sapper Tikhon Parfenov clearly heard a noise and German voices overhead. Nearly three tons of explosives were placed in a chamber under the building. The terrible explosion shook the bank of the Volga. The building in which the Germans had consolidated themselves went up in the air, burying hundreds of Germans under its ruins.

The new methods of conducting battle enabled us to hold out and win.

CONSTANT, CLOSE, COMBINED OPERATIONS

In the battle for the city the Army had eight to ten artillery regiments, five anti-tank artillery regiments, and two to three 'katyushi' rocket-launching regiments.

The density of distribution of our artillery was constantly changing, as a result of losses. In the region of the city it amounted to an average of eight to twelve guns to every half-mile of front.

We tried as far as we could to centralize the organization of artillery fire, and a large amount of good work was done in this connection by the Army's Artillery Commander, Major-General Pozharski, and his staff, under Colonel Khizhnyakov.

General Nikolay Mitrofanovich Pozharski emerged as a real innovator in the use of powerful masses of artillery in the defence of the city, and in the use of artillery counterattacks, as the organizer of powerful mortar groups. Pozharski was able to organize artillery fire in such a way as to enable it to pass freely and easily from one commander to another, and when it was necessary to strike a blow at the most dangerous sector of the front, it could be operated centrally. Convinced from experience that it was important to support the storm groups with artillery fire, he boldly included heavy-calibre guns in the groups.

At that time artillery was our most powerful weapon in the fight against the enemy.

The Army Artillery Commander was able centrally to administer the artillery of all infantry divisions, of the anti-tank artillery regiments, the artillery support regiments and the 'katyushi' units. At the end of September, for example, a substantial enemy attack in the area of Mamayev Kurgan and Banny Gully was broken by an artillery bombardment. Counter-preparations continued for several successive days, and more than two hundred and fifty medium and heavy-calibre guns took part in them along a front of between half a mile and a mile.

In the November fighting, in the Barrikady factory area, a

concentrated bombardment was made by the artillery of eight divisions, two anti-tank artillery regiments, three artillery support regiments, and also two regiments of the Front artillery group.

The administration of the artillery was organized so as to make it possible, when the need arose, for the artillery batteries and regiments to come entirely under the orders of the Army Artillery Commander. For this purpose, all artillery reinforcement units were in contact with the divisional artillery commander and at the same time directly with the Army Artillery Commander also. The Army and Front artillery regiments also came under the Army's long-range artillery group, which at any moment could support one division or another in any area.

At the same time as organizing powerful, concentrated artillery fire, the Army's artillery staff planned fire against a group of targets or even an individual target (for example, the water-tanks on Mamayev Kurgan or the baths building in the workers' settlement). Divisional artillery staffs in similar circumstances were called on to organize such close, combined operations with other troops, so that the effects of concentrated artillery fire could be put to full advantage by infantry and tanks.

For example, the 39th Guards Infantry Division, in the fighting for the Krasny Oktyabr factory, even used 203-mm. guns for direct fire at a distance of two hundred to three hundred yards. If our artillerymen had been told previously that such powerful artillery would be used in that way, they would not have believed it possible.

The conditions of street fighting made it necessary to organize a system of forward artillery observation posts, in the companies and platoons, that is, with the storm groups themselves.

Small-calibre artillery and regimental cannon, which were intended for use as anti-tank weapons, were successfully used for firing at buildings point-blank—into windows, doors, attic rooms and at roofs. High explosive shells were a serious danger to men, and 45-mm. anti-tank incendiary shells destroyed simple enemy fortifications in buildings.

Short-range weapons were extremely effective, particularly against enemy armoured cars and tanks.

A considerable percentage of our artillery on the right bank, in the city itself, was rapidly put out of action by the constant bombing, and also by the concentrated enemy artillery and mortar fire. Although artillery was needed all the time, everywhere, we kept a regiment of the Army's rocket artillery in reserve (mortars on caterpillar tracks). We attached it to no one in particular, and it often came to our aid at critical moments to halt enemy attacks.

In the battle for the city an important role was played by anti-tank hand grenades and anti-personnel hand grenades. In the whole of the rest of the war, right through to Berlin, the 62nd Army did not use as many grenades as it used on the banks of the Volga. Our men treated grenades with great respect and gave them pet names: they called the 'F-1' grenade 'Fenyusha' and the anti-tank grenade 'Tanyusha'. Every soldier tried to have five to ten grenades in hand, saving them primarily for assault operations and beating off enemy attacks when there was not enough room for such 'long-range' weapons as rifles.

Grenades were essential for the storm groups, in the closest fighting. With a grenade the soldier in the storm group went into the assault of a stronghold, with a grenade he made a path for himself through the labyrinth of buildings, cellars, rooms and corridors, and the grenade helped him to smoke the enemy out of fortifications against which artillery and aerial bombardment were powerless. In the skilled hands of cool-headed men hand-grenades were always a reliable source of help.

There were very few armoured units in Stalingrad, because the conditions of city battle made it impossible to use large masses of tanks; we had no way of ferrying them across the Volga. Special ferries are needed for heavy tanks, and the Army did not have enough of them.

What tanks the Army did have, however, we used to the full: those that were broken down were used as stationary firing positions, and those still in action as a shock force for counter-attacks. In areas accessible to the enemy's tanks they provided a skeleton framework for our anti-tank defences. We posted them some two hundred to three hundred yards behind our forward positions, camouflaged them well, dug them in as far as the turret, and gave them covering fire from infantry, which also dug itself in or consolidated itself in buildings.

Fire from stationary tanks, ambushing enemy tanks, which appeared in large numbers in the streets and squares, was most effective.

This was precisely how, on September 14 and 15, we managed to stop the German tanks which tried to break quickly through into the city. They were met by devastating fire from ambushes, and, after suffering heavy losses, turned back.

On those days, on the single sector occupied by the armoured brigades of Colonel Krichman and Lieutenant-Colonel Udovichenko, in which there were thirty T-34 tanks, and two regiments of anti-tank artillery, the enemy threw in more than four hundred tanks of various kinds. However, in spite of their manifest numerical superiority, the German tanks failed to break through our defences and reach the Volga.

That is why, in the second half of September, the German generals stopped their attacks with massed tanks and started to throw them into battle only with infantry, in small groups, and with air and artillery support.

On September 19, for example, in an attempt to take possession of Mamayev Kurgan, German tanks in groups of ten to fifteen launched an attack from three sides—north, west and south. In all, more than forty tanks took part. On this sector we had a total of five T-34 and three T-60 tanks.

The first of our tanks to go into action on the south-western slopes of Mamayev Kurgan was commanded by Sergeant-Major Smekhotvorov. He had barely managed to fire a shot, when the enemy turned a wall of fire from every kind of weapon at his tank. One enemy shell burst about five yards from his tank, but the crew did not lose their heads. With a second shot Smekhotvorov hit a German tank, which went up in flames. Another shot, and smoke belched from another German tank. When the Germans started to jump out of the tanks they fell an easy prey to our machine-gunners. The rest of the German tanks then turned back, and the infantry would not advance without them.

A section from Udovichenko's brigade (to take another

example of city battle), consisting of three tanks and an eighteen-man platoon of infantry, were instructed to wipe out some German tommy-gunners who had infiltrated through to some buildings at the corner of Respublikanskaya and Kievskaya Streets. The section was under the command of Lieutenant Morozov, commander of the group of tanks. Unnoticed by the enemy he withdrew his tanks from the eastern slopes of Mamayev Kurgan, put the infantrymen on the tanks, and from approximately half a mile away opened fire at the buildings at great speed. When the tanks approached the buildings, our infantrymen rushed forward, seized a block, and completely wiped out the German tommy-gunners ensconced there.

When this task had been completed Morozov was instructed to take his tanks out to the western outskirts of the Krasny Oktyabr settlement, where the next enemy attack was expected.

Our tanks, therefore, moved from one end of the factory district to the other several times a day.

On September 27 the enemy threw some two battalions of infantry and sixteen tanks against the silicate factory. The factory was being defended by Colonel Krichman's armoured unit. Before the attack the Germans carried out a heavy aerial bombardment of the factory. After the raid our tank crews lit smoke-bombs near their tanks. The Germans fell for the ruse, and believing our tanks to be on fire, rushed into the attack. Allowing them to come up close, our tank and artillery men opened up at them from point-blank range and set fire to eleven German tanks.

When our tanks were put out of action, they were quickly repaired and returned to the battle. We were helped greatly in this by the workers of the Tractor factory, and particularly the workers in No. 5 workshop.

In spite of the factory's being under constant artillery and air bombardment, the tractor workers, led by Colonel Katukov and Major Vovk, worked night and day repairing tanks.

M. G. Weinrub, my deputy in charge of armoured units, went to look at the repair work on broken-down tanks, and afterwards related the following:

Tank No. 214 was towed to the factory from the Krasny

Oktyabr settlement. An armour-piercing shell had penetrated a sheet of armour on the side and damaged the engine. A team under Makarov set to work to repair it. They had not yet removed the last sheet of armour when the Luftwaffe appeared and rained bombs and bullets on the factory . . . They all had to take cover under the tank. But the raids went on, one after the other. The mechanics detailed someone to warn them of approaching aircraft, and only when there was direct danger to the workshop did they stop work and take cover.

The majority of tanks were repaired several times. Tank No. 214, for example, had been repaired four times, and when it was brought in a fifth time, Makarov said:

'No. 214 again?'

'We've only been "wounded",' the crew commander answered apologetically, 'and with your help we'll be back in action tomorrow. But for every time we've been "wounded" we've destroyed a German tank.'

But it was impossible to make up our losses in tanks purely by repairs, and on October 5, to strengthen the Army, Colonel Bely's armoured brigade arrived at the left bank of the Volga. By the morning of October 6, fifteen of this brigade's tanks had been ferried across to the city. On the same morning they took up positions along the railway line and Sculpturnaya Street, and without having had time to consolidate themselves, went straight into battle. This was an exceptionally successful battle. In the first hour eight German tanks and a large number of men were destroyed. (I would point out, by the way, that tank crews did not bother to count the number of enemy soldiers they killed, they preferred to hunt for enemy machines and therefore made little use of their machine-guns. I came to this conclusion while watching the tank crews in action on Sculpturnaya Street. This weakness was soon overcome, and the tanks began to use their machine-guns as well as their cannon.)

In the middle of the day on October 6 the air and artillery barrage on the river slackened off somewhat, and the tanks of Colonel Bely's brigade which were still left on the east bank began to be loaded on to ferries. But no sooner had the first ferry with a T-34 tank on board reached the centre of the river than German dive-bombers swooped on it, dropping small bombs. One of them damaged the steering mechanism and the ferry's engine, and the ferry and the tank started floating down river with the current. The tank commander, Sergeant-Major Petr Zybin, told us:

'At the beginning my crew took cover from shrapnel and machine-gun bullets under the tank, then we all climbed into the tank and waited to see what would happen. Fortunately, a north-west wind was blowing, and the ferry and tank landed on the east bank. We had to get off the ferry and take the tank back to the landing-stage. While the bombing was going on there was a lot of noise, of course, but the only casualty was the ferry's motor-mechanic, who was slightly wounded . . .'

When Colonel Bely's remaining tanks had been ferried across they took up positions on the north-west outskirts of the Barrikady factory.

On October 7, Zholudev's, Gorishny's and Gurtiev's divisions, together with Bely's tanks, waged a fierce battle against two enemy infantry divisions and one hundred and fifty tanks, attacking the western outskirts of the Barrikady factory. All the attacks were beaten off. The enemy left nine hundred dead and sixteen burnt-out tanks on the battlefield. We lost three tanks and their crews.

From October 14–17, in the period of the most intense fighting, when the Germans threw hundreds of tanks into the battle for the Tractor factory and the Barrikady factory, our tank crews fired from ambushes, as I have already described. And although Bely's brigade had only twenty tanks left, they withstood the attack by superior forces, put out of action and burnt out many German tanks, and, most important, prevented the enemy's shock group, consisting of five divisions, from turning to strike south along the Volga against the flank of the Army's main forces.

On October 14 the Germans managed to break into the Tractor factory. Tanks now had to be repaired on the Volga bank and in gullies, with improvised equipment. Repaired tanks were sent straight to positions where they were needed as powerful mobile firing posts; seeing them in action, our infantry units held out and fought considerably more tenaciously and confidently.

The German tanks, despite their superiority in numbers,

were often powerless against our tanks. This was achieved by good reconnaissance, by manœuvre (tanks which could move towed those which could not) and by good camouflage.

In counter-attacks our tanks always operated together with the infantry and sappers. By point-blank fire they made breaches in blank walls, cut off objects of attack from the enemy's main system of defence and, after completing their task, they would either return or stay, carefully camouflaged, under cover.

During our offensive in the city we used small groups of tanks (not more than five in a group) not only because we did not have many of them, but also because in the conditions of fighting in the city, especially one that had been destroyed, it was a complicated business, or rather it was inexpedient, to use them in large numbers.

An army on the offensive in city conditions has to organize combined operations between infantry and tanks and, if that combined operation is broken, it must spare no efforts to restore it.

In an offensive in field conditions, the main elements in combined operations are the battalion, the battery and the tank company. In an offensive in the city these elements of combined operations are more often than not the infantry, tank and artillery platoon.

In city fighting every street and square is a miniature battlefield, requiring special attention and special organization of combined operations by every commander. You will not take it by force alone.

It may be suggested that in my comments on city fighting I am advocating caution and inertia. Such a reproach can be easily rejected by taking examples from our experience.

In September the Germans, approaching the city, had overwhelming superiority in every type of weapon. They had no doubt that with one blow they could throw us into the Volga. I submit that in field conditions with such a balance of forces they would have been able to carry out their plan and rapidly break the 62nd Army's defences, particularly as our defences were at the most a mile deep. In field conditions, to withstand an enemy who has tenfold superiority in strength, on the basis of such a fluid defence as the 62nd Army was able to put up, would have been impossible. There are no such examples in the history of war. But for three months we withstood constant attacks from the enemy's superior forces.

What was the reason? It lies in the fact that in battle it is not always strength which wins the day. Victory is won more by skill than by numbers. And when skill becomes a mass phenomenon an army becomes invincible.

Perhaps I am excessively extolling the virtues of the 62nd Army? I think not.

Without wishing to offend anyone I would like to emphasize the fact that it was the soldiers of the 62nd Army who understood more quickly than anyone else what city fighting means, and learned more quickly and better than the enemy to make use of streets, buildings, basements, staircases, factory chimneys and the roofs of houses. Mastering the art of city battle, all organs of the Army—staffs, political sections and rear—continued to study it, acquired more information and drew more deeply on their experience. The art of street fighting did not spring into existence fully-formed, we perfected it; every soldier tried to devise, and devised, new and usually successful ways of fighting.

What outstanding exploits our reconaissance scouts performed! What pages of extraordinary courage they wrote in the chronicles of the legendary fame of the defenders of the fortress on the Volga!

To find out everything about the enemy, his positions, his intentions, his strength and potential, meant to be able to see clearly how the battle was going to develop, to make it possible to arrive at correct decisions on every occasion, and thereby emerge victorious from the battle. In the days of the fighting in Stalingrad, therefore, reconnaissance had to find out information that would enable us to know what the enemy would be doing, not only tomorrow or next week, but at any given moment, so as not to be caught unawares, and so as to take steps to upset and paralyse the enemy's plans. To achieve this in our situation was exceptionally difficult, almost impossible. The particularly high density of the enemy's formations, the large number of field police and Gestapo among the German troops, the careful shadowing of the local population in the villages occupied by the Germans and in the areas of the city that they occupied—all these made the work of our reconnaissance scouts behind enemy lines extremely difficult.

In our conditions it was hard to organize ground reconnaissance, but to organize air reconnaissance was probably even harder. The enemy's superiority in the air, as long as he retained it, prevented our planes from making frequent flights over the enemy's lines. To try to repeat a flight, to make a second run, frequently meant the end of an aircraft and its crew.

Reconnaissance in a city, where fighting went on in virtually the same place for five months, where the front line went not only through quarters of the city, but through the storeys of houses, staircases and factory workshops, had to be carried out using special methods. It was important in doing this that, adapting themselves to the circumstances, the reconnaissance scouts should obtain the information needed by commanders, should be the eyes and ears of the command.

And however hard it was for them, they found effective ways and means of obtaining reliable information for us. In this connection I must mention the officer in charge of the reconnaissance section of the 62nd Army, Colonel Herman, his political deputy, Boygachev, and his united, resourceful team in the reconnaissance section of Army H.Q. They were a collection of courageous men, who by their own example and efficiency were an inspiration to all the men working on reconnaissance in our Army.

I liked Colonel M. Z. Herman from our first meeting, for his power of concentration and thoughtfulness. He did not say a great deal, but he had carefully thought out every word he did speak.

I had first heard about Herman from the Member of the Military Council, K. A. Gurov, but I was soon able to see for myself what a first-class reconnaissance man he was. If Colonel Herman made a report on the enemy, that meant that he had himself already verified the data and was convinced that it was reliable.

M. Z. Herman never waited for instructions as to where and when reconnaissance needed to be organized. More often than not he reported on his own initiative on the results of reconnaissance and handed on information of interest to us, or asked us what information the Army Command needed, and obtained it at any price. He was a reconnaissance officer who was fully master of campaign tactics and always knew what was happening.

The methods worked out by our reconnaissance men ensured a constant, reliable and timely flow of reconnaissance information.

Foot reconnaissance was the most successful in city conditions. Reconnaissance scouts on foot penetrated behind the enemy's lines, into the positions occupied by the enemy, made observations and obtained the information the Army's commanders needed. However, in view of the continuous barrage of fire from the enemy's forward positions, it was impossible to get through it with a large party or patrol. The enemy would easily have detected a reconnaissance party of fifteen to twenty men. It was decided, therefore, that reconnaissance parties sent behind enemy lines should not contain more than three to five men. These brave spirits, armed with tommy-guns and grenades, with binoculars and radio transmitters, penetrated behind the enemy lines to a depth of two or three miles, and camouflaging themselves, observed everything that was happening.

Such reconnaissance went on all the time. The men set off behind enemy lines only at night-time, and for the most part along the gullies which ran westward from the Volga. These gullies, formed by the waters of the River Tsaritsa, stood us in good stead. The paths through them were difficult ones. To cover them by night, under constant fire, needed a truly strong will, fearless, iron self-control and the special qualities of the pathfinder. Not every bold spirit who expressed the wish to join reconnaissance could be sent behind enemy lines. Only the most courageous and resourceful were recruited to the reconnaissance parties, and the majority of the ones in the groups were Komsomol members, strong in body and spirit.

'Company makes even death pleasant'—says an old Russian proverb. But it was not death that our reconnaissance men were thinking about, when they set off on their missions. They were thinking about life, about life for the Soviet people, who had sent them out to help protect the honour, freedom and independence of their country. For the sake of happiness, in a country rid of the enemy, they were prepared to face death, carrying out their tasks. When they were behind the enemy's lines they knew that the whole Army, the whole Soviet people, all those who were following the battle by the Volga with bated breath, were with them. Not all reconnaissance scouts returned to their units, and of those who returned many went straight to hospital.

Many reconnaissance parties operated heroically during the October fighting. One of them, affectionately called 'Snowball', was known up and down the front. It derived its name from the surname of its commander, Sergeant, afterwards Lieutenant, Snegov.[1] There were seven men in the party, but normally three or five men went out on reconnaissance at any one time, the remainder waited for their comrades to return, and rested in readiness to go out themselves on some dangerous mission, often involving the most unexpected adventures.

This remarkable group operated almost always surely and successfully. It was highly elusive. The men in it could escape notice even when it would have seemed impossible to remain hidden from the enemy's sharp-eyed observers.

When the small parties set off they were normally given instructions to make observations, and avoid any skirmishes with the enemy.

The men in the 'Snowball' group were distinguished by their exceptional courage, and on their return from their missions often brought in prisoners for interrogation, or raided enemy headquarters and stores.

On 8 October 1942, the reconnaissance party was given the job of getting through to the vicinity of Vishnevaya Gully, and finding out what enemy forces were being concentrated there. This was not the easiest of jobs. The group was under Snegov himself. He had three other men with him—Koryakin, Gryzlov and Abel. Their weapons consisted of three tommy-guns, twelve hand-grenades and a small-bore rifle. Apart from weapons, the group took radio equipment, telephone apparatus, rations and medical supplies. They were to set off early that day from the bank of the Volga, heading behind the enemy lines through Banny Gully. They went as

---

[1] From the Russian 'sneg', meaning snow.

far as the main road from the Tractor factory southward to the centre of the city, and here they stopped.

'Let's watch the enemy's movements till nightfall,' Snegov told the others. 'We'll listen, watch and remember everything that will help us to go on further.'

Dusk fell, followed by the darkness of an October evening. Two more hours passed. By scarcely distinguishable sounds Snegov realized that under cover of darkness some Germans were going back into the rear.

'It looks as though they've gone for dinner. Well, let's wish them a good appetite,' said the commander jestingly. 'And now, my friends, off we go!'

And the group set off along the bottom of the gully towards the railway bridge, about five hundred yards south of the Krasny Oktyabr settlement.

To cover this distance, speed was needed, but speed of a special kind. Pressing themselves close to the ground they had to crawl over a mile, literally alongside the enemy. Snegov went ahead, followed by the others, ready to obey his command at any given moment. It took the group about an hour and a half to reach the railway bridge across Banny Gully. Then, finally, there was the railway line. The slightest careless movement, and all was lost. But Snegov and his men had their wits about them.

Snegov gestured to the men to take cover. The group rapidly occupied a position by the railway line, where they could not be seen, but could see what was going on around them. As if sensing the danger the Germans sent up rockets from the top of Mamayev Kurgan and from the Krasny Oktyabr settlement. The Germans were clearly losing their nerve. But the Germans could not see anything. By the light of the rockets, however, the reconnaissance group examined the shattered trucks and engines on the railway tracks. This conglomeration of wood and metal stretched almost in a continuous line north-westward to the Krasny Oktyabr settlement. They were quick to realize that it would be possible to establish an excellent observation post in the shattered trucks, and use them as a shelter for the whole group.

'The Germans surely can't start examining every broken-down truck and engine along the whole of this enormous cemetery of metal,' thought Snegov, and whispered his decision to the others.

'After me!' He gave the command almost soundlessly and crawled along the railway track.

From time to time Snegov stopped, listened to the slightest rustle, and, when he was sure that there was no danger, crawled on again. Crawling on like this for about a mile, the group reached the southern outskirts of the Krasny Oktyabr settlement. But when the men started to approach the railway trucks the Germans again sent up rockets. The night sky became more and more alive with flares and aeroplanes. But all went well. The Germans did not see the reconnaissance group, which, by the light of the enemy rockets, was able to choose one of the metal trucks which was less buckled than the others. It was apparently a truck that had carried coal. Another goods waggon was piled up on top of it. Such a 'two-storey detached residence' would serve as a good observation post. With great care they climbed up to the 'second storey' and decided to rest till morning.

At dawn they took precise bearings of the co-ordinates of the observation post: they were half a mile east of Vishnevaya Gully, and where they needed to be to carry out their mission. They had a reliable shelter, which enabled them to observe the locality for a long way round. To the north of the observation post, some three hundred yards away, was the Krasny Oktyabr settlement. Half a mile or so to the north-west was Hill 107.5. West of the post were orchards, and to the south-east, on Mamayev Kurgan, were the two water-tanks.

The co-ordinates could now be sent by radio to H.Q., together with a report of what had been done, and observations could continue.

From daybreak they could hear the drone of enemy aircraft overhead. At the beginning they were single reconnaissance planes, followed later by bombers, carrying their load of death to the city, to its factories, houses and the positions occupied by the defenders. Almost simultaneously the enemy opened fire with artillery and mortars. In reply, shells and mortar bombs dropped on the enemy not far away, from the direction of the Volga. But where were the Germans firing from? The reconnaissance men soon detected dozens of enemy artillery and mortar batteries posted in the area west of Hill 107.5 and the Krasny Oktyabr settlement. Continuing their observation, they detected movement along the road from Gorodishche, in the region of Gumrak. It appeared to be columns of enemy artillery and mortars. Reaching the afforestation area bordering on the city to the west, they were beginning to take up firing positions. Following the guns came lorries, which began unloading what was presumably boxes of ammunition alongside the guns.

It was difficult to see exactly what all this meant. But they understood that fresh enemy forces were arriving on this sector of the front, and that the enemy was presumably preparing for a strong attack from this area. A report on what they had seen needed to be sent quickly by radio. Using the transmitter was no easy matter, as it might be detected by the enemy, particularly as the reconnaissance party's observation post was right inside the enemy positions.

The information they sent in was of great value to Army H.Q. What was needed now was to know what units the enemy had in the area of Vishnevaya Gully. To find this out a prisoner was needed. The 'Snowball' party was instructed to get one.

On the same day, at 4 p.m., they reported to H.Q.:

'On Hill 107.5 there are a lot of observation posts, and telephone lines are being laid; north of the railway line, in the vicinity of Vishnevaya Gully, there is a build-up of artillery and ammunition taking place. Our task is clear, and tomorrow morning we will study the situation in the area of Vishnevaya Gully.'

During the daytime they observed the enemy without binoculars. German soldiers, alone and in groups, were passing up and down the road from the Krasny Oktyabr settlement alongside the orchards. They had no thought for any danger that might be lurking. On the western outskirts of the Krasny Oktyabr settlement smoke was rising from field kitchens. Soldiers gathered round the water-hydrant, gossiping leisurely as they collected water. Between the reconnaissance group's observation post and the settlement, German signallers were laying a cable along the ground from the west towards Hill 107.5 Shells burst here and there, 'presents' from our artillery . . .

After discussing with the others the best way of capturing a prisoner, the commander of the group decided to organize an ambush along the road between the Krasny Oktyabr settlement and the orchards, and take a prisoner in the evening. If they failed to take one alive, then they would use the German's documents to get among the crowd of enemy soldiers by the kitchens and water-hydrant, and also listen in on the telephone line to what the Germans were talking about.

The most difficult part of the operation was taking the prisoner. The job was going to be done by Snegov, Koryakin, an experienced scout, and Abel, who spoke fluent German. Gryzlov, the radio operator, was to continue his observations and send in radio reports. The three men took their telephone apparatus with them, and also the small-bore rifle, a tommy-gun, daggers and hand grenades. Abel, in addition, had a policeman's rubber truncheon, captured on one of their previous missions.

When darkness fell, the three of them left the truck and set off towards the railway crossing south of the Krasny Oktyabr settlement. Finding the telephone line, they set about tapping it. They then carefully moved the cable ten or so yards to the side of the road, into the bushes, and cut it. Snegov and Koryakin then moved off in different directions to wait for the German telephonists who would come looking for the break in the line. Abel stayed by the cable. A German signaller soon appeared from the direction of the orchards, flashing a torch on the cable, looking for the break. The torch-light worried our men, because they might be seen by it. Snegov took a quick decision. Koryakin and Abel hid in the bushes and waited until the German signaller came up to the point where they had cut the cable. Snegov hid some distance away. When the German came up close and switched on the torch to examine the cable, there was a click from the breech of the rifle in Koryakin's hands, and the German fell. Abel leaped from behind the bushes with the rubber truncheon ready, but the German showed no signs of life. They dragged the dead German into the bushes, and Abel emerged dressed as a German soldier, with documents in the name of Hans Müller. Leaving Koryakin on watch, Snegov and Abel listened in at the end of the line from the Krasny

Oktyabr direction. They could hear a rustling sound in the receiver, and then a call. Abel answered the call in German, asking:

'Who's on line duty?'

'Willi, one of our telephonists. Who's coming to meet him?'

'I am, Hans,' answered Abel. 'I've found the break. But there's not enough cable to join the ends. Send a few yards with Willi.'

'Right,' came the answer.

At the end of the conversation 'Hans' asked for Willi to come as soon as possible to the railway line.

'I'll meet him there,' said Abel.

And Abel went towards the railway line and stood at the top of the slope, so that he could be seen from a distance; five yards from Abel, with the small-bore rifle, Snegov lay hidden.

Soon they heard steps, and then they made out an approaching silhouette. This was presumably Willi. He crossed the railway line and started to climb up the steep slope. 'Hans' shone his torch on him and stretched out his hand to help him to the top. When the signaller gave him his hand, Abel gripped it hard and brought the rubber truncheon down hard on the man's head . . .

After gagging the unconscious German, the two men dragged him to the railway trucks. Then, together with Koryakin, they joined the broken ends of the cable and repaired the line. This would reassure whoever had sent the signallers to repair the damage, so that they would not send anyone else. Leaving Koryakin to keep a look out, Snegov told Gryzlov to get the transmitter ready to send a report. The prisoner had by now come to, and the interrogation could begin.

But how were they going to interrogate him? What if he suddenly yelled out?

'Ask him questions, and let him answer them on paper. We're not taking his gag off,' ordered Snegov.

Abel translated Snegov's instructions, and so that the German could write, they freed his right hand, and gave him a pencil and paper. The decision was a very sensible one. By answering the questions in writing, the German could not cry out and attract the attention of his compatriots, and at the same time our men obtained an important document. The German would now hardly do anything that would lead to the capture of our men with this document in their possession.

'Your Christian name, surname, unit and where you are posted?' Abel asked the prisoner.

'Willi Brandt, of the 274th Regiment,' wrote the prisoner.

The prisoner stopped answering questions, and begged for water. The reconnaissance men had no choice but to try to satisfy his request. Unfortunately, they had no water left. What were they going to do? Taking two billy-cans, and taking advantage of the darkness, Abel strode off towards the Krasny Oktyabr settlement for water. He walked confidently through the settlement, answering the greetings of German soldiers he met. On the western outskirts of the settlement he even thought of going up to a group of soldiers waiting for their evening meal, so as to listen to what they were talking about, but he resisted the temptation. As soon as he had got some water he returned to his comrades.

When the prisoner's gag was taken off and he could speak, he gave not only his name and regiment, but his unit and where he was posted. After he had drunk a few mouthfuls he was ready to give more information.

He told them that the 274th Infantry Regiment was being incorporated into the 94th Infantry Division, which had arrived here from the vicinity of Sadovaya Station and Minina suburb at the beginning of October. He also told them that, as a signaller, he had recently listened to a telephone conversation between officers of regimental H.Q. From this conversation he had gathered that the 24th Panzer Division, with more than a hundred and fifty tanks, had arrived, that units of a light infantry division had been sent to the Krasny Oktyabr settlement, that Hitler had demanded that the city be occupied by October 15, and that preparations were therefore going ahead for a decisive offensive.

The veracity of what Willi Brandt had told them was confirmed by the information that they had already gleaned.

'You have betrayed a military secret,' Snegov told the prisoner. 'And if your regiment finds out, you will be shot.'

The German was now not overjoyed at the idea of returning to his unit, and his expression showed the fact.

'Don't be afraid,' Abel reassured him. 'We are not going to give you away. But you are not to tell a soul what has happened, and at every available opportunity you should tell your mates that the Russians don't shoot their prisoners and that German soldiers don't need to be afraid of captivity, and the main thing is that they ought not to fight against the Soviet people.'

The prisoner listened to him, then asked:

'And how am I going to explain the bump on my head and my long absence? It's a long time since I was sent out on the line . . .'

They told him how to get out of his difficulty:

'Tell them you fell down the railway embankment and knocked yourself unconscious.'

He cheered up a bit.

They then led him to the spot where they had taken him prisoner, gave him some telephone cable, and showed him how to get back to Hill 107.5.

Continuing to look mistrustfully at the rifle, Willi Brandt started down the slope. When he was sure that he was safe, he waved his hand and said: *'Danke, Kamerad'*, did not look back any more, and set off along the path they had shown him.

Who knows what happened to that soldier? Probably, like hundreds of thousands of others, deceived and made fools of by the Nazis, he was killed by the Volga; or perhaps he survived and is among the millions of Germans who are building a new life in Democratic Germany, knowing clearly who is Germany's friend and who her foe.

Gryzlov quickly reported the information we had obtained from Brandt to 62nd Army H.Q. signals.

With so much valuable information in our possession, we had important details about the forces the enemy had concentrated on this sector of the front, and about his intentions. All this was vital for us, so that we could take correct decisions.

When Gryzlov had finished his transmission, Snegov decided to move the observation post elsewhere, as it was now dangerous to remain where they were.

'After me!' came the familiar words of their commander.

And the four courageous men moved off to fresh fields, to meet fresh dangers and experience fresh adventures.

No less heroic and skilled than our ground reconnaissance were our pilots, who threw themselves into the thick of the battle to observe the enemy's firing positions, his defence works, communications and distribution of the enemy's forces in the rear. The men of the 62nd Army can remember no time in the battle when there were not dozens or hundreds of enemy planes overhead. Until November 23 the enemy had complete superiority in the air. But even in these circumstances our airmen got through to their destinations.

In the daytime we often saw our fighters, with stars on their wings, approach from beyond the Volga, and German planes, with crosses or swastikas on their wings and fuselage, come in to meet them from the west. More often than not the air battles were fought out over the Volga, and to anyone who did not know it would have seemed a jolly game.

Our airmen, not sparing themselves or their aeroplanes, diving steeply and doing somersaults, tried to come up on the enemy's tail and catch him in their sights. This was battle to the death.

At these moments our soldiers would have their eyes riveted on the sky, and one would often hear shouts of: 'Look, look, he's on his tail! Let him have it! Ah, he's got out of the way—it would have been the end of him otherwise!'

Taking advantage of the enemy's preoccupation with the battle taking place, our reconnaissance planes would then slip through to their destinations. They could not go into battle until they had completed their mission. What was asked of them was to reach their target, photograph it, and return to base. Our planes could do this only in the daytime, and not without loss . . .

And at night, when the enemy's planes and anti-aircraft defences were operating blindly (there was no radar), our night-pilots would go out on other missions. When darkness fell the first wave to go in from the east would be PO-2's. From low altitudes they would bomb and machine-gun enemy searchlights. In the after-glow of the fires in the city our reconnaissance planes would seek out their targets, drop their load of bombs and return to their aerodromes.

The Germans spoke contemptuously of our PO-2's, calling them 'Russian plywood'. But when the PO-2's started bombing them at night-time, the Germans realized what was what. But the enemy did not suspect what valuable reconnaissance information these unpretentious planes provided for the Army.

I am not quoting any concrete examples of the heroism of our airmen, who did not hesitate to give their lives in the battle for the honour and independence of their country. It would be no exaggeration to say, however, that all of them deserve the very highest praise.

Co-ordinated operations by all the different branches of an army are, as we know, the basis of success. In the period of the defence of Stalingrad the forms of such combined operations were various, but in essence they amounted to one and the same thing—everyone, from the commander to the private, tried to help his neighbour to right and left, and spared no effort, not even life itself, to achieve the common aim—victory over the enemy.

That is why one must mention the often neglected work of such men as the engineers, whose operations added many a glorious page to the story of the defence of the city. They not only constructed ferries, but fought in the Army's forward units as well. Explosives and mines in the hands of courageous sappers became formidable weapons. When the enemy seemed in an invulnerable position, along came the sappers and blew him up. When the enemy could not be approached by normal means, the sappers would dig an underground tunnel as far as the enemy's fortified position and let explosives do the rest.

Such terms as 'underground mine-tunnels' and 'saps' sound archaic nowadays. But in the fight against the enemy the sappers of the 62nd Army did not hesitate to use the experience of the famous Russian miners who defended Sevastopol in the middle of the last century.

Scores of enemy tanks were put out of action by mines laid by the sappers. They were an integral part of the storm groups and performed great feats.

When, for example, the enemy was attacking the northern part of the city, a group of sappers under Major G. N.

Vanyakin laid two minefields in the vicinity of Mokraya Mechetka Gully. Eight enemy tanks were blown up in them.

On one of the sectors occupied by the 13th Guards Division, the enemy tried to break through twice in one night. This sector had to be held. A group of engineers, under the command of a Communist, Lieutenant F. Levadny, under fire from the enemy laid four hundred mines, and the enemy, suffering losses from our fire and the mines, had to transfer his attacks elsewhere.

The enemy established a powerful strongpoint in the grounds of the oil combine, surrounded by an embankment. From here he was shelling Banny Gully and the bank of the Volga. The embankment prevented us from correcting our fire. It was discovered by reconnaissance that one of the oil-tanks in the grounds of the combine was not occupied by the enemy. A group of sappers of the 8th Guards Battalion dug a tunnel from Dolgi Gully under this tank, blew a hole in the bottom of the tank, and established two firing posts and an observation post in it. The work of the sappers was camouflaged by specially organized artillery and mortar fire. With the occupation of the oil-tank the enemy strongpoint was paralysed.

Preparing to storm the foundry shop at the Krasny Oktyabr factory, the sappers on the 39th Guards Division's sector used explosives to make communication trenches, making it possible to approach within the distance of a grenade-throw from the enemy lines, attack him successfully and seize a strongly-fortified enemy strongpoint.

On the 45th Division's sector north-west of the Krasny Oktyabr factory, at the foot of Mamayev Kurgan, was an enemy position from which our positions were being fired on. Sappers prepared a barrel of explosives, and with the fuse ignited, rolled it down on the enemy's strongpoint. The explosion that ensued destroyed the firing position and the Germans in it.

The enemy took cover in the basement of the famous 'L-shaped house' and prevented our units from completing their occupation of the building. Sappers from the storm groups, under Second Lieutenant P. D. Ivanitski, laid and blew up over 5 cwt of explosives. Information provided by

345

prisoners showed that over one hundred and fifty Germans were killed in the explosion.

The engineers, of course, worked together with the rest of the troops; their operations were part of the Army's overall operations. It must be pointed out, however, that the sappers were particularly ingenious, resourceful and quick-thinking. There seemed to be no situation that our sappers could not find a solution to.

The sappers ensured that the ferries were working, stormed buildings occupied by the enemy, consolidated positions occupied by our troops, and made shelters and dugouts.

Winter drew on. But however difficult the military situation might be, soldiers had to be kept warm and be provided with washing facilities. Baths, made by the sappers, appeared in the battle-torn city. And the men expressed their sincere gratitude to their friends in the engineers.

The fighting by the Volga died away; the enemy had been partly destroyed, partly taken prisoner. The Army moved out of the city to prepare for new battles, but the sound of explosions could be heard for a long time afterwards in the city. This was the engineers destroying mines, unexploded shells and bombs.

The rebuilding of the destroyed city and its industry began, in accordance with a decision of the Party and the government, immediately after the fighting was over. The sappers were the first to take part in this great work. By clearing the city of thousands of dangerous mines and shells, the sappers made it possible for the work of reconstruction to begin.

The Army's communications had to work smoothly, twenty-four hours a day, as all signals from unit commanders in forward positions had to be communicated as rapidly and clearly as possible, just as the nervous system of the body transmits messages to the brain about all changes that take place in the organism.

In the fighting by the Volga communications were of especial importance, because on their clear, uninterrupted operation depended the fate of the city's defence. Whereas in field conditions reports on military operations can take an hour or more to go from the forward positions through divisional H.Q. to Army H.Q.; in the conditions of city battle this is inadmissible. For instance, if an Army H.Q. duty officer receives a report during the night from a division operating with broad room for manœuvre, he can think about whether to wake the commander or give him the report in the morning, but in our case such a delay could have meant disaster for the Army.

That is literally true. In field conditions, when in an hour's fighting or a night's fighting the enemy might advance a mile or two, he only makes a dent in the defences. In the city, however, where in places the depth of our defence positions was measured in hundreds of yards, such an enemy advance really would mean disaster. Here, therefore, we had to know the enemy's intentions beforehand, so as to prevent him from delivering a surprise attack. It was necessary, therefore, for our weapons to be kept at the ready, and for our men to be prepared to go into battle at any moment and repulse the enemy swiftly and effectively. Could all this really be achieved without good communications with our reconnaissance, with our guard posts, with observation posts, the artillery and its firing positions across the Volga, the commanders of reserve units, and all the units and services supporting and supplying the men in action? Of course not. Only clear and continuous communication by radio and telephone, and properly thought-out signalling with lights, could ensure effective administration of the Army and forestall an attack prepared by the enemy. More often than not we meet such an attack at the approaches to our positions and at their concentration points, when the enemy's men and material were coming out of their shelter. Without communications we could not have administered the Army, could not have moved our guns and mortars, sent in aeroplanes and other means of resisting an enemy attack on the threatened sector.

Divisional and Army command posts were on the right bank of the Volga, anything from about 300 to 1,000 yards from the forward positions. With our administrative posts so close to the troops, it was possible for commanders at all levels to sense the way a battle was going, examine changes in the situation and take appropriate decisions in good time. The most effective form of administration was personal contact between senior commanders and their subordinates. But that does not mean that the telephone and the radio lost their importance. They were, in fact, our constant preoccupation. But the organization of a continuously operating radio and telephone network was very difficult, for the following reasons:

1: constant bombardment, especially from the air, of command posts and our various sectors, led to our telephone lines being constantly burnt and broken, and to heavy losses among our signals units;

2: the Army was split three times right to the Volga, and was fighting simultaneously along three unconnected sectors of front;

3: because of the enemy's strong fire-power, it was impossible to use radio transmitters at the Army command post;

4: the presence of a broad stretch of water at the Army's rear was also a serious obstacle.

Retaining the basic principles of the organization of signals—from top to bottom, from right to left and from specialized units to infantry—we often adapted them to suit the operational conditions, and in some areas the communications system recommended for defensive fighting broke down.

The operational situation, the tactical position of our troops, and the location of our H.Q.'s meant that the Army had to resort to a hybrid scheme: communications were established between our troops on one flank and those on the other, and from this axis cables were led off to the divisions. In the divisions and regiments cables were usually laid along the sector of the front.

I can still see the strained faces of the Army Chief of Staff, N. I. Krylov, and the Chief Signals Officer, Colonel, later General, M. P. Yurin, sitting at night over their maps, examining old, and thinking up new, ways of organizing signals and administration.

Communications in warfare, like the nervous system of the body, remain invisible, but a lot depends on them. Destroy an army's signals centre, and the army is paralysed. I therefore used to joke about Comrades Krylov and Yurin as neuropathologists, who, without even seeing the root cause of the disease, treated the patient by instinct.

One cable often served two or three divisions at the same time, and to ensure stable communication these divisions

348

were provided with supplementary links to auxiliary posts, forming a complete circuit.

At the principal monitoring posts and at all auxiliary centres, emergency repair parties were organized.

The telephone network was as a rule duplicated by a radio network, and the marines also used flag signalling.

In the divisions, telephone networks normally consisted of two or three lines with monitoring posts.

The Army's main radio centre consisted of low-power RB, RBM, 12-RP and 13-RA radio transmitters, and was immediately alongside the command post. An auxiliary centre, consisting of powerful radio transmitters, was on the other bank of the Volga, about six miles from Army H.Q., and through it we maintained contact with Front H.Q., the air force and our rear.

For greater efficiency in operation, and to provide for direct conversations between Army H.Q. and unit H.Q.'s, all radio transmitters had to operate with microphones, limiting the content of conversation transmissions.

Radio, on the whole, was a reliable form of communication, and on some occasions the only form (communication with Gorokhov's group and the 13th Division was maintained almost exclusively by radio).

I must mention one other, and perhaps the most difficult, part of the work of the 62nd Army's signallers—the laying of a telephone cable across the bed of the Volga. The Army had no special equipment, and our signallers had to use ordinary telephone cable to establish communication between the Army command post and the east bank of the Volga. (The Army had an emergency H.Q. command post across the river, through which Gorokhov's group, the artillery and the rear were administered, and in October, that is in the middle of the most difficult time in the fighting, it was through this emergency command post that the troops in the centre of the city and in the factory district were administered, and the telephone line across the Volga, therefore, also had to work continuously and without interruptions.)

The cable, with weights attached to it, was lowered into the water and laid along the bed of the river. But no more than three or four days later the signallers had to lay another cable. And that went on from start to finish of the fighting in

349

the city. On this sector the signallers suffered heavy losses, but their nerves were, as they say, stronger than steel, and they carried out their tasks with honour.

At the beginning of the fighting in the centre of the city, the Army's base was moved to the town of Leninsk, and the main supplies units were in the villages of Burkovski, Gospitomnik and Verkhnyaya Akhtuba. On the left bank of the Volga supplies were brought up to the ferries by military transport, and from the landing-stages on the right bank they were carried to the units by hand, as there was not, and could not be, any transport in the city.

To ensure that supplies were transported properly across the Volga, special teams were set up at the ferries, to see to the loading and unloading of boats, the control of traffic, the maintenance of order and, especially, the camouflaging of men and supplies at the landing-stages.

During the fighting in the city, strict regulations for reserve supplies were established, laying down that units on the right bank of the Volga would keep one complete set of ammunition and four days' rations in stock, and that divisional and Army stores, on the left bank of the Volga, would have in stock three-quarters of a set of ammunition, two refuellings of fuel and oil, and six days' rations and fodder.

The conditions in which the Army's rear units worked in the period of the battle for the city were extremely difficult. The loading area on the left bank of the Volga and the unloading area on the right bank, were churned up with trenches, holes and dug-outs, in which supplies were kept and men waited to be ferried across to the city, or evacuated from it.

The nearer the enemy came to the Volga, the more difficult it was to deliver supplies from the left bank to the right. There were days and even weeks when ammunition deliveries fell so drastically that the Army Military Council gave orders to use ammunition economically, at the same time as urgently pressing the Front Military Council to take vigorous measures to get ammunition through to the city.

However, in asking the Front Command to give urgent assistance with ammunition, we realized that the resources available to the Front were also restricted, and, the most important factor, that it was incapable of preventing the Germans from slackening their fire or of restraining the elements on the Volga during the period of drifting ice.

The chief of staff of every kind of Army unit in the rear, be he engineer, artilleryman or chemist, looked for and, in spite of the exceptional difficulties, found ways and means of delivering military stores to the city.

Our hearts filled with pride when we watched the steamers and armoured boats of the Volga fleet forcing their way through the ice to the Army's landing-stages, or PO-2 aircraft flying down to a height of ten to fifteen yards above the narrow strip of icy bank, dropping their cargoes and risking the danger of piling up against the steep bank of the river.

In order to ensure the uninterrupted delivery of supplies to the city, every available means of ferrying cargoes across the river was used, and primarily the civil river fleet, the boats of the Volga navy, and also naval pontoons, fishing boats, rafts and footbridges, made by the Army's engineering units from whatever materials they could find in the locality.

At different times the right bank of the Volga was linked with the left bank by three crossings:

1. *The Central Crossing.* This worked with engine-driven ferries, had the biggest carrying capacity, and linked the central city landing-stage with Krasnaya Sloboda, by the shortest route. Unfortunately, from September 14 the enemy began firing on it with every kind of weapon, and it had to be abandoned in the second half of September.

2. *The Skudri Crossing.* This served the northern sector of the Army's front. At different periods ferries, armoured boats and steamers operated on this crossing. This crossing was used to take supplies to Gorokhov's group (in the vicinity of Rynok), and also to the Tractor, Barrikady and Krasny Oktyabr factories.

3. *Crossing '62'.* This was the main crossing used by our Army. On the right bank it had a group of moorings at the Krasny Oktyabr and Barrikady factories. These moorings received cargoes from Skudri, Tumak, Srednyaya and Verkhnyaya Akhtuba. When the enemy came close to the Volga bank in the factory district, these moorings were virtually not used at all for the delivery of the main cargoes and the

evacuation of the wounded, and if they were used, then it was only at night, as during the day the enemy subjected them to an intense artillery and air bombardment. For the landing of cargoes and reinforcements, and also for the evacuation for the bulk of the wounded, four moorings south of Banny Gully were used.

The incessant mortar and artillery barrage and bombing of the moorings killed personnel running the ferries, destroyed landing-stages and boats. From November 7–28, for example, the 44th Pontoon and Bridge-Building Battalion, serving the ferries, lost thirty-six men (eleven killed and twenty-five wounded). In the same period the enemy put out of action, sent up in flames or to the bottom of the river, the steamers *Dubrovka, Sovkhoznitsa, Kapitan Ivanishchev, Pozharski, Abkhazets, Donbass, Tramvay No. 1, BMK, SP-19*, seven ferries, and thirty-five *N-2-P* type pontoons. The majority of these vessels were put out of action, not while crossing the river, but while being loaded, or, most of all, while resting at their moorings during the day.

On October 28, the fleet's base and main loading point was moved to Srednyaya Akhtuba. As a result of such losses, boats were not kept at the moorings. There were, of course, direct hits with mortar bombs and shells on moving vessels. After being repaired, all boats were brought back into service.

Because of the drifting ice, and then the icing over of the river, we had to move the loading point and base for the fleet from Srednyaya Akhtuba to the left arm of the Volga, to the village of Tumak.

The Army's main ferry was therefore moved three times on the left bank of the Volga, which inevitably had an effect on the efficiency of the work of the ferries.

Side by side with the Army's central ferry worked the Army boat-station, directly under the command of Army engineering H.Q. It was operated by teams from the 119th Army Motor and Engineering Battalion on the right bank and the 327th Army Engineering Battalion on the left bank. The boatmen helped the ferries, bringing across reinforcements, ammunition and provisions, evacuating the wounded and taking across urgent cargoes, especially when engine-driven vessels were not working.

The boat crews were grouped in five detachments. One

special-purpose detachment was put directly under Army H.Q., under the command of the Member of the Military Council, K. A. Gurov, who decided on the use to which it was to be put in the most critical situations. For the evacuation of the seriously wounded a special medical landing-stage was used, working round the clock.

Divisions and brigades also had boat stations, but they operated with fewer boats. Their operations were under the control of the divisional and brigade commanders.

When darkness fell, first of all the wounded, who had accumulated near the crossings before the engine-driven boats arrived, were moved to the moorings. Great assistance was given with the ferrying across of the wounded by the boatmen. On 8 November 1943, for example, out of a total of 1,060 wounded ferried across, 360 were taken in rowing-boats.

To supplement the ferries, in the early days of October, in the area of the Tractor and Barrikady factories, three foot-bridges, each almost 300 yards in length, were built, linking the Stalingrad bank of the river with Zaitsevski Island across the Denezhnaya Volozhka branch of the Volga.

The bridge built at the southern extremity of the island consisted of a series of wooden rafts and barrels, linked by laps of bar iron and steel hawser. A flooring of boards was laid over the cross-beams. This bridge, though it would not carry any heavy weight and was not very steady even when the surface of the water was disturbed only slightly, lasted for more than a month. In that time several thousand men crossed it in both directions. Countless attacks by German dive-bombers, the incessant artillery and mortar fire, did little harm to the bridge, and repairs were soon made.

The second footbridge, to the north of the first one, lasted only three days: a bomb broke the hawser and the bridge was carried away with the current.

A third footbridge was built across the Denezhnaya Volozhka in the vicinity of the Tractor factory. This one differed from the other two in that its floating supports consisted of anchored iron casks.

The work at the moorings was hard and dangerous, and was carried out under fire the whole time. For example, on October 26 alone, at the moorings at Banny Gully the Germans dropped a hundred or so bombs, 130 mortar bombs and over 120 shells.

In describing the activities of the men on the Volga crossings, and of the engineering units in the city, I cannot omit to mention the part played by the man in charge of the 62nd Army's engineering troops, now a Hero of the Soviet Union, Lieutenant-General Vladimir Matveyevich Tkachenko.

Tkachenko, then a lieutenant-colonel, arrived in the second half of October, in the days of the grimmest defensive fighting. Organizing the work of the crossings, from the very first days he showed the tenacity with which he set about achieving his aim. Modest by nature, he disliked showing off and preening himself on his achievements. And though he was sometimes given tasks to do, when, seemingly, he had neither the strength nor the resources to accomplish them, he would take correct decisions, mobilize his engineering units to the full, and carry out his tasks, usually well and in good time.

When I met him after the war we talked about the slogan 'For us, there is no land across the Volga!'

'That motto,' said Tkachenko, 'was relevant to everyone who took part in the fighting. But it doesn't mean that the men fighting under the motto felt themselves to be doomed. No, everyone was well aware of the fact that there was indeed land across the Volga, precious Soviet land, that from the land across the Volga the country was sending us a stream of reinforcements, weapons, ammunition and provisions. Seeing the support we were being given by the country, the defenders of the city solemnly vowed not to return across the Volga without having won victory first.'

Tkachenko was in personal command of the ferries, and met with difficulties galore. It was particularly difficult in October, when the enemy succeeded in splitting the Army's front and reaching the Volga at a number of points. Then the autumn period of drifting ice set in comparatively early. And though the meteorologists forecast that the river would ice over shortly after November 20, it did not do so until December 17. The unusually steep drop in the temperature of the river, resulting from the ice-jams in the upper reaches of the river, created additional difficulties for the movement of large-draught vessels.

In those days, the Volga, congested as it was with a

continuous stream of ice and under incessant enemy fire, seemed an insurmountable obstacle. The sappers, pontooniers, boatmen and ships' crews managed to surmount it, however. At the beginning of October the Army had only very few pontoons, fewer than ten extremely worn-out armoured boats, a few dozen fishing-boats and some ten ships of the civil river fleet, which carried the greatest volume of cargo.

I cannot omit to mention some of these vessels and their heroic crews. There were the tugs *Kochegar Hetman, Uzbek, Lastochka, No. 2, Abkhazets* and *Kuznets,* passenger boats *Emelyan Pugachev, Spartakovets* and *General Panfilov,* the ice-breaker *Gromoboy,* the armoured boat *Eric,* and barges *Svyazist* and *No. 1,002.* The legendary armoured boat *No. 61* deserves special mention. It made its crossings in any conditions. Neither enemy fire nor the drifting ice could prevent it from carrying out its missions. This boat many times sailed along the bank occupied by the enemy, in order to reach the isolated groups of Gorokhov and Lyudnikov, delivering reinforcements, supplies and provisions.

Together with the ships' crews, great courage and resourcefulness were shown by the buoy keepers. Nikolay Lunev tells this story:

My post was buoy number 443. One mid-day, after an air battle, I noticed one of the planes dropping steeply, with a trail of smoke coming from one engine. With one wing it touched the water, span round in a circle, and came to a halt alongside the upper red buoy. I could not make out whose plane it was, and rowed out towards it. I had to save the men in the water near the sinking aeroplane. There were three of them.

I rowed up to them and heard a foreign language. What was I to do? I had no weapon with me whatsoever. When I saw that they were gasping for breath I rowed up closer. But I took one of the oars and got it ready to defend myself with ...

When two of them were on the boat they helped the third man to clamber in. He was badly burned. Once they felt themselves to be safe, all three of them started pointing to the bank ...

I understood them to mean that they wanted to get to

the bank and hide in the forest, but I pretended that I could not manage the oars and nosed round, not towards the bank, but with the current towards the naval vessels down river. When a motor-boat came in sight, my prisoners started to mutter. To gain time I asked them whether the injured man needed his wounds bandaging, and gripped my oar in readiness. Realizing that I was waiting for the motor-boat to draw near, they started to shout at me, and one of them, with two iron crosses, started to go for his gun ... But the motor-boat containing seamen had already come up close. The seamen trained their tommy-guns on my 'passengers', and I gestured to the Germans to drop their guns and put up their hands. Of course, they did.

We disarmed the three men and made them prisoner. It turned out they were from a special German reconaissance squadron ...

We remember the Volga river men with great gratitude.

To administer the boats on the crossings as well as possible, we used radio, which made it possible at any given moment to check on the work of every boat separately, issue instructions to them, and give them help when the occasion arose.

Special centres were established for repairing damaged ships, and they went back into service again extremely quickly. Boats which had sunk were located by special detachments. The *Uzbek*, barge *No. 1,002* and other boats were found in this way, raised to the surface and repaired.

Waiting for the river to freeze solid, our sappers, in order to strengthen the thin and precarious ice, prepared in advance several thousand square yards of a planking and brushwood surface, prepared hundreds of special sledges with long runners for carrying ammunition and evacuating the wounded across the ice, not yet frozen solid. As soon as the ice-drift came to a halt, the sappers laid their wooden surface and splendid crossings over the ice were soon ready.

To end my description of the Volga crossings I would like to quote a few figures. In the period from the second half of October until the drifting ice came to a standstill, more than 28,000 men and more than 3,000 tons of ammunition and other cargoes were carried across the river. The crossings over the ice, from the moment the drifting ice stopped to the end of operations in the city, carried over 18,000 lorries, 263 caterpillars (tanks and tractors), 325 pieces of artillery and more than 17,000 other vehicles.

The 62nd Army's medical service was set up in the spring of 1942, at the same time as the Army itself was formed.

The Army's medical establishments and units contained young personnel without sufficient practical medical or military experience. The medium- and lower-level staff, for the most part, had been called up from the reserve. The medical posts of our Army units and formations, and the Army's medical and health establishments, were inadequately supplied with necessary equipment, bedding, etc.

The Army's medical service had no special ambulance transport whatever; the Army's casualty-clearing establishments contained a total of 2,300 beds.

The Army lacked a great deal, a very great deal, in its work of helping the wounded; nevertheless, in spite of all the difficult, sometimes intolerable conditions, particularly in the days of street fighting in the city, the 62nd Army's medical staff did its job successfully.

The Army's medical service was under the command of the Chief Medical Officer, Mikhail Prokopievich Boyko.

I first met him in the city at the crossings, shortly after my arrival in the city. He was of medium height, lively, and the first impression I had of him was a good one. At the crossings he was supervising the work of the orderlies, dealing with the evacuation of the wounded across the Volga. As I watched him working, I felt that he was a very strong-willed person, and that, if you asked him, he would go straight off to join a counter-attack with grenade and tommy-gun. A good organizer, a man who really knows his job, a disciplined officer and Communist—that was my first impression of Boyko. I did not change my opinion throughout the war.

In a war, as a rule, there is a shortage of something or other. Many people, particularly those in charge of one aspect or another of the work, used to mention the fact, in order to emphasize, to over-emphasize, their own merits. M. P. Boyko understood the position better than men in charge of other sections, and he never complained about difficulties; he simply, after estimating the possibilities, put forward his proposals, and, showing the way to carry them out, promptly set about doing so.

The battle by the Volga lasted 180 days. With the build-up of military strength on both sides it was impossible to achieve victory by a single thrust, by a single effort, however heroic. What was needed was cool-headed, calculating care. It was no good letting the grass grow under one's feet. You may ask: 'But did not the Army have a Military Council; it had a Commander and a headquarters, who should have foreseen events several months ahead'.

This is true, but only in theory. Could the Army H.Q., Front H.Q., or even G.H.Q. have foreseen that the battle of the Don and the Volga would continue from July 1942 to February 1943? Of course not! But there were some things that could be foreseen and planned, if not at Front level, certainly at 62nd Army level. I am thinking of Colonel Boyko, who understood the course of events and in his own way was able to look far into the future. Foreseeing difficulties that lay ahead, he took steps which later, a month, two months later, enabled him to overcome the difficulties. This was the foresight of the practical worker, who, fully aware of his duty, can live up to the task he has been set. One day, at the height of the bitterest fighting in the factory district, when every soldier counted, Boyko was able to convince me of the need to issue an order for every 'divisional and brigade commander to prepare warm dug-outs and shelters for the medical posts, for the wounded'. It was at his insistence in September, when it was still warm, even hot, when no one was thinking about cold weather, that warm dug-outs were begun, and completed, dug-outs which later, in November and December, helped us to save the lives of thousands of soldiers.

The conditions in which our medical services worked can be judged from the daily reports sent in by the men in charge of it:

September 13. The evacuation of the wounded yesterday and today was made especially difficult by the exceptional scale of the enemy's air operations . . .

September 21. Fighting is in progress on a large scale.

Over the past two days the transporting of the wounded to the left bank has become even more difficult. Bombing is going on the whole time; the ferry is working only during the hours of darkness, and even then with interruptions . . .

September 30. Repeated attempts by armoured boats to approach the bank of the river during the night of September 28–29 were unsuccessful. During the night No. 689 mobile field hospital came under heavy mortar fire; there were casualties. At the same time and in the same area the 112th Medical Battalion suffered heavy losses from a direct hit on a dressing-station . . .

Colonel-General E. I. Smirnov, the medical officer in charge of the Supreme Medical Administration of the Ministry of Defence, in his book on *Problems of Medicine in War*, wrote about our medical service as follows:

The presence of a major water obstacle, the Volga, in the Army's rear, made treatment and evacuation much more difficult. The ferrying of the wounded across the Volga was possible only at night, and then under heavy enemy artillery and mortar fire. The Army medical service worked not only under mortar and artillery fire, but also under fire from enemy tommy-gunners.

In these conditions . . . one cannot talk about individual cases of heroism and courage. It was a case of mass heroism, mass courage by the medical workers, particularly those of the 62nd Army.

We put every effort into achieving the best possible organization of the medical and evacuation services, providing skilled medical assistance in the Army's mobile field hospital units. The wounded and the sick, with the exception of those who could not be transported, were taken by various means to the Army's rear, to casualty-reception hospitals, where they were given full skilled medical attention.

The wounded and the sick in need of long treatment were evacuated along the river to Astrakhan and Saratov, and by rail to Leninsk and Elton.

Mobile field hospital unit No. 80 and casualty-reception

centre no. 54 did a particularly difficult and crucial job. To all intents and purposes they dealt with the entire stream of wounded from the front line, and gave them the medical attention they needed. They had also dealt with the ferrying of the wounded across the Don. All this work was carried out under non-stop bombing, as a result of which the accommodation being used by both of these units was largely destroyed. Mobile field hospital unit No. 80 had fourteen of its staff killed, and a number of wounded and shell-shock cases.

Casualty-reception centre No. 54 and medical battalions were set up in the city, to receive the wounded and the sick, evacuate them to the east bank of the Volga and attend to the ferries.

First-aid was given to the wounded on the battlefield, and then they were evacuated behind the lines without delay, from one stage of the casualty-clearing service to the next; they were given nonsurgical attention at battalion medical posts, initial treatment by a doctor at regimental medical posts, and skilled medical attention at divisional medical posts.

Considering the particular conditions in which the battle was being fought, and the creation of storm groups and detachments, the Army's medical service had to look for new ways of working, so as to provide medical attention as close as possible to the units themselves. Particular attention was paid to the provision of lower-level units (platoons, companies and battalions) with medical teams, and the provision of such teams with the necessary equipment. Storm groups and detachments had men attached to them with the special job of evacuating the wounded from each small garrison, after giving first-aid on the spot. Medical orderlies and instructors, therefore, were always to be found in battle formations, in garrisons, storm groups and strongpoints.

Medical auxiliaries equipped battalion posts immediately behind the battalions' battle formations, in various kinds of shelter (dugouts, the cellars of buildings, etc.), giving nonsurgical treatment to those wounded in battle.

Immediately behind the battalion battle formations, the regimental medical posts were also set up in dug-outs, with doctors giving preliminary treatment. Behind the regimental formations, the divisions established the forward operating groups of the medical battalions, giving urgent surgical attention.

Below the banks of the Volga, in dug-outs, reception and sorting centres, operating and dressing hospitals were established, for the wounded who could not be transported across the river. Accommodation was provided for the surgical group of the 39th Infantry Division in mine adits. The surgical group of General Rodimtsev's division was housed in a sewer-pipe.

On the bank of the river, in cellars and dug-outs, was the surgical group of casualty-reception centre No. 54, which, apart from collecting the wounded and evacuating them across to the left bank, established an operating and dressing-station, and provided highly-skilled surgical treatment.

The Army's epidemiological section carried on its work of medical and epidemiological inspection in the area of military operations. It was also accommodated in dug-outs.

But probably the most difficult work the medical service had to perform was the evacuation of the wounded across the Volga, as we had no special resources for doing this, and as a rule used the vessels of the Volga fleet on their return journeys, after they had delivered men, ammunition and their other cargoes to the city.

The medical battalions set up at the beginning of September could not provide a continuous wounded-evacuation service, as almost all their boats were soon taken over by the Army to keep the crossings working, and the medical battalions were left only with the divisions' boat-crossings.

On 17 September 1942, on the proposal of Colonel Boyko, the Army Military Council instructed the officers in charge of casualty-reception centre No. 54 and field mobile hospital unit No. 689 to attend only to the Volga crossings.

The casualty-reception centre occupied the basement of the restaurant by the central landing-stage. It received the bulk of the wounded, the number of which grew hour by hour. But at the same time the enemy was beginning his drive towards the central landing-stage, and the casualty-reception centre found itself in an extremely difficult situation. A German tank entrenched itself not far from the restaurant. At the Khalzunov monument, on the road leading to the restaurant, the Germans set up machine-guns, and tommy-gunners ensconced themselves in the transforming station and the Engineers' House. The casualty-reception centre was therefore in a state of siege.

For several days the wounded and the medical workers were unable to leave the basement to go to the moorings.

On September 25 armoured boats were sent to the besieged casualty-reception centre; the boats fought their way through to the landing-stages and, pushing the enemy back from the bank, brought the wounded out of the basement.

The evacuation of the wounded went slowly, since the Volga was at this point under enemy artillery and machine-gun fire. Soldiers were sent in from battle units to help the medical personnel and carry the seriously wounded to the armoured boats.

In these conditions, with the help of naval boats of the Volga fleet and guardsmen from Rodimtsev's division, 711 people were evacuated from the restaurant building on September 25 and 550 on September 26.

On the night of the 26th the enemy approached right up to the restaurant building. Under cover of fire from the boats, the final wounded and equipment were brought from the basement and loaded on to the boats. The medical personnel also crossed to the left bank on this trip. Two hours later the restaurant was occupied by German tommy-gunners.

Between September 20–27 the personnel of casualty-reception centre No. 54 lost four dead, eleven wounded and five missing.

Wounded were also evacuated by Crossing '62'. Here it was the personnel of mobile field hospital unit No. 689 who looked after the wounded. Armoured boats, ferries and other vessels were plying on this sector. The wounded were evacuated only at night.

By September 23 this unit had organized a surgical and dressing centre in underground shelters, where duty teams from this hospital unit and from divisional medical battalions were at work. The wounded were given surgical treatment. The Luftwaffe took no notice of the hospitals' red crosses and bombed them unmercifully. One bomb fell on the operating theatre. Dr Tatyana Vasilievna Barkova, a nurse, two orderlies and twenty-two wounded soldiers were killed.

The small staff of mobile field hospital unit No. 689,

working in exceptionally difficult conditions, every day received and evacuated to the left bank between six hundred and eight hundred wounded. Outstanding services were rendered here by the leading surgeon, Medical Officer 2nd class Krivonos and Medical Officer 3rd class Panchenko. When the enemy destroyed the operating theatre, they made a new one under an upturned boat, putting tables underneath it and giving the wounded urgent surgery.

Our Soviet doctors, especially the surgeons, were models of self-sacrificing service to the country. Regardless of difficulties, and often at the risk of their own lives, they fought to save the lives of the soldiers in all circumstances.

I remember the pump-house on the very bank of the Volga, south of the mouth of the Banny Gully. One day, walking along the bank, I saw a group of soldiers and officers, crouched against the wall of the destroyed building. When I came up close I found them to be seriously wounded. Many of them had crawled here themselves, some had been brought on stretchers by orderlies. But why were they here, against the wall? Was there really no room for them in the cellar?

I opened the door and went down the steep, narrow, iron stairs. It was extremely stuffy and smelled strongly of ether. The wounded were groaning. By the stairs, on about ten square yards of concrete floor about a dozen wounded men were lying in two rows.

I strode across them to the door, or rather to the two sheets which did for a door, behind which a bright light was burning. It was an operating theatre. A wounded soldier was lying on the table. Three people in white coats were bending over him. To one side, on an upturned iron barrel, a primus stove was hissing, with water boiling on it in a pan.

The doctor, seeing me, gestured to his assistants to straighten their coats. The coats had, of course, once been white, but were now covered with brown patches. Only their white caps looked at all fresh.

'What are you doing here?' I asked the doctor.

Without taking his eyes off the operating table he pointed to a small table in the corner, on which was a thick exercise book—a register. The numbers of the entries ran into three figures.

'Who did all these, and when?' I asked, pointing to the three-figure entries of operations carried out.

The doctor looked at the nurses by the table. Everything was suddenly clear, particularly as all the entries had been made by the same hand.

It was the leading surgeon of the Army field hospital, Eisenberg. He had organized this operating theatre with two assistants, and had carried out over two hundred operations.

Later, there were people who told me that there was a high mortality rate among Dr Eisenberg's patients. But my answer was: 'And how many men would have died, if Eisenberg had not organized help for them?'

The Army Military Council decorated the whole of Eisenberg's group.

At the beginning of October the wounded were also evacuated by the footbridge to Zaitsevski Island, where there was a medical group from the 112th Medical Battalion and a second group from casualty-reception centre No. 54. When the seriously wounded had been given treatment they were carried on stretchers to the moorings a mile away and sent back to the rear.

During the period of drifting ice on theVolga, boats landed in different places, according to conditions on the river. What we called the 'flying ferries' were then organized, with the wounded being loaded on to the armoured boats wherever they could manage to land.

The medical service, therefore, had to be extremely efficient and mobile, using every man and all resources to get the sick and the wounded evacuated rapidly to the rear medical battalions and the appropriate mobile field hospitals.

In the latter part of November, at Tumak landing-stage on the east bank of the river, a reception centre was organized to provide the wounded with warmth and food. A detachment of mobile field hospital unit No. 689 was also posted there, with an operating theatre and a dressing-station for the wounded who could not be transported any further.

Great help in ferrying the wounded across the river during the period of drifting ice was given by the ice-breaker. When it was put out of action by a collision, it was replaced by armoured tugs.

At this period it was extremely difficult to evacuate the

wounded of Lyudnikov's division, which was cut off from the Army's main forces, and was conducting a defensive operation, as we know, on a small sector in the vicinity of the Barrikady factory.

Armoured boats fought their way through towards the division, but did not always reach their goal. Every boat which got through to Lyudnikov's division had a medical auxiliary or nurse on board, with stretcher-bearers. They loaded and unloaded the wounded and looked after them during the crossing. To keep the wounded warm, the boats always carried blankets and chemical-filled hot-water bottles.

As a result of the unstinting efforts of the crews of the armoured boats and the medical workers, the bulk of the wounded were evacuated from Lyudnikov's sector to the left bank.

In the period of drifting ice, Medical Officer 2nd class Serdyuk was put in charge of the evacuation of the wounded across the Volga and of communications with the medical services.

I first saw Comrade Serdyuk when the Army command post's dug-outs were in flames, and burning oil was enveloping the boats standing by the bank, waiting to take away the wounded. In the flames and smoke I saw a man of medium height in a leather coat. He was untying boats from the burning moorings and moving them away from the flames.

Five or so boatmen were doing the same. Serdyuk was giving orders and instructions in a soft, but powerful voice. At first I thought that our new superintendent for the landing-stage had arrived and I was delighted: he would be able to introduce some order into the loading and unloading. But when I went up closer I saw the badge of the medical service in his buttonhole.

When he saw me, Serdyuk came over to me and reported:

'Medical Officer 2nd class Serdyuk. I'm putting the landing-stage into some kind of order.'

I warmly shook him by the hand and said:

'Well done! I hope that as a doctor and a man you'll always behave like this in the future.'

At that moment a wall of earth and sand rose into the air as German mortar bombs exploded near the landing-stage.

Serdyuk did not flinch, and I thought—this is a man with iron nerves. He went right through from the Volga to the Spree, and was in Berlin when the war ended.

When the Volga iced over, it became possible to transfer the medical and casualty-clearance work to the divisional medical battalions, which themselves saw to the further evacuation of the wounded to the Army's base hospital, as directed by the medical service.

On the east bank of the river, in dug-outs and warm tents some thirty miles from the landing-stages, were the divisions' rear medical battalions, reception and sorting centres, operating theatres and dressing-stations, hospital and evacuation centres, with surgeons and therapists on hand. The wounded and the sick spent from four to fifteen days here. The convalescent were given military and political training. The men who were convalescing after slight injuries and illnesses formed a reserve from which divisions were reinforced.

The wounded who needed long, special treatment were sent to the Army's mobile field hospitals, either the more forward ones, some nine to fifteen miles from the front line, at Kolkhoznaya Akhtuba, Verkhnyaya Akhtuba, Srednyaya Akhtuba and Zaplavnoye, or those further in the rear, twenty-five to thirty miles away, at Leninsk, Solodovka, Tokarevy Peski and elsewhere.

These latter medical establishments confined themselves to cases requiring treatment for up to two months, and cases of infectious diseases until they were cured.

The self-sacrificing efforts of the medical workers, who were, in fact, in the front line of battle, helped the 62nd Army to carry out its mission.

The best, the most reliable indication of the good work done by the medical service at the front was the low mortality rate among the wounded operated on and given hospital treatment. The 62nd Army's medical service showed in practice that you can fight to save human life in any circumstances. Fewer wounded died in the 62nd Army than in other armies, where conditions were not quite so difficult. This was made possible by the fact that medical posts and skilled surgery were available for the wounded rapidly, directly behind the front line, that is, right in the battle-torn city.

There is still a great deal one could tell about what happened during the fighting in Stalingrad. I have talked about what I saw and experienced myself.

After describing the particular features of the military operations which took place by the Volga, I would like to put forward for my military readers a few conclusions I have come to:

1. Anyone studying the art of warfare must realize that it is no good being a pedant and clinging to abstract theories worked out in the departments of the academies. Any sane-minded person needs to be given more historical examples and told not to repeat them, but to use them intelligently and partially, in accordance with the precise situation.

2. Don't stand on your dignity, if the ideas of students and lower-ranking officers prove better than those given out from the rostrum; acknowledge the fact and give them their deserts. This will bring good results in battle, when they will be taking decisions independently.

3. Don't cling blindly to regulations. You need to know, study and repeat them, but the important thing is to be able to adapt one's knowledge to match the circumstances.

The storm groups of Stalingrad stood us in good stead in the battles for the cities which we took on the road to Berlin, but in field conditions our troops successfully used new forms of doing battle, such as reconnaissance developing into attack, 'special echelons' and 'artillery raids' instead of long artillery preparation. These methods were not used in the battle for Stalingrad, but in field conditions they had a stunning effect on the enemy, being a complete surprise to him.

I was in Volgograd not long ago, and there I met some veterans of the defence of the city: Alexander Rodimtsev, Mikhail Shumilov, Jacob Pavlov, Vasili Zaitsev, Ilya Voronov and other renowned defenders of the fortress on the Volga. I walked round the city for a long time without recognizing it. In place of the endless ruins a fine city has arisen, with gardens, theatres, squares and beautiful blocks of flats. One could not but feel a sense of pleasure.

I only recognized two buildings—the elevator and a mill near 'Pavlov's House'. The elevator had changed somewhat, with new outhouses round it, but the mill was exactly as it had been in the autumn of 1942, having been preserved as a relic of the twentieth century—literally every square inch of its walls bears the traces of shot and shell. The brick chimney, half destroyed by shells, towers in solitary splendour above the ruins.

The secretary of the district committee of the party, Ivan Kuzmich Zhegalin, showed me Komsomolskaya Street. I drove down it with him in a car, and my heart was bursting with pleasure: in gratitude to the Komsomol heroes of the battle, the citizens of Volgograd had named the finest street in the city after it.

We went to Mamayev Kurgan, where, on 12 September 1942, I took over command of the 62nd Army.

Going down into a gully I immediately found the spot from where, in September of 1942, under constant enemy fire, the Army Military Council and the Army H.Q. administered the Army.

And I remembered the day when the burning oil engulfed the dug-outs. General Rodimtsev sent some of his reconnaissance men to find out what had happened to the Military Council. On their return they reported:

'The Military Council has moved . . .'

'Where to, the left bank?'

'No, nearer the front line.'

Remembering this incident, I could again hear Nikita Sergeyevich Khrushchev speaking to me on 12 September 1942, when the German armies had already approached the bank of the Volga:

'Remember, Vasili Ivanovich, that we must hold the city, and strengthen our people's confidence in our Army's ability to defeat the enemy.'

Could the Military Council really cross to the right bank when our Army was threatened by the greatest danger of all—the loss of the nation's confidence? I think that we, the Communists of the 62nd Army, correctly understood the words of the Member of the Front Military Council, in deciding to stay in the city and fight to the death.

The Commander of the 39th Guards Division, Major-General Stepan Savelevich Guriev, on 5 February 1943, in the presence of all the Army's divisional commanders, said:

'Could we, as divisional commanders, think of retreating across the Volga, when the Army Military Council was with us? "It's difficult for you," we said to those under our command, pointing to the burning dug-outs of the Military Council, "but isn't it difficult for the Military Council? They are being attacked, bombed, burned, the same as we are, and even worse . . ." This had the strongest effect on the troops, and they all fought to the bitter end.'

There, by the Volga, we went through a stern school of courage and military skill. The experience can still stand our soldiers in good stead.

MAPS

KEY TO MAP ABBREVIATIONS

A—army
AC—army corps
Bn—battalion
CC—cavalry corps
CD—cavalry division
comp bn—composite battalion
G—guards
IBr—infantry brigade
ID—infantry division
IR—infantry regiment
It—Italian
km—kilometre
m—metre
MC—motorized corps
MD—motorized division
MIBr—marine infantry brigade
MTS—machine and tractor station
Rum—Rumanian
sett—settlement
SFa—state farm
St—station
StF—Stalingrad Front
TA—tank (armoured, panzer) army
TBr— ”   ”   ”   brigade
TC — ”   ”   ”   corps
TD — ”   ”   ”   division

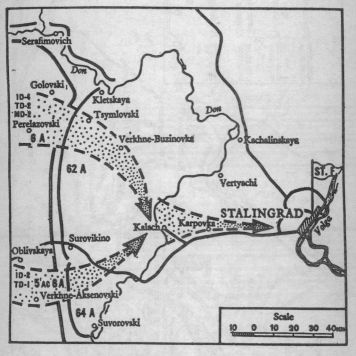

Plan of the enemy attack on Stalingrad

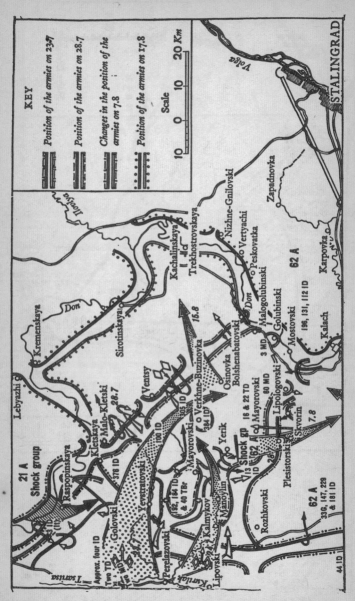

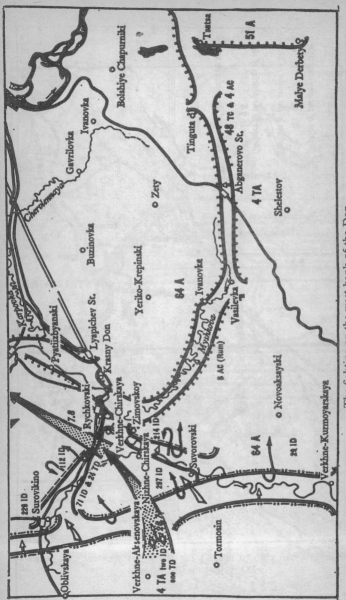

The fighting on the west bank of the Don

373

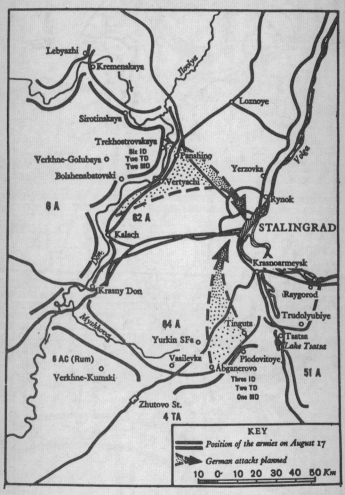

The German plan to destroy the Soviet armies near the Volga by concentrated attacks

The Stalingrad Front

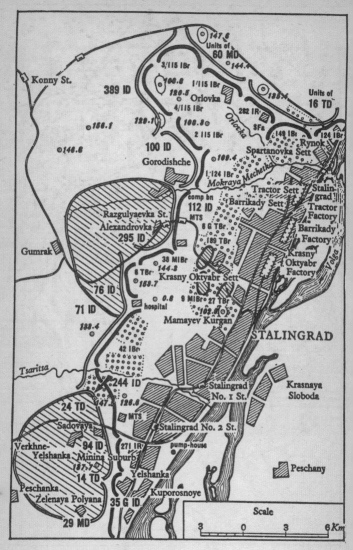

The situation on September 13

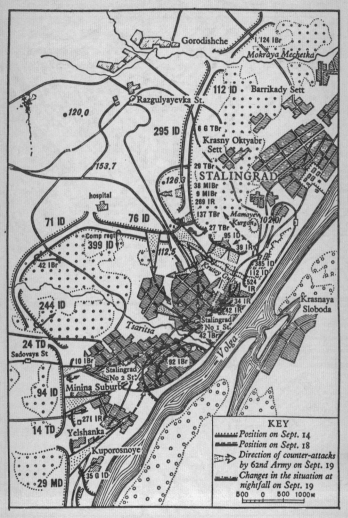

The fighting in the central and southern districts of the city
September 14-26

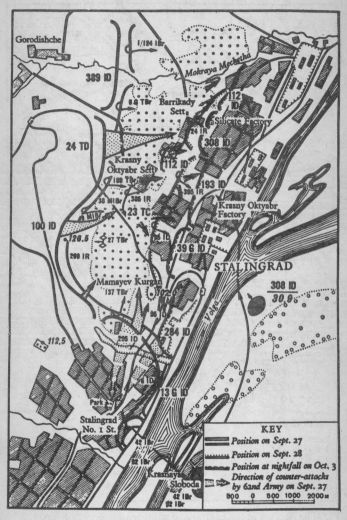

The fighting for the Krasny Oktyabr and Barrikady settlements

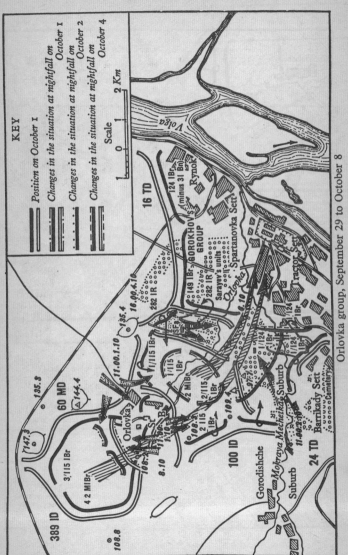

KEY

	Position on October 1
	Changes in the situation at nightfall on October 1
	Changes in the situation at nightfall on October 2
	Changes in the situation at nightfall on October 4

Scale

1   0   1   2 Km

Orlovka group, September 29 to October 8

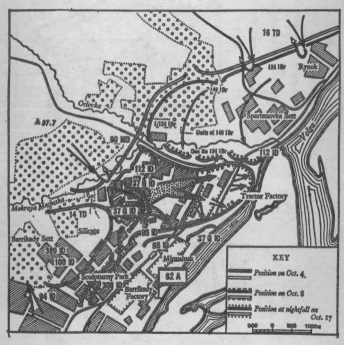

The fighting for the Tractor Factory, October 4-14

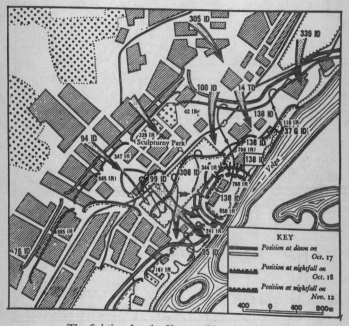

The fighting for the Krasny Oktyabr Factory

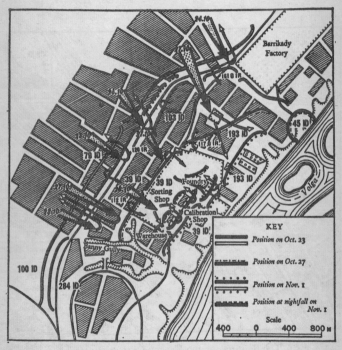

The fighting for the Barrikady Factory

INDEX OF NAMES

N.B. In this book units are frequently referred to by the name of the commander instead of the number of the unit, e.g. *Rodimtsev's division* for *13th Infantry Division*. I have not listed such references in the index, except to include the first reference to the arrival of a unit (and therefore its commander) in the city, and any vital reference, such as the encirclement of a unit, e.g. of *Lyudnikov's division*.